W9-BZC-692

Designing Interfaces

Jenifer Tidwell

BEIJING • CAMBRIDGE • FARNHAM • KÖLN • PARIS • SEBASTOPOL • TAIPEI • TOKYO

Designing Interfaces
by Jenifer Tidwell

Copyright © 2006 O'Reilly Media, Inc. All rights
reserved. Printed in the United States of America.

Published by O'Reilly Media, Inc.,
1005 Gravenstein Highway North,
Sebastopol, CA 95472.

O'Reilly books may be purchased for educational,
business, or sales promotional use. Online editions
are also available for most titles (*safari.oreilly.com*).
For more information, contact our corporate/
institutional sales department: (800) 998-9938 or
corporate@oreilly.com.

Editors: Andrew Odewahn and Mary O'Brien
Production Editor: Genevieve d'Entremont
Cover Designer: Mike Kohnke
Interior Designer: NOON

Printing History:
November 2005: First Edition.

Nutshell Handbook, the Nutshell Handbook logo,
and the O'Reilly logo are registered trademarks of
O'Reilly Media, Inc. *Designing Interfaces* and
related trade dress are trademarks of O'Reilly
Media, Inc.

Many of the designations used by manufacturers
and sellers to distinguish their products are
claimed as trademarks. Where those designations
appear in this book, and O'Reilly Media, Inc., was
aware of a trademark claim, the designations have
been printed in caps or initial caps.

While every precaution has been taken in the
preparation of this book, the publisher and author
assume no responsibility for errors or omissions,
or for damages resulting from the use of the
information contained herein.

This book uses RepKover, a durable and flexible
lay-flat binding.

ISBN: 0-596-00803-1

ISBN13: 978-0-596-00803-1

[C]
[11/06]

Jenifer Tidwell is an interaction designer and software developer for The MathWorks, makers of technical computing software. She specializes in the design and construction of data analysis and visualization tools, and has been working on new designs for the data tools in MATLAB, which is used by researchers, students, and engineers worldwide to develop cars, planes, proteins, and theories about the universe. She has been known to design web sites, and was an early enthusiast for rich Internet application (RIA) technology, having helped design and develop Curl in the early 2000s.

Jenifer received her technical education at MIT and her design education at the Massachusetts College of Art, but she's not finished learning yet. She has been researching user interface patterns since 1997. Photography and writing are her creative outlets, and she spends as much time as she can in the New England outdoors—on a bike, on a boat, on foot, on skis, and on belay.

Jenifer's personal web site can be found at *http://jtidwell.net*.

COLOPHON

Our look is the result of reader comments, our own experimentation, and feedback from distribution channels. Distinctive covers complement our distinctive approach to technical topics, breathing personality and life into potentially dry subjects.

The animal on the cover of this book is a Mandarin duck (*Aix galericulata*), one of the most beautiful of the duck species. Originating in China, these colorful birds can be found in southeast Russia, northern China, Japan, southern England, and Siberia.

The males have diverse and colorful plumage, characterized by an iridescent crown, chestnut-colored cheeks, and a white eye stripe that extends from their red bills to the back of their heads. Females are less flamboyant in appearance and tend to be gray, white, brown, and greenish brown, with a white throat and foreneck.

These birds live in woodland areas near streams and lakes. Being omnivorous, they tend to have a seasonal diet, eating acorns and grains in autumn; insects, land snails, and aquatic plants in spring; and dew worms, grasshoppers, frogs, fish, and mollusks during the summer months.

The mating ritual of Mandarin ducks begins with an elaborate and complex courtship dance that involves shaking movements, mimed drinking gestures, and preening. Males fight each other to win a female, but it is ultimately the female who decides her mate. Mandarin ducklings instinctively follow their notoriously protective mothers, who will feign injury to distract predators such as otters, raccoon dogs, mink, polecats, eagle owls, and grass snakes.

Mandarin ducks are not an endangered species, but they are considered to be threatened. Loggers continuously encroach upon their habitats, and hunters and poachers prize the males for their plumage. Their meat is considered unpalatable by humans, and they are generally not hunted for food.

Genevieve d'Entremont was the production editor and proofreader for *Designing Interface*s. Ann Schirmer was the copyeditor. Susan Honeywell was the page compositor. Phil Dangler and Claire Cloutier provided quality control. Kelly Talbot and Johnna VanHoose Dinse wrote the index.

Mike Kohnke designed the cover of this book, based on a series design by Edie Freedman. The cover image is from *Johnson's Natural History*. Karen Montgomery produced the cover layout in Adobe InDesign CS, using Adobe's ITC Garmond font.

NOON (*www.designatnoon.com*) designed the interior layout. This book was converted by Joe Wizda to Adobe InDesign CS. The text fonts are Gotham Book and Adobe Garamond; the heading fonts are Univers and Gotham Bold. The illustrations that appear in the book were produced by Robert Romano, Jessamyn Read, and Lesley Borash using Macromedia FreeHand MX and Adobe Photoshop CS. This colophon was written by Jansen Fernald.

CONTENTS

Put two side-by-side panels on the interface. In the first, show a set of items that the user can select at will; in the other, show the content of the selected item.

Place an iconic palette next to a blank canvas; the user clicks on the palette buttons to create objects on the canvas.

Show each of the application's pages within a single window. As a user drills down through a menu of options, or into an object's details, replace the window contents completely with the new page.

Let the user choose among alternative views that are structurally different, not just cosmetically different, from the default view.

Lead the user through the interface step by step, doing tasks in a prescribed order.

Show the most important content up front, but hide the rest. Let the user reach it via a single, simple gesture.

Place links to interesting content in unexpected places, and label them in a way that attracts the curious user.

Use a mixture of lightweight and heavyweight help techniques to support users with varying needs.

Present only a few entry points into the interface; make them task-oriented and descriptive.

Using a small section of every page, show a consistent set of links or buttons that take the user to key sections of the site or application.

04 ORGANIZING THE PAGE:
LAYOUT OF PAGE ELEMENTS

09 MAKING IT LOOK GOOD:
VISUAL STYLE AND AESTHETICS   268

PREFACE

Once upon a time, interface designers worked with a woefully small toolbox.

We had a handful of simple controls: text fields, buttons, menus, tiny icons, and modal dialogs. We carefully put them together according to the Windows Style Guide or the Macintosh Human Interface Guidelines, and we hoped that users would understand the resulting interface—and too often, they didn't. We designed for small screens, few colors, slow CPUs, and slow networks (if the user was connected at all). We made them gray.

Things have changed. If you design interfaces today, you work with a much bigger palette of components and ideas. You have a choice of many more user interface toolkits than before, such as Java™ Swing, Qt, HTML and Javascript, Flash, and numerous open-source options. Apple's and Microsoft's native UI toolkits are richer and nicer-looking than they used to be. Display technology is better. Web applications often look as professionally designed as the web sites they're embedded in, and while desktop-UI ideas like drag-and-drop are integrated into web applications slowly, some of those web sensibilities are migrating back into desktop applications in the form of blue underlined links, Back/Next buttons, daring fonts and background images, and nice, non-gray color schemes.

But it's still not easy to design *good* interfaces. Let's say you're not a trained or self-taught interface designer. If you just use the UI toolkits the way they should be used, and if you follow the various style guides or imitate existing applications, you can probably create a mediocre but passable interface.

Alas, that may not be enough anymore. Users' expectations are higher than they used to be—if your interface isn't easy to use "out of the box," users will not think well of it. Even if the interface obeys all the standards, you may have misunderstood users' preferred workflow, used the wrong vocabulary, or made it too hard to figure out what the software even does. Impatient users often won't give you the benefit of the doubt. Worse, if you've built an unusable web site or web application, frustrated users can give up and switch to your competitor with just the click of a button. So the cost of building a mediocre interface is higher than it used to be, too.

It's even tougher if you design products outside of the desktop and web worlds, because there's very little good design advice out there. Palmtops, cell phones, car navigation systems, digital TV recorders—designers are still figuring out what works and what doesn't, often from basic principles. (And their users often tolerate difficult interfaces—but that won't last long.)

Devices like phones, TVs, and car dashboards once were the exclusive domain of industrial designers. But now those devices have become smart. Increasingly powerful computers drive them, and software-based features and applications are multiplying in response to market demands. They're here to stay, whether or not they are easy to use. At this rate, good interface and interaction design may be the only hope for our collective sanity in 10 years.

SMALL INTERFACE PIECES, LOOSELY JOINED

As an interface designer trying to make sense of all the technology changes in the last few years, I see two big effects on the craft of interface design. One is the proliferation of *interface idioms*: recognizable types or styles of interfaces, each with its own vocabulary of objects, actions, and visuals. You probably recognize all the ones shown in the figure on the next page, and more are being invented all the time.

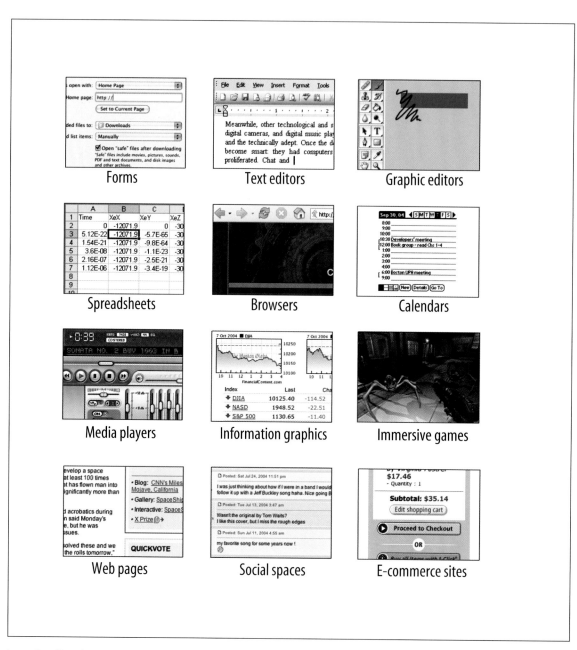

A sampler of interface idioms

The second effect is a loosening of the rules for putting together interfaces from these idioms. It no longer surprises anyone to see several of these idioms mixed up in one interface, for instance, or to see parts of some controls mixed up with parts of other controls. Online help pages, which have long been formatted in hypertext anyway, might now have interactive applets in them, animations, or links to a web-based bulletin board. Interfaces themselves might have help texts on them, interleaved with forms or editors; this used to be rare. Combo boxes' dropdown menus might have funky layouts, like color grids or sliders, instead of the standard column of text items. You might see web applications that look like document-centered paint programs, but have no menu bars, and save the finished work only to a database somewhere.

The freeform-ness of web pages seems to have taught users to relax their expectations with respect to graphics and interactivity. It's okay now to break the old Windows style-guide strictures, as long as users can figure out what you're doing.

And that's the hard part. Some applications, devices, and web applications are easy to use. Many aren't. Following style guides never guaranteed usability anyhow, but now designers have even more choices than before (which, paradoxically, can make design a *lot* harder). What characterizes interfaces that are easy to use?

One could say, "The applications that are easy to use are designed to be intuitive." Well, yes. That's almost a tautology.

Except that the word "intuitive" is a little bit deceptive. Jef Raskin once pointed out that when we say "intuitive" in the context of software, we really mean "familiar." Computer mice aren't intuitive to someone who's never seen one (though a growling grizzly bear would be). There's nothing innate or instinctive in the human brain to account for it. But once you've taken 10 seconds to learn to use a mouse, it's familiar, and you'll never forget it. Same for blue underlined text, play/pause buttons, and so on.

Rephrased: "The applications that are easy to use are designed to be *familiar*."

Now we're getting somewhere. "Familiar" doesn't necessarily mean that everything about a given application is identical to some genre-defining product (e.g., Word, Photoshop, Mac OS, or a Walkman). People are smarter than that. As long as the parts are recognizable enough, and the relationships among the parts are clear, then people can apply their previous knowledge to a novel interface and figure it out.

That's where patterns come in. This book catalogs many of those familiar parts, in ways you can reuse in many different contexts. Patterns capture a common structure—usually a very "local" one, like funky layouts on a combo box—without being too concrete on the details, which gives you flexibility to be creative.

If you know what users expect of your application, and if you choose carefully from your toolbox of idioms (large-scale), controls (small-scale), and patterns (covering the range), then you can put together something which "feels familiar" while remaining original.

And that gets you the best of both worlds.

ABOUT PATTERNS IN GENERAL

In essence, patterns are structural and behavioral features that improve the "habitability" of something—a user interface, a web site, an object-oriented program, or even a building. They make things easier to understand or more beautiful; they make tools more useful and usable.

As such, patterns can be a description of best practices within a given design domain. They capture common solutions to design tensions (usually called "forces" in pattern literature) and thus, by definition, are not novel. They aren't off-the-shelf components; each implementation of a pattern differs a little from every other. They aren't simple rules or heuristics either. And they won't walk you through an entire set of design decisions—if you're looking for a complete step-by-step description of how to design an interface, a pattern catalog isn't the place!

This book describes patterns literally as solutions to design problems because part of their value lies in the way they resolve tensions in various design contexts. For instance, an interface designer who needs to pack a lot of stuff into a too-small space can use a Card Stack. What remains for the designer is information architecture—how to split up the content into pieces, what to name them, etc.—and what exactly the Card Stack will look like when it's done. Tabs? A lefthand-side list or tree? That's up to the designer's judgment.

Some very complete sets of patterns make up a "pattern language." These patterns resemble visual languages, in that they cover the entire vocabulary of elements used in a design (though pattern languages are more abstract and behavioral; visual languages talk about shapes, icons, colors, fonts, etc.). This set isn't nearly so complete, and it contains techniques that don't qualify as traditional patterns. But it's concise enough to be manageable and useful.

OTHER PATTERN COLLECTIONS

The text that started it all dealt with physical buildings, not software. Christopher Alexander's *A Pattern Language*, and its companion book, *The Timeless Way of Building* (both Oxford University Press), established the concept of patterns and described a 250-pattern multilayered pattern language. It is often considered the gold standard for a pattern language because of its completeness, its rich interconnectedness, and its grounding in the human response to our built world.

In the mid-1990s, the publication of *Design Patterns,* (Addison-Wesley) by Erich Gamma, Richard Helm, Ralph Johnson, and John Vlissides profoundly changed the practice of commercial software architecture. This book is a collection of patterns describing object-oriented "micro-architectures." If you have a background in software engineering, this is the book that probably introduced you to the idea of patterns. Many other authors have written books about software patterns since *Design Patterns*. Software patterns such as these do make software more habitable—for those who write the software, not those who use it!

The first substantial set of user-interface patterns was the predecessor of this patterns collection, "Common Ground."[1] Many other collections and languages followed, notably Martijn van Welie's "Interaction Design Patterns,"[2] and Jan Borchers's book *A Pattern Approach to Interaction Design* (Wiley). More recently, a full-fledged web site pattern language was published, called *The Design of Sites* (Addison-Wesley). I highly recommend it, especially if you're designing traditional web sites. If you're building web or desktop applications, or if you're pushing the boundaries in either domain, look at all of these publications; you might find inspiration in any of them.

ABOUT THE PATTERNS IN THIS BOOK

So there's nothing really new in here. If you've done any web or UI design, or even thought much about it, you should say, "Oh, right, I know what that is" to most of these patterns. But a few of them might be new to you, and some of the familiar ones may not be part of your usual design repertoire.

These patterns work for both desktop and web-based applications. Many patterns also apply to such digital devices as palmtops, cell phones, and TV-based devices like digital recorders. Ordinary web sites might also benefit, but I'll talk more about that topic in the next section.

Though this book won't exhaustively describe all the interface idioms mentioned earlier, they organize part of the book. Three chapters focus on the more common idioms: forms, information graphics, and WYSIWYG editors (like those used for text and graphics). Other chapters address subjects that are useful across many idioms, such as organization, navigation, actions, and visual style.

This book is intended to be read by people who have some knowledge of such interface design concepts and terminology such as dialog boxes, selection, combo boxes, navigation bars, and white space. It does not identify many widely accepted techniques, such as copy-and-paste, since you already know what they are. But, at the risk of belaboring the obvious, this book describes some common techniques to encourage their use in other contexts—for instance, many desktop applications could better use Global Navigation—or to discuss them alongside alternative solutions.

This book does *not* present a complete process for constructing an interface design. When doing design, a sound process is critical. You need to have certain elements in a design process:

- Field research, to find out what the intended users are like and what they already do
- Goal and task analysis, to describe and clarify what users will do with what you're building
- Design models, such as personas (models of users), scenarios (models of common tasks and situations), and prototypes (models of the interface itself)

1. *http://www.mit.edu/~jtidwell/common_ground.html*

2. *http://www.welie.com/patterns*

- Empirical testing of the design at various points during development, like usability testing and *in situ* observations of the design used by real users
- Enough time to iterate over several versions of the design, because you won't get it right the first time

The topic of design process transcends the scope of this book, and plenty of other books and workshops out there cover it well. Read them; they're good.

But there's a deeper reason why this book won't give you a recipe for designing an interface. Good design can't be reduced to a recipe. It's a creative process, and one that changes under you as you work—in any given project, for instance, you won't understand some design issues until you've designed your way into a dead end. I've personally done that many times.

And design isn't linear. Most chapters in this book are arranged more or less by scale, and therefore by their approximate order in the design progression: large decisions about content and scope are made first, followed by navigation, page design, and, eventually, the details of interactions with forms and canvases and such. But you'll often find yourself moving back and forth through this progression. Maybe you'll know very early in a project how a certain screen should look, and that's a "fixed point"; you may have to work backward from there to figure out the right navigational structure. (No, it's not ideal, but things like this do happen in real life.)

That said, here are some ways you can use these patterns:

Learning

If you don't have years of design experience already, a set of patterns may serve as a learning tool. You may want to read over it to get ideas, or refer back to specific patterns as the need arises. Just as expanding your vocabulary helps you express ideas in language, expanding your interface design "vocabulary" helps you create more expressive designs.

Examples

Each pattern in this book has at least one example. Some have many; they might be useful to you as a sourcebook. You may find wisdom in the examples that is missing in the text of the pattern.

Terminology

If you talk to users, engineers, or managers about interface design, or if you write specifications, then you could use the pattern names as a way of communicating and discussing ideas. This is another well-known benefit of pattern languages. (The terms "singleton" and "factory," for instance, were originally pattern names, but they're now in common usage among software engineers.)

Inspiration

Each pattern description tries to capture the reasons why the pattern works to make an interface easier or more fun. If you get it, but want to do something a little different from the examples, you can be creative with your "eyes open."

One more word of caution: a catalog of patterns is not a checklist. You cannot measure the quality of a thing by counting the patterns in it. Each design project has a unique context, and even if you need to solve a common design problem (such as how to fit too much content onto a page), a given pattern might be a poor solution within that context. No reference can substitute for good design judgment. Nor can it substitute for a good design process, which helps you find and recover from design mistakes.

Ultimately, you should be able to leave a reference like this behind. As you become an experienced designer, you will have internalized these ideas to the point at which you don't notice you use them anymore; the patterns become second nature. They're part of your toolbox from then on.

AUDIENCE

If you design user interfaces in any capacity, you might find this book useful. It's intended for people who work on:

- Desktop applications
- Web applications or "rich internet applications" (RIAs)
- Highly interactive web sites
- Software for handhelds, cell phones, or other consumer electronics
- Turnkey systems, such as kiosks
- Operating systems

The list might also include traditional web sites such as corporate home pages, but I deliberately did not focus on web sites. They are amply covered by the existing literature, and talking more about them here seems redundant. Also, most of them don't have the degree of interactivity taken for granted in many patterns; there's a qualitative difference between a "read-only" site and one that actually interacts with its users.

Of course, profound differences exist among all these design platforms. However, I believe they have more in common than we generally think. You'll see examples from many different platforms in these patterns, and that's deliberate—they often use the same patterns to achieve the same ends.

This book isn't Design 101; it's more like Design 225. As mentioned earlier, it's expected that you already know the basics of UI design, such as available toolkits and control sets, concepts like drag-and-drop and focus, and the importance of usability testing and user feedback. If you don't, some excellent books listed in the references can get you started with the essentials.

Specifically, this book targets the following audiences:

- Software developers who need to design the UIs that they build.
- Web page designers who are now asked to design web apps or sites with more interactivity.
- New interface designers and usability specialists.

- More experienced designers who want to see how other designs solve certain problems; the examples can serve as a sourcebook for ideas.

- Professionals in adjacent fields, such as technical writing, product design, and information architecture.

- Managers who want to understand what's involved in good interface design.

- Open-source developers and enthusiasts. This isn't quite "open-source design," but the idea here is to open up interface design best practices for everyone's benefit.

HOW THIS BOOK IS ORGANIZED

These patterns are grouped into thematic chapters, and each chapter has an introduction that briefly covers the concepts those patterns are built upon. I want to emphasize *briefly*. Some of these concepts could have entire books written about them. But the introductions will give you some context; if you already know this stuff, they'll be review material, and if not, they'll tell you what topics you might want to learn more about.

The first set of chapters are applicable to almost any interface you might design, whether it's a desktop application, web application, web site, hardware device, or whatever you can think of:

- Chapter 1, *What Users Do,* talks about common behavior and usage patterns supported well by good interfaces.

- Chapter 2, *Organizing the Content,* discusses information architecture as it applies to highly interactive interfaces. It deals with different organizational models, the amount of content a user sees at one time, and the best way to use windows, panels, and pages.

- Chapter 3, *Getting Around,* discusses navigation. It describes patterns for moving around an interface—between pages, among windows, and within large virtual spaces.

- Chapter 4, *Organizing the Page,* describes patterns for the layout and placement of page elements. It talks about how to communicate meaning simply by putting things in the right places.

- Chapter 5, *Doing Things,* talks about how to present actions and commands; use these patterns to handle the "verbs" of an interface.

Next comes a set of chapters that deal with specific idioms. It's fine to read them all, but real-life projects probably won't use all of them. Chapters 6 and 7 are the most broadly applicable, since most modern interfaces use trees, tables, or forms in some fashion.

- Chapter 6, *Showing Complex Data,* contains patterns for trees, tables, charts, and information graphics in general. It discusses the cognitive aspects of data presentation, and how to use them to communicate knowledge and meaning.

- Chapter 7, *Getting Input from Users,* deals with forms and controls. Along with the patterns, this chapter has a table that maps data types to various controls that can represent them.

- Chapter 8, *Builders and Editors,* discusses techniques and patterns often used in WYSIWYG graphic editors and text editors.

Finally, the last chapter comes at the end of the design progression, but it too applies to almost anything you design.

- Chapter 9, *Making It Look Good,* deals with aesthetics and fit-and-finish. It uses graphic-design principles and patterns to show how (and why) to polish the look-and-feel of an interface, once its behavior is established.

I chose this book's examples based on many factors. The most important factor is how well an example demonstrates a given pattern or concept, of course, but other considerations include general design fitness, printability, platform variety—desktop applications, web sites, devices, etc.—and how well-known and accessible these applications might be to readers. As such, the examples are weighted heavily toward Microsoft and Apple software, certain web sites, and easily-found consumer software and devices. This is not to say that they are always paragons of good design. They're not, and I do not mean to slight the excellent work done by countless designers on less well-known applications. If you know of examples that might meet these criteria, please suggest them to me.

COMMENTS AND QUESTIONS

Please address comments and questions concerning this book to the publisher:

> O'Reilly Media, Inc.
> 1005 Gravenstein Highway North
> Sebastopol, CA 95472
> (800) 998-9938 (in the United States or Canada)
> (707) 829-0515 (international or local)
> (707) 829-0104 (fax)

We have a web page for this book, where we list errata, examples, and any additional information. You can access this page at:

> *http://www.oreilly.com/catalog/designinterfaces*

Visit *http://designinginterfaces.com* for more information.

To comment or ask technical questions about this book, send email to:

> *bookquestions@oreilly.com*

For more information about our books, conferences, Resource Centers, and the O'Reilly Network, see our web site at:

> *http://www.oreilly.com*

ACKNOWLEDGMENTS

First, my deepest thanks to the technical reviewers of this book: Eric Freeman, Peter Morville, William Wake, Robert Reimann, Jeff Johnson, Martijn van Welie, and Ron Jeffries. Your suggestions unquestionably made this book better.

Other readers, reviewers, and suggestion-makers include Andrea Midtmoen Fease, Jan Stetson, Helen Rennie, Rhon Porter, Geoff Dutton, Steve Eddins, Lynn Cherny, Tom Lane, Joe Conti, Will Schroeder, Janice Kutz, Tim Wright, Ben Bederson, Robert Nero, and Michael Del Gaudio. You all offered your time and energy to help with this project—thank you. And extra thanks to my other colleagues at The MathWorks, especially Chris Wood, for all your patience while I was so busy writing this.

Thanks to the really early reviewers, Ralph Johnson and the Software Architecture Group at the University of Illinois at Urbana-Champaign: Tankut Baris Aktemur, John Bordan, John Brant, Nicholas Bray, Danny Dig, Christos Evaggelou, Alejandra Garrido, Brian Foote, Munawar Hafiz, Thuc Si Mau Ho, Pablo Montesinos, Jeff Overbey, Weerasak Witthawaskul, Spiros Xanthos, and Joseph Yoder. (I'm sure I missed some of you because your names on the recordings were so faint!)

Doug Hull, Tom Lane, Gerard Torenvliet, Alex Conn, Amy Groden-Morrison, Susan Fowler, and Robert Nero all supplied material and links that I've included as key examples—thank you all for those screenshots and suggestions, and I hope the text does them credit.

At O'Reilly, thanks to Nat Torkington, who "found" the original web site and contacted me; Mike Hendrickson, for guiding me through the early stages of the book and coming up with some terrific ideas for it; and Andrew Odewahn and Mary O'Brien, my helpful and kind editors during the later stages of writing the draft.

The thousands of anonymous visitors to my UI patterns web site are the reason why this book exists. Without your log records, I'd never have known how heavily used the site actually is. And thanks to those of you who took the time to write and tell me you liked it. I hope this book meets your expectations!

Many, many thanks to my family and friends, especially Rich. You all encouraged me to turn the web site into a book, and supported me wholeheartedly throughout the writing process.

Finally, I want to thank our local champions: the 2003 and 2004 New England Patriots and the 2004 Boston Red Sox. You all helped us believe that anything—anything!—can be possible if we try hard enough.

Even writing a book.

01

WHAT USERS DO

This book is almost entirely about the look and behavior of applications, web applications, and interactive devices. But this first chapter will be the exception to the rule. No screenshots here; no layouts, no navigation, no diagrams, and no visuals at all.

Why not? After all, that's why you may have picked up this book in the first place.

It's because good interface design doesn't start with pictures. It starts with an understanding of people: what they're like, why they use a given piece of software, and how they might interact with it. The more you know about them, and the more you empathize with them, the more effectively you can design for them. Software, after all, is merely a means to an end for the people who use it. The better you satisfy those ends, the happier those users will be.

Each time someone uses an application, or any digital product, they carry on a conversation with the machine. It may be literal, as with a command line or phone menu, or tacit, like the "conversation" an artist has with her paints and canvas—the give and take between the craftsperson and the thing being built. With social software, it may even be a conversation by proxy. Whatever the case, the user interface mediates that conversation, helping the user achieve whatever ends he or she had in mind.

As the user interface designer, then, you get to script that conversation, or at least define its terms. And if you're going to script a conversation, you should understand the human's side as well as possible. What are the user's motives and intentions? What "vocabulary" of words, icons, and gestures does the user expect to use? How can the application set expectations appropriately for the user? How do the user and the machine finally end up communicating meaning to each other?

There's a maxim in the field of interface design: "Know thy users, for they are not you!"

So this chapter will talk about people. It covers a few fundamental ideas briefly in this introduction, and then discusses the patterns themselves. These patterns differ from those in the rest of the book. They describe human behaviors—as opposed to system behaviors—that the software you design may need to support. Software that supports these human behaviors help users achieve their goals.

A MEANS TO AN END

Everyone who uses a tool, software or otherwise, has a reason to use it. For instance:

- Finding some fact or object
- Learning something
- Performing a transaction
- Controlling or monitoring something
- Creating something
- Conversing with other people
- Being entertained

Well-known idioms, user behaviors, and design patterns can support each of these abstract goals. Interaction designers have learned, for example, how to help people search through vast amounts of online information for specific facts. They've learned how to present tasks so that it's easy to walk through them. They are learning ways to support the building of documents, illustrations, and code.

The first step in designing an interface is figuring out what its users are really trying to accomplish. Filling out a form, for example, almost never is a goal in and of itself—people only do it because they're trying to buy something online, get their driver's license renewed, or install a networked printer.[1] They're performing some kind of transaction.

Asking the right questions can help you connect user goals to the design process. Users and clients typically speak to you in terms of desired features and solutions, not of needs and problems. When a user or client tells you he wants a certain feature, ask why he wants it— determine his immediate goal. Then, to the answer of this question, ask "why" again. And again. Keep asking until you move well beyond the boundaries of the immediate design problem.[2]

Why should you ask these questions if you have clear requirements? Because if you love designing things, it's easy to get caught up in an interesting interface-design problem. Maybe you're good at building forms that ask for just the right information, with the right controls, all laid out nicely. But the real art of interface design lies in *solving the right problem*.

So don't get too fond of designing that form. If there's any way to finish the transaction without making the user go through that form at all, get rid of it altogether. That gets the user closer to his goal, with less time and effort spent on his part. (And maybe yours, too.)

Let's use the "why" approach to dig a little deeper into some typical design scenarios.

- Why does a mid-level manager use an email client? Yes, of course—"to read email." Why does she read and send email in the first place? To converse with other people. Of course, other means might achieve the same ends: the phone, a hallway conversation, a formal document. But apparently email fills some needs that the other methods don't. What are they, and why are they important to her? Privacy? The ability to archive a conversation? Social convention? What else?

- A father goes to an online travel agent, types in the city where his family will take a summer vacation, and tries to find plane ticket prices on various dates. He's learning from what he finds, but his goal isn't just browsing and exploring different options. Ask why. His goal is actually a transaction: buying plane tickets. Again, he could have done that at many different web sites, or over the phone with a live travel agent. How is this site better than those other options? Is it faster? Friendlier? More likely to find a better deal?

1. See Eric Raymond's essay, "The Luxury of Ignorance: An Open-Source Horror Story," about his travails with a Linux print utility at *http://www.catb.org/-esr/writings/cups-horror.html*.

2. This is the same principle that underlies a well-known technique called "root cause analysis." However, root cause analysis is a tool for fixing organizational failures; here, you use its "five whys" (more or less) to understand everyday user behaviors and feature requests.

- A cell phone user wants a way to search through his phone list more quickly. You, as the designer, can come up with some clever ideas to save keystrokes while searching. But why did he want it? It turns out that he makes a lot of calls while driving, and he doesn't want to take his eyes off the road more than he has to—he wants to make calls while staying safe (to the extent that that's possible). The ideal case is that he doesn't have to look at the phone at all! A better solution is voice dialing: all he has to do is speak the name, and the phone makes the call for him.

- Sometimes goal analysis really isn't straightforward at all. A snowboarding site might provide information (for learning), an online store (transactions), and a set of Flash movies (entertainment). Let's say someone visits the site for a purchase, but she gets sidetracked into the information on snowboarding tricks—she switched goals from accomplishing a transaction to browsing and learning. Maybe she'll go back to purchasing something, maybe not. And does the entertainment part of the site successfully entertain both the twelve-year-old and the thirty-five-year-old? Will the thirty-five-year-old go elsewhere to buy his new board if he doesn't feel at home there, or does he not care?

It's deceptively easy to model users as a single faceless entity—"The User"—walking through a set of simple use cases, with one task-oriented goal in mind. But that won't necessarily reflect your users' reality.

To do design well, you need to take many "softer" factors into account: gut reactions, preferences, social context, beliefs, and values. All of these factors could affect the design of an application or site. Among these "softer" factors, you may find the critical feature or design factor that makes your application more appealing and successful.

So be curious. Specialize in it. Find out what your users are really like, and what they really think and feel.

THE BASICS OF USER RESEARCH

Empirical discovery is the only really good way to obtain this information. To get a design started, you'll need to characterize the kinds of people who will use whatever you design (including the "softer" categories just mentioned), and the best way to do that is to go out and meet them.

Each user group is unique, of course. The target audience for, say, a new cell phone will differ dramatically from that for a piece of scientific software. Even if the same person uses both, his expectations for each are different—a researcher using scientific software might tolerate a less-polished interface in exchange for high functionality, whereas that same person may trade in his new phone if he finds its UI to be too hard to use after a few days.

Every user is unique, too. What one person finds difficult, the next one won't. The trick is to figure out what *generally* true about your users, which means learning about enough individual users to separate the quirks from the common behavior patterns.

Specifically, you'll want to learn:

- Their goals in using the software you design
- The specific tasks they undertake in pursuit of those goals
- The language and words they use to describe what they're doing
- Their skill at using software similar to what you're designing
- Their attitudes toward the kind of thing you're designing, and how different designs might affect those attitudes

I can't tell you what your particular target audience is like. You need to find out what they might do with the software you design, and how it fits into the broader context of their lives. Difficult though it may be, try to describe your potential audience in terms of how and why they might use your software. You might get several distinct answers, representing distinct user groups; that's okay. You might be tempted to throw up your hands and say, "I don't know who the users are," or, "Everyone is a potential user." That doesn't help you focus your design at all—without a concrete and honest description of those people, your design will proceed with no grounding in reality.

Unfortunately, this user-discovery phase will consume serious time early in the design cycle. It's expensive, but always worth it, because you stand a better chance at solving the right problem—you'll build the right thing in the first place.

Fortunately, lots of books, courses, and methodologies now exist to help you. Although this book does not address user research, here are some methods and topics to consider.

Direct observation

Interviews and on-site user visits put you directly into the user's world. You can ask users about what their goals are and what tasks they typically do. Usually done "on location," where users would actually use the software (e.g., in a workplace or at home), interviews can be structured—with a predefined set of questions—or unstructured, in which you might probe whatever subject comes up. Interviews give you a lot of flexibility; you can do many or a few, long or short, formal or informal, on the phone or in person. These are great opportunities to learn what you don't know. Ask why. Ask it again.

Case studies

Case studies give you deep, detailed views into a few representative users or groups of users. You can sometimes use them to explore "extreme" users that push the boundaries of what the software can do, especially when the goal is a redesign of existing software. You also can use them as longitudinal studies—exploring the context of use over weeks, months, or even years. Finally, if you design custom software for a single user or site, you'll want to learn as much as possible about the actual context of use.

Surveys

Written surveys can collect information from many users. You can actually get statistically significant numbers of respondents with these. Since there's no direct human contact, you will miss a lot of extra information—whatever you don't ask about, you won't learn about—but you can get a very clear picture of certain aspects of your target audience. Careful survey design is essential. If you want reliable numbers instead of a qualitative "feel" for the target audience, you absolutely must write the questions correctly, pick the survey recipients correctly, and analyze the answers correctly—and that's a science.

Personas

Personas aren't a data-gathering method, but they do help you figure out what to do with that data once you've got it. This is a design technique that "models" the target audiences. For each major user group, you create a fictional person that captures the most important aspects of the users in that group: what tasks they're trying to accomplish, their ultimate goals, and their experience levels in the subject domain and with computers in general. They help you stay focused. As your design proceeds, you can ask yourself questions like, "Would this fictional person really do X? What would she do instead?"

And there's more. You might notice that some of these methods and topics, like interviews and surveys, sound suspiciously like marketing activities. That's exactly what they are. Focus groups can be useful too (though not so much as the others), and the concept of market segmentation resembles the definition of target audiences we've used here. In both cases, the whole point is to understand the audience as best you can.

The difference is that as a designer, you're trying to understand the people who use the software. A marketing professional tries to understand those who buy it.

It's not easy to understand the real issues that underlie users' interaction with a system. Users don't always have the language or introspective skill to explain what they really need to accomplish their goals, and it takes a lot of work on your part to ferret out useful design concepts from what they *can* tell you—self-reported observations usually are biased in subtle ways.

Some of these techniques are very formal, and some aren't. Formal and quantitative methods are valuable because they're good science. When applied correctly, they help you see the world as it actually is, not how you think it is. If you do user research haphazardly, without accounting for biases like the self-selection of users, you may end up with data that doesn't reflect your actual target audience—and that can only hurt your design in the long run.

But if you don't have time for formal methods, it's better to just meet a few users informally than to not do any discovery at all. Talking with users is good for the soul. If you're able to empathize with users and imagine those individuals actually using your design, you'll produce something much better.

USERS' MOTIVATION TO LEARN

Before you start the design process, consider your overall approach. Think about how you might design its overall interaction style—its personality, if you will.

When you carry on a conversation with someone about a given subject, you adjust what you say according to your understanding of the other person. You might consider how much he cares about the subject, how much he already knows about it, how receptive he is to learning from you, and whether he's even interested in the conversation in the first place. If you get any of that wrong, then bad things happen—he might feel patronized, uninterested, impatient, or utterly baffled.

This analogy leads to some obvious design advice. The subject-specific vocabulary you use in your interface, for instance, should match your users' level of knowledge; if some users won't know that vocabulary, give them a way to learn the unfamiliar terms. If they don't know computers very well, don't make them use sophisticated widgetry or uncommon interface-design conventions. If their level of interest might be low, respect that, and don't ask for too much effort for too little reward.

Some of these concerns permeate the whole interface design in subtle ways. For example, do your users expect a short, tightly focused exchange about something very specific, or do they look for a conversation that's more of a free-ranging exploration? In other words, how much openness is there in the interface? Too little, and your users feel trapped and unsatisfied; too much, and they stand there paralyzed, not knowing what to do next, unprepared for that level of interaction.

Therefore, you need to choose how much freedom your users have to act arbitrarily. At one end of the scale might be a software installation wizard: the user is carried through it with no opportunity to use anything other than Next, Previous, or Cancel. It's tightly focused and specific, but quite efficient—and satisfying, to the extent that it works and is quick. At the other end might be an application like Excel, an "open floor plan" interface that exposes a huge number of features in one place. At any given time, the user has about 872 things that she can do next, but that's considered good because self-directed, skilled users can do a lot with that interface. Again, it's satisfying, but for entirely different reasons.

Here's an even more fundamental question: how much effort are your users willing to spend to learn your interface?

It's easy to overestimate. Maybe they use it every day on the job—clearly they'd be motivated to learn it well in that case, but that's rare. Maybe they use it sometimes, and learn it only well enough to get by. Maybe they'll only see it once, for 30 seconds. Be honest: can you expect most users to become intermediate-to-expert users, or will most users remain perpetual beginners?

Software designed for intermediate-to-expert users include:

- Photoshop
- Dreamweaver
- Emacs
- Code development environments
- System-administration tools for web servers

In contrast, here are some things designed for occasional users:

- Kiosks in tourist centers or museums
- Windows or Mac OS controls for setting desktop backgrounds
- Purchase pages for online stores

- Installation wizards
- Automated teller machines

The differences between the two groups are dramatic. Assumptions about users' tool knowledge permeate these interfaces, showing up in their screen-space usage, labeling, widget sophistication, and the places where help is (or isn't) offered.

The applications in the first group have lots of complex functionality, but they don't generally walk the user through tasks step-by-step. They assume users already know what to do, and they optimize for efficient operation, not learnability; they tend to be document-centered or list-driven (with a few being command-line applications). They often have entire books and courses written about them. Their learning curves are steep.

The applications in the second group are the opposite: restrained in functionality but helpful about explaining it along the way. They present simplified interfaces, assuming no prior knowledge of document- or list-centered application styles (e.g., menu bars, multiple selection, etc.). Wizards frequently show up, removing attention-focusing responsibility from the user. The key is that users aren't motivated to work hard at learning these interfaces—it's usually just not worth it!

Now that you've seen the extremes, look at the applications in the middle of the continuum:

- Microsoft Office
- Email clients
- Web browsers
- Cell phone applications
- PalmOS

The truth is, most applications fall into this middle ground. They need to serve people on both ends adequately—to help new users learn the tool (and satisfy their need for instant gratification), while enabling frequent-user intermediates to get their work done smoothly. Their designers probably knew that people wouldn't take a three-day course to learn an email client. Yet the interfaces hold up under repeated usage. People quickly learn the basics, reach a proficiency level that satisfies them, and don't bother learning more until they are motivated to do so for specific purposes.

Alan Cooper coined the terms "sovereign posture" and "transient posture" to discuss these approaches. Sovereign-posture applications work with users as partners; users spend time in them, give them their full attention, learn them well, and expand them to full-screen size. Transient-posture programs are brought up briefly, used, and dismissed. These roughly correspond to the two extremes I posited, but not entirely. See the book *About Face 2.0: The Essentials of Interaction Design* for a more nuanced explanation of postures.

Someday you will find yourself in tension between the two ends of this spectrum. Naturally you want people to be able to use your application "out of the box," but you also might want to support frequent or expert users as much as possible. Find a balance that works for your situation. Organizational patterns in Chapter 2 such as **Multi-Level Help**, **Intriguing Branches**, and **Extras on Demand** can help you serve both constituencies.

THE PATTERNS

Even though individuals are unique, people behave predictably. Designers have been doing site visits and user observations for years; cognitive scientists and other researchers have spent many hundreds of hours watching how people do things and how they think about what they do.

So when you observe people using your software, or performing whatever activity you want to support with new software, you can expect them to do certain things. The behavioral patterns listed below often are seen in user observations. Odds are good that you'll see them too, especially if you look for them.

A note for patterns enthusiasts: These patterns aren't like the others in this book. They describe human behaviors, not interface elements, and they're not prescriptive like the patterns in other chapters. Instead of being structured like the other patterns, these are presented as small essays.

Again, an interface that supports these patterns well will help users achieve their goals far more effectively than interfaces that don't support them. And the patterns are not just about the interface, either. Sometimes the entire package—interface, underlying architecture, feature choice, and documentation—needs to be considered in light of these behaviors. But as the interface designer or interaction designer, you should think about these as much as anyone on your team. You may be in the best position to advocate for the users.

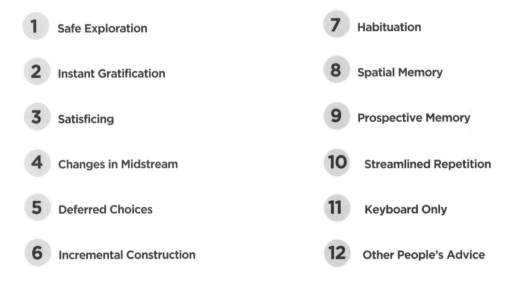

1   **Safe Exploration**

2   **Instant Gratification**

3   **Satisficing**

4   **Changes in Midstream**

5   **Deferred Choices**

6   **Incremental Construction**

7   **Habituation**

8   **Spatial Memory**

9   **Prospective Memory**

10   **Streamlined Repetition**

11   **Keyboard Only**

12   **Other People's Advice**

1 safe exploration

"Let me explore without getting lost or getting into trouble."

When someone feels like she can explore an interface and not suffer dire consequences, she's likely to learn more—and feel more positive about it—than someone who doesn't explore. Good software allows people to try something unfamiliar, back out, and try something else, all without stress.

Those "dire consequences" don't even have to be very bad. Mere annoyance can be enough to deter someone from trying things out voluntarily. Clicking away popup windows, re-entering data mistakenly erased, suddenly muting the volume on one's laptop when a web site unexpectedly plays loud music—all can be discouraging. When you design almost any kind of software interface, make many avenues of exploration available for users to experiment with, without costing the user anything.

Here are some examples:

- A photographer tries out a few image filters in an image-processing application. He then decides he doesn't like the results and hits "Undo" a few times to get back to where he was. Then he tries another filter, and another—each time being able to back out of what he did. (The pattern named **Multi-Level Undo**, in Chapter 5, describes how this works.)

- A new visitor to a company's home page clicks various links just to see what's there, trusting that the Back button will always get her back to the main page. No extra windows or popups open, and the Back button keeps working predictably. You can imagine that if a web application does something different in response to the Back button—or if an application offers a button that seems like a Back button, but doesn't behave quite like it—then confusion might ensue. The user can get disoriented while navigating, and may abandon the application altogether.

- A cell phone user wants to try out some intriguing new online functionality, like getting sports scores for the World Series in real time. But he's hesitant to try it because the last time he used an online service, he was charged an exorbitant amount of money just for experimenting with it for a few minutes.

2 instant gratification

"I want to accomplish something now, not later."

People like to see immediate results from the actions they take—it's human nature. If someone starts using an application and gets a "success experience" within the first few seconds, that's gratifying! He'll be more likely to keep using it, even if it gets harder later. He will feel more confident in the application, and more confident in himself, than if it had taken a while to figure things out.

The need to support instant gratification has many design ramifications. For instance, if you can predict the first thing a new user is likely to do, then you should design the UI to make that first thing stunningly easy. If the user's goal is to create something, for instance, then show a new canvas and put a palette next to it. If the user's goal is to accomplish some task, point the way toward a typical starting point.

It also means that you shouldn't hide introductory functionality behind anything that needs to be read or waited for, such as registrations, long sets of instructions, slow-to-load screens, or advertisements. These are discouraging because they block users from finishing that first task quickly.

3 satisficing

"This is good enough. I don't want to spend more time learning to do it better."

When people look at a new interface, they don't read every piece of it methodically and then decide, "Hmmm, I think this button has the best chance of getting me what I want." Instead, a user will rapidly scan the interface, pick whatever he sees first that might get him what he wants, and try it—even if it might be wrong.

The term "satisficing" is a combination of "satisfying" and "sufficing." It was devised in 1957 by the social scientist Herbert Simon, who used it to describe the behavior of people in all kinds of economic and social situations. People are willing to accept "good enough" instead of "best" if learning all the alternatives might cost time or effort.

Satisficing is actually a very rational behavior, once you appreciate the mental work necessary to "parse" a complicated interface. As Steve Krug points out in his book *Don't Make Me Think,* (New Riders) people don't like to think any more than they have to—it's work! But if the interface presents an obvious option or two that the user sees immediately, he'll try it. Chances are good that it will be the right choice, and if not, there's little cost in backing out and trying something else (assuming that the interface supports **Safe Exploration**).

This means several things for designers:

- Make labels short, plainly worded, and quick to read. (This includes menu items, buttons, links, and anything else identified by text.) They'll be scanned and guessed about; write them so that a user's first guess about meaning is correct. If he guesses wrong several times, he'll be frustrated and you're both off to a bad start.

- Use the layout of the interface to communicate meaning. Chapter 4, *Layout*, explains how to do so in detail. Users "parse" color and form on sight, and they follow these cues more efficiently than labels that must be read.

- Make it easy to move around the interface, especially for going back to where a wrong choice might have been made hastily. Provide "escape hatches" (see Chapter 3). On typical web sites, using the Back button

is easy, so designing easy forward/backward navigation is especially important for web applications, but it's also important for installed applications and devices.

- Keep in mind that a complicated interface imposes a large cognitive cost on new users. Visual complexity will often tempt nonexperts to satisfice: they look for the first thing that may work.

Satisficing is why many users end up with odd habits after they've been using a system for a while. Long ago, a user may have learned Path A to do something, and even though a later version of the system offers Path B as a better alternative (or was there all along), he sees no benefit in learning it— that takes effort, after all—and he keeps using the less-efficient Path A. It's not necessarily an irrational choice. Breaking old habits and learning something new takes energy, and a small improvement may not be worth the cost to the user.

4   changes in midstream

"I changed my mind about what I was doing."

Occasionally, people change what they're doing in the middle of doing it. Someone may walk into a room with the intent of finding a key she had left there, but while she's there, she finds a newspaper and starts reading it. Or she may visit Amazon to read product reviews, but ends up buying a book instead. Maybe she's just sidetracked; maybe the change is deliberate. Either way, the user's goal changes while she's using the interface you designed.

What this means for designers is that you should provide opportunities for people to do that. Make choices available. Don't lock users into a choice-poor environment with no global navigation, or no connections to other pages or functionality, unless there's a good reason to do so. Those reasons do exist. See the patterns called **Wizard** (Chapter 2), **Hub and Spoke** (Chapter 3), and **Modal Panel** (Chapter 3) for examples.

You also can make it easy for someone to start a process, stop in the middle, and come back to it later to pick up where he left off—a property often called "reentrance." For instance, a lawyer may start entering information into a form on a PDA. Then when a client comes into the room, the lawyer has to turn off the PDA with the intent of coming back to finish the form later. The entered information shouldn't be lost.

To support reentrance, you can make dialog boxes remember values typed previously (see **Good Defaults** in Chapter 7), and they don't usually need to be modal; if they're not modal, a user can drag them aside on the screen for later use. Builder-style applications—text editors, code development environments, and paint programs—can let a user work on multiple projects at one time, thus letting the user put any number of projects aside while she works on another one.

Online surveys hosted by surveymonkey.com sometimes offer a button on each page of a survey that says, "I'll finish it later." This button closes the browser page, records the choices made up to that point, and lets the user come back to finish the survey later.

5 deferred choices

"I don't want to answer that now; just let me finish!"

This follows from people's desire for instant gratification. If you ask a user several seemingly unnecessary questions while he's trying to get something done, he'd often rather skip the questions and come back to them later.

For example, some web-based bulletin boards have long and complicated procedures for registering users. Screen names, email addresses, privacy preferences, avatars, self-descriptions...the list goes on and on. "But I just wanted to post one little thing," says the user plaintively. Why not skip most of the questions, answer the bare minimum, and come back later (if ever) to fill in the rest? Otherwise he

might be there for half an hour answering essay questions and finding the perfect avatar image.

Another example is creating a new project in Dreamweaver or other web site editors. There are some things you do have to decide up front, like the name of the project, but you can defer other choices easily—where on the server are you going to put this when you're done? I don't know yet!

Sometimes it's just a matter of not wanting to answer the questions. At other times, the user may not have enough information to answer yet. What if a music-writing software package asked you up front for the title, key, and tempo of a new song, before you've even started writing it? (See Apple's GarageBand for this lovely bit of design.)

The implications for interface design are simple to understand, though not always easy to implement:

- Don't accost the user with too many up-front choices in the first place.

- On the forms that he does have to use, clearly mark the required fields, and don't make too many of them required. Let him move on without answering the optional ones.

- Sometimes you can separate the few important questions or options from others that are less important. Present the short list; hide the long list. See the **Extras on Demand** pattern in Chapter 2.

- Use **Good Defaults** (Chapter 7) wherever possible, to give users some reasonable default answers to start with. But keep in mind that prefilled answers still require the user to look at them, just in case they need to be changed. They have a small cost, too.

- Make it possible for users to return to the deferred fields later, and make them accessible in obvious places. Some dialog boxes show the user a short statement such as "You can always change this later by clicking the Edit Project button." Some web sites store a user's half-finished form entries or other persistent data, like shopping carts with unpurchased items.

- If registration is required at a web site that provides useful services, users may be far more likely to register if they're first allowed to experience the web site—drawn in and engaged—and then asked later about who they are. In fact, TurboTax 2005 allows a user to work through an entire tax form before creating a username.

6 incremental construction

"Let me change this. That doesn't look right; let me change it again. That's better."

When people create things, they don't usually do it all at once. Even an expert doesn't start at the beginning, work through the creation process methodically, and come out with something perfect and finished at the end.

Quite the opposite. Instead, she starts with some small piece of it, works on it, steps back and looks at it, tests it (if it's code or some other "runnable" thing), fixes what's wrong, and starts to build other parts of it. Or maybe she starts over if she really doesn't like it. The creative process goes in fits and starts. It moves backwards as much as forwards sometimes, and it's often incremental, done in a series of small changes instead of a few big ones. Sometimes it's top-down; sometimes it's bottom-up.

Builder-style interfaces need to support that style of work. Make it easy to build small pieces one at a time. Keep the interface responsive to quick changes and saves. Feedback is critical: constantly show the user what the whole thing looks and behaves like while the user works. If you deal with code, simulations, or other executable things, make the "compile" part of the cycle as short as possible so the operational feedback feels immediate—leave little or no delay between the user making changes and seeing the results.

When good tools support creative activities, the activities can induce a state of "flow" in the user. This is a state of full absorption in the activity, during which time distorts, other distractions fall away, and the person can remain engaged for hours—the enjoyment of the activity is its own reward. Artists, athletes, and programmers all know this state.

Bad tools will keep someone distracted, guaranteed. If the user has to wait even half a minute to see the results of the incremental change she just made, then her concentration is broken; flow is disrupted.

If you want to read more about flow, look at the books by Mihaly Csikszentmihalyi, who studied it for years.

7 habituation

"That gesture works everywhere else; why doesn't it work here, too?"

When one uses an interface repeatedly, some frequently used physical actions become reflexive: typing Control-S to save a document, clicking the Back button to leave a web page, pressing Return to close a modal dialog box, using gestures to show and hide windows, or even pressing a car's brake pedal. The user no longer needs to think consciously about these actions. They've become habitual.

This tendency certainly helps people become expert users of a tool (and it helps create a sense of flow, too). Habituation measurably improves efficiency, as you can imagine. But it can also lay traps for the user. If a gesture becomes a habit and the user tries to use it in a situation when it doesn't work—or, worse, does something destructive—then the user is caught short. He suddenly must think about the tool again (What did I just do? How do I do what I intended?), and he might have to undo any damage done by the gesture.

For instance, Control-X, Control-S is the "save this file" key sequence used by the emacs text editor.

Control-A moves the text-entry cursor to the beginning of a line. These acts become habitual for emacs users. When a user types Control-A, Control-X, Control-S at emacs, it performs a fairly innocuous pair of operations.

Now what happens when he types that same habituated sequence in Microsoft Word?

1. Control-A: select all
2. Control-X: cut the selection (the whole document, in this case)
3. Control-S: save the document (whoops)

This is why consistency across applications is important!

Just as important, though, is consistency within an application. Some applications are evil because they establish an expectation that some gesture will do Action X, except in one special mode, where it suddenly does Action Y. Don't do that. It's a sure bet that users will make mistakes, and the more experienced they are—i.e., the more habituated they are—the more likely they are to make that mistake.

This is also why confirmation dialog boxes often don't work to protect a user against accidental changes. When modal dialog boxes pop up, the user can easily get rid of them just by clicking "OK" or hitting Return (if the OK button is the default button). If dialogs pop up all the time when the user is making intended changes, such as deleting files, it becomes a habituated response. Then when it actually matters, the dialog box doesn't have any effect, because it slips right under the user's consciousness.

I've seen at least one application that sets up the confirmation dialog box's buttons randomly from one invocation to another. One actually has to *read* the buttons to figure out what to click! This isn't necessarily the best way to do a confirmation dialog box—in fact, it's better to not have them at all under most circumstances—but at least this design sidesteps habituation creatively.

8 spatial memory

"I swear that button was here a minute ago. Where did it go?"

When people manipulate objects and documents, they often find them again later by remembering where they are, not what they're named.

Take the Windows, Mac, or Linux desktop. Many people use the desktop background as a place to put documents, frequently used applications, and other such things. It turns out that people tend to use spatial memory to find things on the desktop, and it's very effective. People devise their own groupings, for instance, or recall that "the document was at the top right over by such-and-such." (Naturally, there are real-world equivalents too. Many people's desks are "organized chaos," an apparent mess in which the office owner can find anything instantly. But heaven forbid that someone should clean it up for them.)

Many applications put their dialog buttons—OK, Cancel, etc.—in predictable places, partly because spatial memory for them is so strong. In complex applications, people also may find things by remembering where they are relative to other things: tools on toolbars, objects in hierarchies, and so on. Therefore, you should use patterns like **Responsive Disclosure** (Chapter 4) carefully. Adding something to an interface doesn't usually cause problems, but rearranging existing controls can disrupt spatial memory and make things harder to find. It depends. Try it out on your users if you're not sure.

Along with habituation, which is closely related, spatial memory is another reason why consistency across and within applications is good. People may expect to find similar functionality in similar places.

Spatial memory explains why it's good to provide user-arranged areas for storing documents and objects, like the aforementioned desktops. Such things aren't always practical, especially with large numbers of objects, but it works quite well with small numbers. When people arrange things themselves, they're likely to remember where they put them. (Just don't rearrange things for them unless they ask!) The **Movable Panels** pattern in Chapter 4 describes one way to do this.

Also, this is why changing menus dynamically sometimes backfires. People get used to seeing certain items on the tops and bottoms of menus. Rearranging or compacting menu items "helpfully" can work against habituation and lead to user errors.

Incidentally, the tops and bottoms of lists and menus are special locations, cognitively speaking. People notice and remember them more than stuff in the middle of menus. They are the worst items to change out from under the user.

9 prospective memory

"I'm putting this here to remind myself to deal with it later."

Prospective memory is a well-known phenomenon in psychology that doesn't seem to have gained much traction yet in interface design. But I think it should.

We engage in prospective memory when we plan to do something in the future, and we arrange some way of reminding ourselves to do it. For example, if you need to bring a book to work the next day, you might put it on a table beside the front door the night before. If you need to respond to someone's email later (just not right now!), you might leave that email on your screen as a physical reminder. Or, if you tend to miss meetings, you might arrange for Outlook or your Palm to ring an alarm tone five minutes before each meeting.

Basically, this is something almost everyone does. It's part of how we cope with our complicated, highly scheduled, multitasked lives: we use knowledge "in the world" to aid our own imperfect memories. We need to be able to do it well.

Some software does support prospective remembering. Outlook and PalmOS, as mentioned above,

implement it directly and actively; they have calendars (as do many other software systems), and they sound alarms. But what else can you use for prospective memory?

- Notes to oneself, like virtual "sticky notes"
- Windows left onscreen
- Annotations put directly into documents (like "Finish me!")
- Browser bookmarks, for web sites to be viewed later
- Documents stored on the desktop, rather than in the usual places in the filesystem
- Email kept in an inbox (and maybe flagged) instead of filed away

People use all kinds of artifacts to support passive prospective remembering. But notice that almost none of the techniques in the list above were designed with that in mind! What they *were* designed for is flexibility—and a laissez-faire attitude toward how users organize their information. A good email client lets you create folders with any names you want, and it doesn't care what you do with messages in your inbox. Text editors don't care what you type, or what giant bold magenta text means to you; code editors don't care that you have a "Finish this" comment in a method header. Browsers don't know why you keep certain bookmarks around.

In many cases, that kind of hands-off flexibility is all you really need. Give people the tools to create their own reminder systems. Just don't try to design a system that's too smart for its own good. For instance, don't assume that just because a window's been idle for a while, no one's using it and it should be closed. In general, don't "helpfully" clean up files or objects that the system may think are useless; someone may be leaving them around for a reason. Also, don't organize or sort things automatically unless the user asks the system to do so.

As a designer, is there anything positive you can do for prospective memory? If someone leaves a form half-finished and closes it temporarily, you could retain the data in it for the next time—it will help remind the user where she left off. Similarly, many applications recall the last few objects or documents they edited. You could offer bookmarks-like lists of "objects of interest"—both past and future—and make that list easily available for reading and editing.

Here's a bigger challenge: if the user starts tasks and leaves them without finishing them, think about how to leave some artifacts around, other than open windows, that identify the unfinished tasks. Another one: how might a user gather reminders from different sources (email, documents, calendars, etc.) into one place? Be creative!

10 streamlined repetition

"I have to repeat this how many times?"

In many kinds of applications, users sometimes find themselves having to perform the same operation over and over again. The easier it is for them, the better. If you can help reduce that operation down to one keystroke or click per repetition—or, better, just a few keystrokes or clicks for all repetitions—then you will spare users much tedium.

Find and Replace dialog boxes, often found in text editors (Word, email composers, etc.), are one good adaptation to this behavior. In these dialog boxes, the user types the old phrase and the new phrase. Then it takes only one "Replace" button click per occurrence in the whole document. And that's only if the user wanted to see or veto each replacement—if they're confident that they really should replace all occurrences, then they can click the "Replace All" button. One gesture does the whole job.

Here's a more general example. Photoshop lets you record "actions" when you want to perform some arbitrary sequence of operations with a single click. If you want to resize, crop, brighten, and save 20 images, you can record those four steps as they're done to the first image, and then click that action's "Play" button for each of the remaining 19.

See the **Macros** pattern in Chapter 5 for more information.

Scripting environments are even more general. Unix and its variants allow you to script anything you can type into a shell. You can recall and execute single commands, even long ones, with a Control-P and return. You can take any set of commands you issue to the command line, put them in a for-loop, and execute them by hitting the Return key once. Or you can put them in a shellscript (or in a for-loop in a shellscript!) and execute them as a single command. Scripting is very powerful, and as it gets more complex, it becomes full-fledged programming.

Other variants include copy-and-paste capability (preventing the need to retype the same thing in a million places), user-defined "shortcuts" to applications on operating-system desktops (preventing the need to find those applications' directories in the filesystem), browser bookmarks (so users don't have to type URLs), and even keyboard shortcuts.

Direct observation of users can help you find out just what kinds of repetitive tasks you need to support. Users won't always tell you outright. They may not even be aware that they're doing repetitive things that they could streamline with the right tools—they may have been doing it so long that they don't even notice anymore. By watching them work, you may see what they don't see.

In any case, the idea is to offer users ways to streamline the repetitive tasks that could otherwise be time consuming, tedious, and error prone.

11 keyboard only

"Please don't make me use the mouse."

Some people have real physical trouble using a mouse. Others prefer not to keep switching between the mouse and keyboard because that takes time and effort—they'd rather keep their hands on the keyboard at all times. Still others can't see the screen, and their assistive technologies often interact with the software using just the keyboard API.

For the sakes of these users, some applications are designed to be "driven" entirely via the keyboard. They're usually mouse-driven too, but there is no operation that must be done with *only* the mouse—keyboard-only users aren't shut out of any functionality.

Several standard techniques exist for keyboard-only usage:

- You can define keyboard shortcuts, accelerators, and mnemonics for operations reachable via application menu bars, like Control-S for Save. See your platform style guide for the standard ones.

- Selection from lists, even multiple selection, usually is possible using arrow keys in combination with modifiers (like the Shift key), though this depends on which platform you use.

- The Tab key typically moves the keyboard focus—the control that gets keyboard entries at the moment—from one control to the next, and Shift-Tab moves backwards. This is sometimes called "tab traversal." Many users expect it to work on form-style interfaces.

- Most standard controls, even radio buttons and combo boxes, let users change their values from the keyboard by using arrow keys, the Return key, or the spacebar.

- Dialog boxes and web pages often have a "default button"—a button representing an action that says "I'm done with this task now." On web pages, it's often Submit or Done; on dialog boxes, OK or Cancel. When users hit the Return key on this page or dialog box, that's the operation that occurs. Then it moves the user to the next page or returns him to the previous window.

There are more techniques. Forms, control panels, and standard web pages are fairly easy to drive from the keyboard. Graphic editors, and anything else that's mostly spatial, are much harder, though not impossible. See **Spring-Loaded Mode**, in Chapter 8, for one way to use keyboards in graphic editors.

Keyboard-only usage is particularly important for data-entry applications. In these, speed of data entry is critical, and users can't afford to move their hands off the keyboard to the mouse every time they want to move from one field to another, or even from one page to another. (In fact, many of these forms don't even require users to hit the Tab key to traverse between controls; it's done automatically.)

12 other people's advice

"What did everyone else say about this?"

People are social. As strong as our opinions may sometimes be, what our peers think tends to influence us.

Witness the spectacular growth of online "user comments": Amazon for books, IMDb.com for movies, photo.net and flickr for photographs, and countless retailers who offer space for user-submitted product reviews. Auction sites like eBay formalize user opinions into actual prices. Blogs offer unlimited soapbox space for people to opine about anything they want, from products to programming to politics.

The advice of peers, whether direct or indirect, influences people's choices when they decide any number of things. Finding things online, performing transactions (should I buy this product?), playing games (what have other players done here?), and even building things—people can be more effective when aided by others. If not, they might at least be happier with the outcome.

Here's a more subtle example. Programmers use the MATLAB application to do scientific and mathematical tasks. Every few months, the company that makes MATLAB holds a public programming contest; for a few days, every contestant writes the best MATLAB code they can to solve a difficult science problem. The fastest, most accurate code wins. The catch is that every player can see everyone else's code—and copying is encouraged! The "advice" in this case is indirect, taking the form of shared code, but it's quite influential. In the end, the winning program is never truly original, but it's undoubtedly better code than any single solo effort would have been. (In many respects, it's a microcosm of open-source software development, which is driven by a powerful set of social dynamics.)

Not all applications and software systems can accommodate a social component, and not all should try. But consider whether it might enhance the user experience to do so. And you could be more creative than just tacking a web-based bulletin board onto an ordinary site. How can you persuade users to take part constructively? How can you integrate it into the typical user's workflow?

If the task is creative, maybe you can encourage people to post their creations for the public to view. If the goal is to find some fact or object, perhaps you can make it easy for users to see what other people found in similar searches.

Of the patterns in this book, **Multi-Level Help** (Chapter 2), most directly addresses this idea; an online support community is a valuable part of a complete help system for some applications.

ORGANIZING THE CONTENT:
INFORMATION ARCHITECTURE AND
APPLICATION STRUCTURE

At this point, you may know what your users want out of your application. You may know which idiom or interface type to use, such as a graphic editor, a form, web-like hypertext, or a media player—or an idea of how to combine several of them. If you're really on the ball, you've written down some typical scenarios that describe how people might use high-level elements of the application to accomplish their goals. You have a clear idea of what value this application adds to people's lives.

Now what?

You could start making sketches of the interface. Many visual thinkers do that at this stage. If you're the kind of person who likes to think visually, and needs to play with sketches while working out the broad strokes of the design, go for it.

But if you're not a visual thinker by nature (and sometimes even if you are), then hold off on the interface sketches. They might lock your thinking into the first visual designs you manage to put on paper. You need to stay flexible and creative for a little while, until you work out the overall organization of the application.

High-level organization is a wickedly difficult topic. It helps to think about it from several angles, so this introduction takes two aspects that I've found useful and discusses them in some depth.

The first, "Dividing Stuff Up," encourages you to try separating the content of the application entirely from its physical presentation. Rather than thinking in terms of windows, tree views, and links, you might think abstractly about how to organize the actions and objects in your application in the way truest to your subject matter. You can postpone the decisions about using specific windows and widgets. Clearly this separation of concerns is useful when you design multimodal applications (e.g., the same content presented both on the Web and on a palmtop, with very different physical presentations), but it's also good for brand new applications or deep redesigns. This approach forces you to think about the right things first: organization and task flows.

Second, "Physical Structure" gets into the presentation of the material in pages, windows, and panels. In truth, it's very difficult to completely separate presentation from organization of the content; they're interdependent. The physical forms of devices and web pages can place tight constraints on a design, and on the desktop, an application's window structure is a major design choice. So it earns a place in this chapter.

THE BASICS OF INFORMATION ARCHITECTURE: DIVIDING STUFF UP

In the Preface, I talked a bit about interface idioms.[1] These, you might recall, are interface types or styles that have become familiar to some user populations. They include text editors, forms, games, command lines, and spreadsheets. They're useful because they let you start a design with a set of familiar conventions; you don't have to start from first principles. And once a first-time user recognizes the idiom being used, she has a head start on understanding the interface.

Whatever it is you're building, you've probably decided which idioms to use. But what may not be so obvious is how to organize the "stuff" you're presenting via these idioms. If your application is small enough to fit on one page or physical panel, great—you're off and running. But odds are good that you're dealing with a lot of features, tools, or content areas. The nature of the high-tech industry is to keep cramming more stuff into these interfaces, since features usually are what sell.

If you've done any work on web sites, you may know the term "information architecture." That's essentially what you'll be doing first. You need to figure out how to structure all this content and functionality: how to organize it, label it, and guide a user through the interface to get what they came for. Like a real-world architect, you're planning the informational "space" where people will dwell.

But applications are different from traditional web sites. Think about it in terms of "nouns" versus "verbs." In web sites and many other media—books, movies, music, graphic design— you work with nouns. You arrange them, present them, categorize them, and index them. Users know what to do with text and images and such. But applications, by definition, exist so people can get things done: write, draw, perform transactions, interact with others, and keep track of things. You're manipulating verbs now. You need to structure the interface so users always know what to do next (or at least have a good idea where to look).

Most applications (and many web sites) are organized according to one or more of the following approaches. Some use nouns, others use verbs:

- Lists of objects—e.g., an inbox full of email messages
- Lists of actions or tasks—e.g., browse, buy, sell, or register
- Lists of subject categories—e.g., health, science, or technology
- Lists of tools—e.g., calendar, address book, or notepad

You should base your choice on several interrelated factors: the nature and domain (subject matter) of the application, users' domain knowledge, users' comfort level with computers in general, and, most of all, how closely your application needs to match the *mental models* that users already have of the domain. (Mental models represent what users believe to be true about something, based on previous experience or understanding: classifications, vocabulary, processes, cause and effect, and so on.)

---

1. The term "idiom" comes from Scott McCloud's *Understanding Comics*, where it's used to describe a genre of work that has developed its own vocabulary of styles, gestures, and content. Another term might be "type," as used in Malcolm McCullough's *Digital Ground* to describe architectural forms and conventions.

You can trace many problems in UI design to a poor choice here, or worse, a confusing mixture of more than one type of organization—like tools and subject categories mixed into one navigation bar with ambiguous titles.

On the other hand, sometimes a mixed organization works fine. Some of the more interesting small-scale UI innovations have come from mixing nouns with verbs on the same menu, for instance; its usability depends on context. Also, you can apply these divisions not only to the top level of the application, but to numerous levels inside them. Different parts of an interface demand different organizational approaches.

Again, this isn't rocket science; you've seen these concepts before. But sometimes it's easy to choose one kind of division by default and not think carefully about which might be best. By calling them out, we make them visible and amenable to discussion. This will be true about many patterns and organizational models described in this book.

Let's take a closer look at these four categorizations and see what they're each best for.

LISTS OF OBJECTS

Most of the time, it will be pretty obvious when to use this categorization. Collections of email messages, songs, books, images (see the iPhoto example in Figure 2-1), search results, and financial transactions—we cope with them in the software we use every day. From these lists, we reach various familiar interface idioms: forms to edit things, media players to play things, and web pages to view things.

FIGURE 2-1 / Lists of photos in iPhoto, sorted by album and displayed as thumbnails in a table

You will find these objects in selectable lists, tables, trees, or whatever is appropriate; some UIs are very creative. At one extreme, cell phone phonebooks may be short and linear, comprising only a few entries that you can scan quickly on a tiny screen. But TiVos list their recorded TV shows in multilevel hierarchies that you must traverse with several clicks, and the most sophisticated email clients allow all kinds of complex sorting and filtering. When you build these kinds of interfaces, make sure the design scales up appropriately, and take care to match the capabilities and needs of users with the functionality your interface provides.

There's much to be said about organizing and presenting the objects in such an interface. That's your next task as information architect. These models are most common:

- Linear, usually sorted
- 2D tables, also sorted, which often let the user sort via column headers, or filter according to various criteria
- A hierarchy that groups items into categories (and possibly subcategories)
- A hierarchy that reveals relationships: parent/child, containers, etc.
- Spatial organizations, such as maps, charts, or desktop-like areas in which users can place things where they want

In fact, all of these models (except 2D tables) apply to all four approaches to dividing up an interface: objects, tasks, categories, and tools. Your choice should depend upon what people want to do with the application, what best fits their mental models, and what best suits the natural organization—if any—of the objects in question.

If you present timetables for city buses, for instance, the natural organization is by bus or route number. A linear list of routes is a valid way to organize it. But not everyone will know what bus number they want; a spatial organization, like an interactive city map, may be more useful. You also might consider a hierarchy of areas, stations in those areas, and routes leaving those stations.

Chapter 6, *Showing Complex Data*, covers these organizational models for "nouns" in more detail. Of the patterns in this chapter, **Two-Panel Selector** is commonly used to structure this kind of interface, as is **One-Window Drilldown**.

Then, once the user has selected some object, what do they do with it? Read on!

LISTS OF ACTIONS

This approach is verb- instead of noun-centered. Instead of asking the user, "What do you want to work on?", these kinds of interfaces ask, "What do you want to do?" Such interfaces range from TurboTax's high-level decision tree (one screen of which is shown in Figure 2-2) to long menus of actions to be performed on an edited document or selected object.

What's nice about these is that they're often described in plain English. People can take them at face value. When you understand the application's domain well enough to define the correct set of tasks, the interface you design becomes quite usable, even to first-time users.

The hard part is dealing with the proliferation of actions that might be available to the user. Too many actions, more so than too many objects, can make it very hard for users to figure out what to do.

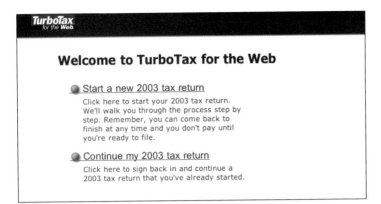

Welcome to TurboTax for the Web

● Start a new 2003 tax return

Click here to start your 2003 tax return. We'll walk you through the process step by step. Remember, you can come back to finish at any time and you don't pay until you're ready to file.

● Continue my 2003 tax return

Click here to sign back in and continue a 2003 tax return that you've already started.

FIGURE 2-2 / A friendly task-based organization at *http://turbotax.com*, described in terms of verbs—"Start" and "Continue"—and supplemented by helpful explanations

Desktop applications have menu bars and toolbars available for displaying large numbers of actions at once; most users understand these familiar conventions, at least superficially. Applications that use the **One-Window Drilldown** pattern can present whole-page menus, provided they're not too long. And the **Canvas Plus Palette** pattern talks about one very typical way to organize creational actions for use in many kinds of visual builders. In fact, all of Chapter 5 is devoted to various ways of placing, sorting, and organizing actions on an interface.

But the designers of small device interfaces, such as cell phones and PDAs, have interesting constraints. All they can easily do is present single-click choices of a few functions: three at a time if they're lucky, but usually only one or two. For them, it's critical to prioritize which actions are the most frequently chosen at any given point in the interaction, so they can be assigned to those one or two "softkeys" or buttons (see Figure 2-3). That careful prioritization is good discipline, even for web and desktop applications.

FIGURE 2-3 / This cell phone contains a linear list of entries in a phone book. At the bottom of the screen, you see a pair of softkeys—changeable labels for the hardware buttons underneath them—labeled "Exit" and "View." The lefthand button is almost always Exit for all applications (users thus can become habituated to that button). However, the righthand button changes according to what you're doing—it's always the most common action.

All other possible actions are hidden inside a menu, reachable via the middle softkey with the T-shaped icon on it. This division of common versus not-so-common is an example of **Extras On Demand**, a pattern in this chapter. The designers had to make a difficult choice about which action was most important, since showing all of them at once wasn't an option.

Web sites and online references divide up their content by subject category all the time. They have large amounts of stuff for people to browse through, and it often makes the most sense to organize it by subject, or by a similar categorization. But the success of a category-based organization, like that of tasks, depends on how well you've anticipated what users are looking for when they first see your interface. Again, you need to understand the application's domain well enough to match the mental models that your users already have.

Most applications aren't organized this way. Subject categories are better for sorting out nouns than verbs, and action-oriented software usually isn't a good fit for it. That said, help systems—which should be an integral part of an application's design—often do use it, and if an application really does combine knowledge lookup with actions (like medical applications or mapping software), this could come in handy.

Figure 2-4 shows a popular example. The iTunes Music Store organizes its thousands of songs by album, artist, and then genre; that's how its users browse the catalog when they're not using the search facility. What if it were organized by some other means, like the musicians' hair length at the time of the 2004 Grammy Awards? That organization doesn't match most people's mental models of the music universe (hopefully). No one could find anything they were looking for.

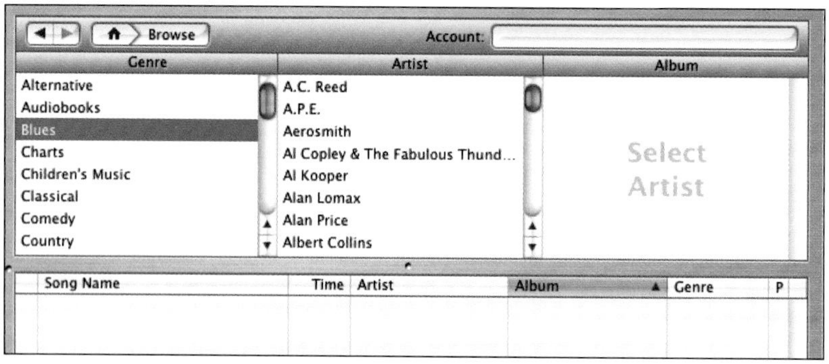

FIGURE 2-4 / The iTunes Music Store categorizes songs by album, artist, and genre. iTunes itself adds playlists as a category. This organizational model, combined with the familiar media-player idiom, really is the heart of the iTunes application.

In any case, organization by subject category might be useful to your application. Related types of organizations include alphabetical, chronological, geographical, and even audience type (like frequent users versus first-time users). See the book *Information Architecture for the World Wide Web* (O'Reilly) for more information.

Operating systems, palmtops, and cell phones all provide access to a range of tools, or sub-applications, used within their physical frameworks. Some applications, such as Microsoft Money, work that way too, and some web sites offer self-contained web applications such as wizards or games.

Once again, this works best when users have a clear, predictable expectation of what the tools should be. Calendars and phone lists are pretty recognizable. So are check-balancing programs and investment interfaces, as one might find in financial applications like MS Money. If your web site offers some novel and strangely named web apps, and they are mixed in with subject categories, users generally are not going to "get it" (unless they're very motivated).

For some reason, a tool-based organizational model fails particularly badly when the names of tools mix with actions, tasks, or objects. Mixing them tends to break people's expectations of what those items do—whether presented as menu choices, list items, buttons, or links—especially for new users who don't know what the names of the tools are yet. Users you observe often do not articulate this confusion well, so beware. You should watch them for subtle signs of confusion, but don't ask them about it directly.

On the other hand, if the user's goal isn't to get something important done, but rather to explore and play, then this strategy might work. Interesting names might attract attention and cause people to click on them just to see what they are. (See the **Intriguing Branches** pattern in this chapter.) But in this case, predictability isn't necessarily a huge benefit. In most software, predictability is quite important.

How can you organize the presentation of a list of tools? Linear organizations are common, since there usually aren't many of them in the first place. PalmOS and many other small devices use a grid of them (see Figure 2-5), which essentially is a linear list. Usually they're sorted alphabetically, for ease of lookup, or by expected frequency of use. When there are a lot of tools—and users might add lots more—then you might group them by category, like the Windows start bar does. Some systems let the users place tools wherever they want.

In the next chapter, on navigation, there's a pattern called **Hub and Spoke**. It's often used to structure an application around a tool-based organizational model.

FIGURE 2-5 / The PalmOS applications screen is a simple linear list of tools.

PHYSICAL STRUCTURE

Once you've come up with the beginnings of a design, you have to translate it into a physical structure of windows, pages, and controls. That's one of the first aspects of an application that people perceive, especially on the desktop, which can host all the types of window arrangements described here.

I've heard this debate many times before: should an application use multiple windows, a single window with several tiled panes, or one window whose content "swaps out" like a web page? Should it use some combination thereof? See Figure 2-6.

You may already know by now which to use—the technology you're using often will set your course. Handhelds, cell phones, and most other consumer electronics simply don't give you the option for multiple windows or multiple panes. Even if you could, it's a bad idea, simply because users will find it too hard to navigate without a mouse.

Desktop software and large-screen web applications give you more choices. There aren't any hard-and-fast rules for determining what's best for any given design, but the sections that follow provide some guidelines. Before you decide, analyze the kinds of tasks your users will perform—especially whether they need to work in two or more UI areas at the same time. Do they need to refer to panel A while editing something in panel B? Do they need to compare A and B side-by-side? Do they need to keep panel A in view at all times to monitor something? Let your understanding of users' tasks drive your decisions.

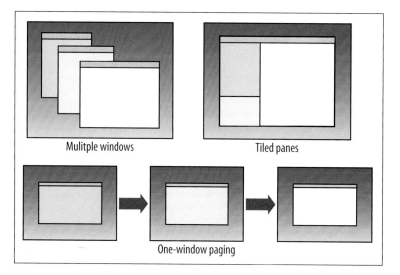

Mulitple windows   Tiled panes

One-window paging

FIGURE 2-6 / Three different physical structures

MULTIPLE WINDOWS

Multiple windows sometimes are the right choice, but not often. They work best in sophisticated applications when users want to customize the layout of their screen. Infrequent users, and sometimes frequent users too, may find multiple windows irritating or confusing.

ORGANIZING THE CONTENT

Sometimes users simply lose them if there are too many of them onscreen at once. On the other hand, if users really need to see two or more windows "in parallel," you need either this or the tiled-pane model.

Simple web applications work best with a single-window paging model, which can show one page at a time. It's how the Web has worked from Day One, after all, and people are very familiar with that model. Also, because it conserves space so well—there's nothing else on-screen to compete with the viewed content—it's the best choice for small handhelds and cell phones. (You couldn't fit tiled or multiple windows, anyhow.) See the **One-Window Drill-down** pattern for more; it shows how to fit a hierarchical list-driven or task-centered interface into a one-window model.

Many applications and web applications use tiled panes on one window. It's great for users who want to see a lot at once while expending little effort on window management. Countless windows and dialog boxes are designed with a two-pane structure, and three is becoming more common, thanks to the prevalence of Outlook and similar applications. People intuitively grasp the idea that you "click in one pane to see something in the other."

Tiled panes can take up a lot of screen space, however. I've sometimes had to switch to a multiple window approach when the number of panes got too high, and users just couldn't fit enough of them in the window at once.

The first pattern in this chapter, **Two-Panel Selector**, describes one situation that depends upon tiled panes for its effectiveness. You can structure **Canvas Plus Palette** with them, too. Some web sites arrange small modules of interactive content onto otherwise ordinary pages; individually, these modules might behave like single-pane windows, but on the page, they're tiled.

The tiled and multiple-windows approaches together constitute the "open floor plan" idea mentioned in Chapter 1, in the discussion of focused versus open interfaces. Layouts that use tiled or multiple windows provide access to several things at once, and users take responsibility for focusing their attention on the various panels or windows at the right times. Sometimes technology prevents you from using tiled or multiple windows; at other times you ought to choose not to indulge in them, but instead use a single window to lead the user through the interface along carefully predesigned paths.

So it's all about tradeoffs. Of course, this is always true. In the end, what matters is whether or not your users—novices, intermediates, and experts—can use what you build and enjoy it. Play with the design. Draw pictures and build prototypes. Try them out on yourself, your colleagues, and, most importantly, the users themselves.

THE PATTERNS

This chapter's patterns cover both of the approaches to application design just discussed. Some of them mix content structure with physical structure. They illustrate combinations that are known to work exceedingly well, such as the first four patterns:

 Two-Panel Selector

 Canvas Plus Palette

 One-Window Drilldown

 Alternative Views

The next few patterns don't go much into physical presentation, but instead deal with content in the abstract. **Wizard** talks about "linearizing" a path through a task; it can be implemented as any number of physical presentations. **Extras on Demand** and **Intriguing Branches** describe additional ways to divide up content.

 Wizard

 Extras on Demand

19 **Intriguing Branches**

Many patterns, here and elsewhere in the book, contribute in varying degrees to the learnability of an interface. **Multi-Level Help** sets out ways to integrate help directly into the application, thus supporting learnability for a broad number of users and situations.

20 **Multi-Level Help**

13 two-panel selector

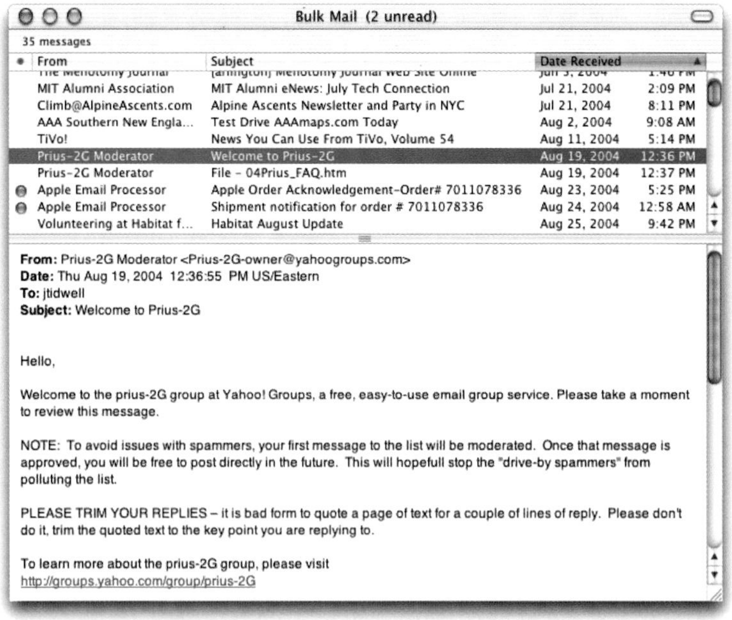

FIGURE 2-7 / Mac Mail

Put two side-by-side panels on the interface. In the first, show a set of items that the user can select at will; in the other, show the content of the selected item.

use when

You're presenting a list of objects, categories, or even actions. Messages in a mailbox, sections of a web site, songs or images in a library, database records, files—all are good candidates. Each item has interesting content associated with it, such as the text of an email message or details about a file's size or date. You want the user to see the overall structure of the list, but you also want the user to walk through the items at his own pace, in an order of his choosing.

Physically, the display you work with is large enough to show two separate panels at once. Very small cell phone displays cannot cope with this pattern, but a screen such as the Blackberry's can.

why

The Two-Panel Selector is a learned convention, but an extremely common and powerful one. People quickly learn that they're supposed to select an item in one panel to see its contents in the other. They might learn it from their email clients, from Windows Explorer, or from web sites; whatever the case, they apply the concept to other applications that look similar.

When both panels are visible side-by-side, users can quickly shift their attention back and forth, looking now at the overall structure of the list ("How many more unread email messages do I have?"), and now at an object's details ("What does this email say?"). This tight integration has several advantages over other physical structures, such as two separate windows or **One-Window Drilldown**:

- It reduces physical effort. The user's eyes don't have to travel a long distance between the panels, and he can change the selection with a single mouse click or key press, rather than first navigating between windows or screens (which can take an extra mouse click).

- It reduces visual cognitive load. When a window pops to the top, or when a page's contents are completely changed (as happens with **One-Window Drilldown**), the user suddenly has to pay more attention to what he's now looking at; when the window stays mostly stable, as in a Two-Panel Selector, the user can focus on the smaller area that did change.

- It reduces the user's memory burden. Think about the email example again: when the user looks at just the text of an email message, there's nothing onscreen to remind him where that message is in the context of his inbox. If he wants to know, he has to remember or navigate back to the list. But if the list is already onscreen, he merely has to look, not remember. The list thus serves as a "You are here" signpost (see Chapter 3 for an explanation of signposts).

how

Place the selectable list on the top or left panel, and the details panel below it or to its right. This takes advantage of the visual flow that most users who read left-to-right languages expect. (Try reversing it for right-to-left language speakers.)

When the user selects an item, immediately show its contents or details in the second panel. Selection should be done with a single click. But while you're at it, give the user a way to change selection from the keyboard, particularly with the arrow keys—this reduces both the physical effort and the time required for browsing, and contributes to keyboard-only usability (see **Keyboard Only**, in Chapter 1).

Make the selected item visually obvious. Most GUI toolkits have a particular way of showing selection, e.g., reversing the foreground and background of the selected list item. If that doesn't look good, or if you're not using a GUI toolkit with this feature, try to make the selected item a different color and brightness than the unselected ones—that helps it stand out.

What should the selectable list look like? It depends—on the inherent structure of the content, or perhaps on the task to be done. For instance, most filesystem viewers show the directory hierarchy, since that's how filesystems are structured. Animation and video-editing software use interactive timelines. A GUI builder simply may use the layout canvas itself; selected objects on it then show their properties in a **Property Sheet** (Chapter 4) next to the canvas.

Consider using one of the models described in the "List of objects" section of this chapter's introduction:

- Linear, usually sorted
- 2D tables, also sorted, which often let the user sort via column headers or filter according to various criteria
- A hierarchy that groups items into categories (and possibly subcategories)
- A hierarchy that reveals relationships: parent/child, containers, etc.
- Spatial organizations, such as maps, charts, or desktop-like areas in which users can place things where they want

You also can use information-presentation patterns such as **Sortable Table** and **Tree-Table** (both found in Chapter 6) in Two-Panel Selectors, along with simpler components such as lists and trees. **Card Stack** (Chapter 4) closely relates to Two-Panel Selector; so does **Overview Plus Detail** (Chapter 6).

When the select-and-show concept extends through multiple panels, to facilitate navigation through a hierarchical information architecture, you get the **Cascading Lists** pattern (also Chapter 6).

examples

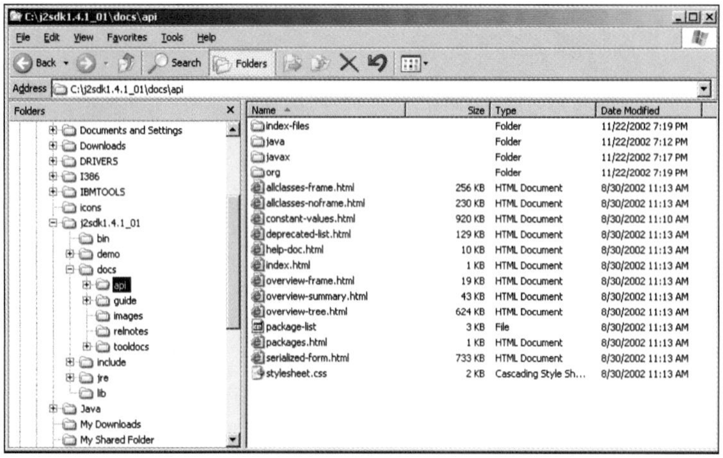

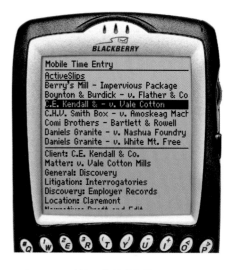

FIGURE 2-8 / The Windows Explorer is probably one of the most familiar uses of Two-Panel Selector. Its content is organized hierarchically, using a selectable tree; in contrast, the Mac Mail example (Figure 2-7) uses a selectable table, which has a strictly linear organization. In both UIs, the dark backgrounds indicate the selected item.

FIGURE 2-9 / Nortel's Mobile Time Entry application is a rare example of Two-Panel Selector use in a handheld device. The Blackberry screen offers just enough space for two usefully sized panes; when you select an item in the top pane, its contents appear on the bottom pane. (Both are scrollable with the Blackberry's scroll wheel, barely visible on the right side.)

In practice, this interface was quite effective. The lawyers who used this time-billing application could easily find items that they wanted—the two views together give enough context, but also enough details, to identify items quickly and accurately.

14 canvas plus palette

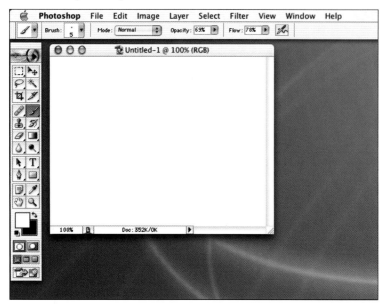

FIGURE 2-10 / Photoshop

what

Place an iconic palette next to a blank canvas; the user clicks on the palette buttons to create objects on the canvas.

use when

You're designing any kind of graphical editor. A typical use case involves creating new objects and arranging them on some virtual space.

why

This pair of panels—a palette with which to create things, and a canvas on which to put them—is so common that almost every user of desktop software has seen it. It's a natural mapping from familiar physical objects to the virtual onscreen world. And the palette takes advantage of visual recognition: the most common icons (paintbrush, hand, magnifying glass, etc.) are reused over and over again in different applications, with the same meaning each time.

how

Present a large, empty area to the user as a canvas. It might be in its own window, as in Photoshop (in Figure 2-10), in a tiled panel, or embedded in a single page with other tools. It works no matter what physical structure you've chosen, as long as you can see the canvas side-by-side with the palette.

The palette itself should be a grid of iconic buttons or button-like areas. They can have text in them if the icons are too cryptic; some GUI-builder palettes list the names of GUI components alongside their icons. So does Visio, with its palettes of complex visual constructs tailored for specific domains. But the presence of icons appears necessary for users to recognize the palette for what it is.

Place the palette to the left or top of the canvas. (It's likely that speakers of right-to-left languages might prefer it to the right of the canvas, not the left; usability-test it if this is an issue for you.) It can be divided into subgroups, and you may want to use a **Card Stack**, such as tabs, to present those subgroups.

ORGANIZING THE CONTENT

Most palette buttons should create the pictured object on the canvas. But some builders have successfully integrated other things, like zoom mode and lassoing, into the palette. This started early; MacPaint mixed its modes into its palette (see Figure 2-12), and people have learned what the arrow, hand, and other icons do. But be careful. I recommend not mixing other actions into a creational palette—it can be very confusing for users.

The gestures used to create items on a palette vary from one application to another. Some use drag-and-drop only; some use a single click on the palette and single click on the canvas; and some use **One-off Modes** (see Chapter 8), **Spring-Loaded Modes**, and other carefully designed gestures. I have always found that usability testing in this area is particularly important, since users' expectations vary greatly.

examples

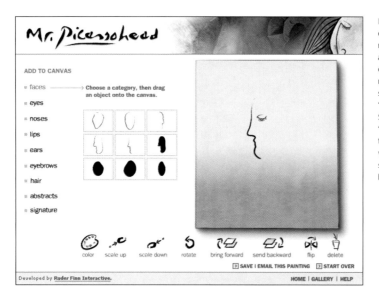

FIGURE 2-11 / You don't need all the trappings of a document-centered desktop application to make Canvas Plus Palette work. This web application, Mr. Picassohead, is a whimsical twist on this familiar pattern. The palette itself is merely a grid of icons, and it doesn't look like a set of buttons at all; the palette is subdivided and "tabbed" by category (a use of Two-Panel Selector). When you click on the words "eyes," "noses," or "lips," the palette changes to show those objects. The canvas itself is neutral, but not white. Its purpose is clear to the first-time user simply because it's a big open space, framed by a border. See *http://mrpicassohead.com*.

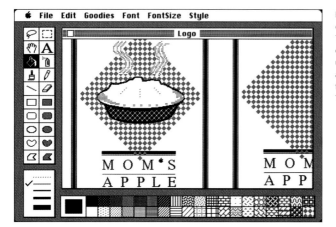

FIGURE 2-12 / Taking a trip back in time, let's look at one of the interfaces that popularized this pattern: MacPaint. The pattern hasn't changed much since 1984—the basic elements are all there, in the same spatial configuration used by contemporary software such as Mr. Picassohead and Photoshop. Photoshop and other visual builders, in fact, still use many of MacPaint's icons over 20 years later. The screenshot is from *http://mac512.com*.

15 **one-window drilldown**

FIGURE 2-13 / Two iPod menus

what

Show each of the application's pages within a single window. As a user drills down through a menu of options, or into an object's details, replace the window contents completely with the new page.

use when

Your application consists of many pages or panels of content for the user to navigate through. They might be arranged linearly, in an arbitrary hyperlinked network, or—most commonly—in a menu hierarchy. Address books, calendars, web-based email readers, and other familiar applications often use this pattern.

One or both of these constraints might apply to you:

- You are building for a device with tight space restrictions, such as a handheld (see Figure 2-13), a cell phone, or a TV. On these miniature screens, **Two-Panel Selector**—and tiled panes in general—are impractical because there just isn't enough room to use them well. Traversing from one panel to another on a TV screen also is difficult, since TVs have no mice.

- Even if you build for a desktop or laptop screen, you may have a complexity limit. Your users may not be habitual computer users—having many application windows open at once may confuse them, or they may not deal well with complex screens or fiddly input devices. Users of information kiosks fall into this category, as do novice PC users.

why

Keep it simple. When everything's on one screen or window, the options at each stage are clear, and users know they don't need to focus their attention anywhere else.

Besides, everyone these days knows how to use a web browser, with its single window and simple back/forward page model. People expect that when they click on a link or button, the page they're looking at will be replaced, and when they click "Back," they'll go back to where they were before.

You could use multiple windows to show the different spaces that a user navigates through—a click in a main window may bring up a second window, a click in that window brings up a third, etc. But that can be confusing. Even sophisticated users can easily lose track of where their windows are (though they can see several windows side-by-side and place them where they want).

One-Window Drilldown is an alternative to several of the higher-density patterns and techniques discussed here. As pointed out earlier, **Two-Panel Selector** may not fit, or it may make the screen layout or interactions too complex for the typical user. Tiled windows, **Closable Panels**, **Movable Pieces**, and **Cascading Lists** (the last three are patterns in Chapter 4) also have space and complexity issues. They don't work on miniature screens, and they complicate interfaces intended for novice computer users.

how

You are given one window to work with—a miniature screen, a full-sized screen, a browser window, or an application window that lives on the desktop alongside other applications. Structure your content into panels that fit gracefully into that window: not too large and not too small.

On these panels, design obvious "doors" into other UI spaces, such as underlined links, buttons, or clickable table rows. When the user clicks on one of these, replace the current panel with the new one. Thus the user "drills down" deeper into the content of the application.

How does the user go back? If you're designing for a device with back/forward buttons, that's one solution. If not, create those buttons and put them in one permanent place on the window—usually the upper left, where browsers put them. You should put "Done" or "Cancel" controls on panels where the user completes a task or selection; these controls give the user a sense of closure, of "being done."

Remember that with no graphic depiction of the application's structure, nor of where they are in that structure, a one-window application forces the user to rely on a mental picture of how all these spaces fit together. Simple linear or hierarchical structures work best. In usability tests, make sure people can use the thing without getting lost! **Breadcrumbs** and **Sequence Maps** can help if they do; see Chapter 3, *Navigation*.

Implementations of **Hub and Spoke** often use One-Window Drilldown, especially on the Web and miniature screens. Again, see Chapter 3.

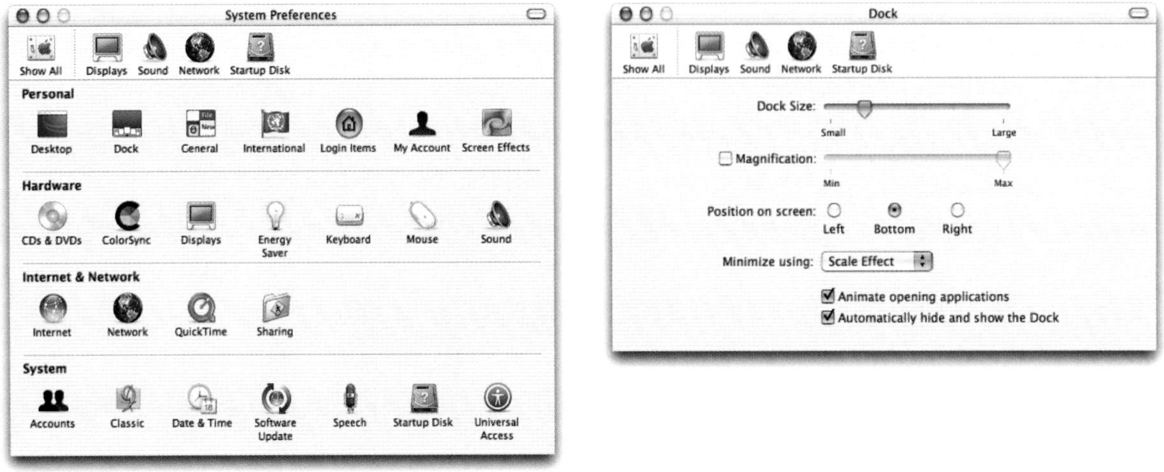

FIGURE 2-14 / The Mac OS X System Properties tool keeps everything within one window. The main panel is on the left; a drilldown panel (for the Dock) is shown on the right. There's only one level of drilldown panels. The user goes back to the main panel via the "Show All" button in the upper left.

Mac screens often are large, and OS X users are varied in their levels of experience. The System Properties designers may have chosen a One-Window Drilldown approach not because of small screens, but because of the sheer number and diversity of subpanels. That main panel takes up a lot of space, and it probably didn't work well in a tiled **Two-Panel Selector** window.

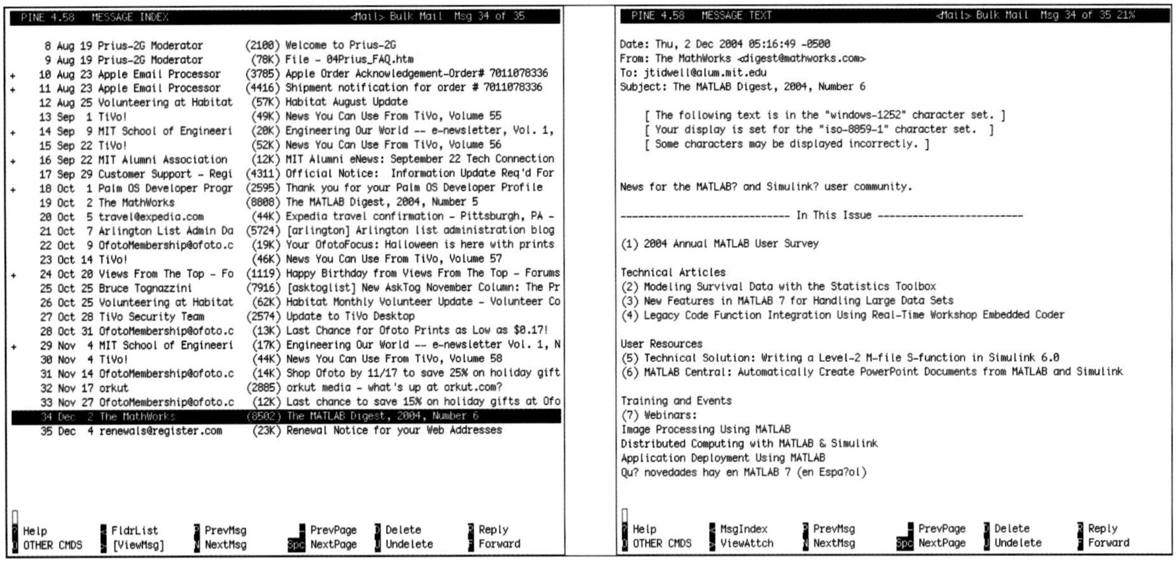

FIGURE 2-15 / The Pine email client is a lightweight, text-only user interface driven entirely from the keyboard. The greater-than and less-than keys navigate the application's hierarchy: the main screen, the list of mailboxes, the list of messages within the selected mailbox (left), the text of the selected message (right), and the attachments to the message.

Pine thus contains a deep hierarchy of UI "spaces," but it works well within one window. Compare this screenshot to that of Mac Mail in the **Two-Panel Selector** pattern—both are good interfaces, but they have very different designs. We might guess that two stringent requirements drove Pine's One-Window Drilldown design: to run in a text-based terminal window, and to be operated with only the keyboard.

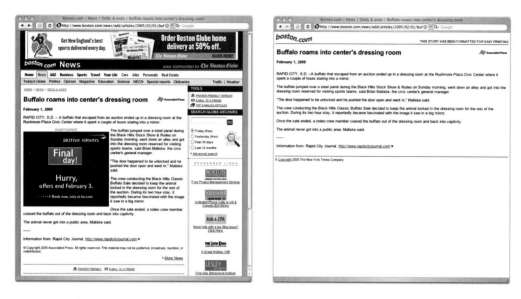

FIGURE 2-16 / A boston.com article in standard format and in printer-friendly format

what

Let the user choose among alternative views that are structurally different, not just cosmetically different, from the default view.

use when

You're building a web page, an editor, a map application, or anything that displays formatted content of any kind. People will use it under many conditions. Maybe you already provide some customizability—font sizes, languages, sort order, zoom level, etc.—but those lightweight changes don't go far enough to accommodate all the things people typically do with it.

why

Try as you might, you can't always accommodate all possible usage scenarios in a single design. For instance, printing is typically problematic for applications because the information display requirements differ—navigation and interactive gizmos should be removed, for instance, and the remaining content reformatted to fit the printer paper. See the news article example above (Figure 2-16) for what that can look like.

Beyond different usage scenarios, you should use Alternative Views for several other reasons:

- Different technologies at the user's end— one person might view the application on a desktop, but another person would view it on a PDA, and a third would use a screen reader such as JAWS.
- Users' preferences with regard to speed, visual style, and other factors.
- A need to temporarily view something differently, in order to gain insight.

how

Choose a few usage scenarios that the application's (or page's) normal mode of operation cannot easily serve. Design specialized views for them, and present those views as alternatives within the same window or screen.

In these alternative views, some information might be added, and some might be taken away, but the primary content should remain more or less the same. If you need to strip down the interface—for use by a printer or screen reader, for instance—then consider removing secondary content, shrinking or eliminating images, and cutting out all navigation but the most basic.

Stuffing content into a PDA or cell phone screen is trickier; it could force you to redesign the navigation itself. Rather than showing a lot of content on one screen or page, as you could with a desktop computer or TV, you might split it up into multiple pages, each of which fits gracefully onto a smaller screen.

Put a "switch" for the mode somewhere on the main interface. It doesn't have to be prominent; Power-point and Word (as you'll see in Figure 2-19) put their mode buttons in the lower-left corner, which is an easily overlooked spot on any interface. Most applications represent the alternative views with iconic buttons. Make sure it's easy to switch back to the default view, too. As the user switches back and forth, preserve all of the application's current state—selections, the user's location in the document, uncommitted changes, Undo/Redo operations, etc. Losing them will surprise the user.

Applications that "remember" their users often retain the user's alternative-view choice from one use to the next. In other words, if a user decides to switch to an alternative view, the application will just use that view by default next time. Web sites can do this with cookies; desktop applications can keep track of preferences per user; an app on a digital device like a cell phone can simply remember what view it used the last time it was invoked.

Web pages may have the option of implementing Alternative Views as alternative CSS pages. This is how some sites cope with print-suitable views, for example.

examples

FIGURE 2-17 / Both the Windows Explorer and the Mac Finder permit several alternative views of the files in a filesystem. This example shows two views: a sortable multicolumn list (see the **Sortable Table** pattern in Chapter 6) and a grid of icons.

Each view has pros and cons. The table is terrific for managing lots of information—the user can find things by sorting on the columns, for instance. But the icons work better if she is looking for a particular image that she can recognize on sight. These views address different use contexts, and a user might go back and forth among them at one sitting.

ORGANIZING THE CONTENT

> [PDF] Microsoft PowerPoint - L8.ppt
> File Format: PDF/Adobe Acrobat - View as HTML
> ... With a **spring-loaded mode**, the user has to do something active to
> **mode**, essentially eliminating the chance that they'll forget what ...
> classes.csail.mit.edu/6.831/lectures/L8.pdf - Similar pages
>
> [PDF] Zustände
> File Format: PDF/Adobe Acrobat - View as HTML
> ... Zustand „**Spring-Loaded Mode**" mit einer physischen Feder gekoppe
> Loslassen bewirktVerlassen des Zustands. „**Spring-Loaded Mode**" Pa¢
> www.soft.uni-linz.ac.at/.../Vorlesungen/_Mensch-Maschine-
> Kommunikation/Folien%20(PDF)/06Zustaende.pdf - Similar pages

FIGURE 2-18 / Google's search results can return not just ordinary HTML Web pages, but PDF, Word, and Powerpoint documents as well. What if you don't have Word or Powerpoint on your client machine? That technology problem dictates the use of an alternative view: the HTML "translation." What if you really don't want to download a large Powerpoint slideshow and just want to skim the HTML translation in a hurry? That's a user preference.

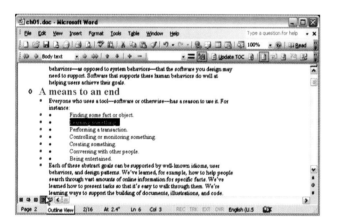

FIGURE 2-19 / Of course, we have Word and Powerpoint themselves. Both full-fledged WYSIWYG editors can construct fairly complex documents—a Powerpoint presentation has a sequence, a template, perhaps notes for some slides, fancy transitions from one slide to another, and even code to support interactivity. A user who's authoring the slideshow may need to see all that. A user who's just running the slideshow doesn't. Again, these are different use contexts.

Word's views include the normal view, intended for most editing tasks; a "print layout" view, which shows how the document might appear on printed pages; a "reading" mode for uncluttered viewing; and an "outline" view, which shows the structure of the document. Someone might use the outline view to gain insight—if you loaded a large, unfamiliar document, for instance, you might switch to outline mode just to see a "table of contents" overview of it. Both applications put the Alternative Views buttons in the lower lefthand corner of the document's window.

Note that in these Word examples, the selected text remains the same as the user switches from one view to another. The position in the document also stays the same through most transitions. However, different toolbars come and go, the zoom level changes, and some kinds of content—notably footnotes and annotations—are visible only in the print layout view.

17 wizard

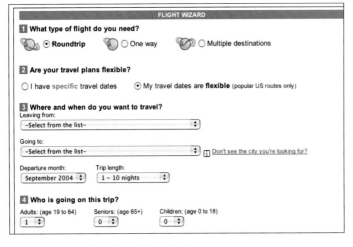

FIGURE 2-20 / Flight Wizard from *http://expedia.com*

what

Lead the user through the interface step by step, doing tasks in a prescribed order.

use when

You are designing a UI for a task that is long or complicated, and that will be novel for the user—it's not something that they do often or want much fine-grained control over. You're reasonably certain that those of you who design the UI will know more than the user does about how best to get the task done.

Tasks that seem well-suited for this approach tend to be either branched or very long and tedious—they consist of a series of user-made decisions that affect downstream choices.

The catch is that the user *must* be willing to surrender control over what happens when. In many contexts, that works out fine, since making decisions is an unwelcome burden for people doing certain things: "Don't make me think, just tell me what to do next." Think about moving through an unfamiliar airport—it's often easier to follow a series of signs than it is to figure out the airport's overall structure. You don't get to learn much about how the airport is designed, but you don't care about that.

But in other contexts, it backfires. Expert users often find Wizards frustratingly rigid and limiting. This is particularly true for software that supports creative processes—writing, art, or coding. It's also true for users who actually *do* want to learn the software; wizards don't show users what their actions really do, nor what application state is changed as choices are made. That can be infuriating to some people. Know your users well!

why

Divide and conquer. By splitting up the task into a sequence of chunks, each of which the user can deal with in a discrete "mental space," you effectively simplify the task. You have put together a preplanned road map through the task, thus sparing the user the effort of figuring out the task's structure—all they need to do is address each step in turn, trusting that if they follow the instructions, things will turn out OK.

"CHUNKING" THE TASK

Break up the operations constituting the task into a series of chunks, or groups of operations. You may need to present these groups in a strict sequence, or not; there is value in breaking up a task into Steps 1, 2, 3, and 4 just for convenience.

A thematic breakdown for an online purchase may include screens for product selection, payment information, a billing address, and a shipping address. The presentation order doesn't much matter, because later choices don't depend on earlier choices. Putting related choices together just simplifies things for people filling out those forms.

You may decide to split up the task at decision points so that choices made by the user can change the downstream steps dynamically. In a software installation wizard, for example, the user may choose to install optional packages that require yet more choices; if they choose not to do a custom installation, those steps are skipped. Dynamic UIs are good at presenting branched tasks such as this because the user never has to see what is irrelevant to the choices she made.

In either case, the hard part of designing this kind of UI is striking a balance between the sizes of the chunks and the number of them. It's silly to have a two-step wizard, and a fifteen-step wizard is tedious. On the other hand, each chunk shouldn't be overwhelmingly large, or you've lost some benefits of this pattern.

PHYSICAL STRUCTURE

Wizards that present each step in a separate page, navigated with Back and Next buttons, are the most obvious and well-known implementation of this pattern. They're not always the right choice, though, because now each step is an isolated UI space that shows no context—the user can't see what went before or what comes next. But an advantage of such wizards is that they can devote an entire page to each step, including illustrations and explanations.

If you do this, allow the user to move back and forth at will through the task sequence. There's nothing more frustrating than having to start a task over just because the software won't let you change your mind about a previous decision. Back buttons are, of course, standard equipment on separate-page wizards; use them, and make sure the underlying software supports stepping backwards. Additionally, many UIs show a selectable map or overview of all the steps, getting some of the benefits of **Two-Panel Selector**. (In contrast to that pattern, Wizard implies a prescribed order— even if it's merely suggested—as opposed to completely random access.)

If you choose to keep all the steps on one page, you could use one of several patterns from Chapter 4:

- **Titled Sections**, with prominent numbers in the titles. This is most useful for tasks that aren't heavily branched, since all steps can be visible at once.

- **Responsive Enabling**, in which all the steps are present on the page, but each remains disabled until the user has finished the previous step.

- **Responsive Disclosure**, in which you wait to show a step on the UI until the user finishes the previous one. Personally, I think this is the most elegant way to implement a short wizard. It's dynamic, compact, and easy to use.

Good Defaults (from Chapter 7) are useful no matter how you arrange the steps. If the user is willing to turn over control of the process to you, then odds are good he's also willing to let you pick reasonable defaults for choices he may not care much about, such as the location of a software installation.

(*The Design of Sites* discusses this concept under the pattern name "Process Funnel." Their pattern aims more at web sites, for tasks such as web shopping, but the concepts generalize well.)

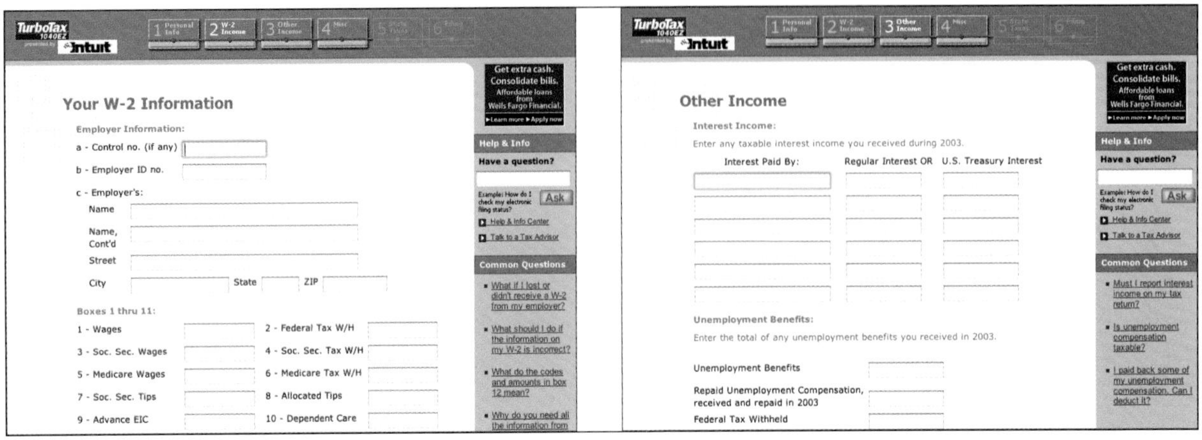

FIGURE 2-21 / TurboTax is a web application that presents several steps in a wizard-like fashion. Each major step is on a different page, and the pages have "Back" and "Continue" (or "Done") links at the ends of the pages, as traditional wizards do. (They're not visible on these screenshots, but trust me, they're there.) A **Sequence Map** at the top shows where you are in the steps at all times. **Good Defaults** generally aren't used here. That may be because sensitive information—personal financial data—is involved, but many users will find themselves entering "0" for a lot of fields.

FIGURE 2-22 / The Expedia example showed a wizard structured with **Titled Sections** (Chapter 4); the TurboTax example uses a paged model, replacing the contents of the browser window with each successive step. This example uses a **Card Stack** (also Chapter 4) to fit all steps into a very limited space. When the user selects a date from this calendar and clicks "Next Step," panel 2 opens up. When that step is done, the user moves on to Panel 3. The user can go back to previous steps anytime by clicking on the yellow titlebars.

Also note the use of a **Preview** (Chapter 5) on the righthand pane of the window, entitled "Your Itinerary." This tracks the user's choices (no pun intended) and shows a summary of those choices. This is convenient because only one wizard page is visible at a time; the user can't see all their choices at once. See *http://thetrain.com*.

18 extras on demand

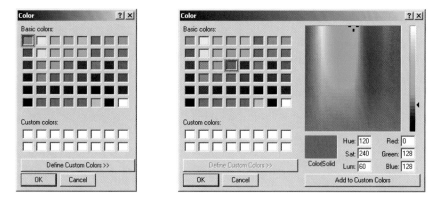

FIGURE 2-23 / The color dialog box in Windows 2000

what

Show the most important content up front, but hide the rest. Let the user reach it via a single, simple gesture.

use when

There's too much stuff to be shown on the page, but some of it isn't very important. You'd rather have a simpler UI, but you have to put all this content somewhere.

why

A simple UI is often better than a complex one, especially for new users, or users who don't need all the functionality you can provide. Let the user choose when to see the entire UI in its full glory—they're a better judge of that than you are.

If your design makes 80 percent of the use cases easy, and the remaining 20 percent are at least possible (with a little work on the user's part), your design is doing as well as can be expected!

When done correctly, Extras On Demand can save a lot of space on your interface.

how

Ruthlessly prune the UI down to its most commonly used, most important items. Put the remainder into their own page or section. Hide that section by default; on the newly simplified UI, put a clearly marked button or link to the remainder, such as "More Options." Many UIs use arrows or chevrons, ">>", as part of the link or button label. Others use "...", especially if the button launches a new window or page.

That section should have another button or other affordance to let the user close it again. Remember, most users won't need it most of the time. Just make sure the entrance to and exit from this "extras" page are obvious.

In some interfaces, the window literally expands to accommodate the details section, and then shrinks down again when the user puts it away. See the **Closable Panels** pattern (Chapter 4) for one way to do this. Various desktop UIs provide another mechanism: a dropdown for fill color, for instance, contains a "More Fill Colors..." item that brings up a separate dialog box.

Experts warn of possible Web attack

Seeing a rise in hacker activity that could be a prelude to a broad Internet attack, security experts urged computer users to protect their machines by installing a free patch. Internet security firms issued similar warnings, saying they've seen increased chatter in hacker discussion groups and chat rooms. "We are expecting something sooner rather than later," said Dan Ingevaldson, engineering director at Internet Security Systems in Atlanta.

FULL STORY

FIGURE 2-24 / Narratives frequently use Extras On Demand to separate the gist of an article from its full text. A reader can scan the leader, such as this one from CNN, and decide whether or not to read the rest of the article (by clicking "Full Story," or the headline itself). If they don't go to the jump page, that's fine—they've already read the most important part.

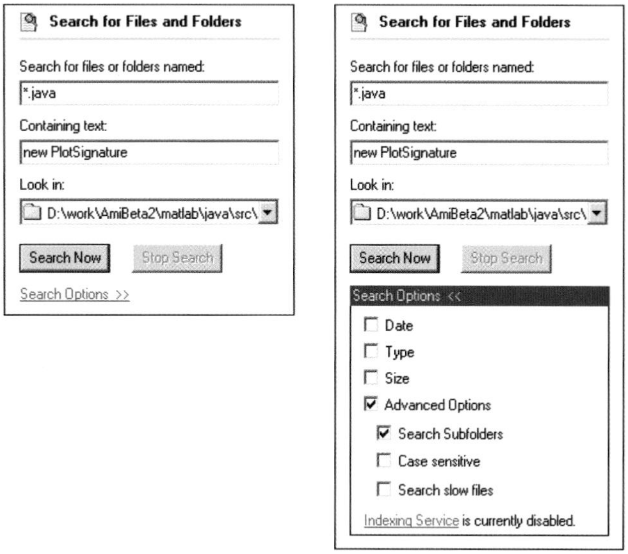

Search for Files and Folders

Search for files or folders named:

`*.java`

Containing text:

`new PlotSignature`

Look in:

D:\work\AmiBeta2\matlab\java\src\

[Search Now] [Stop Search]

Search Options >>

Search for Files and Folders

Search for files or folders named:

`*.java`

Containing text:

`new PlotSignature`

Look in:

D:\work\AmiBeta2\matlab\java\src\

[Search Now] [Stop Search]

Search Options <<

☐ Date
☐ Type
☐ Size
☑ Advanced Options
  ☑ Search Subfolders
  ☐ Case sensitive
  ☐ Search slow files

Indexing Service is currently disabled.

FIGURE 2-25 / This is the file search facility in Windows 2000. Clicking "Search Options" opens a box of extra options. Likewise, clicking the titlebar of the Search Options box, with its "<<" chevron, closes the box. Not shown is another level of Extras on Demand: when the user unchecks "Advanced Options," the indented checkboxes below it disappear. This makes it similar to Responsive Disclosure (Chapter 4), which talks about content that comes and goes as a *side effect* of the choices the user makes, as opposed to **Extras on Demand**, which requires an *intentional* act to open or close content.

19 intriguing branches

A political earthquake in the land of earthquakes (News)
By aphrael
Fri Jul 25th, 2003 at 09:08:32 PM EST

While the rest of the world focuses on the deaths of the Brothers Hussein, the rumblings of a political earthquake are threatening to bring California government to its knees. On Thursday, Lieutenant Governor Cruz Bustamante, prompted by a petition signed by more than 1,600,000 people, called a snap election to recall the state's unpopular Democratic Governor, Gray Davis. It is the first recall of a Governor in the United States since 1921.

Full Story (165 comments, 2611 words in story)

FIGURE 2-26 / From *http://kuro5hin.org*

what

Place links to interesting content in unexpected places, and label them in a way that attracts the curious user.

use when

The user moves along a linear path—a text narrative, a well-defined task, a slideshow, a Flash movie, etc. You want to present additional content that's not the main focus of attention, however. It might be information tangential to a story, as in Figure 2-26. It might be supporting text—examples, explanations of concepts, definitions of terms—or full-fledged help text. Or it could be hidden functionality, like an "Easter egg."

In any case, you want a graceful way of presenting the content so it's ignorable by users trying to get something done quickly, but still available to users for whom it's appropriate.

why

People are curious. If they see something that looks interesting, and they have the time and initiative to check it out, they will. Web surfing would never have become popular without this natural curiosity and willingness to follow links into the unknown. Skillful and playful use of Intriguing Branches can make your interface more fun.

A tradition of creating Intriguing Branches as in-line links (also known as "embedded links") already is well-established on the Web. But functional applications might provide a more interesting use of it. It's well-known that users tend to ignore what is labeled specifically as "Help." But what if you put help-like content behind links (or buttons, or icons) that were labeled in some other way, like "Learn more..."? You can exploit users' natural curiosity to get them into a place where they can learn what they need.

how

Start with a deep understanding of your users. What might interest them? Where in the interface are they likely to take time to explore something further, and where do they just need to get something done?

Create "doors" into the supplemental content that would appeal to users. These doors might be underlined links (even in desktop applications), headlines, buttons, menu items, icons, or clickable image regions—it's up to you to figure out how to label them in a way that inspires curiosity. There's an art to it. When in doubt, usability-test it with a representative sample of your user base.

With particularly obscure affordances, like icons or images, you might want to add tooltips or some other kind of short description to inform the user where they might go when they click on it. (With an Easter egg, though, its very non-obviousness is part of the fun.)

Also, provide an obvious way for the user to get back to their original workflow. The idea is to persuade users to read the branch content, and then go back to what they were originally doing; don't get them stranded in a backwater! Pop-up windows should provide "Close" buttons, and new pages in a browser-like UI should provide "Back" links or buttons.

FIGURE 2-27 / Gmail's settings page offers links that are clearly help-related, but are phrased as suggestions, not as "help." Here, a "Learn more" link is under the Keyboard Shortcuts caption. This is akin to other forms of context-sensitive help, like pop-up menus, help buttons, and function keys. "Learn more" is an active phrase, unlike "Help," though, and it's clearly visible on the page, unlike menus and function keys. One can assume that it opens yet another web page, so its operation is entirely predictable.

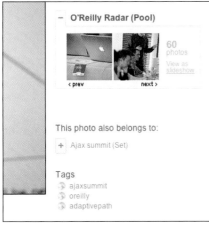

FIGURE 2-28 / Browsing photos in Flickr is often an exercise in following various intriguing branches—it offers "side trips" into other photostreams, image sets, and groups of images with common tags. The result is a thoroughly engaging (and very popular) user experience.

FIGURE 2-29 / A not-so-great example lies in Adobe's PDF reader for Windows. The pink button, "Create an Adobe PDF from your desktop," takes you to a page on Adobe's web site that explains how to use a different product to achieve that task. The button's color and content actually changes every few minutes; it shows a different teaser each time. This is an unusual case of such a link being present in an application—most don't take up valuable toolbar space with something like this.

But these buttons are somewhat self-serving on Adobe's part, since they encourage you to look at other Adobe products and services. Unfortunately, it looks like an advertising device. It would be interesting to know how effective they are, both at cross-selling and at helping users figure out how to do things they need to do anyway.

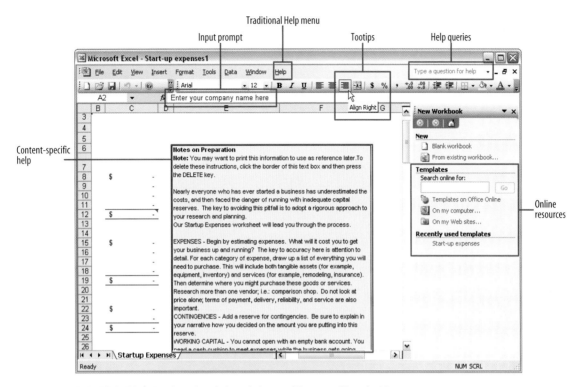

what

Use a mixture of lightweight and heavyweight help techniques to support users with varying needs.

use when

Your application is complex. Some users are likely to need a full-fledged help system, but you know most users won't take the time to use it. You want to support the impatient and/or occasional users too, to the extent you can. In particular, your software may be intended for intermediate-to-expert users—how will you help beginners become experts?

why

Users of almost any software artifact need varying levels of support for the tasks they're trying to accomplish. Someone approaching it for the first time ever (or the first time in a while) needs different support than someone who uses it frequently. Even among first-time users, enormous differences exist in commitment level and learning styles. Some people will want to read a tutorial, some won't; most find tooltips helpful, but a few find them irritating.

Help texts that are provided on many levels at once—even when they don't look like traditional "help systems"— reach everyone who needs them. Many good help techniques put the help texts within easy reach, but not directly in the user's face all the time, so users don't get irritated. However, the techniques need to be familiar to your users. If they don't notice or open a **Closable Panel**, for instance, they'll never see what's inside it.

Create help on several levels, including some techniques (but not necessarily all) from the following list. Think of it as a continuum: each requires more effort from the user than the previous one, but can supply more detailed and nuanced information.

- Captions and instructions directly on the page, including patterns like **Input Hints** and **Input Prompt** (both Chapter 7). Be careful not to go overboard with them. If done with brevity, frequent users won't mind them, but don't use entire paragraphs of text—few users will read them.

- Tooltips. Use them to show brief, one- or two-line descriptions of interface features that aren't self-evident. For icon-only features, tooltips are critical; users can take even nonsensical icons in stride if a rollover says what the icon does! (Not that I'd recommend poor icon design, of course.) Tooltips' disadvantages are that they hide whatever's under them, and that some users don't like them popping up all the time. A short time delay for the mouse hover—e.g., one or two seconds—removes the irritation factor for most people.

- Slightly longer descriptions that are shown dynamically as the user selects or rolls over certain interface elements. Set aside an area on the page itself for this, rather than using a tiny tooltip.

- Longer help texts contained inside **Closable Panels** (see Chapter 4).

- Help shown in a separate window, often in HTML via browsers, but sometimes in WinHelp or Mac Help. Help is often an online manual—an entire book—reached via menu items on a Help menu, or from "Help" buttons on dialog boxes and HTML pages.

- "Live" technical support, usually by email, the Web, or telephone.

- Informal community support, almost always on the Web. This applies only to the most heavily used and invested software—the likes of Photoshop, Linux, Mac OS X, or MATLAB—but users may consider it a highly valuable resource.

MATLAB is a complex, multilayered software application that offers help on all these levels. Each of the following examples comes from it.

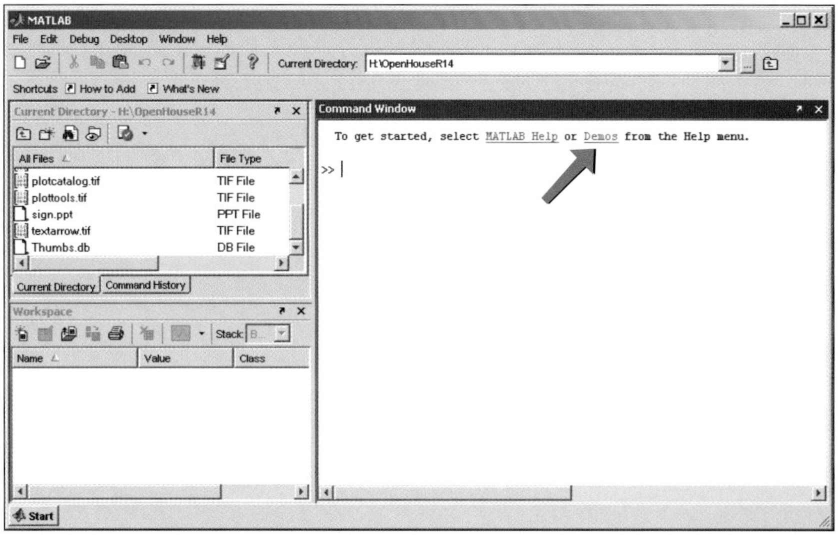

FIGURE 2-31 / When you start MATLAB, the command line immediately directs you to help documents: "To get started, select MATLAB Help or Demos from the Help menu." You also can see captioned items on the Shortcuts toolbar, on which the "How to Add" and "What's New" buttons bring up help texts in separate windows.

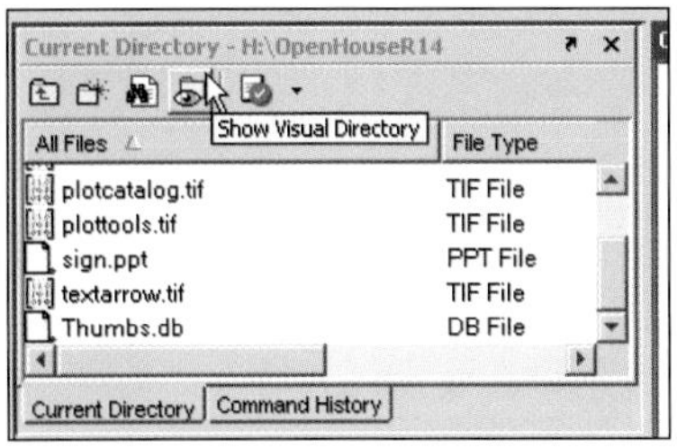

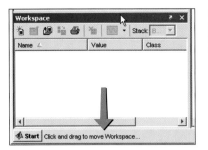

FIGURE 2-32 / Each toolbar button on the main window has a tooltip. Since MATLAB is an application designed for intermediate and expert users, it packs a lot of unusual functionality into small spaces, and tooltips are necessary to learn—or remember—what some of these buttons do.

FIGURE 2-33 / Rollover help is used in a few areas, such as the status bars of movable panels. The sentence shown in this status bar, "Click and drag to move Workspace...," is a little too long to view comfortably in a tooltip. More importantly, the status bar is less obtrusive—a user can ignore it more easily than he can a tooltip.

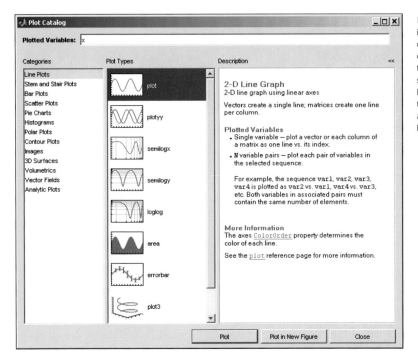

FIGURE 2-34 / Elsewhere in the MATLAB interface, the selection of an object might cause a short description to appear in a closable panel. In this window, selecting a plot type causes the "Description" panel to show a short formatted help page. The help text is longer than often needed (the user can close that panel if he wants), but it's more immediate—and thus more likely to be used—than help in a separate window.

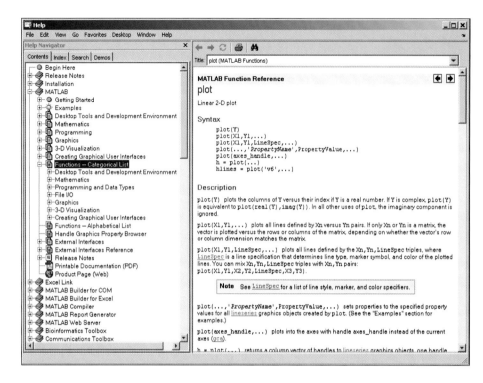

FIGURE 2-35 / In the previous window, clicking the underlined word "plot" in "See the plot reference page for more information" brings up a full-fledged help window. This tool gives the user access to the entire MATLAB manual.

FIGURE 2-36 / MATLAB users also get technical support over the phone and the Web. We've now moved beyond the realm of software design per se, but this is still product design—user experience extends beyond the bits installed on their computers. It includes the interactions they have with the company and its web site.

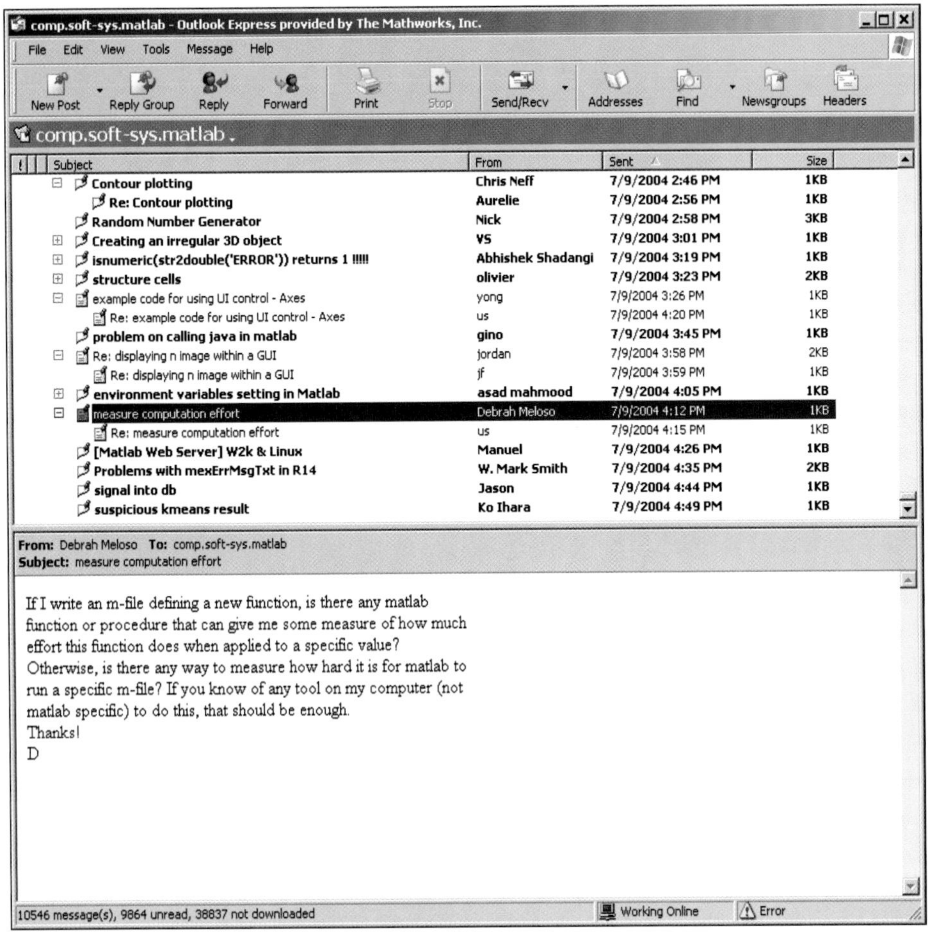

FIGURE 2-37 / Finally, if all other sources of help are exhausted, a user can turn to the wider user community for advice. In the case of MATLAB, users ask and answer one another's questions on a specialized newsgroup, *comp.soft-sys.matlab*. (Web-based discussions can serve the same purpose.) Community-building like this happens only for products in which users become deeply invested, perhaps because they use it every day at work or home, or because they have some emotional attachment to it, as many people do with games, Macs, or open source software.

GETTING AROUND:
NAVIGATION, SIGNPOSTS,
AND WAYFINDING

The patterns in this chapter deal with the problem of navigation. How does a user know where they are now, where to go next, and how to get there from here?

The reason why I call it a "problem" is this. Navigating around a web site or application is like commuting. You have to do it to get where you need to go, but it's dull, it's sometimes infuriating, and the time and energy you spend on it just seems wasted. Can't you do something better with your time, like playing a game or getting some actual work done?

The best kind of commuting—all else being equal—is none at all. Having everything you need right at your fingertips, without having to travel somewhere, is pretty convenient. Likewise, keeping most tools "within reach" on an interface is handy, especially for intermediate-to-expert users (i.e., people who have already learned where everything is). Sometimes you do need to put lesser-used tools in separate dialog boxes, where they don't clutter things up; sometimes you need to group things onto different pages so the interface makes sense. All this is fine, as long as the "distances" that a user has to travel remain short.

So: less is better. Let's talk terminology for a minute and come back to this concept.

STAYING FOUND

Let's say you've built a large web site or application that you've had to break up into sections, subsections, specialized tools, pages, windows, and wizards. How do you help users navigate?

Signposts are features that help users figure out their immediate surroundings. Common signposts include page and window titles, web page logos and other branding devices, tabs, and selection indicators. Patterns such as **Global Navigation**, **Color-Coded Sections**, **Sequence Map**, **Breadcrumbs**, and **Annotated Scrollbar**—all described in this chapter—tell a user where they currently are, and often, where they can go with only one more jump. They help a user stay "found" and plan his next steps.

Wayfinding is what people do as they find their way towards their goal. The term is pretty self-explanatory. But how people actually do it is quite a research subject—specialists from cognitive science, environmental design, and web site design have studied it. These common-sense features help users with wayfinding:

Good signage

Clear, unambiguous labels anticipate what you're looking for and tell you where to go; signs are where you expect them to be, and you're never left standing at a decision point without guidance. You can check this by walking through the artifact you're designing and following the paths of all the major use cases. At each point where a user must decide where to go next, make sure it's signed or labeled appropriately.

Environmental clues

You'd look for restrooms in the back of a restaurant, for instance, or a gate where a walkway intersects a fence. Likewise, you'd look for a Cancel button at the bottom or right of a dialog box, and logos in the upper-left corner of a web page. Keep in mind that these clues often are culturally determined, and someone new to the culture (e.g., someone who's never used a given operating system before) will not be aware of them.

Maps

Sometimes people go sign-to-sign or link-to-link without ever really knowing where they're going in a larger frame of reference. (Ever found your way through a strange airport? That's probably what you did.) But some people might prefer to have a mental picture of the whole space, especially if they're there often. In badly signed or densely built spaces, like urban neighborhoods, maps may be the only navigational aids they have.

In this chapter, the **Clear Entry Points** pattern is an example of careful signage combined with environmental clues—the links should be designed to stand out on the page. A **Sequence Map**, obviously, is a map; you can use **Overview Plus Detail** (Chapter 6) to show maps for virtual spaces, too. **Modal Panel** sort of qualifies as an environmental clue, since the ways out of a modal panel take you right back to where you just were.

I compared virtual spaces to physical ones here. However, virtual spaces have the unique ability to provide a navigational trump card, one that physical spaces can't (yet) provide: the **Escape Hatch**. Wherever you are, click on that link, and you're back to a familiar page. It's like carrying a wormhole with you. Or a pair of ruby slippers.

THE COST OF NAVIGATION

When you walk into an unfamiliar room, you look around. In a fraction of a second, you take in the shape of the room, the furnishings, the light, the ways out, and other clues; very quickly, you make some assumptions about what this room is and how it relates to why you walked in. Then you need to do what you came in to do. Where? How? You might be able to answer immediately—or not. Or maybe you're just distracted by other interesting things in the room.

Similarly, bringing up a web page or opening a window each incur a cognitive cost. Again, you need to figure out this new space: you take in its shape, its layout, its contents, its exits, and how to do what you came to do. All of this takes energy and time. The "context switch" forces you to refocus your attention and adjust to your new surroundings.

Even if you're already familiar with the window (or room) you just went into, it still incurs a cost. Not a large cost, but it adds up—especially when you figure in the actual time it takes to display a window or load a page.

This is true whether you're dealing with web pages, windows, dialog boxes, or device screens. The decisions that users make about where to go are similar, whether they use links or buttons—labels still need to be read, or icons decoded, and the users still will make leaps of faith by clicking on links or buttons they're not sure about.

Knowing that there's a cost associated with jumping from page to page, you can under-stand now why it's important to keep the number of those jumps down. Two of the patterns in this chapter—**Global Navigation** and **Pyramid**—give you specific ways to do that in com-plex applications and sites, by taking common navigation paths and turning them into easy single jumps. Patterns in other chapters, like **Card Stack** (Chapter 4), can help you pack more into a single page, thus sparing you the need to jump to a new one.

But the real efficiency gains come from the structure of the application. One of the nastiest things a designer can do is force a user to go into multiple levels of subpages or dialogs. every time they need to accomplish a simple, everyday task. (Worse is to lead him there, tell him he can't accomplish it because of some missing precondition, and send him back to Square One. Happens to the best of us.)

Can you design your application to do the most common 80 percent of use cases with zero or one "context switches"?

This is hard to do with some kinds of applications. You might think that some kinds of tools just have to be inside dialog boxes, two levels down in your site structure, or wherever. Is a certain tool too big to put on your main page? Try shrinking it: eliminate controls, shorten labels, and use specialized controls that save space (see Chapter 7). Is it too distracting when combined with everything else on the main page? Again, try shrinking it or putting it in an out-of-the-way spot. Do you need that wizard? Maybe its functionality is better ren-dered in one page than many. Be creative!

Now that I've given you a rule to follow, I'll tell you to break it.

Sometimes it's appropriate to bury functionality inside pages that take more than one jump to get to, such as that extra 20 percent left over from the 80 percent you made easily avail-able. It also could be that on your application, simplicity of presentation is more important than saving one or two jumps. **Extras on Demand** is a pattern from Chapter 2 that recom-mends putting little-used functionality behind an extra "door" (also using the 80/20 rule). As always, use your judgment—and usability-test it if you have any doubt.

Designers today seem to be taking all this to heart. Most modern desktop applications now are built around a single main window, often tabbed or tiled, with assorted toolbars and panes around it. It's become less fashionable to use separate windows or dialog boxes for every piece of functionality, and that's a good thing. Web applications also use more client-side validation, progressive disclosure, and other techniques for presenting changeable content without loading a new page each time something changes.

.

Yet sometimes, you still end up four dialog boxes deep in an application (see Figure 3-1).

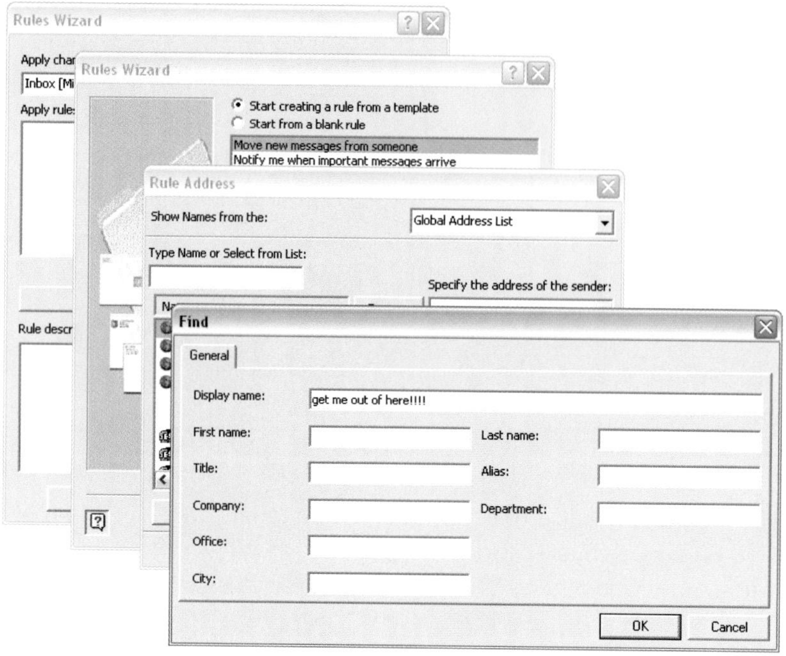

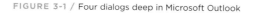

FIGURE 3-1 / Four dialogs deep in Microsoft Outlook

Vocabulary check: dialog boxes, windows, pages, or screens?

On the surface, it seems like web sites and applications are hopelessly different with respect to navigation. They're not. Whereas web sites, web applications, and hardware devices have you move from page to page, applications often make you move from window to window or dialog box. Yes, you can keep several windows in view at once. But users really only can pay attention to one at a time, and there's still a high cost associated with shifting that attention from window to window.

Because pages and windows are similar in this respect, I'm going to simply refer to these virtual rooms as "pages" from here on in this chapter. When you see that term, you can generally assume that whatever I'm talking about also applies to windows, dialog boxes, and screens.

TOO MANY JUMPS

To demonstrate what I mean by reducing the number of jumps, I'll walk through a short case study of an interactive site that's not actually all that bad. The task is probably common, though the site designers obviously didn't optimize the site for this task. You'll see what I mean.

I am visiting Amtrak's web site to find out how much it might cost to ride the train from Boston to New York City. My departure and arrival times are flexible, so I'd like to look at several to find the cheapest ones. To my delight, there's a "Fast Fare Finder" on their home page—I can get this information in one quick step! All I need to do is fill in this mini-form (Figure 3-2), click Go, and I'm there. Right?

FIGURE 3-2 / Amtrak's home page

1. *Click "Go".*

   I guess not. Looks like I'm being asked for the same information again (Figure 3-3).

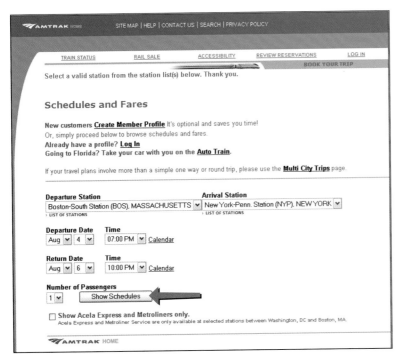

FIGURE 3-3 / Schedules and Fares

2. *Click Show Schedules.*

Close, but no fares are shown here (figure 3-4). I guess I have to choose one of these three options, which probably all have different prices. I'll choose the first one and see what it costs.

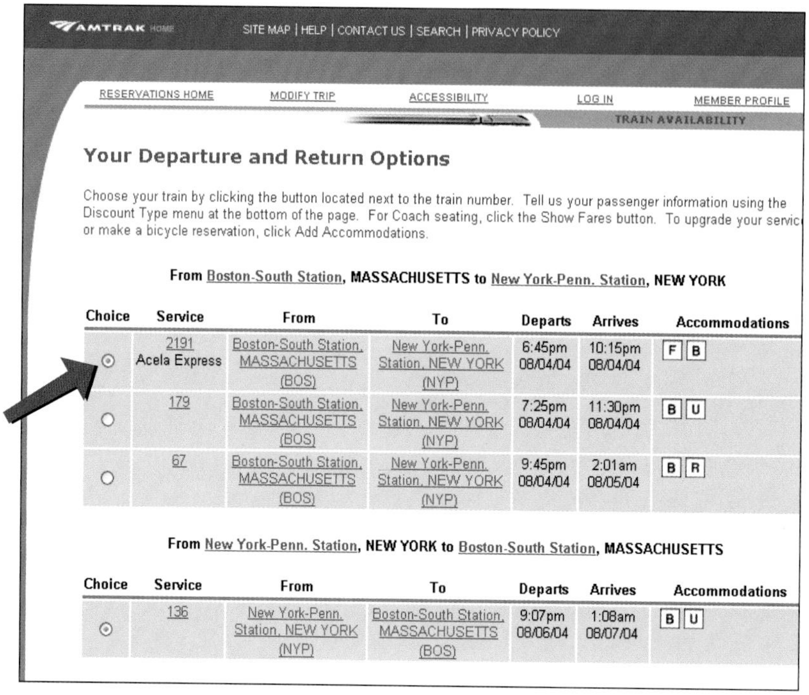

FIGURE 3-4 / Your Departure and Return Options

3. *Pick the first radio button, scroll down, and click a button labeled "Show Fares."*

$156. Finally! Now let me see another one, for comparison.

4. *Click "Return to Train Availability."*

Now, back at "Your Departure and Return Options" (Figure 3-5), I'll pick the second train...

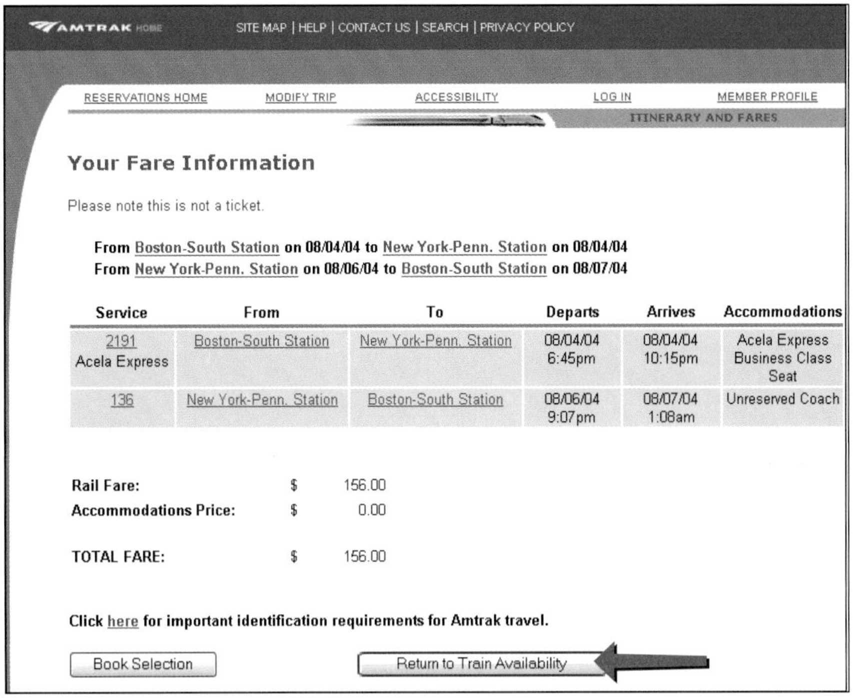

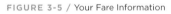

AMTRAK HOME
SITE MAP | HELP | CONTACT US | SEARCH | PRIVACY POLICY
RESERVATIONS HOME
MODIFY TRIP
ACCESSIBILITY
LOG IN
MEMBER PROFILE
ITINERARY AND FARES
Your Fare Information
Please note this is not a ticket.
From Boston-South Station on 08/04/04 to New York-Penn. Station on 08/04/04
From New York-Penn. Station on 08/06/04 to Boston-South Station on 08/07/04
Service
From
To
Departs
Arrives
Accommodations
2191 Acela Express
Boston-South Station
New York-Penn. Station
08/04/04 6:45pm
08/04/04 10:15pm
Acela Express Business Class Seat
136
New York-Penn. Station
Boston-South Station
08/06/04 9:07pm
08/07/04 1:08am
Unreserved Coach
Rail Fare: $ 156.00
Accommodations Price: $ 0.00
TOTAL FARE: $ 156.00
Click here for important identification requirements for Amtrak travel.
Book Selection
Return to Train Availability

FIGURE 3-5 / Your Fare Information

5. *Click "Show Fares" again.*

   $128. Not so bad.

6. *Click "Return to Train Availability" again.*

   And now pick the third train...

7. *Click "Show Fares" again.*

   Also $128.

Seven steps. Seven context switches—and eight page loads—for something that I thought could be done in one step. Remarkable!

Figure 3-6 shows what this use case looks like using a UML sequence diagram hacked for use as a navigation diagram. Each vertical line represents a page, each arrow represents a jump, and each rectangle shows what page I'm on. As you follow the arrows down the page, the diagram shows how the interaction progresses over time.

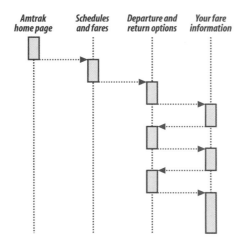

FIGURE 3-6 / Sequence diagram for the Amtrak scenario: four pages and seven jumps

How can we streamline this process down to one jump?

First, can we remove the extraneous "Schedules and Fares" page back at the beginning when we simply confirmed information we'd already typed in? Well, it turns out that that page asks the user for one more critical piece of information: the actual train stations in the source and destination cities. We could solve that problem with two new client-side drop-down lists that fill in with default stations after the cities are typed. (The default train station often is what the user wants anyway.) Alternatively, we could do this on the second page. With that hand-wave, we're one jump gone, five to go.

The next improvement—the big one—is simply to show the fares on the same page as the rest of the train info. We can add a "Fares" column to the table, which eliminates the remaining five jumps! Figure 3-7 shows the much-simplified navigation.

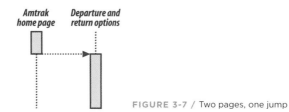

FIGURE 3-7 / Two pages, one jump

THE PATTERNS

To recap, this chapter talks about several aspects of navigation: overall structure, knowing where you are, figuring out where you're going, and getting there efficiently. The patterns address these issues to varying degrees.

The structure of an application or site is tied intimately to navigation within it. It's impossible to separate them, actually. One could arguably put structure-related navigation patterns like **Clear Entry Points**, **Hub and Spoke**, and **Pyramid** into Chapter 2, which discussed how to organize the content, because these patterns talk about how multiple pages interrelate. You can "tack on" some others—**Global Navigation**, **Color-Coded Sections**, **Sequence Map**, **Breadcrumbs**, and **Escape Hatch**—to individual pages after the basic navigational structures are designed, and thus they might move further down the design progression into page layout (the topic of Chapter 4).

And there's one more thing to note. **Clear Entry Points**, **Modal Panel**, and **Hub and Spoke** *restrict* access to navigation, not expand it (as many of the others do). Complete freedom to move anywhere at any time isn't an unalloyed good; sometimes clarity of understanding means that less is better.

In any case, we'll start with the patterns that describe navigational structures: how the pages (or windows or dialog boxes) of a UI interlink. If you draw a picture of the links between the pages of the UI, you might see some of these patterns:

21 Clear Entry Points   **24** Pyramid

22 Global Navigation   **25** Modal Panel

23 Hub and Spoke

The next four patterns work well as "You are here" signposts (as can **Global Navigation**, and Chapter 6's **Overview Plus Detail**). **Sequence Map**, **Breadcrumbs**, and **Annotated Scrollbar** also serve as interactive maps of the content. Annotated Scrollbar is intended more for single spaces, like large documents, than for multiply connected pages. But that's still navigation, after a fashion. It's still important for document users to know where they are, where to go, and how to move around quickly.

26 Sequence Map   **28** Annotated Scrollbar

27 Breadcrumbs   **29** Color-Coded Sections

Animated Transition helps users stay oriented as they move from one place to another. It's a visual trick, and nothing more, but it's very effective at preserving a user's sense of where they are and what's happening.

30 Animated Transition

Finally, **Escape Hatch** is the "navigational trump card" mentioned earlier. With this on the page, users know they can always get back to a familiar place.

31 Escape Hatch

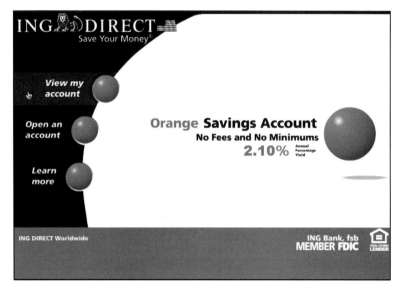

FIGURE 3-8 / From *http://ingdirect.com*

what

Present only a few entry points into the interface; make them task-oriented and descriptive.

use when

You're designing a task-based application, or any other application used largely by first-time or infrequent users. It's also helpful for some web sites. But if the application's purpose is clear to basically everyone who starts it, and if most users might be irritated by one more navigation step than is necessary (like applications designed for intermediate-to-expert users), then don't use it.

why

Some applications and web sites, when opened, present the user with what looks like a morass of information and structure: lots of tiled panels, unfamiliar terms and phrases, irrelevant ads, or toolbars that just sit there disabled. They don't give the hesitant user any clear guidance on what to do first. "Okay, here I am. Now what?"

For these users' sake, list a few options for getting started. If those options match a user's expectations, he can confidently take one of those options and begin work—this contributes to **Instant Gratification** (Chapter 1). If not, at least he knows now what the application actually does because you've defined the important tasks or categories right up front. You've made the application more self-explanatory.

how

When the site is visited, or the application started, present these entry points as "doors" into the main content of the site or application. From these starting points, guide the user gently and unambiguously into the application until he has enough context to continue by himself.

Collectively, these entry points should cover most reasons why anyone would be there. There might be only one or two entry points, or many; it depends on what fits your design. But you should phrase them with language first-time users can understand—this is not the place for application-specific tool names.

Visually, you should show these entry points with emphasis proportional to their importance. In Figure 3-8, for instance, ING Direct clearly wants to point people toward their current special savings account; they put it front-and-center, in bold lettering and colors, surrounded by whitespace. The three other tasks (probably used more frequently by most customers) are rendered in a group, each with equal visual weight. The most commonly used entry point, "View my account," is at the top.

On a page like this, most sites list other navigation links—About, Contact, Privacy Policy, etc.—which are much smaller, visible only to those actually looking for them. They're more specialized; they don't lead you directly into the heart of the site, no more than a garage door leads you directly into the living room of a home.

(Splash screens, by the way, are not a manifestation of Clear Entry Points, since they don't present a decision point to the user. They merely pass the captive user along from one screen to another. Other than being a progress indicator while something is loading, or a demonstration of a designer's prowess, they add no value.)

examples

Small-screen devices benefit from this pattern, too. Most PDAs and cell phones have a **Hub and Spoke** design, in which applications are chosen from a starting screen. But when there gets to be a lot of them, do you present them all together, as PalmOS does, or do you instead split out the most common ones? Presenting too many at once may overload a

first-time user; 80 percent of your use cases may go through only four or five applications. If you do separate them into first-tier and second-tier choices, the users of the second-tier applications incur one or more extra clicks to get where they're going. Only you can decide if that's worth it.

FIGURE 3-9 / Google is best known for doing one thing amazingly well. Its home page design focuses users' attention on that one thing: you can't miss that search box! The other stuff is ranked into secondary (such as Web or Images) and tertiary tiers, plus utility navigation (such as Advanced Search). Like ING Direct's site, this design's cleanness gives a user confidence in taking one of the few major choices.

FIGURE 3-10 / Here, a Motorola cell phone gives single-button-click access to six features: four from the central four-way button, and two from the softkeys at the bottom of the screen. The rest of the phone's applications are two clicks away, in a menu. Sensibly, the phone book is easiest to hit—selectable via a button right under one's left thumb. (This is more about convenience than information overload, I suspect, but it works toward both goals.)

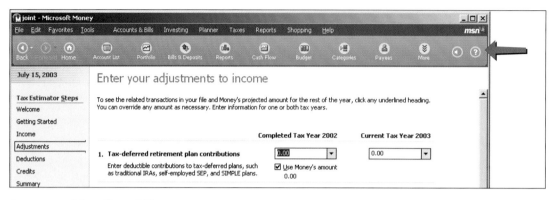

FIGURE 3-11 / From Microsoft Money

what

Using a small section of every page, show a consistent set of links or buttons that take the user to key sections of the site or application.

use when

You build a large web site, or an application with several separate sections or tools. In either case, users are likely to want to move directly from one section to another. You have plenty of space to work with, and you don't mind having extra elements on each page.

Hub and Spoke is an alternative to this pattern. It is better for tools that are more self-contained, with more tightly constrained workflow, or for very small screens.

why

On the Web, a global navigation bar is a well-established convention, so users expect it there. More importantly, though, a set of links or buttons that reflects the UI's highest-order structure makes that structure visible to users from every page. It gives them an overview of the UI and helps them find what they need in it (if the naming scheme

makes sense, anyway). It also facilitates exploration and easy movement by putting each section only one click away from anyplace else.

You can add to the utility of a global navigation panel by making it show what section the user is currently in, like tabs do. Thus it becomes a "You are here" signpost as well as a navigational device.

how

First, devise a sensible organizational structure. Keep the number of sections down to something you can display in the available space, and name the sections well—make them meaningful to the user, don't use too many words, and follow whatever conventions are appropriate (such as "About Us" or "Products").

As for the global navigation panel, design a single panel that looks the same—and goes into the same place—on each page where it appears. On the Web, that should be every page (with the notable exception of applications using a **Hub and Spoke** structure). A desktop UI has far fewer conventional uses of such a thing, but it should probably go into every major application window (not every dialog box). A good global navigation panel is one component of a well-designed **Visual Framework** (see Chapter 4).

To show where the user is now, simply make the link for the current section look different from the others. Use a contrasting color, perhaps, or an unobtrusive graphic like an arrow.

One design issue that you may run into, especially on web pages, is how to present this kind of navigational device along with other sets of links. They ought to be distinct from one another. Users may look to the top of the page for the global navigation; that leaves the left- and righthand sides for other links, or you could put them in the content area itself. You also could also use two very different sets of affordances—simple clickable text for the global navigation, and tabs for more "local" things, for instance.

As with **Center Stage** (Chapter 4), remember that home pages and main windows may require different layouts than other pages in the UI. If getting to the different sections of the UI is a purpose of the home page or opening window, then global navigation may need to be more prominent than everywhere else, and you might want to flesh it out with details or sublinks.

Finally, understand that not every user will use, or even notice, a navigational device like this. Engineers and designers share a common misconception that users will logically look for the overview first, and then decide where to go. They won't. They often don't care to know how the site or UI is organized, but simply follow the nearest and most obvious signposts until they find what they need (this is called **Satisficing**; see Chapter 1). It's analogous to someone looking for the restrooms in an airport—they probably won't bother reading a map if there are signs or architectural clues.

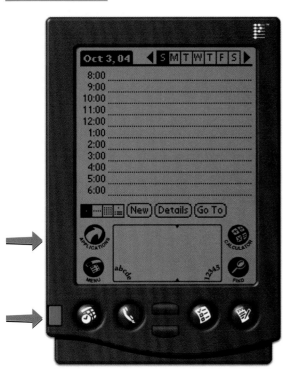

FIGURE 3-12 / Palms and similar PDAs use a hardware form of Global Navigation. The four round buttons at the bottom of the device bring the user directly to the calendar, phone list, To-Do list, and memo pad applications. Similarly, the silkscreened "soft" buttons above it bring the user to the Applications hub, calculator, and two helper tools, Menu and Find.

Notice that the calendar application shown has no explicit "Close" or "Exit" button. I suppose the designers expected that people would use global navigation to move around. This implies that the applications retain their state as the user switches applications, so no changes get lost inadvertently. It's a very different model from **Hub and Spoke** (the next pattern).

23 hub and spoke

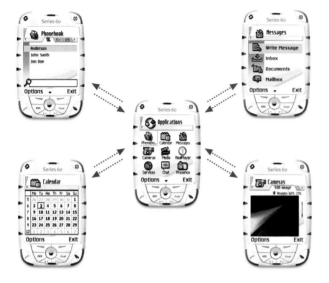

FIGURE 3-13 / Nokia Series 60 phone interface

what

Isolate the sections of the app into mini-applications, each with one way in (from the main page) and one way out (back to the main page).

use when

Your UI contains several discrete tasks, sub-applications, or content elements, such as forms, demos, games, articles, transactions, or self-contained tools. You can reach all of them from one central page or screen. However, you don't want to connect each of them to all the others, for several possible reasons:

- To reinforce the separateness of these sub-applications
- To restrict workflow to force the completion (or explicit cancellation) of a task
- To eliminate visual and cognitive clutter
- Physical space constraints

You may not want to use Hub and Spoke if users have a good reason to move directly between the tools that constitute the spokes. Use **Global Navigation** in that case. These two patterns are different solutions to a similar problem—structuring the users' typical movement paths. (They can coexist, but one usually ends up dominating the other in everyday use.)

Hub and Spoke is especially well-suited for small-screened mobile devices, usually in conjunction with a **One-Window Drilldown** architecture.

why

When you apply Hub and Spoke, you use navigation to structure the user experience into something different from the freeform browsing on the Web, or window-to-window hopping on desktop applications. You ask the user to focus on one section at a time, and then go back to the hub to get to another section. This certainly reduces clutter on the "spoke" pages—the user has less to look at and think about.

But by restricting the available navigation paths through interactive pages, you can also prevent errors—users can't shoot themselves in the foot so easily. With no navigation buttons, they can't leave a web form half-finished by jumping to a different page (the "abandoned edits" problem). With a modal window in a desktop application, they can't "lose" the dialog box on the screen. In general, they have less opportunity to get the UI into a self-inconsistent or confusing state.

Furthermore, restricted navigation means you have much tighter control over what circumstances the interface needs to handle—this often results in simpler (and thus cheaper) implementation. The architecture scales well, too; as more functionality comes on line, it's easy for you to add more spoke links to the hub page.

Finally, you may simply want to design the user's experience of the "spokes" as simple, self-contained UIs. This isn't always appropriate—in fact, it can be downright annoying to users accustomed to free-form navigation!—but the choice is yours. One advantage is that the user will find it very clear what to do, since the Hub and Spoke structure is intuitively obvious in many contexts. You click on a spoke, you do your thing, and you go back to the hub when you need to do something else.

how

Split up the content into self-contained mini-applications, either by task or tool. Design each however you see fit. These are the spokes.

On the hub page, arrange links to the spokes. On each spoke page (and each spoke may have several pages, such as with a **Wizard**), remove all navigation links that distract from the main task flow.

Leave only pertinent actions, such as Back and Next buttons, Cancel, Exit, and perhaps any other actions that won't interfere with the workflow, such as help functions.

When the user reaches the end of whatever task they're doing on the spoke, provide a way for the user to say he's finished, such as well-marked "Done" or "Cancel" buttons. Both should take the user back to the hub.

Bob Baxley's *Making the Web Work: Designing Effective Web Applications* (New Riders) first discussed the notion that a hub-based architecture is useful and good.

examples

In the small-device world, Hub and Spoke is fairly common, but it's rarely seen in its pure form in applications and web applications. I think this is because users find it a bit too constricting on the Web and the desktop. The days of every tool being a modal dialog ended some time ago, and good riddance to them!

Occasionally you do see a web site structured this way. Sites that offer free online games often strip most of the navigation from their actual game-playing pages, for instance. And TurboTax for the Web uses a form of it. TurboTax's home page has the usual large number of links—global navigation, secondary navigation, product links, etc.—but this group of three "products" takes center stage.

FIGURE 3-14 / This fragment of TurboTax's home page offers three products to the user. Clicking "Get Started" on any of them brings you to one of these other pages...

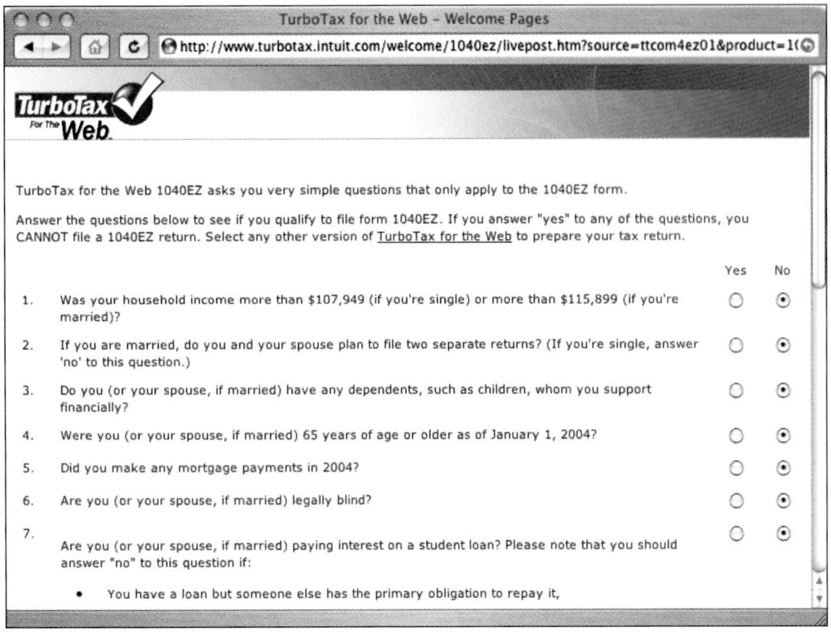

FIGURE 3-15 / These pages have almost no navigation except "Continue" (or "Sign In," or whatever else brings you to the next step) and a few helper links. This figure shows the starting pages for 1040EZ and Basic. Notice the bare-bones headers and sidebars. The users probably don't need any more confusion than that induced by the tax forms themselves!

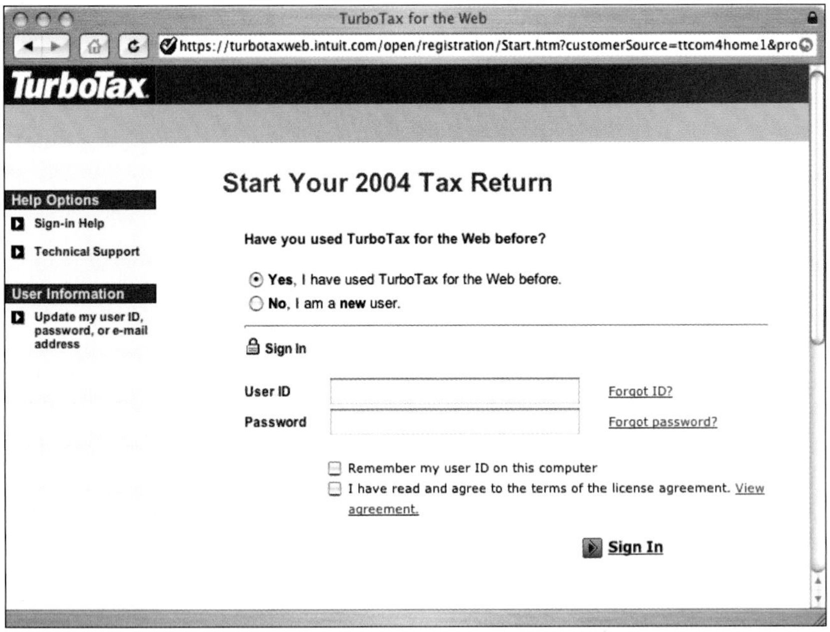

FIGURE 3-16 / This figure shows the first page, but for the Basic tax form.

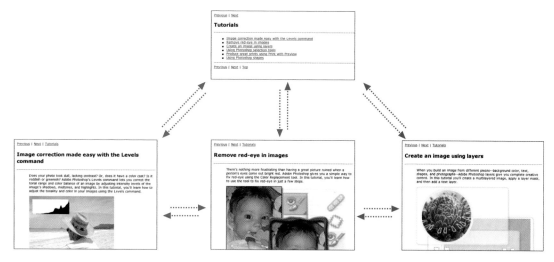

FIGURE 3-17 / Photoshop help tutorials

Link a sequence of pages with Back/Next links. Combine this sequential presentation with a main page that links to and from all pages in the sequence.

The site or application has a sequence of pages that a user normally views one after another, such as a slideshow, a wizard, chapters in a book, or a set of products. The user reaches the first page, and maybe others in the sequence, from a "parent" page that serves as a jumping-off point.

You might also consider using this pattern if you have one page that links to a lot of similar but semantically unconnected pages.

Pyramid seems to be found most often in single-window applications, like those found in devices and web pages. It is often paired with **One-Window Drilldown**.

This pattern reduces the number of clicks it takes to get around. It improves navigation efficiency, while simultaneously expressing a sequential relationship among the pages.

Back/Next (or Previous/Next) links or buttons are all well and good. People know what to do with them. But a user doesn't necessarily want to be locked into a page sequence that he can't easily get out of: having gone seven pages into it, will he need to click the Back button seven times to get back where he started? Not fun!

By putting a link back to the parent page on each sequence page, you increase the user's options. You've now got three main navigation options instead of two—Back, Next, and Up. You haven't made it much more complex, but a casually-browsing user (or one who's changed his mind in midstream) will need far fewer clicks to go where he wants to go. It's more convenient for users.

Likewise, chaining together a set of unconnected pages is kind to users who actually want to see all the pages. Without the Back/Next links, they would jump back and forth to the parent page all the time; they might just give up and leave.

how

This one's pretty simple: put Back, Next, and Up buttons or links on each sequence page, and put links to each sequence page on the parent page. It forms a topology like that shown in Figure 3-18—hence the name "Pyramid."

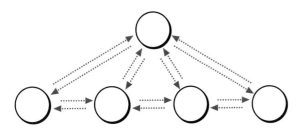

FIGURE 3-18 / Typical Pyramid link topology

You don't need to label these buttons literally "Back," "Next," and "Up"—you can use the actual names of the neighboring pages in the Back and Next labels, for instance, though that wordiness may not be worth the screen space if the user isn't looking for a specific item. Use your judgment. The Up button is generally better labeled "Back to <Page Title Here>," or some variation.

Also, co-locating all three links in one little page area often is handy because it minimizes mouse motion and establishes spatial memory. Even better, put the "Next" links or buttons in exactly the same place on each page—then the user doesn't have to move the mouse at all as he moves from one page to the next!

Most uses of Pyramid are in static linear sequences, like slideshows, where the designer simply placed one page after another. There's no reason why you can't also use it for branched sequences, through which the user chooses a path. Consider it.

Another variation turns a static linear sequence into a loop, by linking the last page back to the first without going back to the parent. It kind of works, but does the user know she's looped all the way back around? Does she recognize the first page in the sequence? Not necessarily—linking back to the parent page instead would be kinder, since it tells her that she's seen all there is to see.

You also can think about this pattern in terms of navigation among list items. A **One-Window Drill-down** application might have a list of objects that you can navigate into (e.g., entries in an address book). Once you've drilled down into one of them, it sometimes would be nice to go directly to the next one, rather than bouncing up to the parent page and down again. Topologically, the problem is identical to links on a web site, though the context is different.[1]

1 This aspect of Pyramid is very well described by Larry Constantine and Lucy Lockwood in a paper called "Usage-Centered Patterns: A Collection of Abstract Design Patterns for Presentation and Interaction Design." Their version of the pattern, intended for lists, is named Detail View Direct Navigation; see *http://foruse.com/patterns/detailnavigation.pdf*.

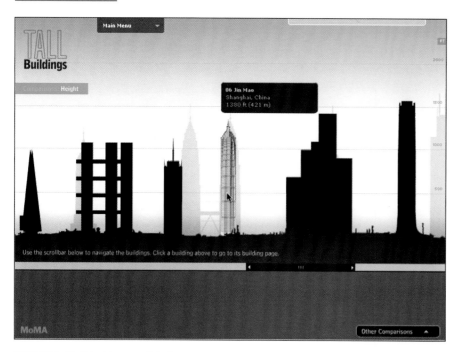

FIGURE 3-19 / The Museum of Modern Art's web site hosts a delightful applet about skyscrapers. It describes each of the twenty-four tallest buildings (and planned buildings) in the world. The user can choose from a sorted list of buildings to drill down into a description of that building; then the user can either go back to the sorted list, or click "Prev" or "Next" to go straight to another building description.

This screen shows the list of buildings by height. It scrolls horizontally; each building silhouette turns into a fully drawn building when the pointer hovers over it, as shown by the "Jin Mao" tooltip.

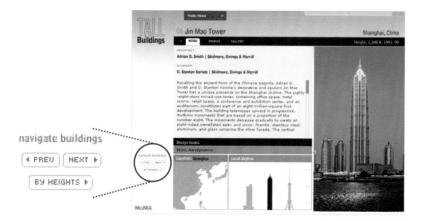

FIGURE 3-20 / This is the page you get when you click on the Jin Mao building. Note the small "Prev," "Next," and "By Heights" buttons, all clustered in a predictable place. See *http://moma.org/exhibitions/2004/tallbuildings*.

25 modal panel

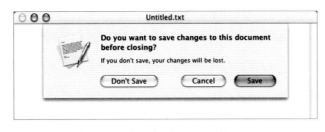

FIGURE 3-21 / The Save dialog box from TextEdit

what

Show only one page, with no other navigation options, until the user solves the immediate problem.

use when

The application is in a state from which it cannot proceed without help from the user. In a document-centric application, for instance, a "save" action might need the user to supply a filename, if one wasn't already given.

why

A modal dialog box (or other modal mechanism) cuts off all other navigation options from the user. He can't ignore the dialog box and go somewhere else in the application: he must deal with it here and now. When it's done, he gets sent back to where he was before.

It's an easy model to understand—and program—though it was overused in applications of past years. A modal panel is disruptive. If the user isn't already prepared to answer whatever the modal panel asks, then it interrupts the user's workflow, possibly forcing him to make a decision about something he just doesn't care about. When used appropriately, a modal panel channels the user's attention into the next decision that he needs to make. There are no other navigation possibilities to distract him.

how

In the same space on the screen where the user's attention lies, place a panel, dialog box, or page that requests the needed information. It should prevent the user from bringing up any other page in that application. This panel ought to be relatively uncluttered, keeping with the need to focus the user's attention onto this new task with minimal distractions.

Remember that this is a navigation-related pattern. You should carefully mark and label the ways out, and there shouldn't be many of them; one, two, or maybe three. In most cases, they are buttons with short, verbish labels, such as "Save," "Don't Save," or "Cancel." Upon clicking them, the user should be taken back to the page she came from.

Web-application designers have a small problem. The browser's Back and Forward buttons (and its history mechanism, bookmarks, URL bar, etc.) will function as they always do, regardless of the designer's wishes to cut off all other navigation options. This will be an interesting area to watch as standards for web applications evolve over the next few years. As of this writing, I don't think there's any good modal-panel solution for web applications, except the one shown in the Google example in Figure 3-23.

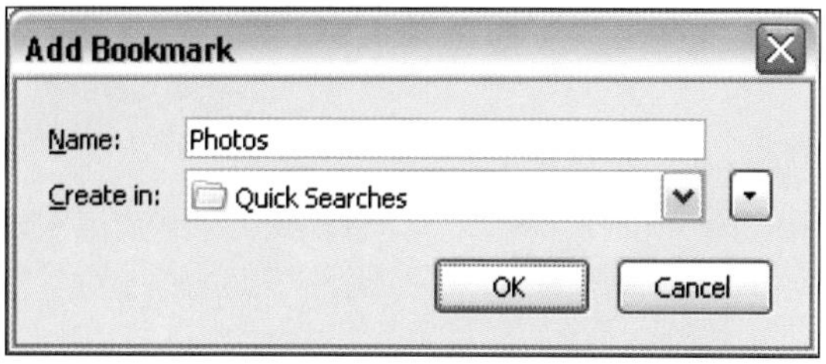

FIGURE 3-22 / This is a typical modal dialog box for Windows applications. It's from Firefox, so its look and feel differs slightly from most Windows applications, but the familiar elements of modal dialog boxes are here: OK and Cancel buttons, a limited number of titlebar options (just a Close button), and content that's tightly focused on one task. However, Firefox may be able to proceed with its usual business—being a web browser—without requiring that this question be answered *right now.* Thus a solution other than a modal dialog box may have been more appropriate (albeit harder to design).

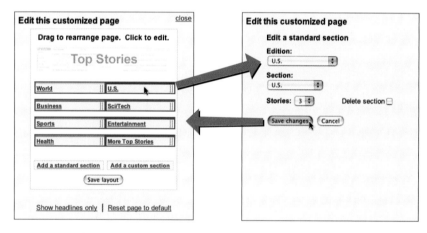

FIGURE 3-23 / Here's a possible solution for web apps. The Google News page contains an interactive "Customize" feature that, like the Firefox dialog box, is focused tightly on one small task. However, it only uses a small panel within the large Google News page. When you double-click on a page icon (such as "World" or "U.S."), the panel changes its contents to show a dialog-like form. When you press "Save changes" or "Cancel"—the only navigation options within this self-contained panel—it shows the previous contents again.

Essentially, it behaves like a **One-Window Drilldown** mini-application within the web page. You can still click the browser's Back or Next buttons, or any other link on the Google News page, but it's clear from context that they lie outside the scope of this customization mini-application.

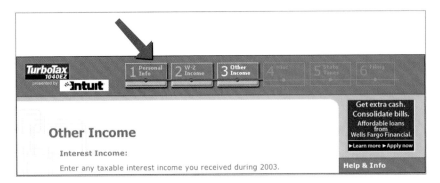

FIGURE 3-24 / TurboTax, 2004 version

what

On each page in a sequence, show a map of all of the pages in order, including a "You are here" indicator.

use when

You've designed a written narrative, a slideshow, a wizard, or anything else through which a user progresses page by page. The user's path is mainly linear.

If the navigation topology is large and hierarchical (as opposed to linear), you may want to consider using **Breadcrumbs** instead, because you won't have room to show a Sequence Map.

why

A computer game player once said in a public forum, "Being lost is not fun." And part of the appeal of such games is the navigation through strange places to accomplish tasks! It's even less fun with applications intended to be serious, where people do not want to waste time figuring out where they are.

Most of the time, actually, "being lost" in an application is not the real problem—it's not knowing how much further you have yet to go. A good map of the page sequence, shown on each page, helps the user stay oriented in several ways: he can see the steps already completed (and possibly the skipped steps or branches too), his current location (with a "You are here" signpost), and how many steps remain.

A Sequence Map should also serve as a navigational device itself; it should let the user jump among different steps by clicking on the map.

how

Near an edge of the page, place a small map of the pages in the sequence. Put it on one line or column if you can, to keep it from competing visually with the actual page content. Give the current page's indicator some special treatment, such as making it lighter or darker than the others; pick another treatment for the already-visited pages.

For the user's convenience, you might want to put the map near or next to the main navigation controls, usually Back and Next buttons.

How should you label each page on the map? If the pages or steps are numbered, then obviously use the numbers—they're short and easy to understand. If not, put the page titles in the map. If the titles are long, that might make it completely unwieldy! Try shortening the titles, or if you can't, try hiding them inside tooltips or small rollover windows.

examples

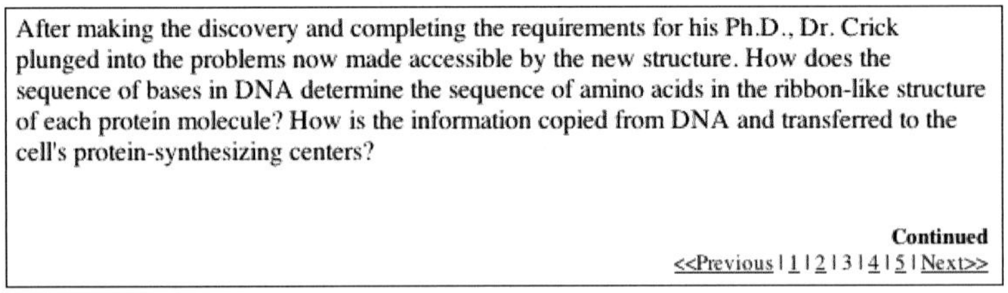

After making the discovery and completing the requirements for his Ph.D., Dr. Crick plunged into the problems now made accessible by the new structure. How does the sequence of bases in DNA determine the sequence of amino acids in the ribbon-like structure of each protein molecule? How is the information copied from DNA and transferred to the cell's protein-synthesizing centers?

Continued
<<Previous | 1 | 2 | 3 | 4 | 5 | Next>>

FIGURE 3-25 / News sites often break up long articles into multiple pages. The New York Times web site places a sequence map at the bottom right of each article segment. The Previous and Next links are placed conveniently on either end, and the previously read pages will turn the same color that followed links would turn—it takes advantage of what users already know (and what CSS already controls) about link behavior.

Note that the tiny numeric links might be a frustratingly small hit target for some users. Will all New York Times readers be young and nimble?

27 breadcrumbs

FIGURE 3-26 / From *http://java.sun.com*

On each page in a hierarchy, show a map of all the parent pages, up to the main page.

Your application or site has a straightforward tree structure, without much interlinking among the tree elements. Users work their way up and down this tree, either via direct navigation or searching. Applications constructed as **One-Window Drill-down** applications frequently use Breadcrumbs. In fact, I've never seen this used for multi-window desktop applications, though tiled panels can use them; see the iTunes screenshot in this pattern for an example of using Breadcrumbs on the main panel.

Breadcrumbs are an alternative to **Sequence Maps**. You may have wanted to use a Sequence Map to help the user stay oriented, but the map would be too large and unwieldy to render into a small space, so you need another solution.

Breadcrumbs show each level of hierarchy leading to the current page, from the top of the application all the way down. In a sense, it shows a single linear "slice" of the overall map of the site or application, thus avoiding the complexity of an entire map.

So, like a Sequence Map, Breadcrumbs help a user figure out where he is. This is especially handy if he's jumped abruptly to somewhere deep in the tree, as he would by following search results (or a bookmark, if it's a web site). Unlike Sequence Map, though, Breadcrumbs don't tell the user where he's headed next, nor where he came from. It deals only with the present.

Many texts tell you that Breadcrumbs—named for the Hansel and Gretel story, in which a child drops breadcrumbs on a forest trail to mark his way home—are most useful for telling the user how he got where he is from the top of the site or application. But that's only true if the user has drilled straight down from the top, with no sidetracking, or following other branches, or dead ends, or searching, or linking directly from other pages...not likely.

Instead, Breadcrumbs are best for telling you where you are relative to the rest of the application or site—it's about context, not history. Look at Figure 3-26 above. I reached this page in Sun's Java web site by some meandering path, but it tells me that I ended up deep in the "Products & Technologies" section, in "Reference." Now I know where to go if I want to learn about other products or find other reference material. Breadcrumbs thus reveal useful clues about the site or application's information architecture.

Finally, Breadcrumbs usually are clickable links or buttons (like **Sequence Maps**), which turns it into a navigational device in its own right.

Near the top of the page, put a line of text or icons indicating the current level of hierarchy. Start with the top level; to its right, put the next level; and so on down to the current page. Between the levels, put a graphic or text character—usually a right-pointing arrow—to indicate movement from one level to the next.

The labels for each page's indicator should be the titles of each page. Users should recognize them if they've been to those pages already; if not, the titles should at least be self-explanatory enough to tell the user what those pages are about. If the titles are too long, try shortening them, or hiding them inside tooltips or small rollover windows.

FIGURE 3-27 / A typical iTunes Music Store screen. I've done a keyword search for a particular song, and I'm at a Search Results page. (I hesitate to call it a "page" because this isn't really a web site in the traditional sense; it's a web-connected desktop application.) Anyway, the breadcrumbs trail shows two levels: Home (shown as an icon), and Search Results. Now I click on the first album I see under "Top Albums," and...

FIGURE 3-28 / ...I get this page. Look at how the breadcrumb trail has changed. Now it shows where I am in iTunes's standard three-level music hierarchy: genre (vocal), artist (Etta James), and album. This gives me one-click access to the genre and artist pages, both of which might be of interest to me. I still could click the Back button—just to the left of the breadcrumbs—to go back to the search results. Again, it's about context, not history.

So the breadcrumbs here have achieved two things: establishing a sense of place in the iTunes world, and providing a rich set of navigation options within that space.

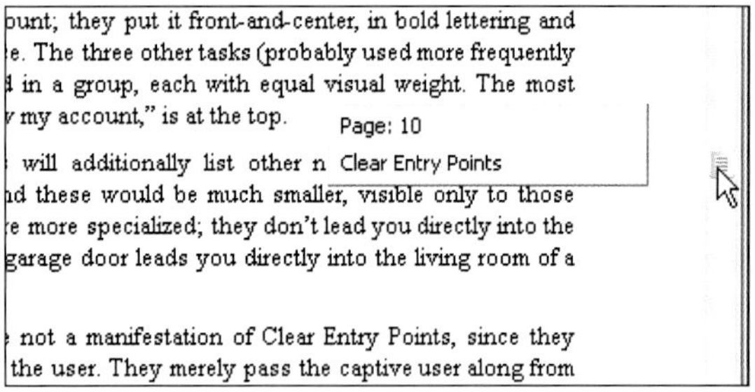

FIGURE 3-29 / Microsoft Word's scrollbar tooltips

what

Make the scrollbar serve double-duty as a map of the content, or as a "You are here" indicator.

use when

You've built a document-centric application, or anything else that contains a large scrolled virtual space, such as a text document, list, or image. Users will scan this application for items of note, such as specific page numbers or landmarks, and they might have trouble keeping track of where they are and where to go next as they scroll.

why

Even though the user remains within one "UI space" as she scrolls through the content, signposts still are useful. When scrolling quickly, it's really hard to read the text flying by (or impossible, if the screen can't refresh quickly enough), so some other indicator of position is necessary. Even if she stops briefly, the part of the document she can see may not contain anything she can orient herself by, like headers.

Why a scrollbar? Because that's where the user's attention is focused. If you put signposts there, the user will see them and use them as she scrolls, rather than trying to look at two different screen areas at once. You can put signposts close to the scrollbar and still get the same effect; the closer, the better.

When the scrollbar shows indicators in the scrollbar track itself, you get something that behaves just like a one-dimensional **Overview Plus Detail** (Chapter 6). The track is the overview; the scrolled window is the detail.

how

Put a position indicator on or near the scrollbar. Either static or dynamic indicators might work—static indicators are those that don't change from second to second, such as blocks of color in the scrollbar track (see the tkdiff screenshot in Figure 3-30). Make sure their purpose is clear, though; such things can baffle users who aren't used to seeing graphics in the scrollbar track!

Dynamic indicators change as the user scrolls, and they often are implemented as tooltips. As the scroll position changes, the tooltip shown next to the scroll thumb changes to show information about the content there. This will vary with the nature of the application. Word, as shown above in Figure 3-29, puts page numbers and headers in these tooltips.

In either case, you'll need to figure out what a user is most likely to be looking for, and thus what you need to put into the annotations. The content structure is a good starting point. If the content is code, you might show the name of the current function or method; if it's a spreadsheet, show the row number; and so on. Also consider whether the user currently is in a specialized mode, such as searching for a string—the annotation should show something about it, if that's what the user is scanning the document for.

This pattern description was taken partially from *About Face: The Essentials of Interaction Design* (Wiley).

examples

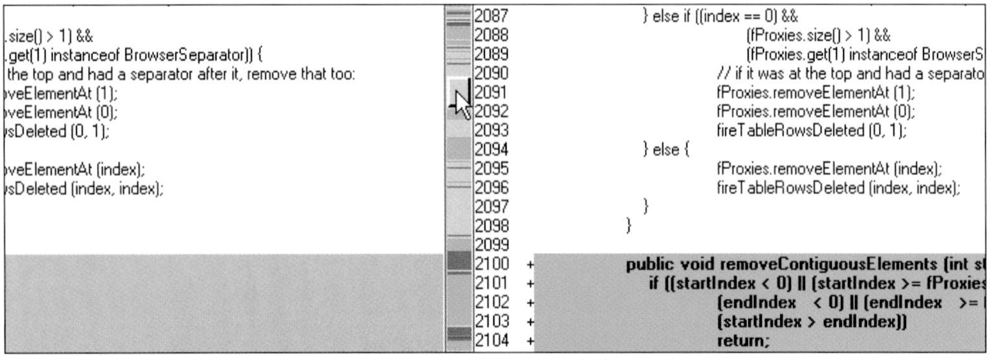

FIGURE 3-30 / Annotated Scrollbar is an uncommon technique. tkdiff is one of very few applications that currently have the flexibility to show nonstandard items in scrollbars. This program visually highlights the differences between two versions of a text file; newly-added sections are marked in green, changed sections in blue, and deleted sections in red. An annotated scrollbar serves as an overall map, thus making large files much easier to comprehend.

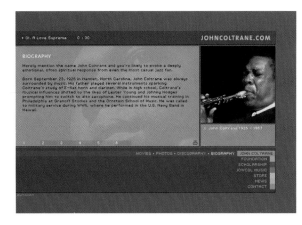 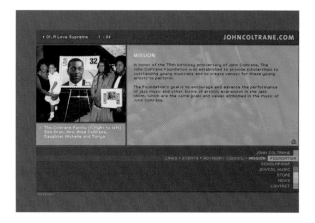

FIGURE 3-31 / From *http://johncoltrane.com*

what

Use color to identify which section of an application or site that a page belongs to.

use when

The UI is a large application with many pages or windows, which can be organized into sections (or chapters, sections, sub-applications, etc.). You might use a **Visual Framework** (Chapter 4) to unify them visually, but you also want each section to have a distinctive look. Perhaps each section needs separate branding, or each has a different purpose or audience.

why

This is an example of a *signpost*—something that gives the user a clue where he is. It does so with some subtlety; colors work visually instead of verbally, and it's not even something that users will necessarily notice immediately (though it's hard to miss in the vivid Coltrane example in Figure 3-31). Once users are attuned to the color schemes, they can use them. Even before then, they'll know when they've left one section for another, if they notice that the color scheme changed.

So color-coding works to distinguish one section from another; it makes the boundaries clear. It's easier for users to mentally map out smaller chunks of a navigational space, such as one section, than the whole space at once—you should do this with a large UI in any case, whether you use color coding or not.

Creative uses of different colors also can make your interface look nicer and less boring. It might even contribute to the branding of the UI—see the Apple example in Figure 3-32.

how

Pick one of the interface colors and change it for each section. Usually, the background color is too much change—the Coltrane example works only because the Visual Framework is so strong and distinctive. Most designs work better with a trim color, like a border, or the background of a small amount of text.

Remember that colorblind users won't necessarily see the differences in colors from one section to another. That's why color never should be the *only* way of distinguishing sections. You also need to have other signposts—indicators on navigation bars, for instance, and page or window titles.

FIGURE 3-32 / Apple's web site provides a more typical example of color coding. Look at the top of each screenshot. The tab and the bar below it change color (and texture!) to match the content—for example, blue for QuickTime or brushed metal for OS X. In the page graphics, you can see the theme colors echoed in titlebars and logos.

The effect is subtle but noticeable. It contributes to both usability and branding, while not detracting from the unity of the overall site. (Note that the tabs are the **Global Navigation** in this web site, while the secondary navigation links live on the colored bar.)

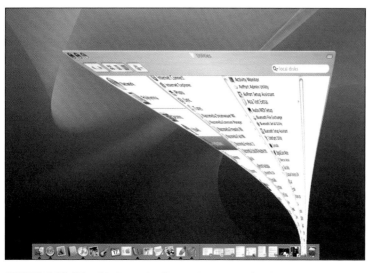

FIGURE 3-33 / Mac OS X's "genie effect" animates a window being minimized.

what

Smooth out a startling or dislocating transition with an animation that makes it feel natural.

use when

Users move through a large virtual space, such as an image, spreadsheet, graph, or text document. They might be able to zoom in to varying degrees, pan or scroll, or rotate the whole thing. This is especially useful for information graphics, such as maps and plots. (See Chapter 6 for more about information graphics.)

Alternatively, the interface might have sections that can be closed and opened again, either by the system or the user—such as trees with closable parent nodes, standalone windows that open and close, or an interface built with **Closable Panels** (Chapter 4). Animated Transition might also be used when users jump from one separate page to another.

why

All of these transformations can disrupt a user's sense of where she is in the virtual space. Zooming in and out, for instance, can throw off her spatial sense when it's done instantaneously, as can rotation and the closing of entire sections that prompt a re-layout of the screen. Even scrolling down a long page of text, when it's jumpy, can slow a reader down.

But when the shift from one state to another is continuous, it's not so bad. In other words, you can animate the transition between states so it looks smooth, not discontinous. This helps keep the user oriented. We can guess that it works because it more closely resembles physical reality—when was the last time you instantly jumped from the ground to 20 feet in the air? Less fancifully, an animated transition gives the user's eyes a chance to track a location while the view changes, rather than try to find the location again after an abrupt change.

When done well, animated transitions bolster your application's "cool factor." They're fun.

how

For each type of transformation that you use in your interface, design a short animation that "connects" the first state with the second state. For zoom and rotate, you might show the in-between zoom or rotate levels; for a closing panel, you may show it shrinking while the other panels expand to take up the space it leaves behind. To the extent possible, make it look like something physical is happening.

If any of these patterns are double-edged swords, this one is. Beware of making the user motion-sick! The animations should be quick and precise, with little or no lag time between the user's initiating gesture and the beginning of the animation. Limit it to the affected part of the screen; don't animate the whole window. And keep it short. My preference would be well under a second, and research shows that 300 milliseconds might be ideal for smooth scrolling.[1] Test it with your users to see what's tolerable.

If the user issues multiple actions in quick succession, such as hitting the down arrow key many times to scroll, combine them into one animated action. Otherwise, the user might sit there through several seconds' worth of animation as the punishment for hitting the down arrow key 10 times. Again: keep it quick and responsive.

examples

The web application "The Secret Lives of Numbers" lets users explore a very wide range of data—

it shows zoomable histograms of number usage across the Web, from 0 to 100,000. It uses animated transitions to transport the user from high-level overviews down to very small, detailed views. Figure 3-34 shows what happens when you hold the mouse button down over one number, in this case 2000: the histogram zooms in slowly, smoothly animating everything on the graph as it goes.

Some things to notice:

- The histogram bars become wider as the viewer zooms in, thus preserving a sense of size and scale. They behave almost like solid objects. When they're wide, you know that you're zoomed way in.

- The number labels on the lefthand margin slowly spread apart, revealing lightly-written minor labels between the white ones. The interval between the white labels also changes, from 25 to 10 to 5, while the pixel distance between them is kept relatively constant. (This is important for looking up numbers; you never want an interesting histogram bar to be too far away from a readable label.)

- The vertical gridlines squish together as the horizontal scale compresses. As the minor gridlines get too close together, they fade into the black background, and the gridline labels are removed selectively. The graph is kept uncluttered.

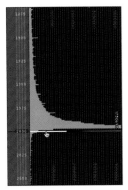 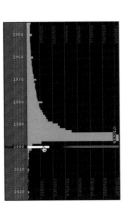 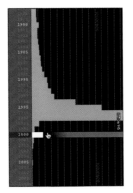

FIGURE 3-34 / Zooming in on "The Secret Lives of Numbers," at *http://www.turbulence.org/Works/nums/applet.html*

1 See "Benefits of Animated Scrolling," *http://hcil.cs.umd.edu/trs/2004-14/2004-14.html*.

31 escape hatch

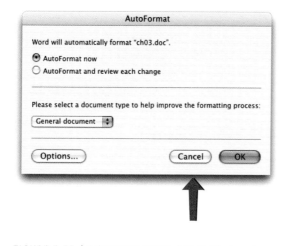

FIGURE 3-35 / A dangerous dialog box from Word, made less so by Cancel

what

On each page that has limited navigation options, place a button or link that clearly gets the user out of that page and back to a known place.

use when

You've got pages that constitute some sort of serial process, like a wizard, or any pages that "lock" the user into a limited navigation situation, like **Hub and Spoke** or **Modal Panel**. Users might be able to reach these pages out of context, as they could do via search results.

(Escape hatches sometimes aren't necessary when you have **Sequence Maps** or **Breadcrumbs** on a page. Users who understand them can use them to get back to a known place.)

why

Limited navigation is one thing, but having no way out is quite another! If you give the user a simple, obvious way to escape from a page, with no strings attached, he's less likely to feel trapped there.

This is the kind of feature that helps people feel like they can safely explore an application or site. It's sort of like an Undo feature—it encourages people to go down paths without feeling like they're committing to them. See the **Safe Exploration** pattern in Chapter 1.

If users can reach these pages via search results, such as web pages in the middle of a step-by-step process, then it's doubly important to put Escape Hatches on each page. Visitors can click them to get to a "normal" page that tells them more about where they actually are.

how

Put a button or link on the page that brings the user back to a "safe place." For example, you can use a home page, a hub page in a **Hub and Spoke** design, or any page with full navigation and something self-explanatory on it. Exactly what it links to depends upon the application's design.

Web pages often use clickable site logos as home-page links, usually in the upper left of a page. These pages provide an Escape Hatch in a familiar place, while helping with branding at the same time.

In some dialogs, a "Cancel" button or the equivalent can serve this purpose. They, too, let the user say "I'm done with this; forget I ever started it."

Have you ever called a company—say, your bank—and had to work your way through a set of phone menus? The menus can be long, confusing, and time consuming. If you find yourself in the wrong menu, you may just hang up and try again from the top. However, many phone menu systems have a hidden Escape Hatch that they don't tell you about: if you dial "0" at any point, you might be connected to a human operator.

ORGANIZING THE PAGE:
LAYOUT OF PAGE ELEMENTS

Page layout is the art of manipulating the user's attention on a page to convey meaning, sequence, and points of interaction.

If the word "manipulating" sounds unseemly to you, think about it this way. Film and television directors make their living by manipulating your attention on the movie or TV screen, and you are presumably a willing participant. Likewise for editors who arrange articles, headlines, and ads on a newspaper. If all this content were presented in a drab monotone, with no graphic emphasis to grab and move your attention, you would actually find it harder to extract meaning—what's supposed to be important, and what's not?

Even though it is ultimately an art, there might be more rationality to good page layout than you think. Some important ideas from graphic design are explained in this chapter introduction; each can guide you in the layout of pages, screens, and dialog boxes. We'll talk about visual hierarchy, visual flow and focal points, and grouping and alignment—all are predictable and rational approaches to page design. This chapter's patterns describe concrete ways to apply those high-level concepts to interface design.

But the changeable, interactive nature of computer displays makes layout easier in some ways, harder in others. We'll talk about why that's true. Some of these patterns work as well in print as they do onscreen, but most of them would be useless in print because they presume that the user will interact with the page.

THE BASICS OF PAGE LAYOUT

This section discusses five major elements of page layout: visual hierarchy, visual flow, grouping and alignment, how to put these three elements together, and how to use dynamic displays.

VISUAL HIERARCHY: WHAT'S IMPORTANT?

The concept of visual hierarchy plays a part in all forms of graphic design. Put simply, the most important content should stand out the most, and the least important should stand out the least. Titles ought to look like titles, and secondary content ought to look like secondary content—in other words, a reader should be able to deduce the informational structure of the page from its layout.

Examples explain this concept best. Figure 4-1 shows text that wasn't formatted with any visual hierarchy at all.

You're invited to Zelda's 30th Birthday Party! Please come dressed as your favorite Gilbert and Sullivan character. Children are welcome. Dinner will be served; if you'd like to bring food, call Stacy at 555-1212. When: October 20th, at 7:00 PM Where: Zelda's house. If you need directions, feel free to call Zelda and ask. Please RSVP to Stacy by October 10th. See you there!

FIGURE 4-1 / No visual hierarchy

Passable, but not great. What's the most important information in that paragraph? You can guess that the first sentence is the most important, but otherwise, it's hard to tell, since the whole block of text is visually monotonous. Once you've read it and realize it's an invitation, you can tell from context—but you had to read it first.

Now let's improve on this example. Whitespace is one of the best tools you have for organizing a visual hierarchy. It's a cheap and graceful way of pulling apart monotonous blocks of information.

You're invited to

Zelda's 30th Birthday Party!

Please come dressed as your favorite Gilbert and Sullivan character. Children are welcome. Dinner will be served; if you'd like to bring food, call Stacy at 555-1212.

When: October 20th, at 7:00 PM
Where: Zelda's house. If you need directions, feel free to call Zelda and ask.

Please RSVP to Stacy by October 10th. See you there!

FIGURE 4-2 / With whitespace

In Figure 4-2, you can at least see distinct groups of information. And the headline at the top—"Zelda's 30th Birthday Party"—stands out a bit more because it has whitespace around it. So does the not-quite-as-important RSVP message at the bottom. But the text that your eye falls on first is probably "You're invited to". It's sitting up there by itself, at the upper left corner, where every speaker of left-to-right languages looks first. That alone gives it unwarranted importance.

You also have typography and positioning at your disposal, which Figure 4-3 applies to the same problem.

FIGURE 4-3 / With typography and alignment

Big, bold fonts do the trick for importance, of course. Our eyes are drawn to dense, contrasted shapes with heavy "visual weight." The invitation's most important line is in a giant font; the second most important line is in a large font, but not as large; the body text is normal sized. Similarly, the tiny lightweight font used for the directions comment indicates "you may want to read this, but it's not that big a deal if you miss it."

Spatial positioning does something a little more complex here. It's being redundant with the whitespace by separating some blocks of text from others. It's also enhancing the apparent importance of the "When" and "Where" text—which are important—by making them stand on the almost-empty left margin, aligned with the headline.

The shapes of some page elements give you clues, too. The comment about directions is indented underneath the "Where" text in the example. You can guess that the directions comment relates to, but is not as important as, the text above it. The same logic applies to tree views, auxiliary text under links, input hints under text fields, and so forth. With these and other familiar structures, like tables, their visual shapes "telegraph" meaning immediately, before the user even starts to read what's in them.

In this chapter, the **Center Stage** pattern deals directly with visual hierarchy by encouraging you to establish a single large area of the UI to do the main task. Using the **Titled Sections** pattern helps define the visual hierarchy, too. And if you develop a **Visual Framework** (another pattern, which encodes how to do visual hierarchy within the whole UI), make sure it accommodates the different levels of hierarchy you need, such as titles, headlines, subheads, lists, navigation bars, and action buttons.

These mechanisms can help you lay out a visual hierarchy:

- Upper-left-corner preference
- Whitespace
- Contrasting fonts: the bigger and bolder, the more important the information
- Contrasting foreground and background colors: putting white text on a black background, for instance, makes a very strong statement on a white page
- Positioning, alignment, and indenting: indented text is subordinate to whatever's above it
- Graphics such as lines, boxes, and colored bars: things in a box or group go together

You'll find that many UIs and printed graphics use several of these mechanisms at once. Web pages frequently use both color and fonts to differentiate headlines from body text; many UIs use both group boxes and whitespace to form visual groups. That's okay. Having all these "variables" to choose from gives you a lot of design freedom, especially since they each have a dual role: to show how the UI is organized, and to communicate branding, emotion, and other non-rational attributes. (I'll return to this fascinating topic in Chapter 9.)

Meanwhile, let's look more deeply at visual organization.

VISUAL FLOW: WHAT SHOULD I LOOK AT NEXT?

Visual flow deals with the tracks that readers' eyes tend to follow as they scan the page. It's intimately related to visual hierarchy, of course—a well-designed visual hierarchy sets up focal points on the page wherever you need to draw attention to the most important elements, and visual flow leads the eyes from those points into the less-important information. As a designer, you should be able to control visual flow on a page so people follow it in approximately the right sequence.

Several forces can work against each other when you try to set up a visual flow. One is our tendency to read top-to-bottom and left-to-right. When faced with a monotonous page of text, that's what you'll do naturally; but any visual focal points on the page can distract you from the usual progression, for better or worse.

"Focal points" are the spots your eyes can't resist going to. You tend to follow them from strongest to weakest, and the better pages have only a few—having too many focal points dilutes the importance of each one. You can set them up in many different ways, such as by using whitespace, high contrast, big chunky fonts, spots of "interesting" color, converging lines, hard edges, faces, and motion. (Yes, this list resembles the one above for visual hierarchy. Titles, logos, and critical sections of text or images use these properties to become focal points.)

The next time you pick up a magazine, look at some well-designed ads and notice what your eyes gravitate toward. The best commercial graphic artists are masters at setting up focal points to manipulate what you see first.

However, if you've ever brought up an ad-filled web page and pointedly ignored the brightly-colored moving ads (so you could read the monotonous blocks of text that you went there to read), then you know that we're not merely slaves to our hardwired visual systems! We can choose to ignore what we think we don't need to look at, and zero in on what we think is the important part of the page. Thus meaning and context also play a big part in visual flow.

If you build a UI in which sequence makes a difference—like a Wizard, or a dialog box in which early choices affect later choices—then think about visual flow. (Even if your UI does not depend upon sequence, you should think about it anyway, since a good visual flow is easier on your users' eyes.) It's not hard to set up a layout that flows well, but be on your guard against layout choices that work against it. Place your controls and buttons along a straightforward visual path. At the end of that path, put the link or button that finishes the task ("Submit," "Return to main page," or "OK") and brings the user somewhere else.

Figure 4-4 shows a dialog box with a nice visual flow. Notice how your eyes start at the top, move straight down the column of text fields (perhaps slowing down at the horizontal lines), and "land" at the four icons. After pausing there to take them in, perhaps, your eyes may hop down to either the Help or the OK and Cancel buttons.

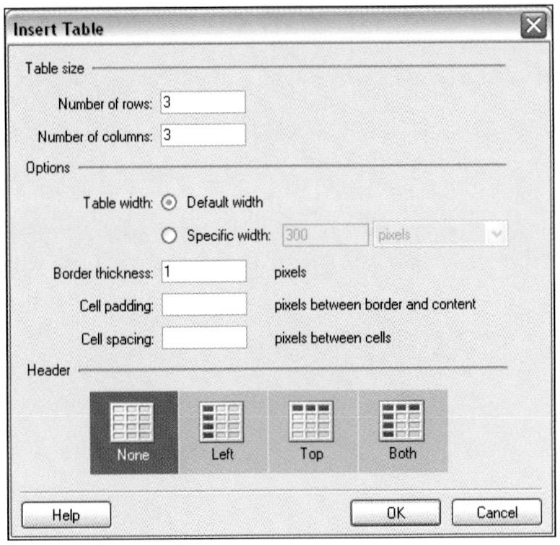

FIGURE 4-4 / Macromedia Contribute's "Insert Table" dialog box

Now, at some point you'll probably take the time to read the labels, but they're so visually lightweight that they likely didn't catch your eye first. The text fields probably did, because they're focal points—white (contrasting against gray), strongly aligned, and semantically important.

In summary:

- Top-to-bottom and left-to-right is the default visual flow.
- Strong focal points will draw the eyes first, followed by weaker ones.
- The perceived meaning of the page content will change where the user chooses to look.

GROUPING AND ALIGNMENT: WHAT GOES WITH WHAT?

You knew this already, but I'll say it anyway because it's so important: by grouping things together visually, you state that they are related. Conversely, if you put two things far away from each other, such as the last field of a form and the form's "Submit" button, then you state that they're not related to each other. If visual flow doesn't step in and lead the user's eyes to the button by some other means, the user may not see it.

Like focal points, grouping and alignment are necessary to forming a clear visual hierarchy. They also help with visual flow, by guiding the viewer's eyes from group to group.

The human visual system craves order. We're wired to see larger forms made from smaller ones, like words from letters or tables from grids of cells. You can take advantage of this need for order by "clustering" related things together, and by separating those clusters with enough whitespace to keep them unambiguously separate. (Whitespace again! It's really okay to use it, even in small spaces. It's better to display less information with more clarity than to crowd a page too much.) This is how you associate a text field with its label, an image with its caption, or a graph with the slider that controls it.

Group boxes can help here, but don't expect them to carry the entire burden of visual grouping; give them "room to breathe" on a crowded page. If you squint your eyes so you can't see the group box's edges, is there enough whitespace that you can still make out the groups? If so, you're doing fine. Also, be careful about nesting group boxes two or more levels deep, since it gets really hard to make out what's what. Try a different approach to designing the visual hierarchy.

Alignment is another, more subtle way to associate things with one another. For instance, if you have two sets of buttons far away from each other on a dialog box, but they do somewhat similar things, you can line up one group under the other and make them the same width to emphasize the similarity. Or if you have two forms on a page, separated by blocks of text, then line up the forms' left edges against one invisible line and the texts' left edges against another.

The theory behind grouping and alignment was developed early in the 20th century by the Gestalt psychologists. They described several layout properties that seem to be hardwired into our visual systems. Among them are the following:

Proximity

Put things close together, and viewers will associate them with one another. This is the basis for strong grouping of content and controls on a UI.

Similarity

If two things are the same shape, size, color, or orientation, then viewers will also associate them with each other.

Continuity

Our eyes want to see continuous lines and curves formed by the alignment of smaller elements.

Closure

We also want to see simple closed forms, like rectangles and blobs of whitespace, that aren't explicitly drawn for us. Groups of things often appear to be closed forms.

Figure 4-5 depicts each property and how you can combine them to create an effective overall design.

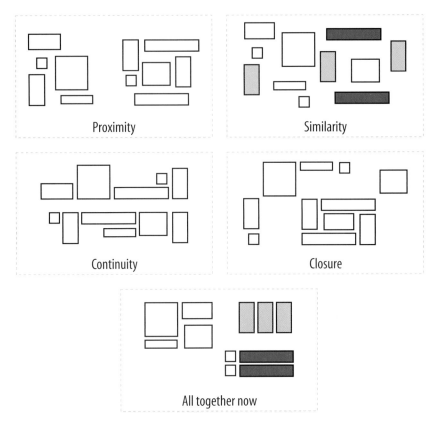

FIGURE 4-5 / Four of the Gestalt principles

As important as they are individually, they're best used in combination with one another. Once again, redundancy is not always bad; the fifth grouping looks more like an actual page layout than a retro-styled mosaic.

Continuity and closure, then, explain alignment. When you align things, you form a continuous line with their edges, and the users follow that line and (perhaps subconsciously) assume a relationship. If the aligned items are coherent enough to form a shape—or to form one out of the whitespace or "negative space" around it—then closure is also at work, adding to the effect.

PUTTING IT ALL TOGETHER

On the web page shown in Figure 4-6, the text is blurred so that you can't read it easily. But I bet you can understand a lot of the page structure.

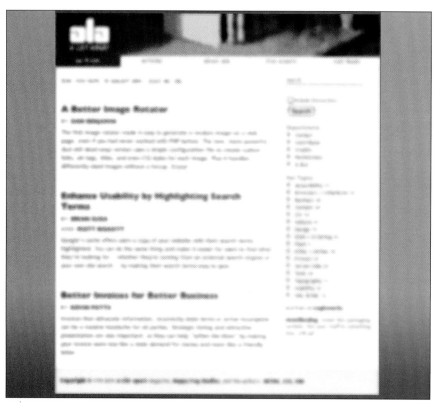

FIGURE 4-6 / From http://www.alistapart.com

In your first glance, you just perceived many of the things we just talked about. Let's deconstruct that first glance. First, what path did your eyes follow? Probably one of those in Figure 4-7, or some variation thereof.

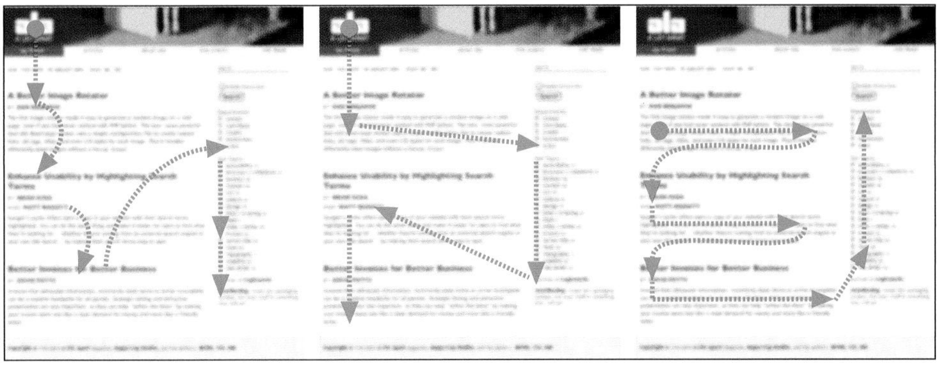

FIGURE 4-7 / Possible visual flows on alistapart.com

The logo is obviously a focal point—it sits where web page headers always sit, and it's a heavy font with high white-on-dark contrast. The headlines draw attention because of their color, size, and whitespace separation. The column on the right looks dense, orange, and visually interesting, so you may have looked at it too.

Note that the third visual-flow variation doesn't start at the logo. Readers who visit a page with single-minded interest in the content may simply ignore the header and start at the upper left of the "white part" of the page—there's no perceived benefit in looking at the page trappings.

Now what about the Gestalt principles we just covered? The page presents three main groups, each of which has big red text, smaller red text, and blocks of body text. Similarity and proximity form these perceptual groups; whitespace sets them apart. The column on the right is set off by a very strong edge—actually, two of them; note the subcolumn along its left side—and its density and color give this shape a strong visual coherence. The dark background of the header comprises another visual form, as does the gray footer, with its single continuous line of text. Figure 4-8 shows the groupings on this page.

FIGURE 4-8 / Grouping on the ALA web page

All this formatting contributes to the visual hierarchy. Context and higher-level mental processing kick in as you start to parse what you see and apply what you already know about web sites.

You can easily distinguish the header, footer, main content, and auxiliary information. Within the main content, there are three points of interest—probably linked articles—each with its header, subheaders (bylines?), and body text. Within the auxiliary information, there's a mini-form (search?), two tables (probably containing links, since they're not black), and other text. The header contains five texts that are aligned and look similar, probably top-level navigation. You can safely ignore the footer, as you probably do on most web pages.

USING DYNAMIC DISPLAYS

Everything I've discussed so far applies equally to UIs, web sites, posters, billboards, and magazine pages. They deal with static aspects of layout. Ah, but you have a dynamic computer display to work with—and suddenly time becomes another dimension of design! Just as importantly, computers permit user interaction with the layout to an extent that most printed things can't.

There are many, many ways you can take advantage of the dynamic nature of computer displays. You can concentrate on space usage, for example—even the biggest consumer-grade computer screens have less usable space than, say, a poster or a newspaper page. That's life. If you work with PDAs or cell phones, you've got an especially tiny space to work in. There are many techniques for using that space to present more content than you can show at one time.

What do you mean, less space?

It's true, your nice 21-inch monitor is physically bigger than a magazine spread. And a wide cinema display might be bigger than a tabloid newspaper. The real problem is resolution. Most UIs contain a lot of text. And as of this writing, most screens just can't render text at a point size as small as print can manage and have it still be readable. So you can't fit as many column-inches (for instance) on a screen that's the same physical size as a piece of paper. Sorry!

Using scrollbars is one common way of presenting a small "viewport" onto a large thing, like text, an image, or a table. Scrollbars let the user move around at will, in one or two dimensions. (But refrain from using horizontal scrolling with text, please).

Or, if you can carve up the content into coherent sections, you have several options—**Card Stacks**, **Closable Panels**, and **Movable Panels** all put some layout control into the user's hands, unlike the more static **Titled Sections**. (You also can split up content over multiple virtual pages and let the user navigate between them; see Chapter 3, *Navigation*.) They invoke time by letting the user see various content at different times of their choosing.

If you want to direct the user through a sequence of steps, **Responsive Enabling** and **Responsive Disclosure** are two well-known, dynamic ways of doing so.

THE PATTERNS

This chapter's patterns give you specific ways to put all these layout concepts into play.

The first two, **Visual Framework** and **Center Stage**, address the visual hierarchy of the whole page, screen, or window, regardless of the type of content you put into that page. You should consider **Visual Framework** early in a project, since it affects all the major pages and windows in an interface.

 Visual Framework    **Center Stage**

The next group of patterns represents four alternative ways of "chunking" content on a page or window. They're useful when you have a lot of stuff to show on the page at once. Once you've made a decision to break up your content into thematic sections, you need to choose how to present them. Should they all be visible at once, or can they (or should they) be viewed independently? Is it okay for users to manipulate those sections on the page? These patterns deal with visual hierarchy, but they also involve interactivity, and will help you choose among the specific mechanisms available in UI toolkits.

 Titled Sections    **Closable Panels**

 Card Stack    **Movable Panels**

Right/Left Alignment and **Diagonal Balance** draw on the concepts of visual flow, alignment, and other things discussed in this introduction. They deal with the spatial relationships among smaller, more static elements on a page, like text and controls.

 Right/Left Alignment   **Diagonal Balance**

The **Property Sheet** pattern is a little unusual. It too talks about spatial relationships among smaller page elements, but it's as much about content and interaction as it is about layout. It's here because when a knowledgeable user recognizes that a page has a Property Sheet on it, their expectations are set quite strongly. The layout tells the user precisely how they should interact with the page.

 Property Sheet

The last three patterns deal with the dynamic aspects of content layout. **Responsive Disclosure** and **Responsive Enabling** are two ways of directing a user through a series of steps or a set of options; they indicate what can be done at any point in time, while preventing the user from straying into areas that will get them into trouble. **Liquid Layout** is a technique for arranging a page that can change size and shape at the user's whim.

 Responsive Disclosure   **Liquid Layout**

 Responsive Enabling

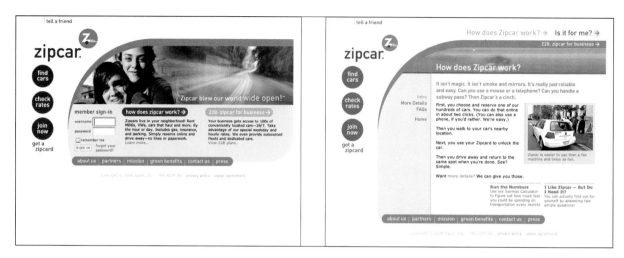

FIGURE 4-9 / From *http://zipcar.com*

what

Design each page to use the same basic layout, colors, and stylistic elements, but give the design enough flexibility to handle varying page content.

use when

You've built a web site with multiple pages, or a UI with multiple windows—in other words, almost any complex software. You want it to "hang together" and look like one thing, deliberately designed; it should be easy to use and navigate.

why

When a UI uses consistent color, font, and layout, and when titles and navigational aids—signposts—are in the same place every time, users know where they are and where to find things. They don't have to figure out a new layout each time they switch context from one page or window to another.

Have you ever seen a book in which the page numbers and headings were in a different place on each page?

A strong visual framework, repeated on each page, helps the page content stand out more. That which is constant fades into the background of the user's awareness; that which changes is noticed. Furthermore, adding character to the design of the visual framework helps with the branding of your web site or product—the pages become recognizable as yours.

how

Draw up an overall look-and-feel for each page or window in the thing you build. Home pages and main windows are "special" and are usually laid out a little differently from subsidiary pages, but they still should share certain characteristics with the rest of the artifact. For example:

- Color: backgrounds, text colors, and accent colors
- Fonts: for titles, subtitles, ordinary text, and minor text

ORGANIZING THE PAGE

- Writing style and grammar: titles, names, content, short descriptions, any long blocks of text, anything that uses language

All other pages or windows should also share the following, as appropriate.

- "You are here" signposts: titles, logos, breadcrumb trails, and **Card Stack** indexes such as tabs or link columns
- Navigational devices: sets of standard links, OK/Cancel buttons, back buttons, "quit" or "exit" buttons, and navigational patterns such as **Global Navigation**, **Sequence Map**, and **Breadcrumbs** (all Chapter 3)
- Techniques used to define **Titled Sections**
- Spacing and alignment: page margins, line spacing, the gaps between labels and their associated controls, and text and label justification
- Overall layout grid: the placement of things on the page, in columns and/or rows, taking

into account the margins and spacing issues listed earlier

If you're familiar with graphic design concepts, you may recognize some of these techniques as comprising a layout grid. A layout grid is a structural template for a set of pages or layouts. Each individual page is different, but all pages use specified margins and align their contents along invisible gridlines. A good Visual Framework does indeed include a layout grid, but it also includes other aspects of look-and-feel, such as colors, visual details, and writing style.

Implementation of a Visual Framework should force you to separate stylistic aspects of the UI from the content. This isn't a bad thing. If you define the framework in only one place—such as a CSS stylesheet or a Java class—it lets you change the framework independently from the content, which means you can tweak it and get it right more easily. (It's also good software engineering practice.)

examples

FIGURE 4-10 / The Windows and Mac OS look-and-feels help to implement a visual framework, since colors, fonts, and controls are fairly standard. But you need to add the higher-level structure, like the layout grid and language. These Excel screenshots both come from the same dialog box—Page Setup—and they illustrate the concept well. All these characteristics are consistent from page to page: location of action buttons in the upper and lower right; margin size, indenting, and vertical distance between text fields; extension of text fields to the right edge; the use of labeled separators (such as "Print titles" and "Orientation") to delimit **Titled Sections**; and capitalization and grammar.

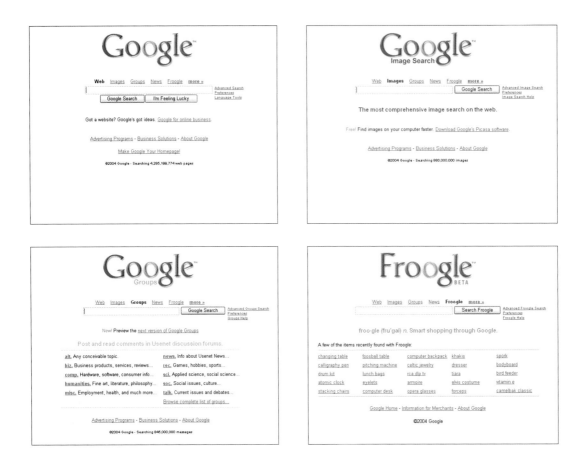

FIGURE 4-11 / Web page designers know how to apply this concept well. Google's pages are simple and unfussy, but very, very recognizable. All signposts are clear and consistent—the logo, the page title and subtitle ("Image Search" and "Groups"), and the other links—and the all-important search field *always* is in the same place!

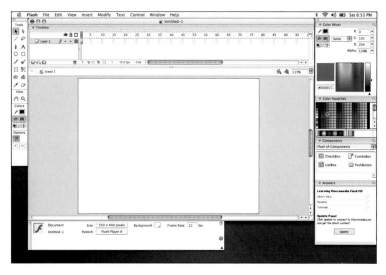

FIGURE 4-12 / Flash MX

Put the most important part of the UI into the largest subsection of the page or window; cluster secondary tools and content around it in smaller panels.

use when

The page's primary job is to show coherent information to the user, let him edit a document, or enable him to perform a certain task. Most applications can use Center Stage—tables and spreadsheets, forms, web pages, and graphical editors all qualify.

why

You should guide the user's eyes immediately to the start of the most important information (or task), rather than letting them wander over the page in confusion. An unambiguous central entity anchors their attention. Just as the lead sentence in a news article establishes the subject matter and purpose of the article, so the entity in Center Stage[1] establishes the purpose of the UI.

Once that's done, the user will assess the items in the periphery in terms of how they relate to what's in the center. This is easier for the user than repeatedly scanning the page, trying to figure it out—what comes first? What's second? How does this relate to that? And so on.

how

Establish a visual hierarchy, with the "center stage" dominating everything else. (See the chapter introduction for a discussion of visual hierarchy.) When designing a Center Stage, consider these factors, though none of them are absolutely required:

Size

> The Center Stage content should be at least twice as wide as whatever is in its side margins, and twice as tall as its top and bottom margins. (The user may change its size, but this is how it should be when the user first sees it.)

---

1 The name of this pattern was first coined in 1998, by P.R. Warren and M. Viljoen, in their paper "Design patterns for user interfaces."

Color

Use a color that contrasts with the information in the margins. In desktop UIs, white works well against Windows gray, especially for tables and trees. As it happens, white often works in web pages too, since ads and navigation bars usually use other colors as their backgrounds; also, web users are "trained" by convention to look for the plain text on a white background.

Headlines

Big headlines are focal points, and can draw the user's eye to the top of the Center Stage. That happens in print media too, of course. See the chapter introduction and **Titled Sections** for more on headlines and focal points.

Context

What does the user expect to see when she opens up the page? A graphic editor? A long text article? A map? A filesystem tree? Work with her preconceptions; put that in center stage and make it recognizable. The user will look for it—this trumps all other rules about visual perception. (But it doesn't mean you can frustrate her by hiding what she's looking for! Some web sites put their main content so far down the page that it's "below the fold" in short windows, requiring the user to scroll down to find it. That's just sadistic.)

Notice that I did not mention one traditional layout variable: position. It doesn't much matter where you put the center stage—top, left, right, bottom, center, all of them can be made to work. If it's big enough, it'll end up more or less in the center anyway. Keep in mind that well-established genres have conventions about what goes into which margins—e.g., toolbars on top of graphic editors, or navigation bars on the left sides of web pages. Be creative, but with your eyes open.

If you're in doubt, take a screenshot of the layout, shrink it down, blur it, and ask someone where on the page they think the main content should start. Again, see the chapter introduction for an example.

FIGURE 4-13 / Most blogs tend to have cluttered layouts; it's a rare blog that sets its main content into a strong center stage. Take a look at this screenshot from *http://boingboing.net*. The ads and other marginal content do attract attention, but the middle column, containing the blog entry, is very wide in comparison. It also starts close to the top of the screen—the header is blessedly short. The eye is drawn easily to the top article.

FIGURE 4-14 / To drive home the point, look what happens when the major page sections are abstracted out as plain rectangles. It may not look very wide in the screenshot, but that center column is over three times as wide as the lefthand column of ads. It needs that much width to compete with the ads' flashy colors and contrast.

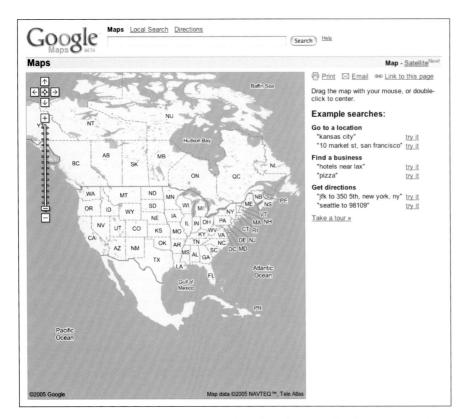

FIGURE 4-15 / Google Maps is a clean, uncluttered interface. The map easily takes center stage by using size and color: it occupies most of the window, and it's colorful, in contrast to the white-background tools at the top and right.

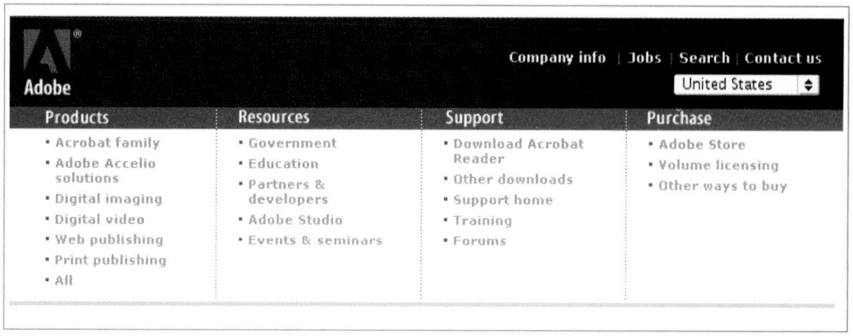

FIGURE 4-16 / http://adobe.com

what

Define separate sections of content by giving each one a visually strong title, and then laying them all out on the page together.

use when

There's a lot of content on the page, but you want to make the page easy to scan and understand. You can group the content into thematic or task-based sections that make sense to the user.

why

Well-defined and well-named sections structure the content into easily digestible chunks, each of which is now understandable at a glance. It makes the information architecture obvious. (See this chapter's introduction for a discussion of visual hierarchy, which is basically about rendering content in a way that communicates its actual structure. See also Chapter 2 for a definition of information architecture.)

When the user sees a page sectioned neatly into chunks like this, it guides her eye along the page more comfortably. The human visual system always looks for bigger patterns, whether they're deliberate or not. So put them in deliberately!

how

First, get the information architecture right—split up the content into coherent chunks, and give them short, memorable names (one or two words, if possible). Next, choose a presentation:

- For titles, use a font that stands out from the rest of the content—bold, wider, larger point size, stronger color, etc. (Remember that nothing's stronger than black, not even red.)

- Try reversing the title against a strip of contrasting color. White on dark can make it look like a Windows titlebar.

- Use whitespace to separate sections.

- Putting sections on different background colors works well on web pages and interfaces that want to look like web pages, though it's unusual on desktop UIs.

- Boxes made from etched, beveled, or raised lines are familiar on desktop UIs. They can get lost—and just become visual noise—if they're too big, too close to each other, or deeply nested. It can be done well when combined with the title; see the examples.

If the page is still too hard to read, try using **Card Stack**, **Two-Panel Selector**, or **Extras on Demand** to manage it all. You can combine some of these patterns with Titled Sections, too. Elsewhere in this chapter, **Closable Panels** and **Movable Panels** are alternative ways of presenting "chunked" content.

If you're having trouble giving reasonable titles to these chunks of content, that may be a sign that the grouping isn't a natural fit for the content. Consider reorganizing it into different chunks that are easier to name and remember. "Miscellaneous" categories may also be a sign of not-quite-right organization, though sometimes they're genuinely necessary.

examples

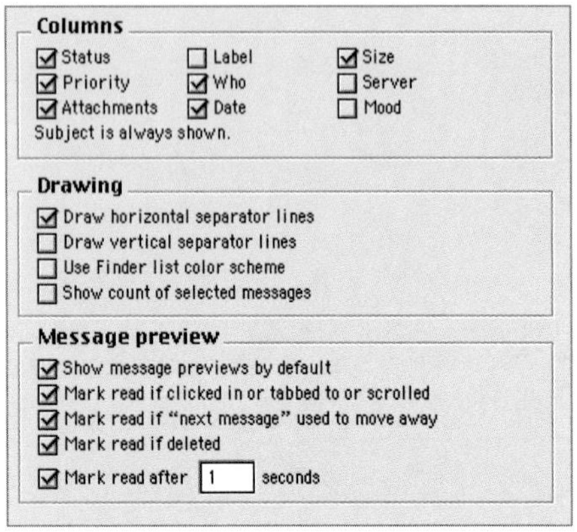

FIGURE 4-17 / Typical usage of Titled Sections in desktop applications. In Eudora's preferences dialog, the boxes look good around the grids of checkboxes, the bold titles stand out clearly, and there is sufficient whitespace between the sections to give them visual "breathing room." (In fact, this example would work even if the boxes were erased.)

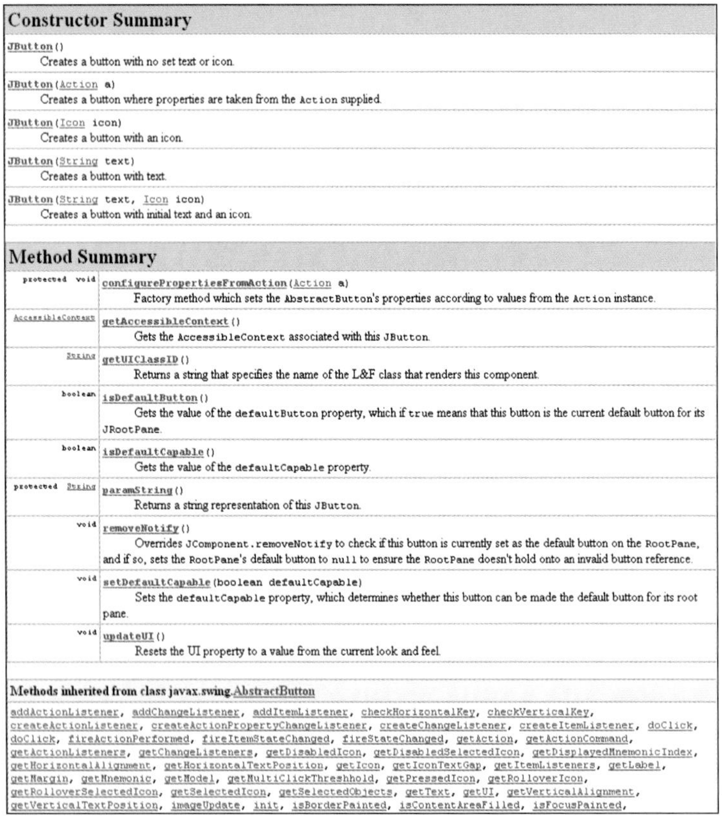

FIGURE 4-18 / This screenshot came from a long page full of Java documentation. Each section is labeled with the blue bars, which are very easy to find and read as the user scrolls rapidly down the page. Notice the use of visual hierarchy here: the main sections are marked with large fonts and darker color, while the minor section at the bottom uses a smaller font and lighter color. At the next level down the hierarchy, the names of classes and methods stand out because they're green and outdented; finally, the body text is small and black, as body text usually is.

35 card stack

FIGURE 4-19 / Internet Explorer properties dialog box

what

Put sections of content onto separate panels or "cards," and stack them up so only one is visible at a time; use tabs or other devices to give users access to them.

use when

There's too much material on the page. A lot of controls or texts are spread across the UI, without the benefit of a very rigid structure (like a **Property Sheet**); the user's attention becomes distracted. You can group the content into **Titled Sections**, but they would be too big to fit on the page all at once. Finally—and this is important—users don't need to see more than one section at one time.

why

The labeled "cards" structure the content into easily-digestible chunks, each of which is now understandable at a glance. Also, tabs, the most common form of Card Stack, are very familiar to users.

how

First, get the information architecture right. Split up the content into coherent chunks, and give them short, memorable titles (one or two words, if possible). Remember that if you split the content up wrong, users must switch back and forth between cards as they enter information or compare things. Be kind to your users and test the way you've organized it.

Then choose a presentation:

- Tabs are great, but they usually require six or fewer cards. Don't "double-row" them, since double rowing is almost never easy to use; scroll them horizontally if they won't fit in one row all at once.

- Vertical tabs let you force a Card Stack into a narrow, tall space that can't accommodate normal tab pages.

- A lefthand column of names works well on many web pages and dialog boxes. You can fit a lot of cards into a column. It lets you organize cards into a hierarchy, too, which you really can't do with tabs. (At some point it becomes more like a **Two-Panel Selector**; there's really no clear boundary between them.)

- Some UIs have a drop-down list at the top of the page, which takes less space than a link column, but at the cost of clarity: drop-down lists usually behave like controls, and a user might not recognize it as a navigational device. It can work if the containment is very obvious; see the OS X example in Figure 4-23. But the user still can't see all the card titles at once.

If you want an alternative to Card Stack that lets people view two or more cards at one time, look at **Closable Panels**. They don't have the metaphoric power of tabs, but they can be quite effective for users who are motivated to learn how to use them.

.

FIGURE 4-20 / You can draw tabs in any number of ways, and they don't have to start on the left side. This is from the Theban Mapping Project web application. See *http://thebanmappingproject.org*.

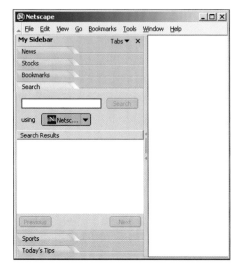

FIGURE 4-21 / Netscape imposes different physical constraints. The "tab" buttons in this sidebar are stacked vertically, and they move from top to bottom as the user clicks them, so now the selected page always has its button directly above it. This is an interesting solution for a constrained, vertically oriented space. (It originally was seen in early versions of Visio.)

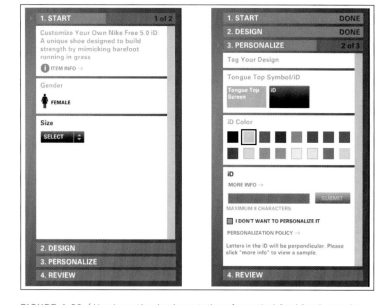

FIGURE 4-22 / Here's another implementation of a vertical Card Stack, one that doesn't even pretend to use tabs. This Nike web application has you click on the orange horizontal bars to show one pane at a time.

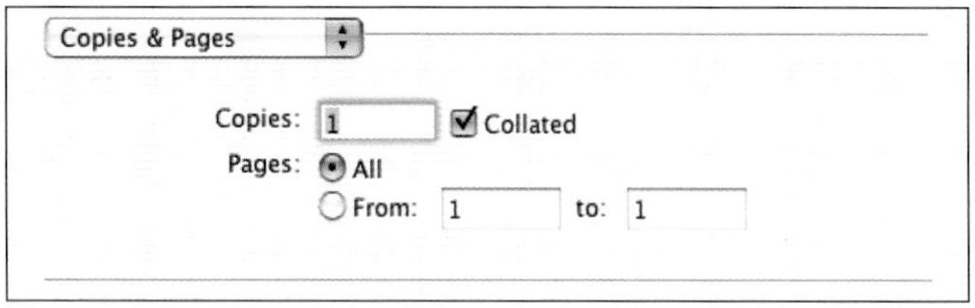

FIGURE 4-23 / Sometimes applications use dropdown lists where tabs might have been used. This is the "Copies & Pages" page in OS X Internet Explorer's print dialog box. Dropdowns are space conserving, and allow long and numerous page names, but the user can't see what other pages are available until she opens the drop-down list. Note the two separators above and below the controls; a user needs this kind of containment to understand what the dropdown does. Otherwise, it just looks like another control, not a navigational device. It's not as easy to use as tabs.

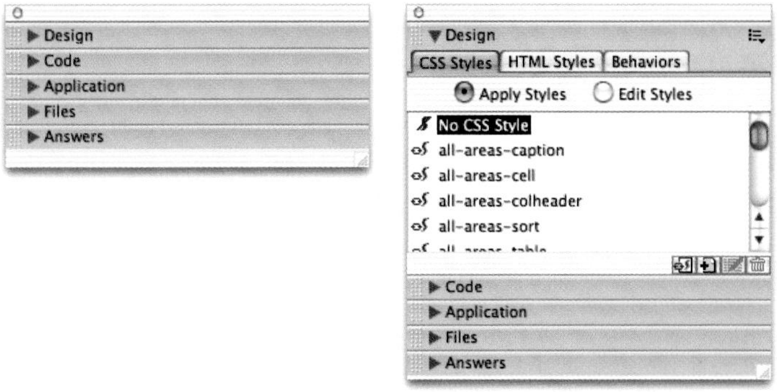

FIGURE 4-24 / Dreamweaver MX

what

Put sections of content onto separate panels, and let the user open and close each of them separately from the others.

use when

There's too much stuff to present on the page, but you want it all only one click away. The content is divisible into clearly named sections, as with **Titled Sections** and **Card Stack**. The user may want to see two or more at a time.

Specifically, this is a useful concrete implementation of Extras on Demand. If you've organized your content using Extras on Demand, you may want to use some form of Closable Panel to hold those extras.

why

You would use Closable Panels in many places where you might use a **Card Stack**—it's a space-saving device that depends on a user clicking it to get at it. However, Closable Panels gives you a little more flexibility:

- It can contain sections of wildly differing sizes. If you used a **Card Stack** with sections of various sizes, the smaller sections would have large areas of whitespace, which is awkward.
- The user can open several sections at once. That's especially nice in authoring tools,

and for "power users" of all kinds of complex applications—at the user's discretion, they can simultaneously open many panels and keep them in view all the time.

- If you create only one closable panel and embed it in a larger page or dialog box, that panel looks less important than the content it's embedded in. If you put both sections into two tab pages, however, they appear to be of equal importance.

There is a cost to using these panels. Tab pages are well understood by most people, but Closable Panels are not as common—they won't be familiar to everyone at first. Usability testing is recommended. Furthermore, the ability to open many sections at once may backfire by making the environment too cluttered and unusable.

how

Divide your content into sections, name them appropriately, and put them into panels that appear and disappear when you click a button or link. Put an arrow, plus sign, triangle, or chevron (">>") on that button or link—doing so hints to the user that something will open or close. In many applications, the triangle points down to the open panel when open, and to the right when closed; these are sometimes termed "twist-downs."

In most applications where you use this device, the window containing the Closable Panel(s) grows and shrinks as the panel is opened and closed. You might also (or additionally) put it in a scrolling panel, or into resizable panes, as in the Dreamweaver example at the top of this pattern.

Also note the use of a **Card Stack** nested inside a Closable Panel. You can use it if you have a very large number of sections to deal with, and if they fit into a two-level hierarchical organization (e.g., the "Design" section contains subsections named "CSS Styles," "HTML Styles," and "Behaviors").

This technique has existed since at least 1993, and possibly earlier. The Motif-based GUI builder called UIM/X used closable panels— even with the twist-down arrows—for its widget palettes.

examples

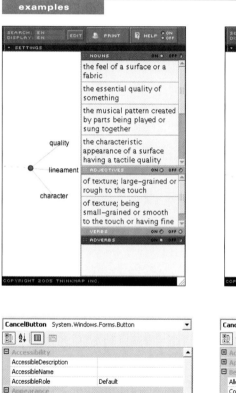

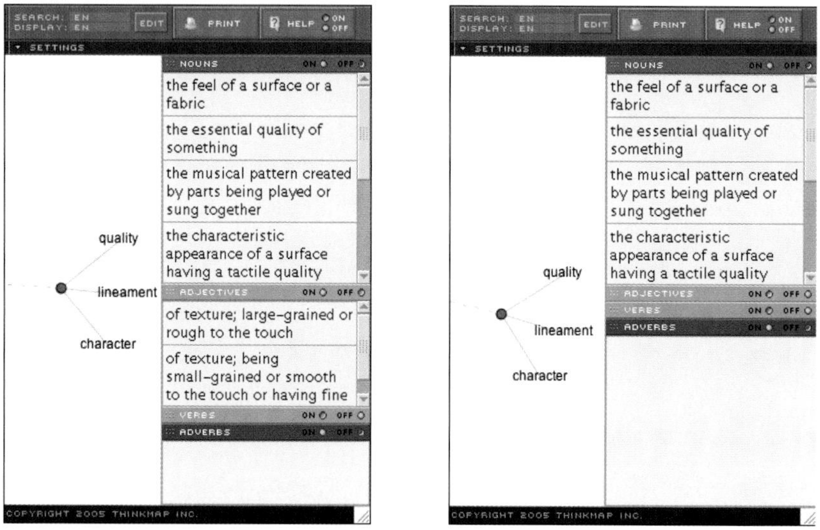

FIGURE 4-25 / Thinkmap's Visual Thesaurus is a web application that uses Closable Panels. The colored titlebars delineate four sections that you can turn on and off at will, via the On/Off radio buttons. You also can drag the titlebars to resize the sections. The user gets more control over what he sees on the interface—if the four sections make it too cluttered, he can turn off the least relevant ones. See http://visualthesaurus.com.

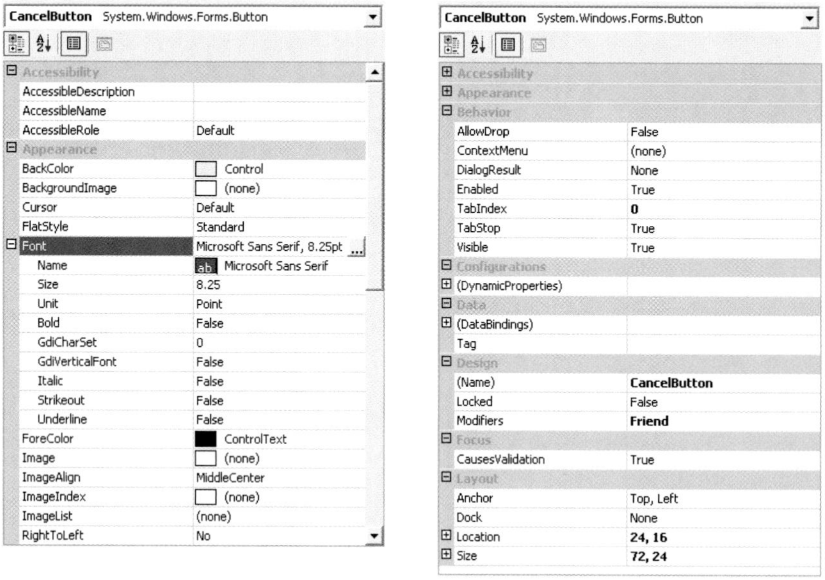

FIGURE 4-26 / Visual Studio's property sheets use Closable Panels to categorize its numerous properties by topic. A user who isn't interested in the Accessibility or Appearance properties, for instance, can close them up while she concentrates on the other properties. Instead of a triangle, Visual Studio uses pluses-in-squares, just like the Windows treeview control. Even though this isn't a treeview, it takes advantage of what users already know: you click on the plus to open something, and click on the minus to close it.

FIGURE 4-27 / Here's an example of this pattern used in a web page. Flickr displays small, delicate closable panels with each image, showing related images or other images in a sequence. You can open and close them with buttons labeled with "+" or "-".

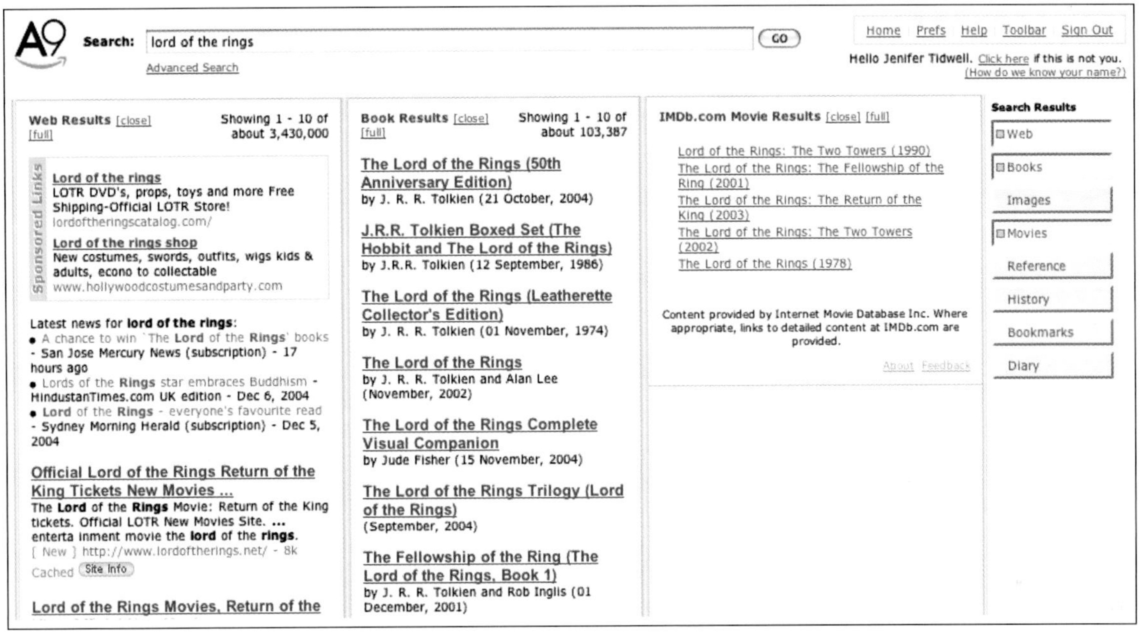

FIGURE 4-28 / This screenshot of A9, Amazon's multidimensional search facility, shows three out of a possible nine (!) panels. Each panel is a resizable vertical column—the bars between them are draggable, so the user can widen or narrow the panels as needed. The button column on the right acts as a control center of sorts, letting the user show and hide various panels; but for local maximizing and closing of the panels, two button-like links beside each panel's titlebar read "[close]" and "[full]." They're redundant with the check-button column, but that's okay.

Notice that the titles of the A9 panels don't really stand out much. There is a visual hierarchy on this page, but it's hard to make out—strong titles would have helped define the three panels. Bolder fonts, horizontal rules below the titles, or colored backgrounds would do the trick. (But consider this: if those titles had been put against stripes of contrasting color, for example, they'd look like actual titlebars. Wouldn't users try to grab and move those titlebars? Would that be a bad thing, if it worked?)

37 movable panels

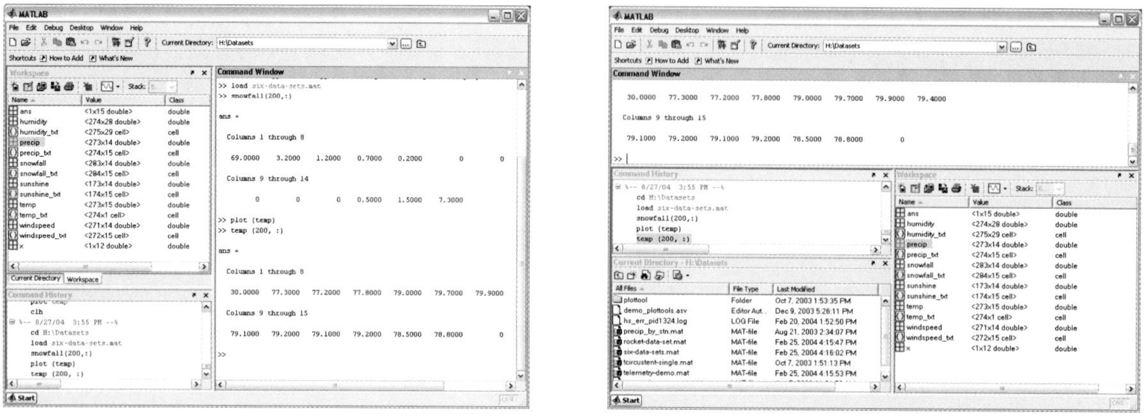

FIGURE 4-29 / MATLAB

---

what

Put different tools or sections of content onto separate panels, and let the user move them around to form a custom layout.

use when

The page has several coherent interface "pieces" that don't really need to be laid out in one single configuration; their meanings are self-evident to users, regardless of their location on the page. You may want users to feel some sense of ownership of the software, or at least have fun playing with it.

why

When they are working on something for a while, people like to rearrange their environment to suit their working style. They can place needed tools close to where they work; hide things they don't need; and use **Spatial Memory** (Chapter 1) to remember where they put things. Rationally speaking, Movable Panels helps users get things done more efficiently and comfortably (in the long run—once they've spent time rearranging it to the way they like it!).

But this kind of personalization seems to appeal to people on some other level, too. They may personalize infrequently visited web sites that provide entertainment, for instance.

how

Let the user move the UI pieces around the page at will. Save the layout for the next time the user resumes using the software, especially if it's an important part of his daily life.

Depending upon the design you've chosen, you may want to give the user freedom to place these pieces anywhere, even if they overlap. Or you may want a prescribed layout grid with "slots" where pieces can be dropped—this lets the page maintain alignment (and some sense of dignity!) without making the user spend too much time fiddling with windows.

If the movable panels react to mouse clicks or mouse drags, such as for text selection, consider putting a "handle" on each piece that the user can grab to move the piece around. Titlebars are good

---

for this. In fact, if you put an "X" on the handle, some users will conclude that that is how they get rid of a piece entirely. (If you implement this, of course, offer a way to recreate the pieces that are gone!)

Your users might appreciate a "Revert to Default Layout" action somewhere on the UI, if they get completely tangled up and just want to start over. When you usability-test Movable Panels, watch especially for accidental panel moves—a user who unintentionally drags a panel into an odd place may not know immediately what he did or how to undo it.

examples

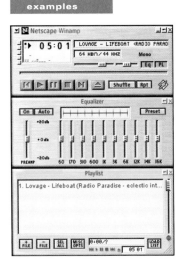

FIGURE 4-30 / The three pieces that make up Winamp can be hidden, shown, rearranged, even separated completely from each other and moved independently. The user can move a piece by dragging its titlebar; that titlebar also has Minimize and Hide buttons. You can bring back hidden pieces via pop up menu items. In this screenshot, you can see Winamp's default configuration.

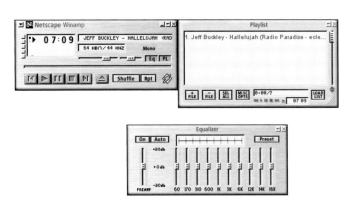

FIGURE 4-31 / Here, Winamp is disassembled and rearranged.

38 right/left alignment

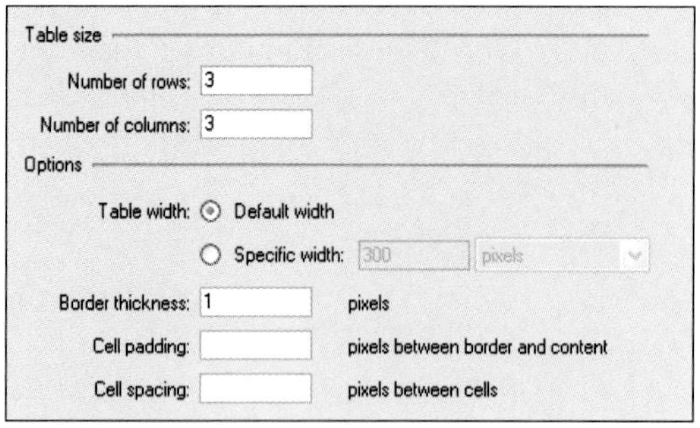

FIGURE 4-32 / Part of a dialog box from Macromedia Contribute

what

When designing a two-column form or table, right-align the labels on the left, and left-align the items on the right.

use when

You're laying out a form, or any other set of items that have text labels in front of them. This also could apply to the internal structure of tables, or any other two-column structure in which the rows should be read left-to-right.

why

When you put text right next to the thing it labels, you form a strong perceptual grouping of that pair—much more so than if they were separated by a large amount of space. If you align variable-length labels along their left sides, the short labels won't be close enough to their controls, and the side-to-side grouping is broken. (This is the Gestalt principle of *proximity* at work.) In short, people more easily connect each label to its associated control when they see right/left alignment.

Meanwhile, you should always left-align controls. When combined with the right-aligned labels and a uniform spacing between them, they help form a nice strong double edge down the middle of the

whole thing (taking advantage of *continuity*, another Gestalt principle). This powerful edge guides the viewer's eyes smoothly down the page, supporting a good visual flow.

In some layouts, right-aligning the labels just doesn't look good. The labels might have widely varying widths, a column of icons might stand to the left of the labels, or perhaps left-aligned titles separate the form's sections—all of these formats can ruin a right/left alignment (though not necessarily). Go with what works.

how

Instead of left-aligning each text label, right-align it. Bring it up close to its control, separated by only a few pixels. The net effect probably will be a ragged (unaligned) left edge—that's usually OK. If some labels are too long to make this work, try breaking them into multiple lines, or resort to putting the labels above the control, in which case this pattern becomes irrelevant.

Then left-align the controls against an imaginary line a few pixels away from the right edges of the labels. Make them precisely aligned, pixel-perfect—if they're not, the controls will look messy. (The human visual system is really good at picking out slight misalignments!)

Again, the other edge of the control column may be ragged. That's not so good if you're dealing with text fields, combo boxes, and other visually "heavy" objects, as in Figure 4-32. Try to stretch them so their right edges are aligned, too, to whatever extent you can. You also can try to align the short ones with one another, and the long ones with one another.

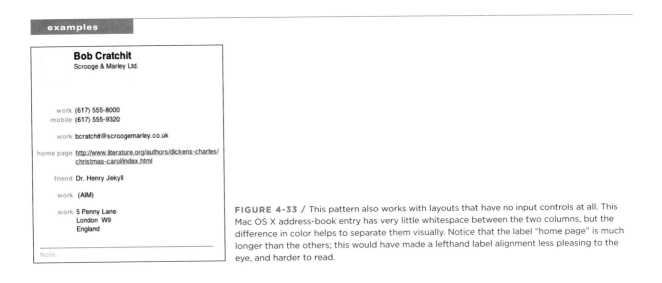

FIGURE 4-33 / This pattern also works with layouts that have no input controls at all. This Mac OS X address-book entry has very little whitespace between the two columns, but the difference in color helps to separate them visually. Notice that the label "home page" is much longer than the others; this would have made a lefthand label alignment less pleasing to the eye, and harder to read.

Method Summary

protected void	**configurePropertiesFromAction**(Action a) Factory method which sets the AbstractButton's properties according to values from the Action instance.
AccessibleContext	**getAccessibleContext**() Gets the AccessibleContext associated with this JButton.
String	**getUIClassID**() Returns a string that specifies the name of the L&F class that renders this component.
boolean	**isDefaultButton**() Gets the value of the defaultButton property, which if true means that this button is the current default button for its JRootPane.
boolean	**isDefaultCapable**() Gets the value of the defaultCapable property.
protected String	**paramString**() Returns a string representation of this JButton.
void	**removeNotify**() Overrides JComponent.removeNotify to check if this button is currently set as the default button on the RootPane, and if so, sets the RootPane's default button to null to ensure the RootPane doesn't hold onto an invalid button reference.
void	**setDefaultCapable**(boolean defaultCapable) Sets the defaultCapable property, which determines whether this button can be made the default button for its root pane.
void	**updateUI**() Resets the UI property to a value from the current look and feel.

FIGURE 4-34 / Again, the widely varying label lengths mean that a lefthand label alignment would put the labels far, far away from their referents. This is easier to read.

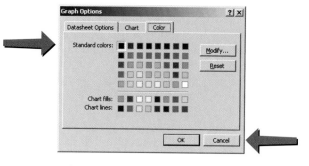

FIGURE 4-35 / Word's Graph Options dialog box

what

Arrange page elements in an asymmetric fashion, but balance it by putting visual weight into both the upper-left and lower-right corners.

use when

You lay out a page or dialog box that has a title or header at the top, and some links or action buttons—such as OK and Cancel, Submit, or Back and Next—at the bottom. The page is short enough to fit on the screen without scrolling.

why

Visually prominent features such as titles, tabs, and buttons should contribute to a balanced composition on the screen. They're already at opposite ends of the page; when you put them on opposite sides too, they often balance one another out. (Think of them as weights—the bigger or more "contrasty" the features are, the heavier they are; the closer to the edge they get, the more you need to put on the other side to compensate.)

Besides being nicer to look at, a diagonal balance also sets up the page so that the user's eye moves easily from the top left to the bottom right—an ideal visual flow for users who speak left-to-right languages. (See the chapter introduction for a discussion of visual flow.) The rest of the page should support this visual flow, too. The eye finally comes to rest on elements representing what the user might do last, like close this UI or go somewhere else.

how

Place the title, tabs, or some other strong element at the upper left of the page; place the button(s) at the lower right. Content of any width goes in between. If the content itself contributes to the balance of the page, so much the better—don't put too much whitespace on only one side, for instance.

Consider what the color dialog box above would look like if you pushed the OK and Cancel buttons to the left edge instead of the right edge. The whole dialog would feel left-weighted and precarious.

In Windows, the placement of the title in the upper left and the conventional placement of buttons in the lower right do this for you automatically. In Mac OS X, many elements, such as title bars, tabs, and action buttons, are centered—so Diagonal Balance is much less common there.

Kevin Mullet's and Darrell Sano's classic pre-Web book *Designing Visual Interfaces* (Sun Microsystems) describes the idea of diagonal balance: "Symmetrical layouts provide...visual equilibrium automatically. Asymmetrical layouts can achieve equilibrium as well, but their tenser, more dramatic form of balance depends on careful manipulation to compensate visually for differences in the size, position, and value of major elements." See below for examples of how you can achieve this balance.

examples

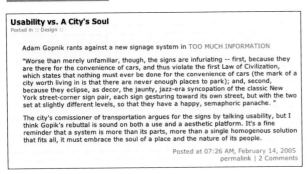

FIGURE 4-36 / A diagonal balance can work with text-only interfaces, too. In this blog entry, the eye goes first to the upper left, reads the content, and then comes to rest on the links at the bottom right. These links are the "next things" the user might want to do with this posting. (The blog is at *http://eleganthack.com*.)

FIGURE 4-37 / Likewise with heavily graphic UIs. The focal points in the site shown here are the logo, the moving car, the "Let's Motor" tag line, and the dealer-locator text field at bottom right—all in a diagonal line (approximately). The motion of the photograph pushes the eye down and right even more forcefully than the other examples. Undoubtedly, the designers of the site wanted to encourage people to use the text field. If it were at the bottom left instead, the page would lose much of its punch, and the text field might get lost in the page. See *http://miniusa.com*.

40 property sheet

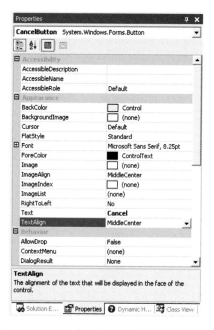

FIGURE 4-38 / Visual Studio property sheet

what

Use a two-column or form-style layout to show the user that an object's properties are edited on this page.

use when

The interface presents an editable object to the user—perhaps something built in a graphical editor, a database record or query, or some domain-specific item (like a car or a stock purchase). The user needs to change the properties or attributes of the object.

why

Most users of visual builders are familiar with the concept of a property sheet—a list of object properties or settings, set forth in a prescribed order, editable via controls appropriate for the property types (such as text fields for strings or dropdowns for one-of-many choices). Well-designed property sheets are generally easy to use, simply because they follow well-understood conventions.

Property sheets can also help the user build a correct mental model of the objects in the UI. A property sheet tells the user what the object's properties are, and what values are available for each of them, especially in applications that mix WYSIWYG editing with programming (such as GUI builders, web page builders, and time-based scripting and animation tools). Property editors thus help the user learn how to use the system.

Alternatives to property sheets might include menus and direct manipulation. A menu can provide access to a small handful of simple boolean or one-of-many properties. If users only need to edit a few properties for an object, then a property sheet may be too heavyweight a solution. A user would need to bring it up, look at it for a fraction of a second, figure out which property to edit, edit it, and maybe close the property sheet again. That's a lot of work, but the advantage is that it scales up well. If the user changes a lot of properties in succession, then that property sheet can stay up and available. They also permit access to vast numbers of properties at once, unlike menus, which stop being usable when they get longer than about eight properties.

Direct manipulation is a different animal entirely. For instance, you can drag, resize, rotate, or layer graphic objects on a canvas with no help from auxiliary windows at all—that covers a lot of properties. Anything that fits into a nice visual metaphor can escape the need for a property sheet. But if it doesn't, property sheets become necessary. (They may also be necessary if some users want the precision of typed numbers for movement, rotation, and similar properties.)

The only commonality here is that the various edit controls are labeled with the names of the properties they edit. When the user finishes filling in values, the new property values are written out to the object.

These issues usually come up when designing property sheets:

Layout
 Some systems use a two-column table, with controls that appear when the user clicks the values shown in the righthand column. (Visual Basic seems to be the de facto standard for this approach.) Others look more like forms or dialog boxes than tables—they might have text fields sitting next to other controls or editors that are several lines tall. Use your judgment. Tables might be more recognizable as property sheets, but forms can be far more flexible in their presentation of the property-editing controls—see the Illustrator example

in Figure 4-39 for an extreme example. With a form-style layout, for instance, you're not constrained to using a single table row for each control. (For many layout variations, consider using **Right/Left Alignment**.)

Property order
 Alphabetical, categorized, or an easy-to-read order that places the most commonly edited properties at the top? They all have advantages. Short property sheets (say, 10 or fewer properties) usually are best with the most common properties listed first. The longer the list gets, the more important it is to categorize them; but if a user looks for one particular property by name, they may want to sort them alphabetically. As always, it's best to give users a choice. However, you're still responsible for picking the right default order, so "let the user choose" still doesn't get you off the hook!

Labels
 Visual Studio and other programming environments often use short, cryptic names for the edited properties. That may be acceptable when the properties represent names that users might use later in programs or scripts (though more descriptive names are always better), but when that's not the case, devise better labels! Use terminology familiar to average users, not jargon. Use multiple words to describe complex things. Tie the whole property sheet into a help system, such as one that shows a description of a property whenever the user starts editing that property.

Control choice
 I could write 50 pages about this. The short version: make sure the property's current value is always visible; choose controls to constrain the input as much as possible—for example, by using non-editable drop-down lists for one-of-many choices; use platform-supplied standard editors for specialized

types like colors, fonts, and filenames. See Chapter 7 for more information about control choice.

When to commit the new property values

Many UIs simply update the object with the new value as soon as the user finishes typing or selecting a value. The more form-like property sheets may wait until the user deliberately commits the whole thing, such as by clicking on an "OK" button. However, if your software can deal well with instant update, go for it—it gives the user more immediate feedback about the change he just made. If you can, provide an undo mechanism. That will help users back out of accidental or unwanted changes, which is especially important with instant update.

"Mixed" values for multiply-selected objects

Some UIs solve this problem by showing no value at all, which can be dangerously misleading if the property actually can have no value (or null, or the empty string). Others show it with a sentinel value, like an asterisk (*), or the word "mixed."

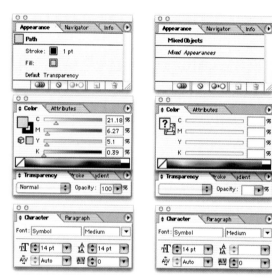

FIGURE 4-39 / Illustrator and Photoshop take the "form-style" layout approach to its logical extreme. This figure shows the property sheet for Illustrator (twice, actually). It is broken up into several **Movable Panels** that float separately on top of the work windows; each panel contains one or more tab pages that group the properties by category. You can hide, rearrange, or drag the tabs from panel to panel. For power users, this dense, flexible, user-configurable approach works well; but it's not something you would use in a casual application, nor with users who aren't already comfortable with software tools this complex.

The first column is a snapshot of the property sheets when a single light-blue rectangle was selected in the work window. In the second column, multiple diverse objects were selected—this shows a few ways of dealing with "mixed" values.

Compare them side-by-side. Notice that no attempt is made to show Stroke and Fill in the second column, since those properties aren't even available on all the selected objects! Color does apply to all of them, however, and gets rendered with question marks and blank text fields—indicating that the source objects have different fill and edge colors. Blank combo boxes also indicate mixed values for transparency, opacity, and text leading (vertical space between letters).

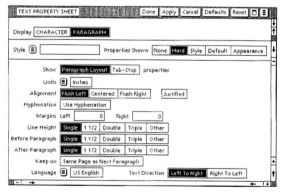

FIGURE 4-40 / This screenshot from the Xerox Star shows a very early property sheet. Some things haven't changed a whole lot: note the two-column layout, the right/left alignment, the use of controls like text fields and radio buttons, and even **Responsive Disclosure** (though you can't see it here).

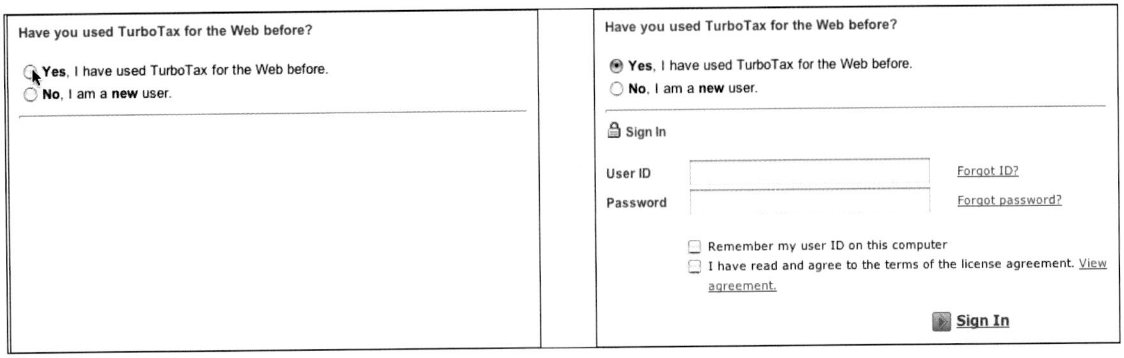

FIGURE 4-41 / From *http://turbotax.com*

what

Starting with a very minimal UI, guide a user through a series of steps by showing more of the UI as he completes each step.

use when

The user should be walked through a complex task step-by-step, perhaps because he is computer-naive or because the task is novel or rarely done (as in a **Wizard**). But you don't want to force the user to go page-by-page at each step—you'd rather keep the whole interface on one single page.

why

In this pattern, the interface actually appears to be "created" in front of the user, one step at a time. At first, the user sees only elements that are necessary for the first step. When the user takes that step, the next set of elements is displayed in addition to the first ones, then the next, etc.

As the user sees the task unfolding directly in front of him via a dynamically growing UI, he can form a correct mental model of the task more quickly and easily. None of the awkward context switches that separate wizard screens impose exist here: the users aren't yanked out of their workflow into a rigid set of modal screens shown one at a time.

Furthermore, since the UI is kept together on one page, the user can easily go back and change his mind about earlier choices. As each step is redone, he immediately sees the effect on subsequent steps. This is better than jumping from one content-starved wizard screen to another.

For occasional tasks, this device can work better than presenting a complex and interlinked set of controls all at once, because it's always obvious what the first step is—and the next. The user never has to think too hard.

How should you choose between this pattern and **Responsive Enabling**? If you use **Responsive Enabling**, you will put all the controls for all choices on the UI—you'll just disable the irrelevant ones until they become relevant (again, in response to the user's choices). Sometimes that can make the UI too cluttered or complicated-looking. It's a judgment call: if you need to fit the UI into a very small space, or if you think too many controls on the UI might look bad or make users nervous, use Responsive Disclosure instead.

Start by showing the controls and text for only the first step. When the user completes that step, show the controls for the next step. Leave the previous steps' controls visible, to let the user go backward if necessary. Keep it all on one page or dialog box, so the user isn't abruptly pushed into a separate "UI space."

In many such step-by-step designs, the choices the user makes at one step alters the rest of the task (i.e., the task is branched, not linear). For instance, an online order form asks whether the billing address is the same as the shipping address. If the user says yes, the UI doesn't even bother showing entry fields for it. Otherwise, there's one more step in the process, and the UI shows the second set of entry fields when appropriate.

This technique is less successful when used to radically change a preexisting UI, instead of adding UI controls to a blank space. Restructuring a UI from under a user can turn his sense of space upside down—it's very disruptive! But when done in an orderly and predictable manner, it provides a compact, space-sensitive way to present a wizard to a user.

The concept of responsive disclosure isn't new. It was used in 1981 in the first commercial WIMP interface, the Xerox Star. Its designers considered "progressive disclosure," a more general concept that includes responsive disclosure, to be a major design principle: "Progressive disclosure dictates that detail be hidden from users until they ask or need to see it. Thus, Star not only provides default settings, it hides settings that users are unlikely to change until users indicate that they want to change them."[2] Indeed.

In the Star's **Property Sheets**, for instance, blank space was reserved for controls that would appear as needed, in response to user choices. When a user chose from a set of values including the word "Other," for instance, an extra text field would appear for the user to enter a number.

"Instructive Interaction: Making Innovative Interfaces Self-Teaching,"[3] by Larry Constantine and Lucy Lockwood, discusses this pattern under the name "Progressive Disclosure."

2 Johnson, J.A., et. al. "The Xerox Star: A Retrospective," IEEE Computer, September 1989, 22(9), pp. 11–29. See also *http://www.digibarn.com/friends/curbow/star/retrospect/*.

3 See *http://foruse.com/articles/instructive.htm*.

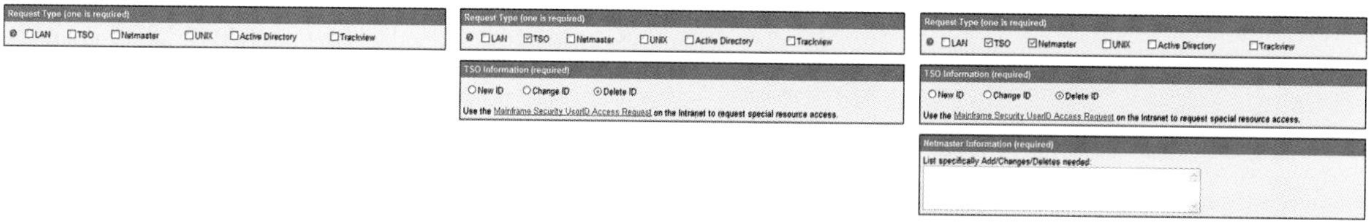

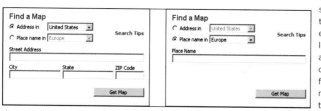

FIGURE 4-42 / This example comes from an internal application at Northwestern Mutual. The user first selects "TSO" for Request Type; the application then shows a new box, asking for TSO Information. When the user then selects "Delete ID," a third box appears. The history of this user's choices remains visible on the page.

FIGURE 4-43 / Now here's an example of doing exactly what I said wasn't a great idea: changing a preexisting interface, rather than adding things to it. However, this example seems small-scale enough to work. It's from Mapblast's UI for entering the spot to be located on a map. It shows two configurations: first for a specific address, and second for a place name without an address. Each is chosen with a radio button. This design might have benefited from first showing no radio button selected, and no address or place name controls at all; when the user then clicks on a radio button, the appropriate controls are shown.

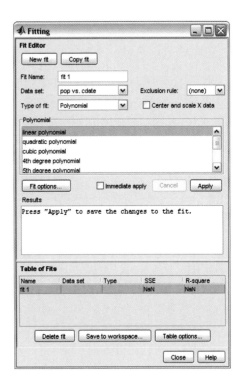

FIGURE 4-44 / MATLAB Curve-Fitting Tool

Starting with a UI that's mostly disabled, guide a user through a series of steps by enabling more of the UI as each step is done.

The UI walks the user through a complex task step-by-step, perhaps because he is computer-naive, or because the task is rarely done (as in a **Wizard**). But you don't want to force the user to go page by page at each step—you'd like to keep the whole interface on one page. Furthermore, you want to keep the interface stable; you'd rather not dynamically reconfigure the page at each step, as you would with **Responsive Disclosure**.

Like **Responsive Disclosure**, this pattern takes advantage of the malleability of computer displays to guide the user through the interface interactively. The user thus gets a chance to form a correct mental model about cause and effect. The UI itself tells him the possible consequences of some choices: if I turn this checkbox on, then I have to fill in these four text fields that just got enabled.

Furthermore, the user can't do things that would get him into trouble, as the UI has "locked out" those actions by disabling them. Unnecessary error messages are thus avoided.

In some applications, such as the GUI in Figure 4-44, most actions on the UI start off disabled—only the actions relevant to the user's first step are available. As the user makes choices and performs actions, more disabled items should be enabled and brought into play. In this respect it's remarkably like **Responsive Disclosure**, since the machine specifies a particular sequence through the interface.

A similar, less sequence-based technique is much more common in desktop UIs. As the user does things on the interface, certain actions or settings become irrelevant or impossible, and those actions get disabled until the user does whatever is necessary to re-enable them. Overall sequence isn't as important. See Figure 4-45 for an example.

Whenever possible, put the disabled items in close proximity to whatever enables them. That helps users find the magic enabling operation and understand the relationship between it and the disabled items. Two of this pattern's examples place that button (or checkbox, respectively) at the top and left of the disabled items, which follows the natural top-to-bottom and left-to-right "flow" of the interface.

When you design an interface that uses **Responsive Enabling** or **Responsive Disclosure**, be sure to disable only things that really can't or shouldn't be used. Be wary of overconstraining the user's experience in an attempt to make the interface friendlier or easier to understand. When you decide what to disable, carefully consider each device: is it disabled for a really good reason? Can you offer that functionality all the time? As usual, usability testing gives users a chance to tell you that you've done it wrong.

Another usability problem to avoid is what Bruce Tognazzini calls the "Mysteriously Dimmed Menu Items"[4]—when the design offers no clue as to why a given device is disabled. Again, minimize the set of things that *have* to be disabled, especially when they're far away from whatever operation turns them on. Also, somewhere on the interface or in its help system, tell the user what causes a feature to be unavailable. Again, this whole problem can be avoided more easily when the disabled controls aren't menus on a menu bar, but instead sit out on the main UI, colocated with whatever switches them on. Spatial proximity is an important clue.

---

4 See "Ten Most Wanted Design Bugs," at *http://www.asktog.com/Bughouse/10MostWantedDesignBugs.html*.

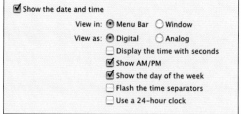

FIGURE 4-45 / The Mac OS X System Preferences provide a typical example of disabling based on a binary choice: should OS X show the date and time on the menu bar, or not? If the user chooses to show it, then she gets a panoply of choices about how it ought to be shown. If not, the choices are irrelevant, so they're disabled. This behavior (plus the indenting of the options under the checkbox) tells the user that these choices affect the date/time display which the checkbox toggled—and nothing else.

FIGURE 4-46 / You also can reverse the sense of this pattern and do "responsive disabling." The navigation system used in Toyota's Prius and Lexus cars employs this technique when a user enters a destination address. Knowing what streets exist in a given search area, the system narrows down the possible street names with each successive letter entered by the user. It then disables the letters that can't possibly follow the currently typed string; the user has fewer buttons to think about, plus some assurance that the system "knows" what they're trying to type. Address entry is thus made easier and more pleasant. (When only a few remaining streets match, the system takes away the keyboard altogether and shows the streets as a list of choices—see the **Autocompletion** pattern in Chapter 5.)

See *http://lexus.com/models/rx_hybrid/interior.html*—the source of these screenshots—for a demo.

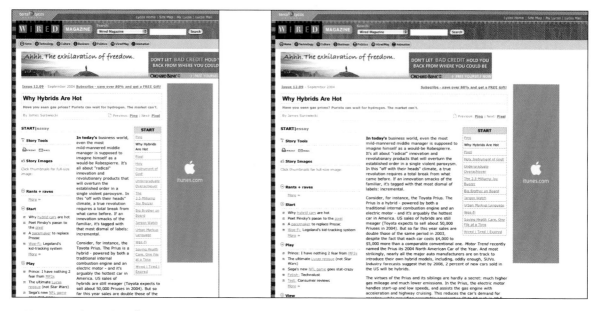

FIGURE 4-47 / From *http://wired.com*

what

As the user resizes the window, resize the page contents along with it so the page is constantly "filled."

use when

The user might want more space—or less—in which to show the content of a window, dialog box, or page. This is likely to happen whenever a page contains a lot of text (as in a web page), or a high-information control like a table or tree, or a graphic editor. It doesn't work as well when the visual design requires a certain amount of screen real estate, and no more or less.

why

Unless you're designing a "closed" UI like a kiosk, a handheld, or a full-screen video game, you can't predict the conditions under which the user views your UI. Screen size, font preferences, other windows on the screen, or the importance of any particular page to the user—none of this is under your control. How, then, can you decide the one optimal page size for all users?

Giving the user a little control over the layout of the page makes your UI more flexible under changing conditions. It also may make the user feel less antagonistic towards the UI, since he can bend it to fit his immediate needs and contexts.

If you need more convincing, consider what happens to a fixed-layout, "non-liquid" UI when the language or font size changes. Do columns still line up? Do pages suddenly become too wide, or even clipped at the margins? If not, great; you have a simple and robust design. But pages engineered to work nicely with window size changes generally also accommodate language or font size changes.

how

Make the page contents continuously "fill" the window as it changes size. Multiline text should wrap at the right margin, until it becomes ten to twelve words wide (more on that later). Trees, tables, graphs, and editors at "center stage" should enlarge generously while their margins stay compact. If the page has anything form-like on it, horizontal stretching should cause text fields to elongate—users will appreciate this if they need to enter anything longer than the text field's normal length. Likewise, anything scrolled (such as lists and tables) should lengthen, and usually widen, too.

Web pages and similar UIs should allow the body content to fill the new space, while keeping navigational devices and signposts anchored to the top and left margins. Background colors and patterns always should fill the new space, even if the content itself cannot.

What happens when the window gets too small for its content? You could put scrollbars around it. Otherwise, whitespace should shrink as necessary; outright clipping may occur when the window gets really tiny, but the most important content hangs in there to the end.

If you deal with paragraphs of text, remember that they become nearly illegible when they're too wide. Graphic designers target an optimal line length for easy reading of text; one metric is 10 to 12 average English words per line. Another metric is 30 to 35 em-widths—that is, the width of your font's lowercase "m". When your text gets much wider than that, users' eyes have to travel too far from the end of one line to the beginning of the next one; if it gets much narrower, it's too choppy to read easily.

(That said, there is evidence that text with a longer line length, such as 100 characters per line, is faster to read than shorter lines, even though users prefer to read lines fewer than 55 characters long.[5])

A well-behaved Liquid Layout can be difficult to implement in complex web pages, especially if you want to dispense with tables and use straight CSS. It's also hard in Visual Basic and Visual C++ (or was, at least, for a long time). However, Java provides several layout managers you can use to implement it.

5 See "Use Reading Performance or User Preference," at *http://usability.gov/guidelines/*.

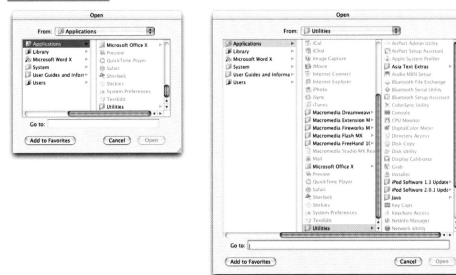

FIGURE 4-48 / Mac OS X allows you to resize the standard "Open" dialog box, which uses a liquid layout. This is good because users can see as much of the filesystem hierarchy as they want, rather than being constrained to a tiny predetermined space. (The **Cascading Lists** pattern is in this dialog box, too.)

05

This chapter is devoted to the "verbs" in the interface. We've spent a lot of pages talking about overall structure and flow, visual layout, and "nouns" such as windows, text, links, and static elements in pages. Chapter 6 spends even more pages on nouns, and Chapter 7 handles traditional (and a few nontraditional) controls and widgets: things that let users supply information and set state, but that don't actually do much.

So now let's talk about buttons and menus.

Sounds exciting, doesn't it? Probably not. Desktop interfaces have been using menu bars as long ago as the first Macintosh, and buttons for even longer. What we think of as "buttons" are only a visual rendering of a physical device that predated GUIs anyway.

It's true that there is a lot of history here, and many best practices to follow. The standard platform style guides, such as Windows, Macintosh, and PalmOS, generally get you pretty close to a workable UI. Most users depend upon learned conventions to negotiate menus and find buttons, so it behooves you to follow those conventions, even when they feel restrictive or nonsensical.

Common functionality like cut, copy, and paste also carries lots of historical baggage—if it could be reinvented now, it probably would work differently, but even moderately experienced desktop computer users have learned how it's "supposed to work." The same is true for pop-up menus (context menus), which some users seem to look for everywhere, and other users never look for at all. Drag-and-drop isn't as bound by history, but it absolutely has to work the way users intuitively expect it to, or the illusion of direct manipulation is broken.

All that said, you can do some cool things to make your interface less dull and more usable. Your goals should be to make the right actions available, label them well, make them easy to find, and support sequences of actions. There are a few creative ways to do it.

First, I'll list the common ways actions are rendered to the user.

Buttons

Buttons are placed directly onto dialog boxes and pages, and usually are grouped semantically. (See the **Button Groups** pattern.) They're big, readable, obvious, and extremely easy to use for even the most inexperienced computer users. But they take up a lot of space on the interface, unlike menu bars and pop-up menus.

Menu bars

Menu bars are standard on most desktop applications. They generally show an application's complete set of actions, organized in a mostly predictable way (such as File, Edit, View). Some actions operate on the entire application, and some operate on individually selected items. Menu bars often duplicate functionality found in context menus and toolbars because they are *accessible*—screenreaders can read them, keyboard accelerators can reach them, and so on. (Accessibility alone makes them indispensable in many products.) Menu bars are starting to appear in some web applications, though not as commonly as they appear in desktop software.

Pop-up menus

Also known as context menus, pop-up menus are raised with a right mouse click or some similar gesture on panels or items. They usually list context-specific, common actions, not all the actions that are possible on the interface. Keep them short.

Dropdown menus

Users raise these menus by clicking on a dropdown control, such as a combo box, and you can find them on many web pages. However, using dropdown menus for actions is usually a bad idea, since dropdown controls are typically used for setting state, not performing actions.

Toolbars

The canonical toolbar is a long, thin row of iconic buttons. Often they have other kinds of buttons or controls on them too, like text fields or **Dropdown Choosers** (see Chapter 7). Iconic toolbars work best when the portrayed actions have obvious visual renderings; when the actions really need to be described with words, try other controls, such as combo boxes or buttons with text labels. Cryptic icons are a classic source of confusion and unusability.

Links

Links are used mostly on web pages, but are now found on many applications too. They also can be blue underlined words or phrases that merely look like links, but actually are implemented as buttons. The point is that anything blue and underlined looks clickable; people will find and use them. That said, many web application designers now make a conscious effort to reduce potential confusion by sticking with buttons for invoking actions, and links to show other content.

Action panels

You might know them as "task panes." Action panels are essentially menus that the user doesn't need to post; they're always visible on the main interface. They are a fine substitute for toolbars when actions are better described verbally than visually. See the **Action Panels** pattern.

Then there are invisible actions, which don't have any labels at all to announce what they do. Users need to know (or guess) that they're there, unless you put written instructions on the UI. Therefore, they don't help with discovery at all. In other words, users can't scan them to find out what actions are possible—with buttons, links, and menus, the UI actions are available for inspection. Users learn from them. In usability tests, I've seen many users look at a new product and methodically walk down the menu bar, item by item, just to find out what it can do.

That said, you almost always need to use one or more invisible actions. People often expect to be able to double-click on items, for example. The keyboard (or the equivalent) sometimes is the only means of access for visually impaired users and people who can't use a mouse. Expert users of some operating systems and applications prefer to work by typing commands into a shell, and/or by using its keyboard actions.

Double-clicking on items

Users tend to view double-clicking as either "open this item" or "do whatever the default thing is with this item," depending on context. In a graphical editor, for instance, double-clicking on an element often means opening a property sheet or specialized editor for it. Double-clicking an application's icon in most operating systems launches that application.

Keyboard actions

Keyboard shortcuts, such as the well-known Control-S to save, should be designed into most desktop applications for accessibility and efficient use. The major UI platforms, including Windows, Mac, GNOME, and PalmOS, each have style guides that describe the standard shortcuts—and they're all very similar. Additionally, menus and controls often have underlined access keys, which let users reach those controls without mouse-clicking or tabbing. (Type the Alt key, then the underlined letter, to invoke these actions.)

Drag-and-drop

Dragging and dropping items on an interface usually means either "move this here" or "do this to that." In other words, someone might drag a file onto an application icon to say "open this file in that application." Or she might drag that file from one place in a file finder to another place, thus moving or copying the item. Drag-and-drop is context-dependent, but it almost always results in one of these two actions.

Typed commands

Command-line interfaces generally allow freeform access to all the actions in the software system, whether it's an OS or an application. I consider these kinds of actions "invisible" because most command-line interfaces (CLIs) don't easily divulge the available commands. They're not very discoverable, though they're quite powerful once you learn what's available—much can be done with a single well-constructed command. As such, CLIs are best for users committed to learning the software very well.

PUSHING THE BOUNDARIES

Some application idioms give you freedom to design nonstandard buttons and controls. Visual editors, media players, applications intended mostly for experts, instant messaging, games, and anything that's supposed to be fun and interesting all have users who might be curious enough to figure out how to use unusual but well-designed interface elements.

Where can you be more creative? Consider the items on the first list above; visible buttons and menus usually are easier to use than keyboard actions. Generalizing from those items, actions could be:

- Clickable icons
- Clickable text that doesn't look like a button
- Something that reacts when the mouse pointer rolls over it
- Something that looks like it may be a manipulable object
- Something placed on almost any piece of screen real estate

How much creativity can you get away with before the application becomes too hard to figure out?

FIGURE 5-1 / GarageBand

For a real-life example, look at the GarageBand application, shown in Figure 5-1. A lot is going on in this interface. Some objects are obviously buttons, like the player controls—rewind, play, fast forward, etc.—and the scrollbar arrows. You will find some sliders and knobs, too.

But look harder at the far right of the window, between the red line and the wood-grain edge. To your eyes, what pieces of the interface look clickable? Why? If you want, you can look ahead to Figure 5-2 and cheat. (And if you already know GarageBand, please bear with me.)

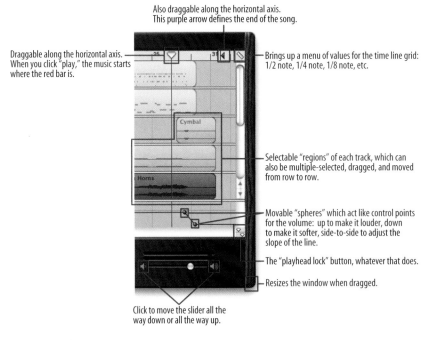

FIGURE 5-2 / GarageBand actions

Figure 5-2 shows which objects on the interface perform actions. You clearly couldn't have known what they all do, since this book doesn't give you the benefit of tooltips, rollover cursors, or experimentation. But did you figure out that some of these objects could be clicked or manipulated? I'm guessing you did.

How? You probably know that interfaces that look like this offer a lot of functionality through direct manipulation, so you have good grounds for just assuming that every interesting visual feature does something. You might know that sliders, like the volume slider at the bottom, sometimes have "jump buttons" at the ends—and you might have recognized the volume slider itself from iTunes. You might guess that tiny squarish icons tend to be buttons, often for presentation-related actions; Word and Powerpoint use a lot of them. You might have seen a vertical line topped with an inverted triangle in some other context—maybe movable, maybe not. (See the **Guides** pattern in Chapter 8.) But didn't this triangle look like it was movable?

When an object looks like it might let you do something, such as click or drag it, then we say it "affords" performing that action. Traditional raised-edge buttons afford pushing; a slider thumb affords dragging; a text field affords typing; a blue underlined word affords clicking. And anything that reacts to the mouse cursor affords something, although you can't necessarily tell what!

Figure 5-2 points out the *affordances* in the GarageBand interface. This is an important concept. In software interfaces, the user doesn't get many sensory clues about what can be tweaked or handled: visuals give most of the clues, and mouse rollovers do the rest. Use them to communicate affordances well.

Here's some specific design advice:

- Follow conventions whenever possible. Reuse UI concepts and controls that people already know, like the volume sliders in the example.
- Use pseudo-3D shading and drop shadows to make things look "raised."
- When the mouse pointer hovers over items that can be clicked or dragged, turn the pointer into something different, like a finger or a hand.
- Use tooltips, or some other descriptive text, to tell the user what the objects under the mouse pointer do. If you don't need them, that's great—you have a self-describing design—but many users expect tooltips anyway.

THE PATTERNS

The first two patterns in this chapter talk about two of the many ways to present actions—one common, one not. When you find yourself reflexively putting actions on an application's menu bar or pop-up menu, stop for a moment and consider using **Button Groups** or **Action Panels** instead.

 44 Button Groups    **45** Action Panel

Prominent "Done" Button improves the single most important button on many web pages and dialog boxes. **Smart Menu Items** is a technique for improving some of the actions you put on menus; this is a very general pattern, useful for many kinds of menus (or buttons and links).

 46 Prominent "Done" Button   **47** Smart Menu Items

We'd like it if we could complete all user-initiated actions in an application instantly, but that's not reality—some actions are time-consuming. **Preview** shows the user what's going to happen before such an action is committed. **Progress Indicator** is a well-known technique for letting the user know what's going on while an operation proceeds, while **Cancelability** refers to a UI's ability to stop an operation when the user asks it to.

 48 Preview   **50** Cancelability

49 Progress Indicator

The last three patterns—**Multi-Level Undo**, **Command History**, and **Macros**—all deal with sequences of actions. These three interlocking patterns are most useful in complex applications, especially those whose users are committed to learning the software well and using it extensively. (That's why the examples come from software such as Linux, Photoshop, Word, and MATLAB.) Be warned that these patterns are not easy to implement. They require the application to model a user's actions as discrete, describable, and sometimes reversible operations, and such a model is very hard to retrofit into existing software architecture. The "Command" pattern in the book *Design Patterns* (Addison-Wesley) is one good place to look for implementation advice.

51 Multi-Level Undo   **53** Macros

52 Command History

And that's as close as this book gets to implementation details. We'll now return to the realm of interface design.

44 button groups

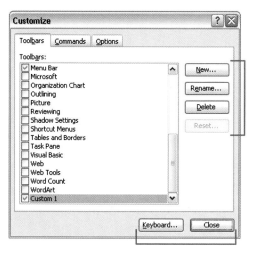

FIGURE 5-3 / Two button groups in a Word's Customize dialog box

what

Present related actions as a small cluster of buttons, aligned either horizontally or vertically. Create several of them if there are more than three or four actions.

use when

You present a small number of actions, say two to five, that are related—they might act on the same things, or have similar or complementary effects. OK, Cancel, Apply, and Close buttons usually are found in groups; they all act on the dialog box as a whole. Likewise, buttons that handle the objects in a list (like Move Up, Move Down, or Delete) should be grouped.

why

Button groups help make an interface self-describing. Well-defined clusters of buttons are easy to pick out of a complex layout, and because they're so visible, they instantly communicate the availability of those actions. They announce, "These are the actions you've got to work with in this context."

The Gestalt principles discussed in Chapter 4 apply here. Proximity hints at relatedness—the buttons are all together, so they probably do similar things. So does visual similarity; if you make all the buttons the same dimensions, for instance, they look like they belong together. Proper sizing and alignment help the button group form a larger composite visual shape (this is the principle of closure).

how

Make a group out of the buttons in question. Label them with short but unambiguous verbs or verb phrases, and don't use jargon unless users expect it. Do not mix buttons that affect different things, or have different scope; see these examples for illustrations of how to do this well. Separate them into different groups.

All buttons in the group should be the same height and width (unless the label length varies widely).

You can line them up in a single column, or arrange them in a single row if they aren't too wide; two or more columns or rows don't look as good.

If the buttons all act on the same object or objects, put the button group to the right of those objects. You could put it below them instead, but users often have a "blind spot" at the bottom of complex UI elements like multicolumn lists and trees—the buttons may not be seen at all. If you have a specific design that works better with the buttons at the bottom, usability-test it and find out. If there are enough buttons, and if they have icons, you could also put them on a toolbar or a toolbar-like strip at the top of the page.

When the buttons affect the whole page or dialog box, like Close or OK, then you should follow the style guide for your platform. Usually they'll be in a column on the far-right margin, or in a row on the bottom-right corner. Users will be habituated to look for them there (see **Habituation** in Chapter 1).

But standalone Close buttons are a special case. Sometimes you can get away with just using a simple "X" icon and placing the button in the upper-right corner—Windows users will instinctively know what to do, and users of other platforms often know that convention too.

examples

The Word dialog box in Figure 5-3 has two button groups—one for list-specific actions, and the other for more general actions. The "scoping" of the button groups is appropriate: the list-specific buttons affect only items on that tab, so they're inside the tab page, whereas the other buttons sit outside the tabs altogether. The "Close" button's position in the lower-right corner is standard for these sorts of dialog boxes, on both Windows and the Mac.

FIGURE 5-4 / Amazon uses pairs of related buttons on its recommendations page. The buttons look alike (yellow and rounded), they're placed next to each other, and they do things that are similar from a user's perspective. Note also that the pairs of buttons all are aligned with each other horizontally. In a whole page full of these book recommendations—only two of which are shown here—they form a strong structural rhythm on the page.

FIGURE 5-5 / iTunes places button groups at each of the four corners of the main window, plus the standard titlebar buttons (such as close or minimize). When the user browses the Music Store, there are even more actions contained in the web-page-like third panel (not shown)—links constitute many of the actions there—and a button for each song in the table.

No fewer than fourteen buttons appear on this interface. I'm not even counting the four scrollbar buttons or the three clickable table headers. There's lots to do here, but thanks to careful visual and semantic organization, the interface is never overwhelming.

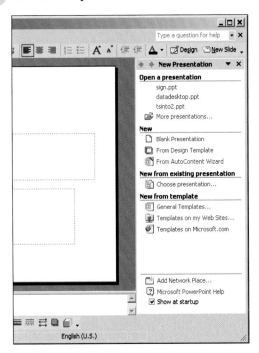

FIGURE 5-6 / Powerpoint's "New Presentation" panel

what

Instead of using menus, present a large group of related actions on a UI panel that's richly organized and always visible.

use when

You need to present many actions—too many for a **Button Group**. You could put them into a menu, but maybe you don't have a menu bar at all, or you'd rather make the actions more obvious. Same for pop-up menus; they're just not visible enough. Your users may not even realize the pop-up menus exist.

Or maybe your set of possible actions is too complex even for a menu. Menus are best at showing a flat set of actions (since pull-right menus, or cascading menus, are hard for some users to manipulate), in a very simple, linear, one-line-per-item presentation. If your actions need to be grouped, and if those groups don't fit the standard top-level menu names—such as File, Edit, View, Tools, or Format—then you might want a different presentation altogether.

This pattern can take up a lot of screen space, so it's not usually a good choice for small devices.

why

The "Use when" section already hinted at the two main reasons for using action panels: visibility and freedom of presentation.

By placing the actions out on the main UI, and not hidden inside a traditional menu, you make those actions fully visible to the user. Really, action panels *are* menus, in the generic sense; they just aren't found in menu bars, dropdowns, or pop-ups. Users don't have to do anything to see what's on an action panel—it's right there in front of them—so your interface is more discoverable. This is particularly nice for users who aren't already familiar with the traditional document model and its menu bars.

There are many, many ways to structure objects on an interface: lists, grids or tables, hierarchies, and just about any custom structure you can devise. But button groups and traditional menus only give you a list (and not a very long one). Action panels are freeform—they give you as much freedom to visually organize verbs as you have for nouns. Use it wisely!

This is one of the places where web design conventions were "back-ported" into desktop applications. Since early web applications couldn't depend on dynamically shown menus, and they certainly couldn't use the browser's menu bar, page designers found other ways of presenting action menus. Vertical columns of links seemed to work fine. (The fact that they're links, not buttons, is sort of irrelevant; if they're labeled as verbs, and if they appear to perform actions, who cares about their implementation? Users don't.)

Set aside a block of space on the interface for the action panel. Place it below or to the side of the target of the action. The target usually is a list, table, or tree of selectable items, but it also might be the **Center Stage** (Chapter 4), like the Powerpoint example in Figure 5-6. Remember that proximity is important. If you place the action panel too far away from whatever it acts on, users may not grasp the relationship between them.

The panel could be a simple rectangle on the page. It could be one of several tiled panels on the page, perhaps a **Movable Panel** (see Chapter 4), a "drawer" in Mac OS X, or even a separate window. That choice depends on the nature of your application. If it's closable, then make it very easy to reopen,

especially if those actions are present only on the action panel and aren't duplicated on a menu!

Odds are good that you'll need to show different actions at different times. The contents of the action panel may depend on the state of the application (e.g., are there any open documents yet?), on the items selected in some list somewhere, or other factors. Let the action panel be dynamic. The changes will attract the user's attention, which is good.

Next, you need to decide how to structure the actions you need to present. Here are some ways you could do it:

- Simple lists
- Multicolumn lists
- Categorized lists, like the Powerpoint example in Figure 5-6
- Tables or grids
- Trees
- **Closable Panels**
- Any combination of these in one panel

If you categorize the actions, consider using a task-centered approach. Group them according to what people intend to do. In the Powerpoint example, for instance, there's an "Open a presentation" group, plus several groups for creating new slideshows.

Still, try to present these groups linearly. Imagine reading the actions aloud to someone who can't see the screen—can you proceed through them in a logical fashion, with obvious start and end points? That, of course, is how a blind user would "hear" the interface.

Incidentally, you also can put controls on an action panel, like a text field next to a "Search" button.

For each action's label, you could use text, icons, or both, depending on what best conveys the nature of the actions. In fact, if you use mostly icons, then you end up with...a traditional toolbar! (Or a palette, if your UI is a visual builder-style application.)

Text labels on an action panel can be longer than those on a menu or a button. You can use multiline labels, for instance—no need to be overly parsimonious with words here. Just remember that longer, more descriptive labels are better for first-time or infrequent users, who need to learn (or be reminded of) what these actions do. The extra space spent on long labels may not be appreciated in dense high-performance interfaces used mostly by experienced users. If there are too many words, even first-time users' eyes will glaze over.

There's often no need to make the actions look like buttons, even if they're implemented as buttons. Phrases written in blue text communicate clickability, since they look like links on a web page; you could enhance the effect by underlining them when the mouse rolls over them. This is what Microsoft does in its interfaces that use action panels. Feel free to experiment. However, usability-test it to make sure users actually see the actions as clickable things, not ordinary text or pictures.

examples

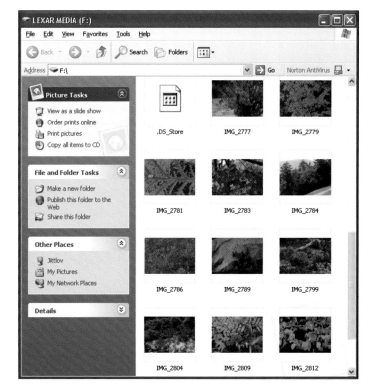

FIGURE 5-7 / This screenshot of the Windows Explorer shows a directory of pictures attached to an action panel. Microsoft calls this feature a "Task Pane." The panel is composed of closable subpanels (see the **Closable Panels** pattern in Chapter 4), each of which contains a manageable handful of related actions.

Note that the first two sections, Picture Tasks and File and Folder Tasks, are completely task-oriented: they're phrased as verbs (View, Order, Print, and Copy), and they anticipate things users will commonly want to do. You might recall that in Chapter 1, we talked about organizing interfaces according to lists of objects, actions, categories, and tools. The first two sections are fine examples of lists of actions. But the third section in this panel, "Other Places," is a list of objects instead.

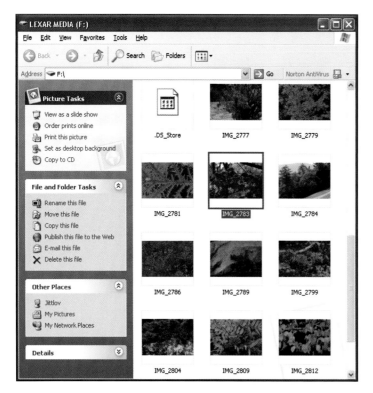

FIGURE 5-8 / The same panel, but with an image file selected. The panel changes dynamically according to context—the listed tasks are not the same as in the other screenshot, in which no files are selected.

46 prominent "done" button

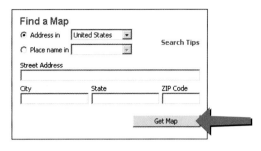

FIGURE 5-9 / From *http://mapblast.com*

what

Place the button that finishes a transaction at the end of the visual flow; make it big and well-labeled.

use when

Whenever you need to put a button like "Done," "Submit," or "OK" on your interface, use this pattern. More generally, use a visually prominent button for the final step of any transaction—like an online purchase—or to commit a group of settings.

why

A well-understood, obvious last step gives your users a sense of closure. There's no doubt that the transaction will be done when that button is clicked; don't leave them hanging, wondering whether or not their work took effect.

Making that last step obvious is what this pattern is really about. Doing it well draws on the layout concepts in Chapter 4—visual hierarchy, visual flow, grouping, and alignment.

how

Create a button that actually looks like a button, not a link; either use platform standards for push buttons, or use a medium-sized button graphic with well-defined borders. This will help the button stand out on the page, and it won't get lost among other things.

When labeling the button, prefer text labels to icons. They're easier to understand for actions like this, especially since most users look for a button labeled "Done," "Submit," or "OK." The text in that label can be a verb or a short verb phrase that describes what will happen, in the user's terms— "Send," "Buy," or "Change Record" are more specific than "Done," and can sometimes communicate more effectively.

Place the button where the user most likely will find it. Trace the task flow down through the page or form or dialog box, and put the button just beyond the last step. Usually that will be on the bottom and/or right of the page. Your page layouts may have a standard place for them (see the **Visual Framework** pattern in Chapter 4), or the platform standard may prescribe it; if so, use the standard.

In any case, make sure the button is near the last text field or control. If it's too far away, then the user may not find it immediately upon finishing his work, and he may look for other affordances in his quest for "what to do next." On the Web, he may end up abandoning the page (and possibly a purchase) without realizing it.

Figure 5-10 shows a typical web form. You probably can see the button in question without even reading the labels, due to visual design alone:

- The orange color stands out. It's a saturated color; it contrasts with the white background, and it echoes the orange of the logo in the upper left—those are the only orange things on the page. (Note the use of the **Diagonal Balance** pattern, anchored by those two orange elements. See Chapter 4.)

- The graphic used for the button looks like a button. It's a rounded or "pill" shape, with a very slight drop shadow, which makes it pop out from the background.

- The button is positioned at the right edge of the form, directly under the body of the form itself. Both the task flow (the user will work from top to bottom) and the visual flow bring the eye to rest at that button.

- The button is set off by whitespace on its left, right, and bottom. That groups it with the form, but there's nothing else around it to compete with it.

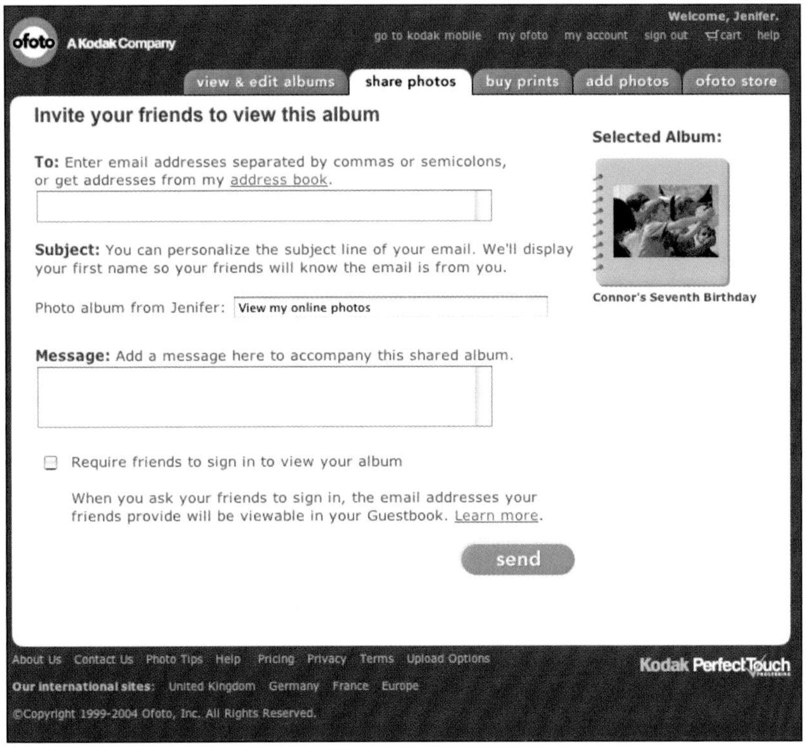

FIGURE 5-10 / From *http://ofoto.com*

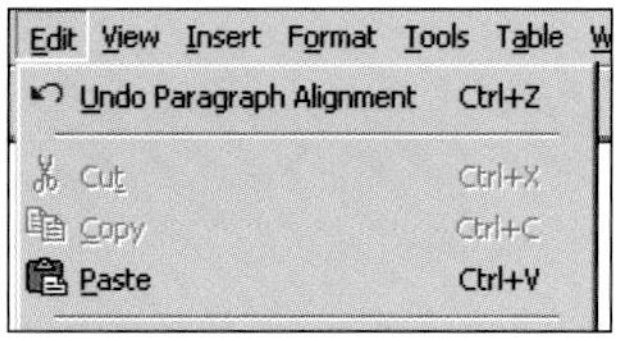

FIGURE 5-11 / Word's Edit menu

what

Change menu labels dynamically to show precisely what they would do when invoked.

use when

Your UI has menu items that operate on specific objects, like Close, or that behave slightly differently in different contexts, like Undo.

why

Menu items that say exactly what they're going to do make the UI self-explanatory. The user doesn't have to think about what object will be affected. She's also less likely to accidentally do something she didn't intend, like deleting "Chapter 8" instead of "Footnote 3." It thus encourages **Safe Exploration**.

how

Every time the user changes the selected object (or current document, last undoable operation, etc.), change the menu items that operate on it to include the specifics of the action. Obviously, if there is no selected object, you should disable the menu item, thus reinforcing the connection between the item and its object.

Incidentally, this pattern also could work for button labels, links, or anything else that is a "verb" in the context of the UI.

What if there are multiple selected objects? There's not a whole lot of guidance out there—in existing software, this pattern mostly applies to documents and undo operations—but you could write in a plural, like "Delete Selected Objects."

example

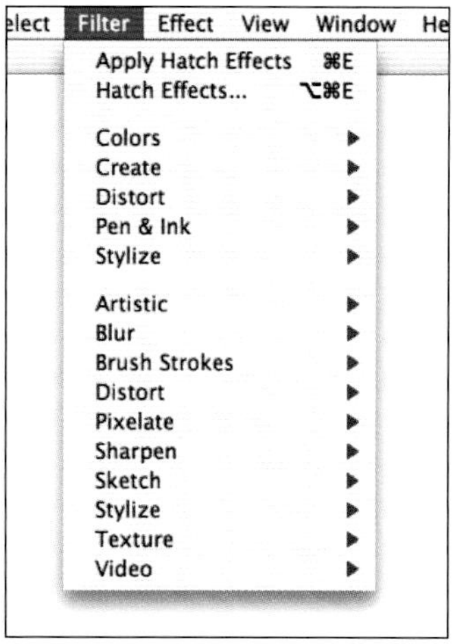

FIGURE 5-12 / A menu from Illustrator's menu bar. The last filter the user applied in this case was the "Hatch Effects" filter. The menu remembers that, so it changes its first two items to (1) reapply the same filter again and (2) modify the filter before reapplying. ("Hatch Effects..." brings up the dialog box to modify it.) The user *might* have applied so many filters that she'd find it useful to be reminded of the last one. And the accelerator keystrokes are handy for repeated application of the same filter!

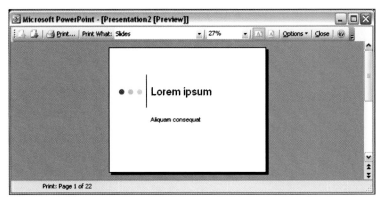

FIGURE 5-13 / PowerPoint's Print Preview screen

what

Show users a preview or summary of what will happen when they perform an action.

use when

The user is just about to do a "heavyweight" action—such as opening a large file, printing a 10-page document, submitting a form that took time to fill out, or committing a purchase over the Web. The user wants some assurance that he's doing it correctly. Doing it wrong would be time-consuming or otherwise costly.

Alternatively, the user might be about to perform a graphic action that isn't particularly heavyweight, but he'd still like to know what it will do in advance.

why

Previews help prevent various errors. A user may have made a typo, or he may have misunderstood something that led up to the action in question (like purchasing the wrong item online). By showing him a summary or visual description of what's about to happen, you give him a chance to back out or correct any mistakes.

Previews also can help an application become more self-describing. If someone's never used a certain action before, or doesn't know what it will do under certain circumstances, a preview explains it better than any documentation—the user learns about the action exactly when and where he needs to.

how

Just before the user commits an action, display whatever information gives him the clearest picture of what's about to happen. If it's a print preview, show what the page will look like on the chosen paper size; if it's an image operation, show a closeup of what the image will look like; if it's a transaction, show a summary of everything the system knows about that transaction. Show what's important—no more, no less.

Give the user a way to commit the action straight from the preview page. There's no need to make the user close the preview or navigate elsewhere.

Likewise, give the user a way to back out. If he can salvage the transaction by correcting previously entered information, give him a chance to do that, too. In many wizards and other linear processes, this is just a matter of navigating a few steps backwards.

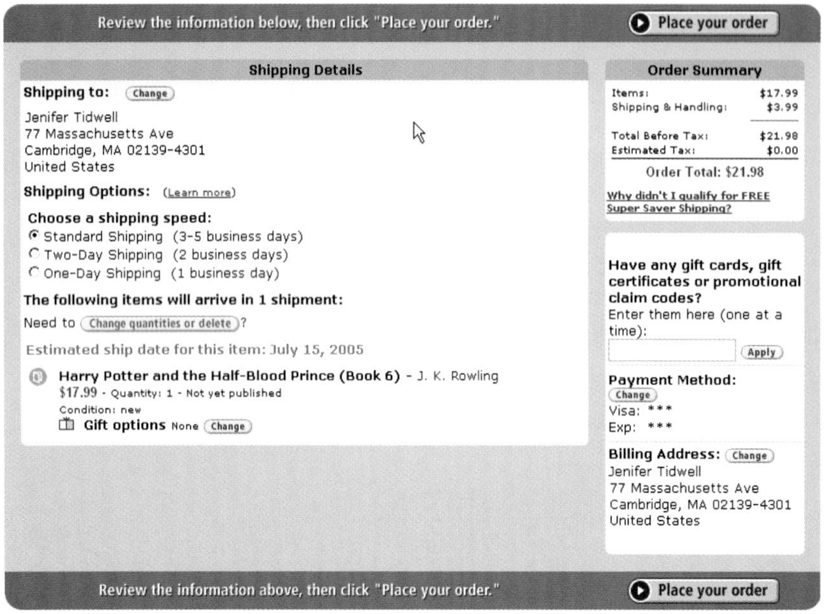

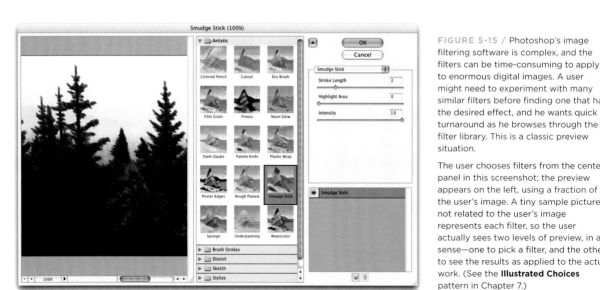

FIGURE 5-14 / Amazon's order summary page comes at the end of a multipage purchase process, during which items were chosen and shipping and payment details were provided. The format is compact and readable, the content is segmented into **Titled Sections** (Chapter 4), and many pieces of information have a convenient "Change" button next to them. The "Place your order" buttons (two, you might notice, for people too rushed to read the whole page) are clear, large, and brightly colored—very easy to find.

FIGURE 5-15 / Photoshop's image filtering software is complex, and the filters can be time-consuming to apply to enormous digital images. A user might need to experiment with many similar filters before finding one that has the desired effect, and he wants quick turnaround as he browses through the filter library. This is a classic preview situation.

The user chooses filters from the center panel in this screenshot; the preview appears on the left, using a fraction of the user's image. A tiny sample picture not related to the user's image represents each filter, so the user actually sees two levels of preview, in a sense—one to pick a filter, and the other to see the results as applied to the actual work. (See the **Illustrated Choices** pattern in Chapter 7.)

49 progress indicator

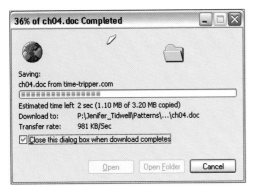

FIGURE 5-16 / Internet Explorer progress dialog box

what

Show the user how much progress was made on a time-consuming operation.

use when

A time-consuming operation interrupts the UI, or runs in the background, for longer than two seconds or so.

why

Users get impatient when the UI just sits there. Even if you change the mouse pointer to a clock or hourglass (which you should in any case, if the rest of the UI is locked out), you don't want to make a user wait for an unspecified length of time.

Experiments show that if users see an indication that something is going on, they're much more patient, even if they have to wait longer than they would without a progress indicator. Maybe it's because they know that "the system is thinking," and it isn't just hung or waiting for them to do something.

how

Show an animated indicator of how much progress has been made. Either verbally or graphically (or both), tell the user:

- What's currently going on
- What proportion of the operation is complete
- How much time remains
- How to stop it

As far as time estimates are concerned, it's okay to be wrong sometimes, as long as your estimates converge on something accurate quickly. But sometimes the UI can't tell how far along it is. In that case, show something animated anyway that is noncommittal about percentages. Think about the browsers' image loops that keep rolling while a page loads.

Most GUI toolboxes provide a widget or dialog box that implements this pattern, like Java Swing's JProgressBar. Beware of potentially tricky threading issues, however—the progress indicator must be updated consistently, while the operation itself proceeds uninhibited. If you can, keep the rest of the UI alive too. Don't lock up the UI while the progress indicator is visible.

If it's possible to cancel the operation whose progress is monitored, offer a cancel button or similar affordance on or near the progress indicator; that's where a user probably will look for it. See the **Cancelability** pattern (next) for more information.

See the **Cancelability** pattern (next) for more information.

example

FIGURE 5-17 / This startup screen uses icons to show what KDE does while it starts—each icon becomes sharply defined when that step is reached. No timing numbers are used, but they aren't really necessary (the user is a captive audience until KDE finishes starting), and they may not be accurate anyway.

50 cancelability

FIGURE 5-18 / Firefox's stop-loading button

what

Provide a way to instantly cancel a time-consuming operation, with no side effects.

use when

A time-consuming operation interrupts the UI, or runs in the background, for longer than two seconds or so—such as when you print a file, query a database, or load a large file. Alternatively, the user is engaged in an activity that literally or apparently shuts out most other interactions with the system, such as when working with a modal dialog box.

why

Users change their minds. Once a time-consuming operation starts, a user may want to stop it, especially if a **Progress Indicator** tells her that it'll take a while. Or the user may have started it by accident in the first place. **Cancelability** certainly helps with error prevention and recovery—a user can cancel out of something she knows will fail, like loading a page from a web server she realizes is down.

A user will feel better about exploring the interface and trying things out if she knows that anything is cancelable. It encourages **Safe Exploration** (see Chapter 1), which in turn makes the interface easier and more fun to learn.

how

First, find out if there's a way to speed up the time-consuming operation so it appears instantaneous. It doesn't even have to be genuinely fast; if a user perceives it as immediate, that's good enough. On the Web or a networked application, this may mean preloading data or code—sending it to the client before it's asked for—or sending data in increments, showing it to the user as it comes in. Remember, people can only read so fast. You might as well use the loading time to let the user read the first page's worth of data, then another page, and so on.

However, if you really do need to cancel it, here's how to do it. Put a cancel button directly on the interface, next to the **Progress Indicator** (which you are using, right?) or wherever the results of the operation appear. Label it with the word Stop or Cancel, and/or put an internationally recognizable stop icon on it: a red octagon, a red circle with a horizontal bar, or an X.

When the user clicks or presses the Cancel button, cancel the operation immediately. If you wait too long, for more than a second or two, the user may doubt that the cancel actually worked (or you may dissuade him from using it, since he might as well wait for the operation to finish). Tell the user that the cancel worked—halt the progress indicator, and show a status message on the interface, for instance.

Multiple parallel operations present a challenge. How does the user cancel a particular one and not others? The cancel button's label or tooltip can state exactly what gets canceled when it's pressed (see the **Smart Menu Items** pattern for a similar concept). If the actions are presented as a list or a set of panels, you might consider providing a separate cancel button for each action, to avoid ambiguity.

If you've ever tried to cancel a photocopier job—maybe you accidentally requested 600 copies of something—it's usually pretty obvious how to do it. There's a big Stop or Cancel button on the copier panel. When you hit it, the copier stops as soon as it's finished the current copy or page.

In Windows, however, if you send a document to the printer and then need to cancel it (maybe you just printed 600 pages by accident), you first must bring up the printer's properties window. It's not immediately obvious how to get there, though there are several ways to do it. Once there, no Cancel button presents itself. You need to use either the menu bar or the context menu (shown here) to cancel the print job. Then a confirmation dialog box asks you if you're really sure. Thus it takes many clicks and a not-so-obvious path to cancel a print job.

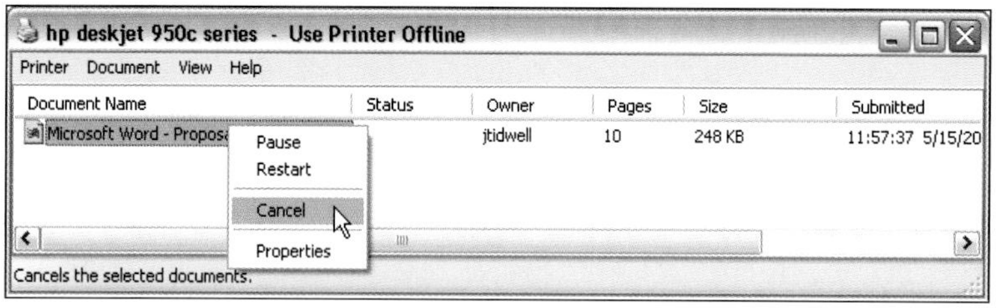

FIGURE 5-19 / Windows XP printer window, with a hard-to-find Cancel operation. Don't do it this way.

51 multi-level undo

FIGURE 5-20 / Photoshop's
visual representation of the "undo
stack"

what

Provide a way to easily reverse a series of actions performed by the user.

use when

You've designed a highly interactive UI that is more complex than simple navigation or form fill-in. This includes mail readers, database software, authoring tools, graphics software, and programming environments.

why

The ability to undo a long sequence of operations lets users feel that the interface is safe to explore. While they learn the interface, they can experiment with it, confident that they aren't making irrevocable changes—even if they accidentally do something "bad." This is true for users of all levels of skill, not just beginners.[1]

Once the user knows the interface well, she can move through it with the confidence that mistakes aren't permanent. If her finger slips and she hits the wrong menu item, no complicated and stressful recovery is necessary; she doesn't have to revert to saved files, shut down and start afresh, or go ask a system administrator to restore a backup file. This spares users wasted time and occasional mental anguish.

Multi-level undo also lets expert users explore work paths quickly and easily. For instance, a Photoshop user might perform a series of filtering operations on an image, study the result to see if she likes it, and then undo back to her starting point. Then she might try out another series of filters, maybe save it, and undo again. She could do this without multi-level undo, but it would take more time (for closing and reloading the image). When a user works creatively, speed and ease-of-use are important for maintaining focus and the experience of flow. See Chapter 1 for more information, especially the **Safe Exploration** and **Incremental Construction** patterns.

how

UNDOABLE OPERATIONS

The software your UI is built on first needs a strong model of what an action is—what it's called, what object it was associated with, and how to reverse it. Then you can build an undo interface on it.

---

1 Alan Cooper and Robert Reimann devote an entire chapter to the Undo concept in their book *About Face 2.0: The Essentials of Interaction Design* (Wiley).

Decide which operations need to be undoable. Any action that might change a file, or anything that could be permanent, should be undoable, while transient or view-related states often are not. Specifically, these kinds of changes are expected to be undoable in most applications:

- Text entry for documents or spreadsheets
- Database transactions
- Modifications to images or painting canvases
- Layout changes—position, size, stacking order, or grouping in graphic applications
- File operations, such as deleting or modifying files
- Creation, deletion, or rearrangement of objects such as email messages or spreadsheet columns
- Any cut, copy, or paste operation

The following kinds of changes generally are not undoable. Even if you think you want to go above and beyond the call of duty and make them undoable, consider that you might thoroughly irritate users by cluttering up the "undo stack" with useless undos:

- Text or object selection
- Navigation between windows or pages
- Mouse cursor and text cursor locations
- Scrollbar position
- Window or panel positions and sizes
- Changes made in an uncommitted or modal dialog box

Some operations are on the borderline. Form fill-in, for instance, sometimes is undoable and sometimes is not. However, if tabbing out of a changed field automatically commits that change, it's probably a good idea to make it undoable.

(Certain kinds of operations are impossible to undo. But usually the nature of the application makes that obvious to users with any experience at all. Impossible undos include the purchase step of an e-commerce transaction, posting a message to a bulletin board or chatroom, or sending an email—as much as we'd sometimes like to undo that!)

In any case, make sure the undoable operations make sense to the user. Be sure to define and name them in terms of how the user thinks about the operations, not how the computer thinks about them. You should undo typed text, for instance, in chunks of words, not letter-by-letter.

DESIGN AN UNDO STACK

Each operation goes on the top of the stack as it is performed, and each Undo reverses the operation at the top, then the next one down, then the next. Redo similarly works its way back up the stack.

The stack should be at least 10 to 12 items long to be useful, and longer if you can manage it. Long-term observation or usability testing may tell you what your usable limit is. (Constantine and Lockwood assert that having more than a dozen items usually is unnecessary, since "users are seldom able to make effective use of more levels."[2] Expert users of high-powered software might tell you differently. As always, know your users.)

PRESENTATION

Finally, decide how to present the undo stack to the user. Most desktop applications put Undo/Redo items on the Edit menu. Also, Undo usually is hooked up to Control-Z or its equivalent. The most well-behaved applications use **Smart Menu Items** to tell the user exactly which operation is next up on the undo stack.

---

2 See Larry Constantine and Lucy Lockwood, "Instructive Interaction: Making Innovative Interfaces Self-Teaching," at *http://foruse.com/articles/instructive.htm*.

But see the screenshot at the top of this pattern (Figure 5-20) for a different, more visual presentation. Photoshop shows a scrolling list of the undo-able operations—including ones that were already undone (one is shown, in gray). It lets the user pick the point in the stack that they want to revert to. A visual command history like this can be quite useful, even just as a reminder of what you've recently done. See the **Command History** pattern for more information.

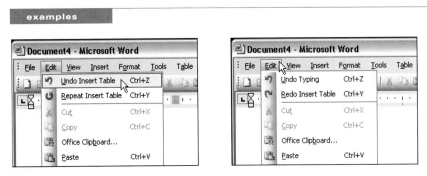

FIGURE 5-21 / A more typical presentation of Multi-Level Undo. In this case, the user typed some text, and then inserted a table. The first Undo removes the table. Once that's done, the following Undo—the next action in the undo stack—is the typed text, and invoking Undo again removes that text. Meanwhile, the user has the opportunity to "undo the undo" with the Redo menu item. If we're at the top of the stack (as in the first screenshot), then there is no Redo, and that menu item is overloaded with a Repeat action.

Confusing? You bet. Most users never will develop a clear mental picture of the algorithms used here; most people don't know what a "stack" is, let alone how it is used in conjunction with Repeat and Redo. That's why the **Smart Menu Items** are absolutely critical to usability here. They explain exactly what's going to happen, which reduces the cognitive burden on the user.

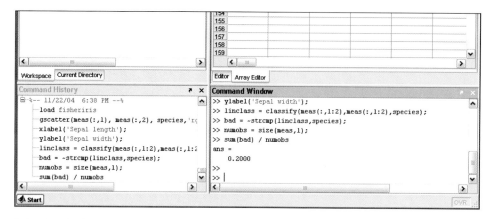

FIGURE 5-22 / MATLAB's command history, shown in the lower left

what

As the user performs actions, keep a visible record of what was done, to what, and when.

use when

Users perform long and complex sequences of actions, either with a GUI or a command line. Most users are fairly experienced, or if not, they at least want an efficient interface that's supportive of long-term and recurring work. Graphical editors and programming environments usually are good candidates for this pattern.

why

Sometimes a user needs to remember or review what he did in the course of working with the software. For instance, he may want to do any of these things:

- Repeat an action or command done earlier, one he doesn't remember well

- Recall the order in which some actions were done

- Repeat a sequence of operations, originally done to one object, on a different object

- Keep a log of his actions, for legal or security reasons

- Convert an interactive series of commands into a script or macro (see the **Macros** pattern in this chapter)

Computers are good at keeping an accurate record of steps taken; people aren't. Take advantage of that.

how

Keep a running list of the actions taken by the user. If the interface is driven from a command line, then you have it easy—just record everything typed there. See Figure 5-22. If you can, keep track of the history across sessions, so the user can see what was done even a week ago or longer.

If it's a graphic interface, or a combination of graphic and command-line interfaces, then things get a little more complicated. Find a way to express each action in one consistent, concise way, usually with words (though there's no reason why it can't be done visually). Make sure you define these with the right granularity—if one action is done en masse to seventeen objects, record it as one action, not seventeen.

What commands should you record, and which ones shouldn't you? See the **Multi-Level Undo** pattern for a thorough discussion of what commands

should "count." If a command is undoable, it should be recorded in the history.

Finally, display the history to the user. That display should be optional in most software, since it will almost certainly play a supporting role in the user's work, not a starring role. Lists of commands—oldest to newest—tend to work well. If you'd like, you could timestamp the history display somehow. MATLAB, shown in Figure 5-22, puts a date and time into the history whenever the program restarts.

```
swing-shift:/var/log/httpd> history
    1  23:55   pwd
    2  23:55   pushd /var/log/httpd/
    3  23:55   ls -l access_log
    4  23:56   tail -1000 access_log | grep "index"
    5  23:56   tail -1000 access_log | grep "index" | wc
    6  23:57   tail -1000 access_log | grep "Diagonal" | wc
    7  23:57   ls -l
    8  23:57   cd jtidwellnet/
    9  23:57   tail -1000 access_log | grep "index" | wc
   10  23:58   tail -200 access_log | more
   11  23:58   tail -200 access_log | grep "google"
   12  23:58   cd ..
   13  23:58   tail -1000 access_log | grep "google"
   14  23:59   tail -1000 access_log | grep "googlebot"
   15  23:59   history
swing-shift:/var/log/httpd> []
```

FIGURE 5-23 / Unix and its many variants use shell programs, such as tcsh and bash, that keep track of their own command histories in files. The user can call it up with the "history" command, as shown here. The history also is accessible through various command-line constructs, like "!!" (reuse the last command), "!3" (reuse the command issued three commands ago), and Control-P, which you can issue repeatedly to show the previous commands one at a time.

FIGURE 5-24 / Photoshop's undo stack, also seen in the **Multi-Level Undo** pattern, is effectively a command history. You can use it to undo what you did, but you don't have to; you can just look at it and scroll through it, reviewing what you did. It uses icons to identify different classes of actions, which is unusual, but nice to use.

53 macros

FIGURE 5-25 / Photoshop's actions list

what

Macros are single actions composed of other, smaller actions. Users can create them by putting together sequences of actions.

use when

Users want to repeat long sequences of actions or commands. They might want to loop over lists of files, images, database records, or other objects, for instance, doing the same things to each object. You might already have implemented **Multi-Level Undo** or **Command History**.

why

No one wants to perform the same set of repetitive interactive tasks over, and over, and over again! This is exactly what computers are supposed to be good at. Chapter 1 described a user-behavior pattern called **Streamlined Repetition**; macros are precisely the kind of mechanism that can support that well.

Macros obviously help users work faster. However, by reducing the number of commands or gestures needed to get something done, they also reduce the possibility of finger-slips, oversights, and similar mistakes.

You might also recall the concept of "flow," also discussed in Chapter 1. When a user can compress a long sequence of actions down to a single command or keyboard shortcut, the experience of flow is enhanced—the user can accomplish more with less effort and time, and she can keep her larger goals in sight without getting bogged down in details.

how

Provide a way for the user to "record" a sequence of actions and easily "play them back" at any time. The playback should be as easy as giving a single command, pressing a single button, or dragging and dropping an object.

DEFINING THE MACRO

The user should be able to give the macro a name of her choice. Let her review the action sequence somehow, so she can check her work or revisit a forgotten sequence to see what it did (as in the **Command History** pattern). Make it possible for one macro to refer to another so they can build on each other.

Users will want to save macros from one day to the next, so make sure they're persistent—save them to files or a database. Present them in a searchable, sortable, and even categorizable list, depending on your users' needs.

DOING THINGS

The macro itself could be played back literally, to keep things simple; or, if it acts upon an object that can change from one invocation to another, you could allow the sequence to be parameterized (e.g., use a placeholder or variable instead of a literal object). Macros also should be able to act on many things at once.

How the names of the macros (or the controls that launch them) are presented depends heavily upon the nature of the application, but consider displaying them with built-in actions rather than making them second-class citizens.

The ability to record these sequences, plus the facility for macros to build on one another, create the potential for a user to invent entirely new linguistic or visual grammar—a grammar that is finely tuned to their own environment and work habits. This is a very powerful capability. In reality, it's programming; but if your users don't think of themselves as programmers, don't call it that or you'll scare them off. ("I don't know how to program anything; I must not be able to do this.")

examples

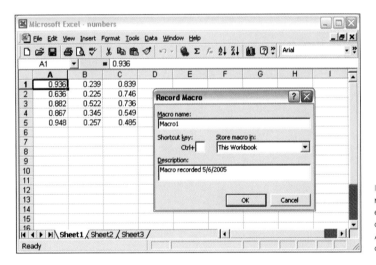

FIGURE 5-26 / Microsoft Excel allows macros to be recorded, named, stored along with the document, and even assigned to a keyboard shortcut. The user also can choose to run it from a button on the toolbar, or an ActiveX control in the document itself (which means you can use them as callbacks for buttons or text fields).

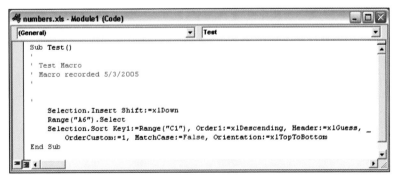

FIGURE 5-27 / These Excel macros are written in Visual Basic, and the user can hand-edit them if desired. This is when it becomes programming. Because Visual Basic provides access to so much general-purpose functionality—most of it not directly related to spreadsheet operations—macros can be a serious security risk for Office applications. By sharply constraining the functionality available to macros and limiting the number of ways users can run macros (e.g., clicking on toolbar buttons), you can trade power for safety.

SHOWING COMPLEX DATA:
TREES, TABLES, AND OTHER
INFORMATION GRAPHICS

Information graphics—including maps, tables, and graphs—communicate knowledge visually rather than verbally. When done well, they let people use their eyes and minds to draw their own conclusions; they show, rather than tell.

These graphics are my favorite kinds of interfaces. However, poor tools or inadequate design can sharply limit what you can do with them, and many information-rich interfaces just don't quite work as well as they could.

The patterns in this chapter will help you make the best of the tools you have, and introduce you to some useful and interesting innovations in visualization design. The ideas described in this introduction can help you sort out which design aspects are most important to you in a given interface.

THE BASICS OF INFORMATION GRAPHICS

"Information graphics" simply means data presented visually, with the goal of imparting knowledge to the user. I'm including tables and tree views in that description because they are inherently visual, even though they're constructed primarily from text instead of lines and polygons. Other familiar static information graphics includes maps, flowcharts, bar plots, and diagrams of real-world objects.

But we're dealing with computers, not paper. You can make almost any good static design better with interactivity. Interactive tools let the user hide and show information as she needs it, and they put the user in the "driver's seat" as she chooses how to view and explore it.

Even the mere act of manipulating and rearranging the data in an interactive graphic has value—the user becomes a participant in the discovery process, not just a passive observer. This can be invaluable. The user may not produce the world's best-designed plot or table, but the process of manipulating that plot or table puts her face-to-face with aspects of data that she may never have noticed on paper.

Ultimately, the user's goal in using information graphics is to learn something. But the designer needs to understand *what* the user needs to learn. The user might look for something very specific, like a particular street on a map, in which case she needs to be able to find it—say by searching directly, or by filtering out extraneous information. She needs to get a "big picture" only to the extent necessary to reach that specific data point. The abilities to search, filter, and zero in on details are critical.

On the other hand, she might try to learn something less concrete. She might look at a map to grasp the layout of a city, rather than to find a specific address. Or she may be a scientist visualizing a biochemical process, trying to understand how it works. Now overviews are important; she needs to see how the parts interconnect into the whole. She may want to zoom in, zoom back out again, look at the details occasionally, and compare one view of the data to another.

Good interactive information graphics offer users answers to these questions:

- How is this data organized?
- What's related to what?
- How can I explore this data?
- Can I rearrange this data to see it differently?
- Show me only what I need to know.
- What are the specific data values?

In these sections, remember that the term "information graphics" is a very big umbrella. It covers plots, graphs, maps, tables, trees, timelines, and diagrams of all sorts. The data can be huge and multilayered, or small and focused. Many of these techniques apply surprisingly well to graphic types that you wouldn't expect.

Before describing the patterns themselves, let's set the stage by discussing some of the questions posed above.

ORGANIZATIONAL MODELS: HOW IS THIS DATA ORGANIZED?

The first thing a user sees in any information visualization is the shape you've chosen for the data. Ideally, the data itself has an inherent structure that suggests this shape to you. Which of these models fits your data best?

Model	Diagram	Common graphics
Linear		List or single-variable plot
Tabular		Spreadsheet, multi-column list, **Sortable Table**, **Multi-Y Plot**, or other multi-variable plots
Hierarchical		**Tree**, **Cascaded Lists**, **Tree Table**, **Treemap**, or directed graph
Network (or organic)		Directed graph or flowchart
Geographic (or spatial)		Map or schematic
Other		Plots of various sorts, such as parallel coordinate plots, or **Treemaps**

Try these models against the data you try to show. If two or more might fit, consider which ones play up which aspects of your data. If your data could be both geographic and tabular, for instance, showing it as only a table may obscure its geographic nature—a viewer may miss interesting features or relationships in the data if you do not show it as a map too.

The organizational model you choose tells the user a lot about the shape of the data. Part of this message operates at a subconscious level; people recognize trees, tables, and maps, and they immediately jump to conclusions about the underlying data before they even start to think consciously about it. But it's not just the shape that does this. The look of the individual data elements also works at a subconscious level in the user's mind: things that look alike must be associated with one another.

If you've read Chapter 4, that should sound familiar—you already know about the Gestalt principles. (If you jumped ahead in the book, this might be a good time to go back and read the introduction to Chapter 4.) Most of those principles, especially similarity and continuity, will come into play here, too. I'll tell you a little more about how they seem to work.

Certain visual features operate "preattentively:" they convey information before the viewer pays conscious attention. Look at Figure 6-1 and find the blue objects.

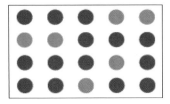

FIGURE 6-1 / Find the blue objects

I'm guessing that you can do that pretty quickly. Now look at Figure 6-2 and do the same.

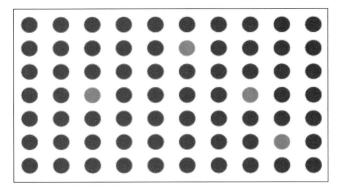

FIGURE 6-2 / Again

You did that pretty quickly too, right? In fact, it doesn't matter how many red objects there are; the amount of time it takes you to find the blue ones is constant! You might think it should be linear with the total number of objects—order-N time, in algorithmic terms—but it's not. Color operates at a primitive cognitive level. Your visual system does the hard work for you, and it seems to work in a "massively parallel" fashion.

On the other hand, visually monotonous text forces you to read the values and think about them. Figure 6-3 shows exactly the same problem with numbers instead of colors. How fast can you find the numbers that are greater than 1?

0.103	0.176	0.387	0.300	0.379	0.276	0.179	0.321	0.192	0.250
0.333	0.384	0.564	0.587	0.857	1.064	0.698	0.621	0.232	0.316
0.421	0.309	0.654	0.729	0.228	0.529	0.832	0.935	0.452	0.426
0.266	0.750	1.056	0.936	0.911	0.820	0.723	1.201	0.935	0.819
0.225	0.326	0.643	0.337	0.721	0.837	0.682	0.987	0.984	0.849
0.187	0.586	0.529	0.340	0.829	0.835	0.873	0.945	1.103	0.710
0.153	0.485	0.560	0.428	0.628	0.335	0.956	0.879	0.699	0.424

FIGURE 6-3 / Find the values greater than one

When dealing with text like this, your "search time" really is linear with the number of items. What if we still used text, but made the target numbers physically larger than the others, as in Figure 6-4?

0.103	0.176	0.387	0.300	0.379	0.276	0.179	0.321	0.192	0.250
0.333	0.384	0.564	0.587	0.857	**1.064**	0.698	0.621	0.232	0.316
0.421	0.309	0.654	0.729	0.228	0.529	0.832	0.935	0.452	0.426
0.266	0.750	**1.056**	0.936	0.911	0.820	0.723	**1.201**	0.935	0.819
0.225	0.326	0.643	0.337	0.721	0.837	0.682	0.987	0.984	0.849
0.187	0.586	0.529	0.340	0.829	0.835	0.873	0.945	**1.103**	0.710
0.153	0.485	0.560	0.428	0.628	0.335	0.956	0.879	0.699	0.424

FIGURE 6-4 / Again

Now we're back to constant time again. Size is, in fact, another preattentive variable. The fact that the larger numbers protrude into their right margins also helps you find them—alignment is yet another preattentive variable.

Figure 6-5 shows many known preattentive variables.

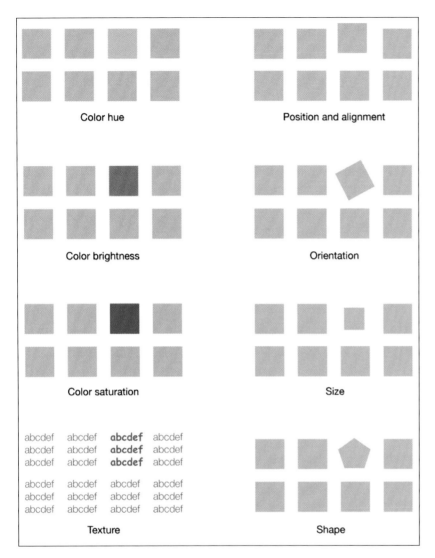

FIGURE 6-5 / Eight preattentive variables

This concept has profound implications for text-based information graphics, like the table of numbers in Figure 6-3. If you want some data points to stand out from the others, you have to make them look different by varying their color, size, or some other preattentive variable. More generally, you can use these variables to differentiate classes or dimensions of data on any kind of information graphic. This is sometimes called "encoding."

When you have to plot a multidimensional data set, you can use several different visual variables to encode all those dimensions in a single static display. Consider the scatter plot shown in Figure 6-6. Position is used along the X and Y axes; color hue encodes a third variable. The shape of the scatter markers could encode yet a fourth variable, but in this case, shape is redundant with color hue. The redundant encoding helps a user visually separate the three data groups.

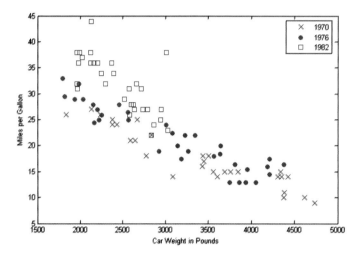

FIGURE 6-6 / Encoding three variables in a scatter plot

Encoding via preattentive factors relates to a general graphic design concept called "layering." When you look at well-designed graphics of any sort, you perceive different classes of information on the page. Preattentive factors like color cause some of them to "pop out" of the page, and similarity causes you to see them as connected to one another, as if each were on a transparent layer over the base graphic. It's an extremely effective way of segmenting data—each layer is simpler than the whole graphic, and the viewer can study each in turn, but relationships among the whole are preserved and emphasized.

NAVIGATION AND BROWSING: HOW CAN I EXPLORE THIS DATA?

A user's first investigation of an interactive data graphic may be browsing—just looking around to see what's there. He also may navigate through it to find some specific thing he's seeking. Filtering and searching can serve that purpose too, but navigation through the "virtual space" of a dataset often is better. **Spatial Memory** (Chapter 1) kicks in, and the user can see points of interest in context with the rest of the data.

A famous mantra in the information visualization field is: "focus plus context." A good visualization should permit a user to focus on a point of interest, while simultaneously showing enough material around that point of interest to give the user a sense of where it is in the big picture.

Here are some common techniques for navigation and browsing:

Scroll and pan

If the data display won't fit onscreen at once, you could put it in a scrolled window, giving the user easy and familiar access to the offscreen portions. Scrollbars are familiar to almost everyone, and are easy to use. However, some displays are too big, or their size is indeterminate (thus making scrollbars inaccurate), or they have data beyond the visible window that you need to retrieve or recalculate (thus making scrollbars too slow to respond). Instead of using scrollbars in those cases, try setting up buttons that the user has to click to retrieve the next screenful of data; think about how MapQuest or MapBlast works. Other applications do panning instead, in which the cursor "grabs" the information graphic and drags it until the point of interest is found, as in Google Maps.

These techniques are appropriate for different situations, but the basic idea is the same: to interactively move the visible part of the graphic. Sometimes **Overview Plus Detail** can help the user stay oriented. A small view of the whole graphic can be shown with an indicator rectangle displaying the visible "viewport;" the user might pan by dragging that rectangle, in addition to scrollbars or whatever else is used.

Zoom

Zooming changes the *scale* of the viewed section, whereas scrolling changes the location. When you present a data-dense map or graph, consider offering the user the ability to zoom in on points of interest. It means you don't have to pack every single data detail into the full view—if you have lots of labels, or very tiny features (especially on maps), it may be impossible anyway. As the user zooms in, those features can emerge when they have enough space.

Most zooms are implemented with a mouse click or button press, and the whole viewing area changes scale at once. But that's not the only way to zoom. Some applications create nonlinear distortions of the information graphic as the user moves the mouse pointer over the graphic: whatever is under the pointer zooms, but the stuff far away from the pointer doesn't change scale. See the **Local Zooming** pattern for more information.

Open and close points of interest

Tree views typically let users open and close parent items at will, so they can inspect the contents of those items. Some hierarchically structured diagrams and graphs also give users the chance to open and close parts of the diagram "in place," without having to open a new window or go to a new screen. With these devices, the user can explore containment or parent/child relationships easily, without leaving that window. The **Cascading Lists** pattern describes another effective way to explore a hierarchy; it works entirely through single-click opening and closing of items.

Drill down into points of interest

Some information graphics just present a "top level" of information. A user might click or double-click on a map to see information about the city she just clicked on, or she might click on key points in a diagram to see subdiagrams. This "drilling down" might reuse the same window, use a separate panel on the same window, or bring up a new one (see Chapter 2 for a discussion of window mechanics). This technique resembles opening and closing points of interest, except that the viewing occurs separately from the graphic, and is not integrated into it.

If you also provide a search facility for an interactive information graphic, consider linking the search results to whatever technique listed previously that you use. In other words, when a user searches for the city of Sydney on a map, show the map zooming and/or panning to that point. Then the search user gets some of the benefits of context and spatial memory.

Sometimes just rearranging an information graphic can reveal unexpected relationships. Look at the following graphic, taken from the National Cancer Institute's online mortality charts (Figure 6-7). It shows the number of deaths from lung cancer in the state of Texas. The major metropolitan regions in Texas are arranged alphabetically—not an unreasonable default order if you look up specific cities, but as presented, the data doesn't prompt many interesting questions. It's not clear why Abilene, Alice, Amarillo, and Austin all seem to have similar numbers, for instance; it may just be chance.

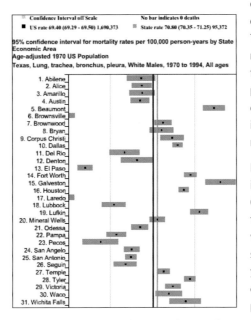

FIGURE 6-7 / From *http://cancer.gov/atlasplus/*, sorted alphabetically

But this web application lets you reorder the data into numerically descending order, as in Figure 6-8. Suddenly the graph becomes much more interesting. Galveston is ranked first—why is that, when its neighbor, Houston, is further down the scale? What's special about Galveston? (Okay, you needed to know something about Texas geography to ask these questions, but you get my point.) Likewise, why the difference between neighbors Dallas and Fort Worth? And apparently, the Mexico-bordering southern cities of El Paso, Brownsville, and Laredo have less lung cancer than the rest of Texas; why might that be?

People who can interact with data graphics this way have more opportunities to learn from the graphic. Sorting and rearranging puts different data points next to each other, thus letting users make different kinds of comparisons—it's far easier to compare neighbors than widely scattered points. And users tend to zero in on the extreme ends of scales, as I did in this example.

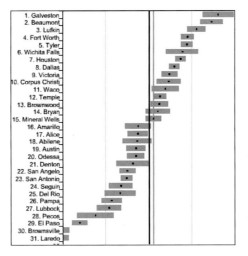

FIGURE 6-8 / The same chart, sorted numerically

How else can you apply this concept? The pattern **Sortable Table** talks about one obvious way: when you have a many-columned table, users might want to sort the rows according to their choice of column. This pattern is pretty common.

(Many table implementations also permit rearrangement of the columns themselves, by dragging.) Trees can have their children reordered. Diagrams and connected graphs might allow spatial repositioning of their elements, while retaining their connectivity. Use your imagination!

Consider these methods of sorting and rearranging:

- Alphabetically
- Numerically
- By date or time
- By physical location
- By category or tag
- Popularity—heavily versus lightly used
- User-designed arrangement
- Completely random (you never know what you might see)

For a subtle example, look at Figure 6-9. Bar charts that show multiple data values on each bar ("stacked" bar charts) might also be amenable to rearranging—the bar segments nearest the baseline are the easiest to evaluate and compare, so you might want to let users determine which variable is next to the baseline.

The light blue variable in this example might be the same height from bar to bar. Does it vary, and how? Which light blue bars are the tallest? You really can't tell until you move that data series to the baseline—that transformation lines up the bases of all blue rectangles. Now a visual comparison is easy: light-blue bars 6 and 12 are the tallest, and the variation seems loosely correlated to the overall bar heights.

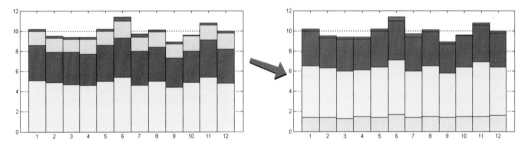

FIGURE 6-9 / Rearrangement of a stacked bar chart

SEARCHING AND FILTERING: SHOW ME ONLY WHAT I NEED TO KNOW.

Sometimes you don't want to see an entire dataset at once. You might start with the whole thing, and then narrow it down to what you need—filtering. Or, you might build up a subset of the data via searching or querying. Most users won't even distinguish between filtering and querying (though there's a big difference from, say, a database's point of view). Whatever term you use, the user's intent is the same: to zero in on whatever part of the data is of interest, and get rid of the rest.

The simplest filtering and querying techniques offer users a choice of which aspects of the data to view. Checkboxes and other one-click controls turn parts of the interactive graphic on and off. A table might show some columns and not others, per the user's choice; a map might show only the points of interest (e.g., restaurants) that the user selects. The **Dynamic Queries** pattern, which can offer rich interaction, is a logical extension of simple filter controls like these.

Sometimes simply highlighting a subset of the data, rather than hiding or removing the rest, is sufficient. That way a user can see that subset in context with the rest of the data. Interactively, you can highlight with simple controls, as described earlier. The **Data Brushing** pattern describes a variation of data highlighting; data brushing highlights the same data in several data graphics at once.

Look at Figure 6-10. This interactive ski-trail map can show four categories of trails, coded by symbol, plus other features like ski lifts and base lodges. When everything is "turned on" at once, it's so crowded that it's hard to read anything! But users can click on the trail symbols, as shown, to turn the data "layers" on and off. The first screenshot shows no highlighted trails; the second switches on the trails rated black-diamond with a single click.

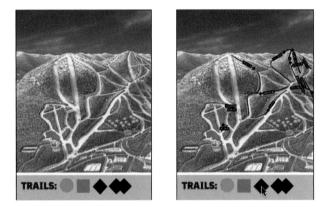

FIGURE 6-10 / From *http://www.sundayriver.com/trailmap.htm*

Searching mechanisms vary heavily from one type of graphic to another. A table or tree should permit textual searches, of course; a map should offer searches on addresses and other physical locations; numeric charts and plots might let users search for specific data values or ranges of values. What are your users interested in searching on?

When the search is done, and results obtained, you might set up the interface to see the results in context, on the graphic—you could scroll the table or map so that the searched-for item is in the middle of the viewport, for instance. Seeing the results in context with the rest of the data helps the user understand the results better. The Jump to Item pattern is a common way to search and scroll in one step.

The best filtering and querying interfaces are:

Highly interactive

They respond as quickly as possible to the user's searching and filtering. Implementing this admittedly isn't easy for web applications and other interfaces that need to get data from across a network.

Iterative

They let a user refine the search, query, or filter until she gets the desired results. They also might combine these operations: a user might do a search, get a screenful of results, and then filter those results down to what she wants.

Contextual

They show results in context with surrounding data to make it easier for a user to understand where they are in a data space. This is also true for other kinds of searches; the best web search engines show a keyword embedded in a sentence, or an image embedded in its web page.

THE ACTUAL DATA: WHAT ARE THE SPECIFIC DATA VALUES?

Several common techniques help a viewer get specific values out of an information graphic. Know your audience—if they're only interested in getting a qualitative sense of the data, then there's no need for you to spend large amounts of time or pixels labeling every little thing. But some actual numbers or text usually are necessary.

Since these techniques all involve text, don't forget the graphic design principles that make text look good: readable fonts, appropriate font size (not too big, not too small), proper visual separation between unrelated text items, alignment of related items, no heavy-bordered boxes, and no unnecessary obscuring of data.

Labels

Many information graphics put labels directly on the graphic, such as town names on a map. Labels also can identify the values of symbols on a scatter plot, bars on a bar graph, and other things that might normally force the user to depend on axes or legends. Labels are easier to use. They communicate data values precisely and unambiguously (when placed correctly), and they're located in or beside the data point of interest—no going back and forth between the data point and a legend. The downside is that they clutter up a graphic when overused, so be careful.

Legends

When you use color, texture, linestyle, symbol, or size on an information graphic to represent values (or categories or value ranges), the legend shows the user what represents what. You should place the legend on the same page as the graphic itself so the user's eyes don't need to travel far between the data and the legend.

Whenever position represents data, as it does on plots and maps (but not on most diagrams), then these techniques tell the user what values those positions represent. They are reference lines or curves on which reference values are marked. The user has to draw an imaginary line from the point of interest to the axis, and maybe interpolate to find the right number. This situation is more of a burden on the user than direct labeling. But labeling clutters things when the data is dense, and many users don't need to derive precise values from graphics; they just want a more general sense of the values involved. For those situations, axes are appropriate.

Datatips

This chapter describes the **Datatips** pattern. Datatips, which are tooltips that show data values when the user hovers over a point of interest, have the physical proximity advantages of labels without the clutter. They work only in interactive graphics, though.

Data brushing

A technique called "data brushing" lets users select a subset of the data in the information graphic and see how that data fits into other contexts. You usually use it with two or more information graphics; for instance, selecting some outliers in a scatter plot highlights those same data points in a table showing the same data. For more information, see the **Data Brushing** pattern in this chapter.

THE PATTERNS

Because this book deals with interactive software, most of these patterns describe ways to interact with the data—moving through it; sorting, selecting, inserting or changing items; and probing for specific values or sets of values. A few deal only with static graphics: information designers have known **Alternating Row Colors**, **Multi-Y Graph**, and **Small Multiples** for a while now, but they translate well to the world of software.

And don't forget the patterns elsewhere in this book. From Chapter 2, recall **Alternative Views** and **Extras On Demand**, both of which can help you structure an interactive graphic. Chapter 3 offers **Annotated Scrollbar** and **Animated Transition**, which help users stay oriented within large and complex data spaces.

The first group of patterns can apply to most varieties of interactive graphics, regardless of the data's underlying structure. (Some are harder to learn and use than others, so don't throw them at every data graphic you create—**Data Brushing** and **Local Zooming**, in particular, are "power tools," best for sophisticated computer users.)

54 Overview Plus Detail   **57** Data Brushing

55 Datatips   **58** Local Zooming

56 Dynamic Queries

Next is a set of patterns for tables and lists.

59 Row Striping   **61** Jump to Item

60 Sortable Table   **62** New-Item Row

Cascading Lists and **Tree Table** are useful for hierarchically structured data. If you use a tree view (also known as an outline view), consider these too.

63 Cascading Lists   **64** Tree Table

The remaining patterns describe ways to construct data graphics for multidimensional data—data that has many attributes or variables.

65 Multi-Y Graph   **67** Treemap

66 Small Multiples

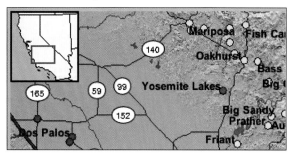

FIGURE 6-11 / From *http://wildfire.usgs.gov*

what

Place an overview of the graphic next to a zoomed "detail view." As the user drags a viewport around the overview, show that part of the graphic in the detail view.

use when

You show a data set drawn as a large information graphic—especially an image or a map. You want users to stay oriented with respect to the "big picture," but you also want them to zoom down into the fine details. Users will browse through the data, inspect small areas, or search for points of interest. High-level overviews are necessary for finding those points of interest, but users don't need to see all available detail for all data points at once—zooming in on a small piece is sufficient for getting fine detail.

why

It's an age-old way of dealing with complexity: present a high-level view of what's going on, and let the users zoom from that view into the details as they need to, keeping both levels visible on the same page for quick iteration.

Edward Tufte uses the terms "micro and macro readings" to describe a similar concept for printed maps, diagrams, and other static information graphics. The user has the large structure in front of them at all times, while being able to peer into the small details at will: "the pace of visualization is condensed, slowed, and personalized." Similarly, users of Overview Plus Detail can scroll methodically through the content, jump around, compare, contrast, move quickly, or move slowly.

Finally, the overview can serve as a "You are here" sign. A user can tell at a glance where they are in the context of the whole data set by looking for the viewport on the overview.

how

Show an overview of the data set at all times. It can be an inset panel, as in the example at the top of the pattern. It also could be a panel beside the detail view, or even another window, in the case of a multiwindow application like Photoshop (see the examples in Figure 6-12).

On that overview, place a viewport. They're usually red boxes, by convention, but they don't have to be—they just need to be visible at a glance, so consider the other colors used in the overview panel. If the graphic typically is dark, make it light; if the graphic is light, make it dark. Make the viewport draggable with the pointer, so users can grab it and slide it around the overview.

The detail view shows a magnified "projection" of what's inside the viewport. The two should be synchronized. If the viewport moves, the detail view changes accordingly; if the viewport is made smaller, the magnification should increase. Likewise, if the detail view has scrollbars or some other panning capability, the viewport should move along with it. The response of one to the other should be immediate, within a tenth of a second (the standard response time for direct manipulation).

examples

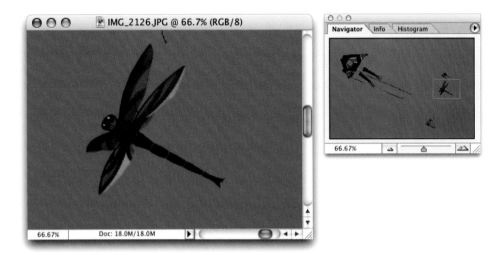

FIGURE 6-12 / Photoshop places the image canvas (the "detail view") on the left, and the overview on the right. The Navigator window shows a view of the whole image, with a red box showing the size and scroll position of the image's canvas window.

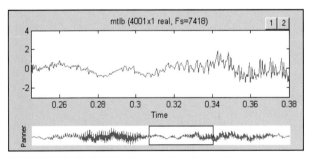

FIGURE 6-13 / In the signal-processing software shown here, the overview panel is on the bottom of the window. The "You Are Here" aspect is particularly important for users who deal with long, complex signals.

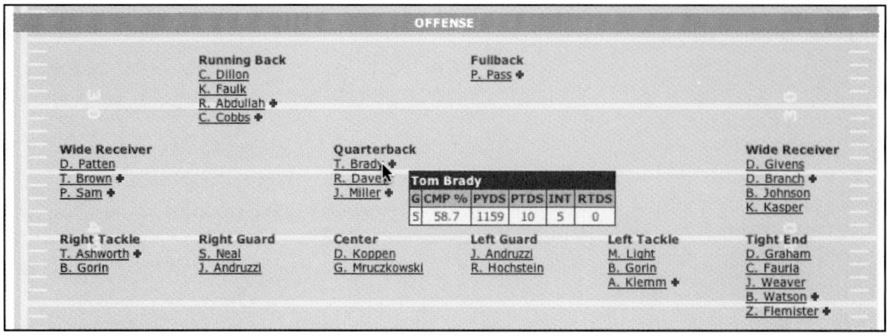

FIGURE 6-14 / From *http://nfl.com/teams/depthcharts/NE*

what

As the mouse rolls over a point of interest on the graphic, put the data values for that point into a tooltip or some other floating window.

use when

You show an overview of a data set, in almost any form. There's more data "hidden behind" specific points on that graphic, such as the names of streets on a map, the values of bars in a bar chart, or data about players on a football team depth chart. The user can "point at" places of interest with a mouse cursor or a touch screen.

why

Looking at specific data values is a common task in data-rich graphics. Users will want the overview, but they also might look for particular facts that aren't present in the overview. Datatips let you present small, targeted chunks of context-dependent data. They put that data right where the user's attention is focused: the mouse pointer. If the overview is reasonably well organized, users find it easy to look up what they need—and you don't need to put it all on the graphic.

Also, some people might just be curious—what else is here? What can I find out? Datatips offer an easy, rewarding form of interactivity. They're quick (no page loading!), they're lightweight, and they offer intriguing little glimpses into an otherwise invisible data set.

If you find yourself trying to use a datatip to show an enlargement of the data that it hovers over, rather than extra data, consider using the **Local Zooming** pattern instead.

how

Use a tooltip-like window to show the data associated with that point. It doesn't technically have to be a "tooltip"—all that matters is that it appears where the pointer is, it's layered atop the graphic, and it's temporary. Users will get the idea pretty quickly.

Inside that window, format the data as appropriate. Denser is usually better, since a tooltip window is expected to be small; don't let the window get so large that it obscures too much of the graphic while it's visible. And place it well. If there's a way to programmatically position it so that it covers as little content as possible (again, see the NFL graphic above), try that.

You might even want to format the datatip differently, depending on the situation. An interactive map might let the user toggle between seeing place names and seeing latitude/longitude coordinates, for example. If you have a few data sets plotted as separate lines on one graph, the datatips might be labeled differently for each line, or have different kinds of data in them.

An alternative way of dynamically showing hidden data is to reserve some panel on or next to the graphic as a static data window. As the user rolls over various points on the graphic, data associated with those points appear in the data window. It's the same idea, but it uses a reserved space rather than a temporary datatip. The user has to shift her attention from the pointer to that panel, but you never have a problem with the rest of the graphic being hidden. Furthermore, if that data window can retain its data, the user can view it while doing something else with the mouse.

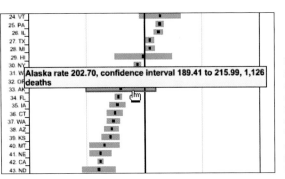

FIGURE 6-15 / A small snippet from a large graph. Each bar represents a state; the location of the bar's center along the X axis indicates the number of cancer-related deaths per state, and the width of each bar shows that figure's confidence interval (ever taken a statistics class?). When the mouse pointer hovers over any bar, a datatip appears. The actual numbers are shown, so the user doesn't have to go scrolling down a long graph to find those numbers.

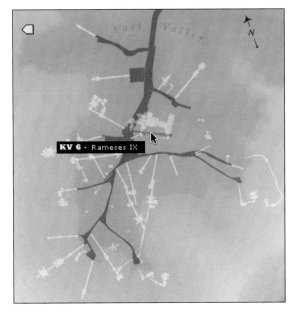

FIGURE 6-16 / You can use datatips to selectively label maps wherever the user puts the mouse, as in this web application from *http://thebanmappingproject.org*.

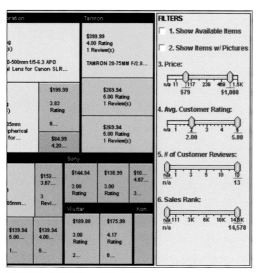

FIGURE 6-17 / From *http://hivegroup.com*

what

Provide ways to filter the data set immediately and interactively. Employ easy-to-use standard controls, such as sliders and checkboxes, to define which parts of the data set get shown. As soon as the user adjusts those controls, the results appear on the data display.

use when

You show the user a large, multivariate data set, of any shape, with any presentation. Users need to filter out some of the data to accomplish any of several objectives—to get rid of irrelevant parts of the data set, to see which data points meet certain criteria, to understand relationships among the various data attributes, or simply to explore the data set and see what's there.

The data set itself has a fixed and predictable set of attributes (or parameters, variables, dimensions, whatever term you prefer) that interest users. They usually are numeric and range-bounded; they also might be sortable strings, dates, categories, or enumerations (sets of numbers representing nonnumeric values). Or they might be visible areas of data on the information display itself, which can be selected interactively.

why

First, dynamic queries are easy to learn. No complicated query language is necessary at the user's end; well-understood controls express common-sense Boolean expressions like "price > $70 AND price < $100". They lack the full expressive power of a query language—only simple queries are possible without making the UI too complicated. But in most cases, it's enough. That's a judgment call you have to make.

Second, the immediate feedback encourages open-ended exploration of the data set. As the user moves a slider thumb, for instance, she sees the visible data contract or expand. As she adds and removes different subsets of the data, she sees where they go and how they change the display. She can concoct long and complex query expressions incrementally, by tweaking this control, then that one, and then another. Thus, a continuous and interactive "question-and-answer session" is carried on between the user and the data. The immediate feedback shortens the iteration loop so that exploration is fun, and a state of flow is possible. (See Chapter 1, **Incremental Construction**.)

Third—and this is a little more subtle—the presence of labeled dynamic-query controls clarifies what the queryable attributes are in the first place. If one of the data attributes is a number that ranges from 0 to 100, for instance, the user learns that just by seeing a slider that has 0 at one end and 100 at the other end.

how

The best way to design a dynamic query depends on your data display, the kinds of queries you think should be made, and your toolkit's capabilities. As mentioned, most programs map data attributes to ordinary controls that live next to the data display. This scenario allows querying on many variables at once, not just those encoded by spatial features on the display. Plus, most people know how to use sliders and buttons.

Other programs afford interactive selection directly on the information display. Usually the user draws a box around a region of interest, and the data in that region is removed (or retained while the rest of the data is removed). This is direct manipulation at its most direct, but it has the disadvantage of being tied to the spatial rendering of the data. If you can't draw a box around it—or otherwise select points of interest—you can't query on it! See the **Data Brushing** pattern for the pros and cons of a similar technique.

Back to controls, then. Picking controls for dynamic queries resembles the act of picking controls for any kind of form: the choices arise from the data type, the kind of query to be made, and the available controls. Some common choices include:

- Sliders to specify a single number within a range.

- Double sliders or slider pairs to specify a subset of a range: "show data points that are greater than this number, but less than this other number."

- Radio buttons or dropdown (combo) boxes to pick one value out of several possible values. You also might use them to pick entire variables or data sets. In either case, "All" frequently is used as an additional metavalue.

- Checkboxes to pick an arbitrary subset of values or boolean variables.

- Text fields to type in single values, perhaps to be used in a **Fill-in-the-Blank** context (see Chapter 7, *Getting Input From Users*). Remember that text fields leave more room for errors and typos than do sliders and buttons.

examples

The example at the top of this pattern shows a set of six filters for a treemap (see the **Treemap** pattern in this chapter). The checkboxes, filters 1 and 2, screen out entire swaths of data with two very simple canned queries: is this item available, and does it have a picture?

The remaining filters use double sliders. Each has two independently movable slider "thumbs" that let a user define a range. The Price slider sets a range of about $80 to about $1000, and as the user moves either end of the range, the whole treemap shifts and changes to reflect the new price range. The same is true for the other sliders.

That example resembles several other implementations, such as the following examples.

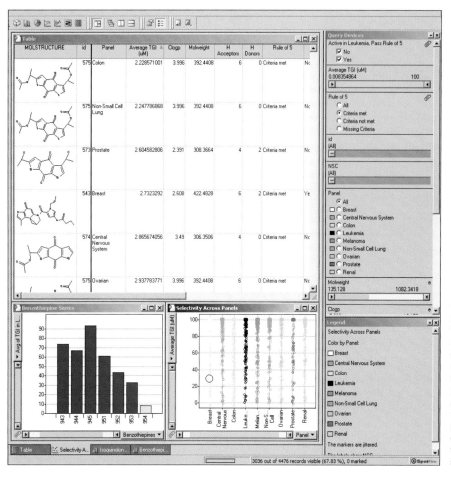

FIGURE 6-18 / Spotfire is a visualization program often used by biotechnology researchers. The "Query Devices" panel is on the right of the window, like the previous example. It too uses checkboxes and double sliders (see the two-toned yellow slider near the middle), plus radio buttons and single sliders. At least eight variables are represented in this dynamic query panel. As the user manipulates the controls, the data in all three of the tables and graphs update themselves.

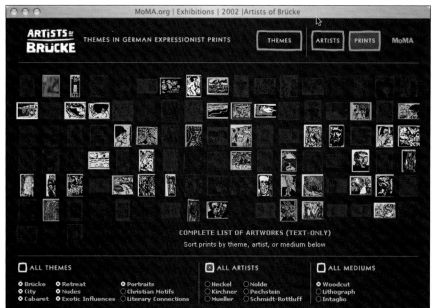

FIGURE 6-19 / This web application lets the user browse through a large set of German expressionist prints. Using the buttons at the bottom of the window, a user can filter out all prints except the woodcuts, for example, or show only portraits by Heckel and Mueller. (The square checkboxes reading "All Themes," etc. unset the round multiple-selection buttons below them—the ones that look like radio buttons, but aren't.)

This interface is powerful enough for an enterprising user to discern themes and relationships among the prints by narrowing down the set in various ways. See *http://www.moma.org/exhibitions/2002/brucke*.

SHOWING COMPLEX DATA

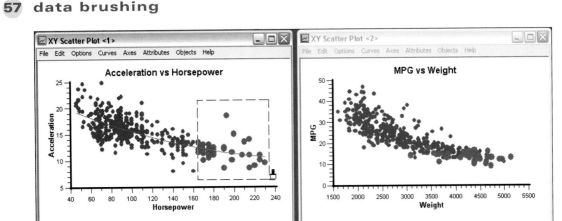

FIGURE 6-20 / BBN Cornerstone

---

what

Let the user select data items in one view; show the same data selected simultaneously in another view.

use when

You show two or more information graphics at a time. You might have two line plots and a scatter plot, a scatter plot and a table, a diagram and a tree, or a map and a table, whatever—as long as each graphic shows the same data set.

why

Data brushing offers a very rich form of interactive data exploration. First, the user can select data points by using an information graphic itself as a "selector." Sometimes it's easier to find points of interest visually than by less direct means, like **Dynamic Queries**—you can see and manipulate outliers on a plot immediately, for instance, while figuring out how to define them numerically could take a few seconds, or longer. "Do I want all points where X > 200 and Y > 5.6? I can't tell; just let me draw a box around that group of points."

Second, by seeing the selected or "brushed" data points simultaneously in the other graphic(s), the user can observe those points in at least one other graphical context. That context can be invaluable. To use the outlier example again, the user might want to know where those outliers are in a different data space, indexed by different variables—and by learning that, he might gain immediate insight into the phenomenon that produced the data.

A larger principle here is *coordinated* or *linked views*. Multiple views on the same data can be linked or synchronized so that certain manipulations—like zooming, panning, and selection—done to one view are shown in the others simultaneously. Coordination reinforces the idea that the views are simply different perspectives on the same data. Again, the user focuses on the same data in different contexts, which can lead to insight.

how

First, how will users select or "brush" the data? It's the same problem you'd have with any selectable collection of objects: users might want one object

---

or several, contiguous or separate, selected all at once or incrementally. Consider these ideas:

- Drawing a rubber band box around the data points (this is very common)

- Single-selection by clicking with the mouse

- Selecting a range (if that makes sense) by shift-clicking, as one can often do with lists

- Adding and subtracting points by control-clicking, also like lists

- Drawing an arbitrary "lasso" shape around the data points

- Inverting the selection via a menu item, button, or key

If you go exclusively with a rubber-band box, consider leaving the box onscreen after the selection gesture. Some systems, like Cornerstone (Figures 6-20 and 6-21), permit interactive resizing of the brushing box. Actually, the user can benefit from any method of interactively expanding or reduc-

ing the brushed set of points because he can see the newly-brushed points "light up" immediately in the other views, which creates more possibility for insight.

As you can see, it's important that the other views react immediately to data brushing. Make sure that the system can handle a fast turnaround.

If the brushed data points appear with the same visual characteristics in all the data views, including the graphic where the brushing occurs, then the user can more easily find and recognize them as brushed. They also form a single perceptual layer (see the "Preattentive Variables" section in this chapter's introduction). Color hue is the preattentive variable most frequently used for brushing, probably because you can see a bright color so easily when your attention is focused elsewhere.

examples

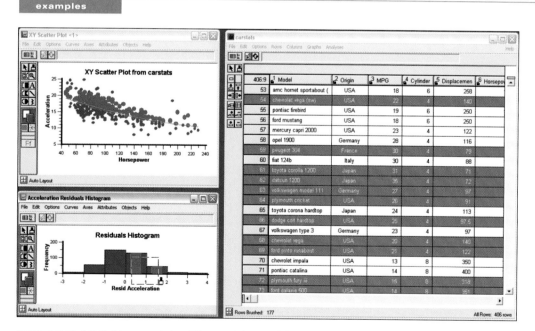

FIGURE 6-21 / Both this screenshot and the one at the top of this pattern are taken from Cornerstone, a statistics and graphing package. The three windows here represent a scatter plot, a histogram of the residuals of one of the plotted variables, and a table of the raw data. All views afford brushing; you can see the brushing box around two of the histogram's columns. Both plots show the brushed data in red, while the table shows it in gray. If you "brushed" a car model in the table, you would see the dot representing that model appear red in the top plot, plus a red strip in the histogram.

SHOWING COMPLEX DATA

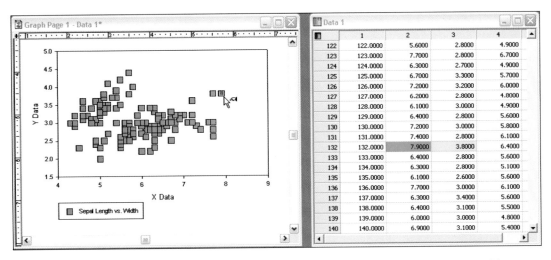

FIGURE 6-22 / Sigmaplot permits the selection of single points. Notice that both this and Cornerstone use special mouse cursors to indicate the brushing mode.

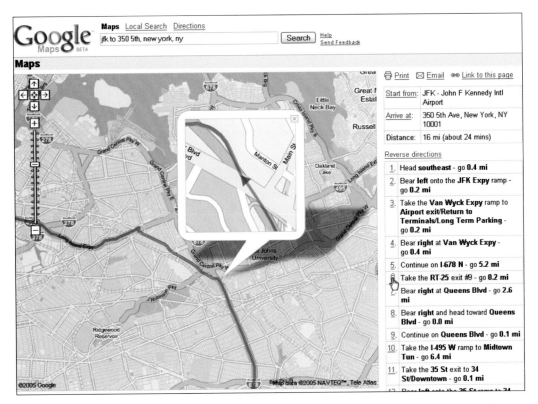

FIGURE 6-23 / Google Maps. It's a bit of a stretch to call this technique "data brushing," but the concept is similar: selection in one view causes the other view to reveal something about that data simultaneously. When the user clicks on a waypoint in the directions, a closeup of that waypoint is magnified on the map. (Incidentally, this is a nice use of **Local Zooming**, which brings us to the next pattern...)

58 local zooming

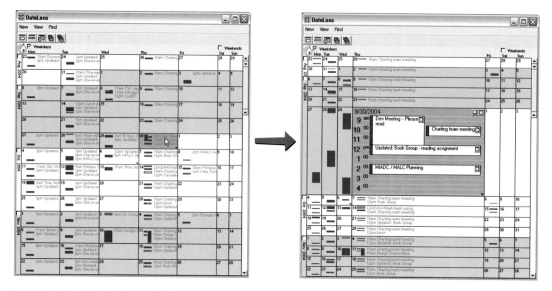

FIGURE 6-24 / The DateLens calendar

what

Show all the data in a single dense page, with small-scale data items. Wherever the mouse goes, distort the page to make those data items large and readable.

use when

You show a large data set using any organizational form—plots, maps, networks, and even tables—on either a large or a small screen. The user can "point at" places of interest with a mouse cursor or touchscreen.

Users will browse through the data or search for points of interest within that organizational structure (e.g., finding a date in a calendar). High-level overviews are necessary for finding those points of interest, but users don't need to see all available detail for all data points at once—zooming in is sufficient for getting fine detail.

Some forms of local zooming, especially fisheye lenses, are appropriate only if your users are willing to learn a new interaction technique to gain

proficiency with a particular application. Using local zooming requires patience. Programmers in particular seem to learn them well.

why

Ordinary zooming works well for most high-density information graphics, but it takes away context: a fully zoomed view no longer shows an overview of the whole dataset. Local zooming focuses on local detail while retaining context. The user remains in the same conceptual space.

One possible cost of local zooming, however, is distortion of that conceptual space. Notice how the introduction of a fisheye—a local zoom that maintains topological continuity between the zoomed area and the rest of the view—changes the landscape in Figure 6-24. Suddenly the overview doesn't look the way it did before: landmarks have moved and spatial relationships have changed ("it used to be halfway down the right side of the screen, but it's not there anymore").

Other kinds of local zooming don't introduce distortion, but hide parts of the overview. With a virtual magnifying glass, for instance, the user can see the zoomed area and part of the larger context, but not what's hidden by the magnifying glass "frame."

The **Overview Plus Detail** pattern is a viable alternative to local zooming. It too offers both detail (focus) and a full overview (context) in the same page, but it separates the two levels of scale into two side-by-side views, rather than integrating them into one distorted view. If local zooming is too difficult to implement, or too hard for users to interact with, fall back to Overview Plus Detail.

The **Datatips** pattern is another viable alternative. Again, you get both overview and detail, but the information shown isn't really a "zoom" as much as a description of the data at that point. A Datatip is an ephemeral item layered over the top of the graphic, whereas Local Zooming can be an integral part of the graphic, and as such you can print and screen-capture it.

how

Fill all the available space with the whole data set, drawn very small. Stretch it to fill the window dynamically (see **Liquid Layout**). Remove detail as necessary. If text is an important structural element, use tiny fonts where you can; if the text still won't fit, use abstract visual representations like solid rectangles or lines that approximate text.

Offer a local zoom mode. When the user turns it on and moves the pointer around, enlarge the small area directly under the pointer.

What the enlargement actually looks like depends on the kind of information graphic you use—it doesn't have to be literal, like a magnifying glass on a page. The DateLens, in Figure 6-24, uses both horizontal and vertical enlargement and compression. But the TableLens, shown in Figure 6-25, uses

only a vertical enlargement and compression because the data points of interest are whole rows, not a single cell in a row. A map or image, however, need to control both directions tightly in order to preserve its scale. In other words, don't stretch or squish a map. It's harder to read that way.

Local zoom lenses can be finicky to "drive" because the user might aim at very tiny hit targets. They don't look tiny—they're magnified under the lens!—but the user actually moves the pointer through the overview space, not the zoomed space. A small motion becomes a big jump. So when the data points are discrete, like table cells or network nodes, you might consider using **Magnetism** (Chapter 8) to aid the user in moving from one focal point to another.

Fisheye views, in particular, are the subject of much academic research in the visualization field. Fisheye views have a lot of promise, but we don't know much about how to make them most effective in production UIs. We're starting to learn that they don't work well for inexperienced computer users, for instance.

examples

The DateLens, shown at the top of the pattern, is a calendar application that works on both the desktop and the PocketPC. It shows an overview of your calendar—each row is a week—with blue blocks where your appointments are. For details, click on a cell. That cell then expands, using an **Animated Transition** (Chapter 3), to show the day's schedule. In this design, the entire graphic compresses to allow room for the focused day, except for the row and the column containing that cell. (That actually provides useful information about the week's schedule, and about other weeks' Thursday appointments.)

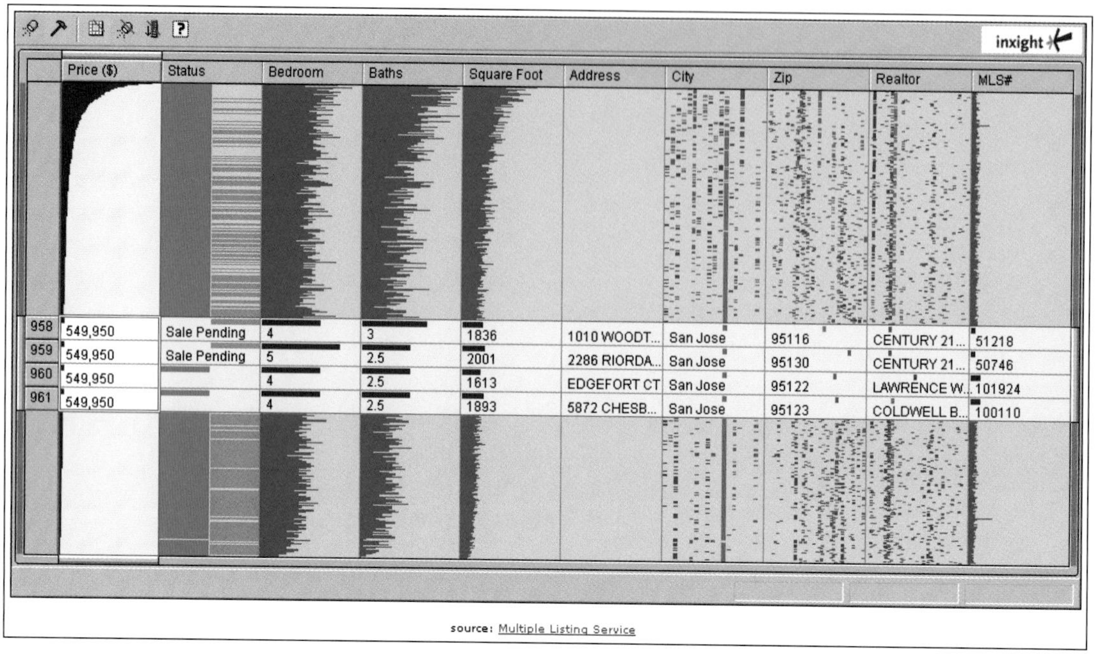

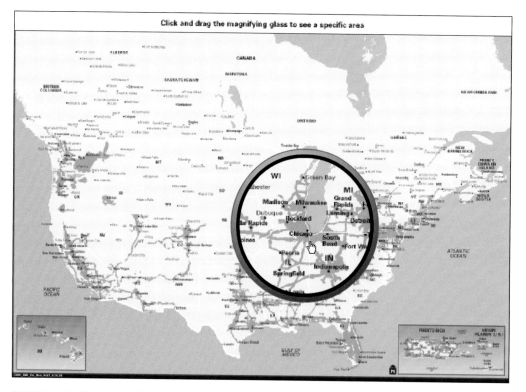

inxight
Price ($)
Status
Bedroom
Baths
Square Foot
Address
City
Zip
Realtor
MLS#
958 549,950 Sale Pending 4 3 1836 1010 WOODT... San Jose 95116 CENTURY 21... 51218
959 549,950 Sale Pending 5 2.5 2001 2286 RIORDA... San Jose 95130 CENTURY 21... 50746
960 549,950 4 2.5 1613 EDGEFORT CT San Jose 95122 LAWRENCE W... 101924
961 549,950 4 2.5 1893 5872 CHESB... San Jose 95123 COLDWELL B... 100110
source: Multiple Listing Service

FIGURE 6-25 / The Inxight TableLens permits the user to open arbitrary numbers of rows and move that "window" up and down the table. This screenshot shows four magnified rows. Note that the only enlargement here is in the vertical direction.

Click and drag the magnifying glass to see a specific area
CANADA
ONTARIO
WI
Green Bay
MI
Madison
Milwaukee
Grand Rapids
Lansing
Dubuque
Rockford
Detroit
Chicago
South Bend
Fort Wa
Peoria
IL
IN
Indianapolis
Springfield
ATLANTIC OCEAN
PACIFIC OCEAN
GULF OF MEXICO

FIGURE 6-26 / A more lens-like example comes to us courtesy of AT&T. This web page shows a low-resolution map of the country. As the user moves the mouse, a literal lens moves with it, magnifying the map to show detailed cellular coverage in that area. See *http://attwireless.com/media/swf/maps/gsmawonnet-nat.swf*.

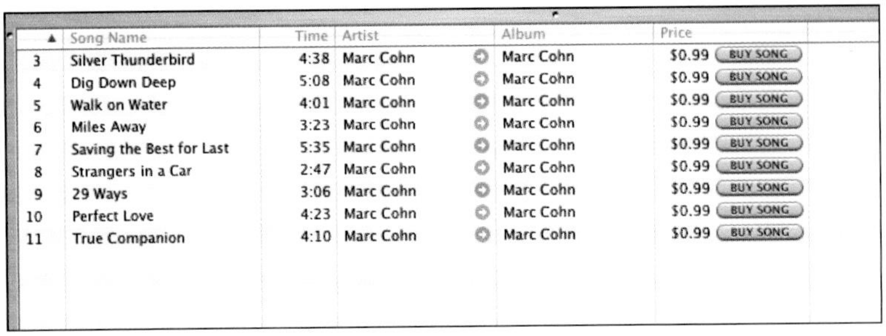

FIGURE 6-27 / iTunes

---

what

Use two similar shades to alternately color the backgrounds of the table rows.

use when

You use a table, but the table's rows are difficult to separate visually, especially when there are many columns (or multiple lines to a row).

why

Blocks of gentle color define and delineate the information contained inside them, even when you can't use whitespace to separate the data into "chunks." Cartographers and graphic designers have known this for ages. (Remember that colored backgrounds are also effective in defining **Titled Sections**.)

When someone looks at a table with a single background color, they will tend to see the columns as coherent objects, due to proximity—the table entries in a column are closer to one another than they are to the other entries in their rows. But you want the viewer to read the table "rowwise" as well as columnwise. By coloring adjacent rows differently, you turn the rows into coherent visual objects, too. (This act takes advantage of the Gestalt principles of continuity and closure; see Chapter 4.)

Specifically, row striping helps a user:

- Follow a row from left to right and back again, without confusing the rows
- See the "footprint" of the table itself, separately from its containing page

how

Pick a pair of quiet, low-saturation colors that are similar in value, but not identical. (In other words, one needs to be a wee bit darker than the other.) Good choices are light blue and white, beige and white, or two similar shades of gray—assuming the text on top of them is dark, anyway. Generally, one of the colors is your page's background color.

Alternate the color from row to row. If the rows are thin, you also could experiment with grouping the rows: the first three are white, the next three are blue, etc.

This pattern virtually eliminates the need for horizontal lines between the rows (though you could use lines, if they are very thin and inconspicuous). If your columns are aligned with one another, you don't need vertical lines or a heavy border around the table—the viewer's sense of visual closure kicks in, and the row colors define the edges of the table for you.

Here are the top women finishers in the 2004 Boston Marathon.

1	Catherine Ndereba	31	Kenya	2:24:27
2	Elfenesh Alemu	28	Ethiopia	2:24:43
3	Olivera Jevtic	26	Serbia and Montenegro	2:27:34
4	Jelena Prokopcuka	27	Latvia	2:30:16
5	Nuta Olaru	33	Romania	2:30:44
6	Lyubov Denisova	32	Russian Federation	2:31:17
7	Malgorzata Sobanska	34	Poland	2:32:23
8	Victoria Klimina	28	Russian Federation	2:33:20
9	Ramilia Burangulova	42	Russian Federation	2:34:08
10	Ai Yamamoto	25	Japan	2:34:32
11	Rika Tabashi	22	Japan	2:41:41
12	Jessica Rodriguez Galvan	27	Mexico	2:50:57
13	Andrea Niggemeier	34	Germany	2:50:59
14	Greta Varchi	31	Italy	2:54:15
15	Yumiko Une	32	Japan	2:54:59
16	Julie S. Spencer	27	Baraboo, WI	2:56:39
17	Angela M. Batsford	23	Canada	2:57:06
18	Mary Ann Protz	47	St. Petersburg, FL	2:57:58
19	Kim A. Donaldson	42	St. Petersburg, FL	2:58:15
20	Lee Di Pietro	46	Ruxton, MD	2:58:59
21	Tracy Fischer	35	Jamul, CA	2:59:36
22	Stephanie Hodge	38	Canada	3:00:00
23	Simonetta Piergentili	39	Woburn, MA	3:01:00

FIGURE 6-28 / The women's top finishers in the 2004 Boston marathon, taken from *http://boston.com*

Here are the top women finishers in the 2004 Boston Marathon.

1	Catherine Ndereba	31	Kenya	2:24:27
2	Elfenesh Alemu	28	Ethiopia	2:24:43
3	Olivera Jevtic	26	Serbia and Montenegro	2:27:34
4	Jelena Prokopcuka	27	Latvia	2:30:16
5	Nuta Olaru	33	Romania	2:30:44
6	Lyubov Denisova	32	Russian Federation	2:31:17
7	Malgorzata Sobanska	34	Poland	2:32:23
8	Victoria Klimina	28	Russian Federation	2:33:20
9	Ramilia Burangulova	42	Russian Federation	2:34:08
10	Ai Yamamoto	25	Japan	2:34:32
11	Rika Tabashi	22	Japan	2:41:41
12	Jessica Rodriguez Galvan	27	Mexico	2:50:57
13	Andrea Niggemeier	34	Germany	2:50:59
14	Greta Varchi	31	Italy	2:54:15
15	Yumiko Une	32	Japan	2:54:59
16	Julie S. Spencer	27	Baraboo, WI	2:56:39
17	Angela M. Batsford	23	Canada	2:57:06
18	Mary Ann Protz	47	St. Petersburg, FL	2:57:58
19	Kim A. Donaldson	42	St. Petersburg, FL	2:58:15
20	Lee Di Pietro	46	Ruxton, MD	2:58:59
21	Tracy Fischer	35	Jamul, CA	2:59:36
22	Stephanie Hodge	38	Canada	3:00:00
23	Simonetta Piergentili	39	Woburn, MA	3:01:00

FIGURE 6-29 / But look what happens when the gray row backgrounds are stripped away. The columns suddenly become much stronger visually, and each row is harder to read from left to right. Some designers, however, find this design cleaner and more pleasing. There is no absolutely correct answer about whether to use **Row Striping**.

SHOWING COMPLEX DATA

60 sortable table

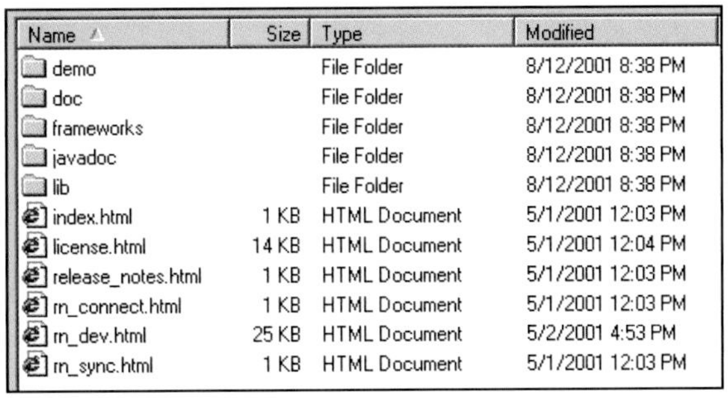

Name △	Size	Type	Modified
📁 demo		File Folder	8/12/2001 8:38 PM
📁 doc		File Folder	8/12/2001 8:38 PM
📁 frameworks		File Folder	8/12/2001 8:38 PM
📁 javadoc		File Folder	8/12/2001 8:38 PM
📁 lib		File Folder	8/12/2001 8:38 PM
index.html	1 KB	HTML Document	5/1/2001 12:03 PM
license.html	14 KB	HTML Document	5/1/2001 12:04 PM
release_notes.html	1 KB	HTML Document	5/1/2001 12:03 PM
rn_connect.html	1 KB	HTML Document	5/1/2001 12:03 PM
rn_dev.html	25 KB	HTML Document	5/2/2001 4:53 PM
rn_sync.html	1 KB	HTML Document	5/1/2001 12:03 PM

FIGURE 6-30 / Windows Explorer

what

Show the data in a table, and let the user sort the table rows according to the column values.

use when

The interface shows multivariate information that the user may want to explore, reorder, customize, search through for a single item, or simply understand on the basis of those different variables.

why

Giving the user the ability to change the sorting order of a table has powerful effects. First, it facilitates exploration. A user can now learn things from the data that he may never have seen otherwise—how many of this kind? what proportion of this to that? is there only one of these? what's first or last? Suddenly finding specific items becomes easier, too; a user need only remember one attribute of the item in question (e.g., its last-edited date), sort on that attribute, and look up the value he remembers.

Furthermore, if the sort order is retained from one invocation of the software to another, the user now can effectively customize the UI for his preferred usage patterns. Some users want the table sorted first to last; some last to first; and some by a variable no one else thinks is interesting. It's good to give users that kind of control.

Finally, the clickable-header concept is familiar to many users now, and they may expect it even if you don't provide it.

how

Choose the columns (i.e., the variables) carefully. What would a user want to sort by or search for? Conversely, what *doesn't* need to be shown in this table? What can be hidden until the user asks for more detail about a specific item?

The table headers should have some visual affordance that can be clicked on. Most have beveled, button-like borders, or blue underlined text. You should use up-or-down arrows to show whether the sort is in ascending or descending order. (The presence of an arrow shows which column was last sorted on—a fortuitous side effect!) Consider using rollover effects, like highlighting or cursor changes, on the headers to reinforce the impression of clickability.

Use a stable sort algorithm. What this means is that if a user sorts first by name, and then by date, the resulting list will show ordered groups of same-date items, each sorted by name within the group. In other words, the table retains the current sort order in the next sort, to the extent possible. Subtle, but very useful.

If your UI technology permits, users can reorder the columns by dragging and dropping. Java Swing has this feature.

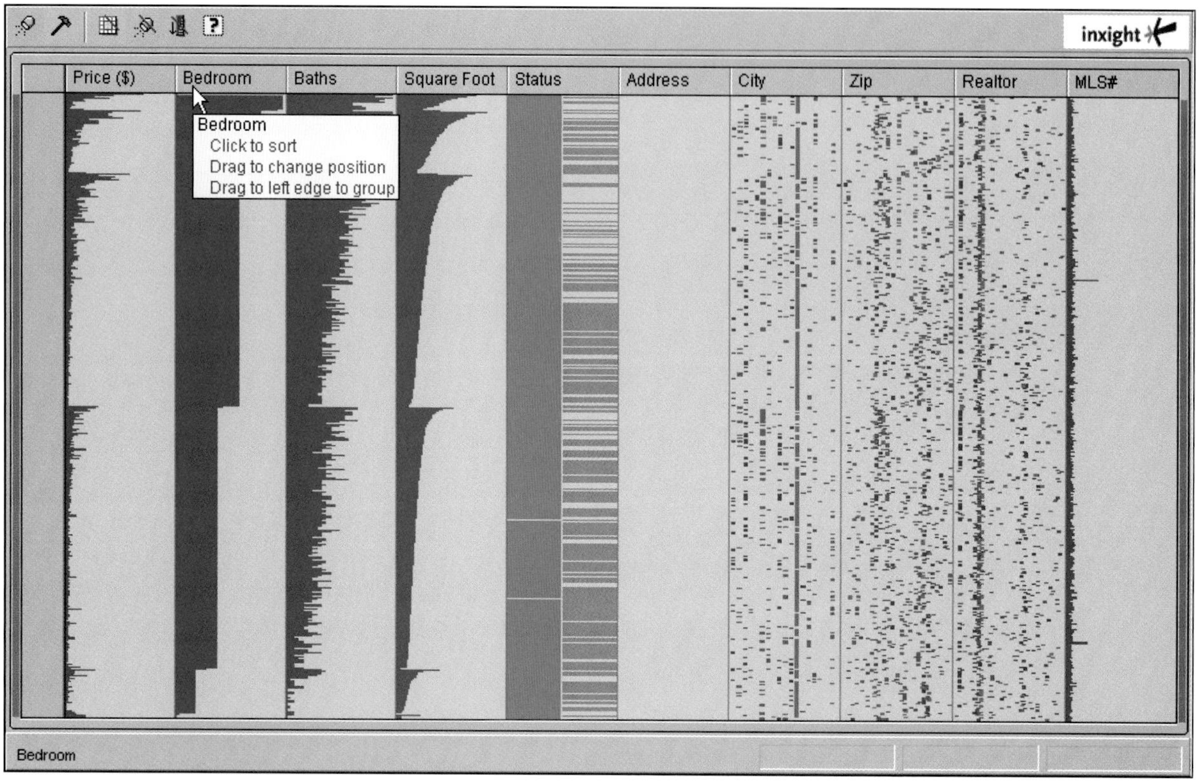

FIGURE 6-31 / Inxight's TableLens is a table whose rows compress down into tiny bars, the length of which represent the values of the table cells. (Users can click on specific rows to see ordinary-looking table rows, but that's not what I want to talk about here.) One of the wonderful things about this visualization is its ability to sort on any column—when the data is highly correlated, as in this example, the user can see that correlation easily.

The dataset shown here is houses for sale in Santa Clara County, California. In this screenshot, the user has clicked on the Bedroom column header, thus sorting on that variable: the more bedrooms, the longer the blue bar. Previously, the stable-sorted table was sorted on Square Foot (representing the size of the house), so you see a secondary "sawtooth" pattern there; it sorts all houses with four bedrooms, for instance, by size. The Baths variable almost mirrors the Square Foot attribute, and so does Price, which indicates a rough correlation. It makes intuitive sense—the more bedrooms a house has, the more bathrooms it's likely to have, and the bigger it's likely to be.

You can imagine other questions you can answer by this kind of interactive graphic. Does ZIP code correlate to price? How strong is the correlation between price and square footage? Do certain realtors work only in certain cities? How many realtors are there?

61 jump to item

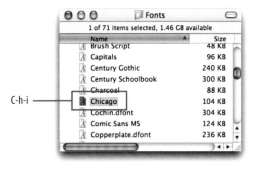

C-h-i

FIGURE 6-32 / From the Mac OS X Finder

what

When the user types the name of an item, jump straight to that item and select it.

use when

The interface uses a scrolling list, table, dropdown, combo box, or tree to present a long set of items. These items are usually sorted, either alphabetically or numerically. The user wants to select one particular item quickly and accurately, and preferably with the keyboard.

This pattern often is used in file finders, long lists of names, and dropdown boxes for state or country selection. You also can use it for numbers—such as years or dollar amounts—or even calendar time, like months or days of the week.

why

People aren't good at scanning down long lists of words or numbers. But computers are. Let them do what they're good at!

Another nice thing about this technique is that it lets the user keep her hands on the keyboard. As a user moves through a form or dialog box, she might find it nice to select from a list simply by typing the first few characters of the item she wants—the system then picks the item for her, and she can continue on to the next thing. No scrolling or clicking is necessary; the user's hand never has to move from the keyboard to the mouse.

how

When the user types the first letter or number of the item she's looking for, jump to the first item that matches what the user typed: automatically scroll the list so that the item is visible, and select it.

As the user types more characters in rapid succession, keep changing the selection to the first exact match for the whole user-typed string. If there is no match, stay put at the nearest match, and don't scroll back to the top of the list. You may want to beep at the user to tell her that there's no match— some applications do, some don't.

Martijn van Welie, in his patterns collection, defined a pattern very similar to this one entitled Continuous Filter.[1]

---

1 See http://www.welie.com/patterns/gui/index.html.

```
emacs@TIDWELLJ                                                    _ |□| x|
File  Edit  Options  Buffers  Tools  HTML  SGML  Help
    <td class="content">
      You are designing a UI that contains several discrete tasks or
      content elements:  forms, demos, games, articles, transactions,
      entire applications, etc.  All are reachable from one central
      page or window.  But you don't want to link all the
      sections or "spokes" to every other one, for several
      possible reasons:
      <ul>
          <li> space constraints,
          <li> absence of visual and/or cognitive clutter,
          <li> restricted workflow to force the completion (or explicit
               cancellation) of a task.
      </ul>
    </td>
  </tr>

  <tr>
    <td valign="top" align="right"> <h4> Why:</h4> </td>
    <td class="content">
      Primarily, you are using navigation to <b>structure
      the user experience</b> into something different from the
      free-form hypertext browsing offered by the Web.  You are asking
      the user to focus on <b>one section at a time,</b> then go back
      to the hub and navigate to another section.  This
      certainly reduces clutter on the "spoke" pages -- the user
      has less to look at, and less to think about.
      <p>
-1\**  hub-and-spoke.html        (HTML Isearch)--L54--56%-----------------
I-search: the
```

FIGURE 6-33 / A variant of Jump to Item is used by the GNU Emacs incremental-search facility. After the user enters i-search mode via Control-S, each typed character brings the user to the first instance of that cumulative string in the document. It doesn't matter that the original material wasn't sorted.

Once an occurrence of the string is found, the user can find subsequent ones by hitting Control-S repeatedly. In some ways, this incremental search is more convenient—and certainly faster—than typical desktop "Find" dialog boxes, which don't update continuously as you type the search string.

Furthermore, recent versions of Emacs highlight all other instances of that string in the document, in addition to scrolling to the first one. This gives the user lots of extra contextual information about the search they're performing: is it a common string, or not? Are they clustered together, or scattered?

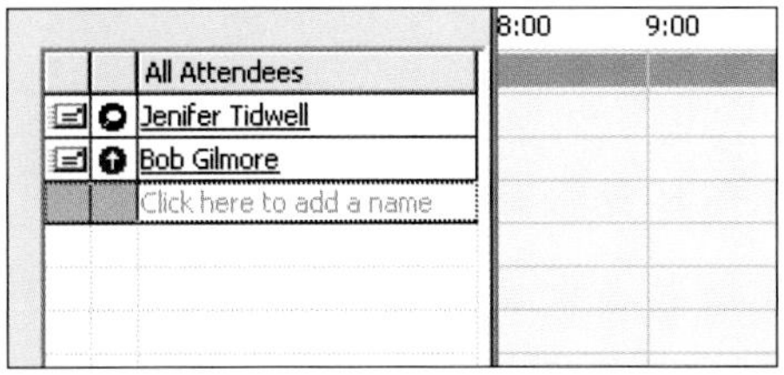

FIGURE 6-34 / An editable table in Outlook

what

Use the last row in the table to create a new item in place.

use when

The interface contains a table, list, tree view, or any other vertical presentation of a set of items (one item per row). At some point, the user needs to add new items to it. But you don't have a lot of room to spare on the UI for extra buttons or options, and you want to make item creation very efficient and easy for the user.

why

By letting the user type directly into the end of the table, you put the act of creation into the same place where the item will ultimately "live." It's conceptually more coherent than putting it in some other part of the UI. Also, it makes the interface more elegant when you don't have an entirely different UI for item creation. It uses less screen real estate, reduces the amount of navigation that needs to be done (thus eliminating a "jump" to another window), and is less work for your users.

how

Give the user an easy and obvious way to initiate a new object from the first empty table row. A single mouse click in that row might start editing, for instance, or the row might contain a "New Whatever" pushbutton, or it might contain a dummy item as shown in Figure 6-34.

At that point, the UI should create the new item and put it in that row. Each column in the table (if it's a multicolumn table) should then be editable, thus letting the user set up the values of that item. The cells could have text fields in them, dropdown lists, or whatever else is necessary to set the values quickly and precisely. As with any form-like user input, **Good Defaults** (Chapter 7) helps save the user work by prefilling those values; the user doesn't have to edit every column.

There are still some loose ends to clean up, though. What happens if the user abandons the new item before finishing? You can establish a valid item right from the beginning—if the user abandons the edits anytime, the item still exists until the user goes back and deletes it. Again, **Good Defaults** helps by prefilling valid values if there are multiple fields.

Depending on how it's implemented, this pattern can resemble **Input Prompt** (Chapter 7). In both cases, a dummy value is set up for the user to edit into a real value, and that dummy value is worded as a "prompt" that shows the user what to do.

FIGURE 6-35 / This cell phone contact list affords the addition of new entries via a New-Item Row. The last row is selectable in the same way other entries are selectable, and clicking the "Select" button below it leads to an editing screen that lets you enter data for the new entry.

63 cascading lists

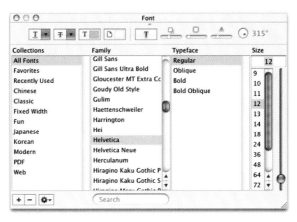

FIGURE 6-36 / Font dialog box from TextEdit

what

Express a hierarchy by showing selectable lists of the items in each hierarchy level. Selection of any item shows that item's children in the next list.

use when

Your data is tree-shaped. The hierarchy might be deep, and it might have many items on each level. A tree view (outline) would work, but the user would scroll up and down a lot to see all the items, and he wouldn't get a good overview of the items at higher levels in the hierarchy.

The hierarchy may be literal, such as a filesystem, or conceptual—this pattern often is used to let a user navigate and choose items within categories, or make a series of interdependent choices, as with the fonts in the example above.

why

By spreading the hierarchy out across several scrolled lists, you show more of it at once. It's that simple. Visibility is helpful when you deal with complex information structures. Also, laying the items out in lists organizes them nicely—a user can more easily keep track of where he is than he could

with an outline format, since the hierarchy levels are in nice, predictable fixed-position lists.

how

Put the first level of the hierarchy in the left-most list (which should use single-selection semantics). When the user selects an item in it, show that item's children in the next list to the right. Do the same with the child items in this second list, and show its selected item's children in the third list.

Once the user reaches items with no children—the "leaf" items, as opposed to "branches"—you might want to show the details of the last-selected item at the far right. The Mac Finder example in Figure 6-37 shows a representation of an image file; you might instead offer a UI for editing an item, reading its content, or whatever is appropriate for your particular application.

A nice thing about this pattern is that you can easily associate buttons with each list: delete the current item, move up, or move down. Many toolkits let you do this in tree controls via direct manipulation, but for those that don't have treeviews, this is a viable alternative.

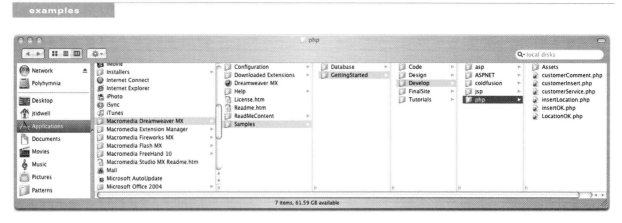

FIGURE 6-37 / This Mac OS X Finder screenshot is an extreme example, with seven levels. But it shows that the pattern scales well, letting the user drill down into deep filesystem hierarchies while staying oriented. (Warning: this pattern can be confusing for people who aren't comfortable with the concept of a hierarchy, especially when the hierarchy is this deep.)

FIGURE 6-38 / It may not look like one, but this Excel chart-type chooser is a two-level cascading list, expressed with two different visual formats. Rather than a literal hierarchy, it uses items grouped into categories. The user's selection in the "Chart sub-type" list includes the item's name and a short description. Also note the use of Card Stack and Illustrated Choices in this dialog box.

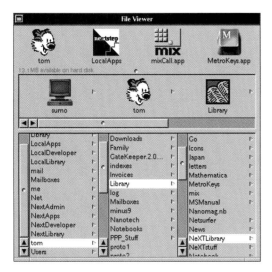

FIGURE 6-39 / NeXTStep originally used this technique in its own File Viewer, circa 1990 or so (screenshot from *http://www120.pair.com/mccarthy/nextstep/intro.htmld/ Workspace.html*).

Subject	From	Sent	Size
⊞ local maxima?	Yuri Strukov	6/3/2002 12:16 PM	1KB
⊟ Problems with for loops...can someone help??	Liz Montabana	6/3/2002 12:18 PM	1KB
⊟ Re: Problems with for loops...can someone help??	Dan Hensley	6/3/2002 12:36 PM	2KB
Re: Problems with for loops...can someone help??	Elizabeth Mont...	6/3/2002 1:10 PM	2KB
⊟ Changing the "zero" element in sparse matrices	Giampiero Salvi	6/3/2002 1:31 PM	1KB
Re: Changing the "zero" element in sparse matrices	Cleve Moler	6/3/2002 2:20 PM	1KB
Re: Changing the "zero" element in sparse matrices	Lars Gregersen	6/3/2002 5:01 PM	2KB
Determining the number of Simulink Systems open?	Joshua Stiff	6/3/2002 2:08 PM	1KB

FIGURE 6-40 / Outlook Express's news reader

what

Put hierarchical data in columns, like a table, but use an indented outline structure in the first column to illustrate the tree structure.

use when

The UI displays multivariate information, so a table works well to show the data (and perhaps allow them to be sorted, as in Sortable Table). But the items are organized primarily as a hierarchy, so you also want a tree to display them most of the time. Your users are relatively sophisticated with respect to GUI usage; this is not an easy pattern for naïve computer users to understand (and the same can be said about most hierarchical views, including trees and **Cascading Lists**).

why

Combining the two data-viewing approaches into one view gives you the best of both worlds, at the cost of some visual and programming complexity. You can show the hierarchy of items, plus a matrix of additional data or item attributes, in one unified structure.

how

The examples show what you need to do: put the tree (really an outline) in the first column, and the item attributes in the subsequent columns. The rows—one item per row—usually are selectable.

Naturally, you can combine this pattern with **Sortable Table** to produce a more browsable, interactive structure. Sorting on the columns disrupts tree ordering, so you'll need to provide an extra button or some other affordance to re-sort the table into the order the tree requires.

This technique seems to have a home in email clients and news readers, where threads of discussion form treelike structures.

example

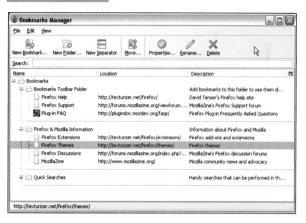

FIGURE 6-41 / The Firefox browser uses a distinctive-looking tree table in one of its dialog boxes. The separators—horizontal lines—help visually group the items in different categories, which isn't a bad idea at all.

65 multi-y graph

©BigCharts.com

FIGURE 6-42 / From *http://nytimes.com*

what

Stack multiple graph lines, one above the other, in one panel; let them all share the same X axis.

use when

You present two or more graphs, usually simple line plots, bar charts, or area charts (or any combination thereof). The data in those graphs all share the same X axis, such as a timeline, but otherwise they're "apples and oranges"—they describe different things. You want to encourage the viewer to find "vertical" relationships among the data sets shown—correlations, similarities, unexpected differences, and so on.

why

Aligning the graphs along the X axis first tells the viewer that these data sets are related, and then it lets the user make side-by-side comparisons of the data. In Figure 6-42, the proximity of the two graphs makes visible the similarity in the curves' shapes; you can see the that the hills and valleys generally line up, and the grid lines enable precise observation. For instance, the vertical grid line for "August" lines up peaks in both curves.

You could have done this by superimposing one graph upon the other. But by showing each graph individually, with its own Y axis, you enable each graph to be viewed on its own merits, without visual interference from the other.

Also, these data sets have very different Y values: one ranges from 7.1 to 8.2, while the other ranges from 20 to over 80! You couldn't even put them on the same Y axis without one of them looking like a flat line. You'd need to draw another Y axis along the left side, and then you'd have to choose a scaling that didn't make the graph look too odd. Even so, direct superimposition encourages the viewer to think that data sets use the same Y scale, and compare them on that basis—"apples to apples," instead of "apples to oranges." If that's not the case, then superimposing them sometimes can be misleading.

how

Stack one graph on top of the other. Use one X axis for both, but separate the Y axes into different vertical spaces. If the Y axes need to overlap somewhat, they can, but try to keep the graphs from visually interfering with each other.

Sometimes you don't need Y axes at all; maybe it's not important to let the user find exact values (or maybe the graph itself contains exact values, like labeled bar charts). In that case, simply move the graph curves up and down until they don't interfere with each other.

Label each graph so its identity is unambiguous. Use vertical grid lines if possible; they let viewers follow an X value from one data set to another, for easier comparison. They also make it possible to discover an exact value for a data point of interest (or one close to it) without making the user take out a straightedge and pencil.

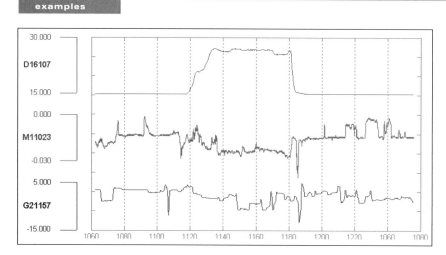

FIGURE 6-43 / An interactive multi-Y graph constructed in MATLAB. You can manipulate the three data traces' Y axes, color-coded on the left, with the mouse—you can drag the traces up and down the graph, "stretch" them vertically by sliding the colored axis endcaps, and change the displayed axis range by editing the Y axis limits in place.

Here's why that's interesting. You might notice that the traces look similar, as if they were correlated—all three drop in value just after the vertical line labeled 1180, for instance. But just how similar are they? Move them and see...

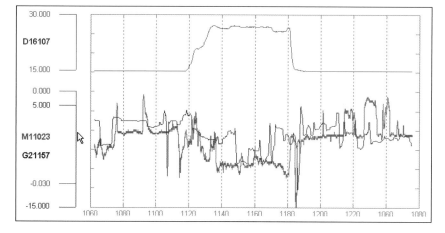

FIGURE 6-44 / Your eyes are very good at discerning relationships among visually rendered data items. By stacking and superimposing these differently scaled plot traces, a user might gain valuable insight into whatever phenomenon produced this data.

66 small multiples

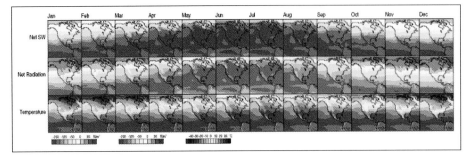

FIGURE 6-45 / From *http://geography.uoregon.edu/shinker/paclim2001*

what

Create many small pictures of the data using two or three data dimensions. Tile them on the page according to one or two additional data dimensions, either in a single comic-strip sequence, or in a 2D matrix.

use when

You need to display a large data set with more than two dimensions or independent variables. It's easy to show a single "slice" of the data as a picture—as a plot, table, map, or image, for instance—but hard to show more dimensions than that. Users might have to look at one plot at a time, flipping back and forth among them to see differences.

When using small multiples, you need to have a fairly large display area available. PDAs and other tiny screens rarely do this well, unless each individual picture is very tiny. But most users will see them on a large screen, or on printed paper.

why

Small multiples are data-rich—they show a lot of information at one time, but in a comprehensible way. Every individual picture tells a story. But when you put them all together and demonstrate how each picture *varies* from one to the next, an even bigger story is told.

As Edward Tufte put it, "Small multiple designs, multivariate and data bountiful, answer directly by visually enforcing comparisons of changes, of the differences among objects, of the scope of alternatives."[2] (Tufte named and popularized small multiples in his famous books about visualization.)

Think about it this way. If you can encode some dimensions in each individual picture, but you need to encode an extra dimension that won't fit in the pictures, how could you do it?

Sequential presentation

Express that dimension as if it varies across time. You can play it like a movie, or use Back/Next buttons to see one graph at a time, for example.

3D presentation

Place the pictures along a third spatial axis, the Z axis.

Small multiples

Reuse the X and Y axes at a larger scale.

Side-by-side placement of pictures lets a user glance from one to the other freely and rapidly. She doesn't have to remember what was shown in a previous screen, as required by a sequential presentation (although a movie can be *very* effective

2 *Envisioning Information*, page 67.

at showing tiny differences between frames). She also doesn't have to decode or rotate a complicated 3D plot, as would be required if you place 2D pictures along a third axis. Sequential and 3D presentations sometimes work very well, but not always, and they often don't work in a noninteractive setting at all.

Choose whether to represent one extra data dimension or two. With only one, you can lay out the images vertically, horizontally, or even line-wrapped, like a comic strip—from the starting point, the user can read through to the end. With two extra data dimensions, you should use a 2D table or matrix—express one data dimension as columns, and the other as rows.

Whether you use one dimension or two, label the small multiples with clear captions—individually, if necessary, otherwise along the sides of the display. Make sure the user understands which data dimension varies across the multiples, and whether you encode one or two data dimensions.

Each image should be similar to the others: use the same size and/or shape, the same axis scaling (if you use plots), and the same kind of content. When you use small multiples, you try to bring out the meaningful differences between the things being shown. Try to eliminate the visual differences that don't mean anything.

Of course you shouldn't use too many small multiples on one page. If one of the data dimensions has a range of 1 to 100, you probably don't want 100 rows or columns of small multiples, so what do you do? You could "bin" those 100 values into, say, 5 bins containing 20 values each. Or you could use a technique called "shingling," which resembles binning, but allows substantial overlap between the bins. (Yes, that means some data points will appear more than once, but that may be a good thing for users trying to discern patterns in the data; just make sure it's labeled well so they know what's going on.)

Note that some small-multiple plots with two extra encoded dimensions are called "trellis plots" or "trellis graphs." William Cleveland, a noted authority on statistical graphing, uses this term, as do the software packages S-PLUS and R.

The North American climate graph, at the top of the pattern, shows many encoded variables. Underlying each small-multiple picture is a 2D geographic map, of course, and overlaid on that is a color-coded "graph" of some climate metric, like temperature. With any one picture, you can see interesting shapes in the color data; they might prompt a viewer to ask questions about why blobs of color appear over certain parts of the continent.

The small multiples as a whole encode two additional variables: each column is a month of the year, and each row represents a climate metric. Your eyes probably followed the changes across the rows, noting changes through the year, and comparisons up and down the columns are easy, too.

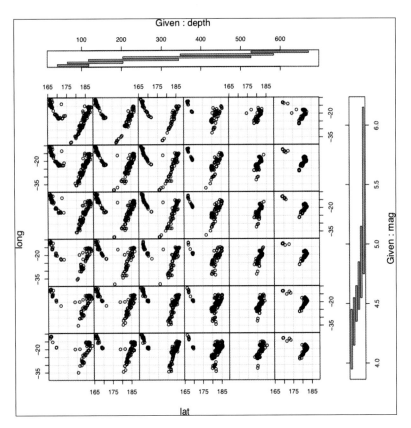

FIGURE 6-46 / A more abstract two-dimensional trellis plot, also called a "coplot" in William Cleveland's *Visualizing Data,* appears in this screenshot. Created with the R software package, this example shows a quantity measured along four dimensions: latitude, longitude, depth, and magnitude. The values along the depth and magnitude dimensions overlap—this is the "shingling" technique mentioned earlier. See *http://www.sph.umich.edu/~nichols/ biostat_bbag-march2001.pdf.*

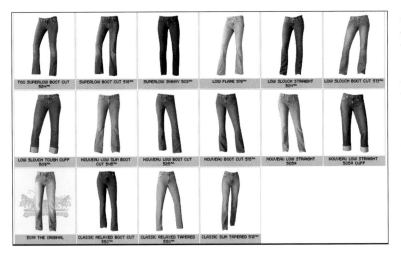

FIGURE 6-47 / Here's a more commercial example. Web sites that sell physical products often use small multiples. The Levis web site uses it to display a choice of jean styles. Because each photograph is so similar to the others—with the same background (except for one special one), approximate pose, and scale—the differences picked out by your eyes actually represent meaningful differences in the jean models.

But wait. The fact that the poses *are* slightly different actually may work to the benefit of this small multiples display. It gives the whole picture a slight roughness, like the natural variations in a piece of fabric; the display is not perfectly uniform, and that makes it feel more relaxed. The different poses also might make individual jeans models slightly more memorable to the user, and easier to pick out of the "lineup" when the user returns to the site later.

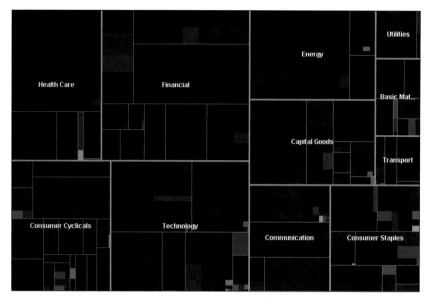

FIGURE 6-48 / SmartMoney's Map of the Market, at *http://smartmoney.com/marketmap*

what

Express multidimensional and/or hierarchical data as rectangles of various sizes. You can nest those rectangles to show the hierarchy, and color or label them to show additional variables.

use when

Your data is tree-shaped. Alternatively, it may be multivariate—each item has several attributes, like size and category, that permit items to be grouped according to those attributes. Users want to see an overview of many data points—maybe hundreds or thousands—and they use screens large enough to accommodate a large display.

Your users should be patient and motivated enough to learn to use an unusual interface. Treemaps are not always easy to read, especially for people who haven't seen them before. Furthermore, they work better onscreen than they do on paper because datatips, dynamic queries, and other interactive mechanisms can help users understand the data.

why

Treemaps encode many data attributes into a single dense diagram. By taking advantage of position, size, containment, color hue and/or value, and labeling, a treemap packs a lot of information into a space that encourages the human visual system to seek out trends, relationships among variables, and specific points of interest.

Look at the the SmartMoney treemap in Figure 6-48, which shows the current performance of 500 publicly traded stocks. It shows the relative sizes of different market sectors, and of companies within those sectors—the blocks of solid color are individual companies. You can instantly see that in that day's market, the big gainers in bright green were small companies (shown as small rectangles), and the big losers in bright red also were small companies. The category Consumer Staples is mostly green, indicating that it did well today; Energy and Health Care are mostly red, so they didn't do as well. But overall, the color is a dark neutral, meaning that the market as a whole was quiet.

This treemap makes it very easy to get an instant overview and spot outliers. It encourages you to see relationships between size and color, size and position, and position and color—all of which give you different kinds of insight into the market. It would take you forever to get that insight from a long table of stock prices.

how

The critical step in designing a treemap is deciding which visual variables encode which data attributes.

Rectangle size

Usually rectangle size encodes a number, such as size, price, or percentage. Make each rectangle's area proportional to that number. If the number has too great a range, you'll end up with some enormous rectangles and some microscopic rectangles, in which case you either could let the user zoom in on them for a closer look, or he could filter out the large ones to let the small ones scale up. **Dynamic Queries** (a pattern in this chapter) often are used for that. See Figure 6-17 for an example of dynamic queries used in conjunction with a treemap.

Grouping and nesting

If your data already is inherently hierarchical, like a taxonomic tree or a filesystem, then you should group and nest the rectangles accordingly. If not, see whether the data items have a natural grouping or categorization that is meaningful to the user. Do they have several possible categorizations? You might consider giving the user a choice on how to group them. Do they have no obvious categorization at all? Then you could take a numeric attribute, like price, and "bin" it into categories ($0 to $5, $5 to $10, etc.). Or you could not group the data items at all. Consider, though, whether some other data display

may be more appropriate; grouping is one of the treemap's strengths.

Color

You can use color to represent a numeric or otherwise ordered value, as in the SmartMoney example in Figure 6-48, or categorization. For a numeric value, choose two colors for the "endpoints" of the range of possible values, like red and green, white and blue, or yellow and red; shades of color between those endpoints represent values in between. For a categorization, use a different hue to represent each category. (If the shades are too similar, though, viewers may assume an ordering where there isn't one.)

Position

A rectangle's position within the treemap is partially dictated by where it belongs in the hierarchy or categorization. But within a category, you might still have freedom to decide where a given rectangle goes. Some treemaps place the largest rectangles in the upper left of a category, and then space-fill the rest of the category so that the smallest rectangles are in the lower right. This establishes a nice rhythm on the page, and helps the user to visually compare the number of small or large rectangles in each main category. In this case, position doesn't encode yet another variable; instead, it's redundant with size and grouping. However, other treemap implementations do encode an order—by age, or alphabetical by name, for example. It depends on how many variables you want to encode at once.

Most treemaps allow users to drill down to the actual data items. Mouse rollovers, for instance, usually produce large tooltips that describe the item in full (see the **Datatips** pattern in this chapter). You usually have to elide some text anyway to fit the descriptions into the treemap blocks, so this is a good practice. Furthermore, a single or double click often brings the user to some other page or window about that item. **Extras On Demand** thus fits into these treemap designs.

As for implementation, it is not trivial to write code to lay out a treemap in a pleasing way. Fortunately, many algorithms exist for drawing a treemap. Some are in academic papers; some are in open-source software or freeware; and others are in products. The different algorithms vary according to how they choose the rectangles' aspect ratios (i.e., the proportion between width and height; the

squarer, the better), how they fill the space for a given category, and their stability with respect to data changes.

Ben Shneiderman invented the treemap in 1990, and he and his colleagues at the University of Maryland have since refined the technique. A history of the treemap, along with many links to papers and implementations, is available at *http://www.cs.umd.edu/hcil/treemap-history/*.

FIGURE 6-49 / The Newsmap web application illustrates the "news landscape" as described by Google News. At any given moment, the Newsmap can collect Google's top headlines and draw a treemap in which the largest blocks represent the most reported stories. The encodings here are:

- Block size: "popularity" of news item; how many news outlets report this story
- Color hue: topic
- Top-level grouping: also topic
- Color value (darkness/lightness): age

Because the headlines' text sizes are proportional to block size, which in turn is proportional to popularity, your eyes are immediately drawn to the biggest news items. (What did you read first? Perhaps the "False warnings" headline, and then "Please Work for Free!"?) The treemap thus is an automatically-constructed visual hierarchy. See *http://www.marumushi.com/apps/newsmap/newsmap.cfm*.

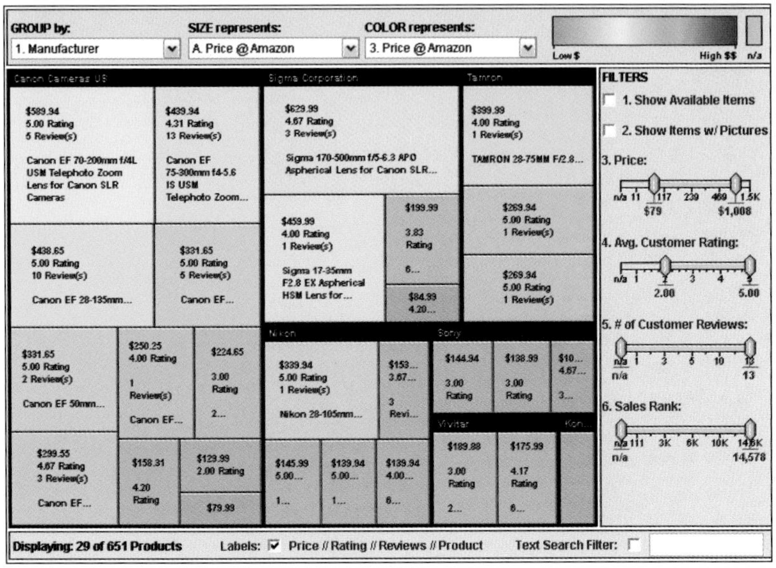

FIGURE 6-50 / From the Hive Group comes a small collection of similar treemap visualizations: items available for purchase from Amazon, world population data, etc. This screenshot shows an example of someone looking for camera lenses on Amazon. Each block represents one product that Amazon sells. At the right is a set of **Dynamic Queries** (again, see the pattern of that name) that lets the user filter out some of the myriad items.

The user can set some of the encodings described in the Newsmap example—block size, color hue, and grouping—with the bar on top ("Group by," "Size represents," and "Color represents"). That kind of customizability is handy in this kind of application. After all, many data attributes are associated with each product—too many to be encoded by the available three or four visual variables. The treemap designers didn't know which attributes each user would be most interested in. They made a good default guess, and put in a simple learnable UI for users to do their own thing. See *http://hivegroup.com*.

GETTING INPUT FROM USERS:
FORMS AND CONTROLS

Sooner or later, the software you design probably will ask the user to answer some kind of a question. It might even happen in the first few minutes of interaction: where should this software be installed? What's your login name? What words do you want to search for?

These kinds of interactions are among the easiest to design. Everyone knows how to use text fields, checkboxes, and combo boxes. These input controls often are the first interface elements novice designers use as they build their first GUIs and web sites.

Still, it doesn't take much to set up a potentially awkward interaction. Here's another sample question: for what location do you want a weather report? The user might wonder, do I specify a location by city, country, or postal code? Are abbreviations okay? What if I misspell it? What if I ask for a city it doesn't know about? Isn't there a map to choose from? And why can't it remember the location I gave it yesterday, anyhow?

This chapter discusses ways to smooth out these problems. The patterns, techniques and controls described here apply mostly to form design—a "form" being simply a series of question/answer pairs. However, they also will be useful in other contexts, like for single controls on web pages or on application toolbars. Input design and form design are core skills for interaction designers, as you can use them in every genre and on every platform.

THE BASICS OF FORM DESIGN

First, a few principles to remember when doing input and form design:

Make sure the user understands what's asked for, and why. This is entirely context-dependent, and any generalizations here risk sounding vapid, but let's try anyway. You should write labels with words that your target users understand—plain language for novice or occasional users, and carefully chosen jargon or specialized vocabulary for domain experts. If you design a long or tedious form, take some space to explain why you need all the information you're asking for. If you're putting a control on a toolbar (or somewhere else equally space-constrained), and its use isn't immediately obvious, use a descriptive tooltip or other type of context-sensitive help to tell the user what it does.

If you can, avoid asking the question at all. Asking the user to answer a question, especially if it comes in the middle of some other task, is a bit of an imposition. You might ask him to break his train of thought and deal with something he hadn't expected to think about. Even in the best of cases, typing into text fields isn't most people's idea of a fun time. Can you "prefill" an input control with already-known or guessable information, as the **Autocompletion** pattern recommends? Can you offer a reasonable default value that removes the burdens of choice from 80 percent of your users? Can you avoid asking for it altogether?

There's one glaring exception to this principle: security. Sometimes we use input controls in a challenge/response context, such as asking for passwords or credit card numbers. You obviously don't want to circumvent these security mechanisms by casually prefilling sensitive information.

Knowledge "in the world" often is more accurate than knowledge "in the head." You can't expect human beings to recall lists of things perfectly. If you ask users to make a choice from a prescribed set of items, try to make that list available to them so they can read over it. (A common exception might be "state or province," often needed for shipping addresses. Obviously, most people can remember the ones they need.) Dropdowns, combo boxes, lists, and other such controls put all the choices out there for the user to review. And when these items have visual renderings, such as images, layouts, and colors, you can use the **Illustrated Choices** pattern to show them.

Similarly, if you ask for input that needs to be formatted in a specific way, like dates or credit card numbers, you might want to offer the user clues about how to format it. Even if the user has used your UI before, he may not remember what's required—a gentle reminder may be welcome. **Good Defaults**, **Structured Format**, and **Input Hints** all serve this purpose. **Autocompletion** goes a step further by telling the user what input is valid, or by reminding the user what he entered some previous time.

Beware of a literal translation from the underlying programming model. Many forms are built to edit database records, or to edit objects in an object-oriented programming language. Given a data structure like these to fill out, it's really easy to design a form to do it. Each structure element gets (1) a label and (2) a control (or a bundle of controls acting together). Put them in some rational order, lay them out top-to-bottom, and you're done. Right?

Not entirely. This kind of implementation-driven form design does work, but it can give you a utilitarian and dull interface—or a difficult one. What if the structure elements don't match up with the input the user expects to give, for instance? And what if the structure is, say, 30 elements long? For some contexts, like property sheets in a programming environment, it's appropriate to show everything the way it's implemented—that's part of the point. But for everything else, a more elegant and user-centered presentation is better.

So here's the challenge: Can you exploit dependencies among the structure elements, familiar graphic constructs (like address labels), unstated assumptions, or knowledge of the user gained from previous interactions to make the form less onerous? Can you turn the problem into one handled by direct manipulation, like drag-and-dropping things around? Be creative!

Usability-test it. For some reason, when input forms are involved, it's particularly easy for designers and users to make radically different assumptions about terminology, possible answers, intrusiveness, and other context-of-use issues. This book has said it before, and will say it again: use usability testing, even if you're sure your design is *good.* This will give you empirical evidence of what works and what doesn't for your particular situation.

Your choice of controls will affect the user's expectation of what is asked for, so choose wisely. A radio box suggests a one-of-many choice, while a one-line text field suggests a short open-ended answer. Consciously or not, people will use the physical form of a control—its type, its size, etc.—to figure out what's being asked for, and they'll set their expectations accordingly. If you use a text field to ask for a number, users may believe that any number is okay; if they enter "12" and you then surprise them with an error dialog box saying, "That number's got to be between 1 and 10," you've yanked the rug out from under them. A slider or spin box would have been better.

The following section gives you a table of possible controls for different input types. You or the engineers you work with will need to decide the semantics of each question. Is it binary? A date or time? One-of-many? Many-of-many? Open-ended but requiring validation? Look it up here, then choose a control based on your particular design constraints.

CONTROL CHOICE

The following charts describe controls and patterns for the kinds of information you might ask from the user, such as numbers and choices from lists. It's not a complete set by any means. In fact, you can probably come up with plenty of others. But the types shown here are common, and the listed controls are among your best choices for clarity and usability.

Consider these factors when choosing among the possible controls for a given information type:

Available space

Some controls take up lots of screen real estate; others are smaller, but may be harder to use than larger ones. Short forms on web pages might be able to spend that screen space on radio buttons or illustrated lists, whereas complex applications may need to pack as much content as possible into small spaces. Toolbars and table-style **Property Sheets** are especially constraining, since they generally allow for only one text line of height, and often not much width either.

User sophistication with respect to general computer usage

Text fields would be familiar to almost all users of anything you'd design, but not everyone would be comfortable using a double-thumbed slider. For that matter, many occasional computer users don't know how to handle a multiple-selection list-box, either.

User sophistication with respect to domain knowledge

A text field might be fine if your users know that, say, only the numbers 1–10 and 20–30 are valid. Beginners will stumble, but if they're a very small part of your user base (and if the context is readily learned), maybe that's okay—a tiny text field might be better than using a big set of interlinked controls.

Bold/Italic/Underline controls are well-known as iconic buttons; it would just be weird to see them as radio buttons instead.

As of this writing, HTML provides only a very small subset of the controls in common usage on the desktop: text fields, radio and checkboxes, scrolled lists, and drop-downs you cannot type into. Commercial and open-source GUI toolkits provide richer sets of controls. Their offerings vary, but many of them are extensible via programming, allowing you to create custom controls for specific situations.

The following sections summarize the various control options for four common input scenarios: lists of items, text, numbers, and dates or times. Each choice is illustrated with a typical example, taken from the Windows 2000 look-and-feel. (Keep in mind that these examples are not necessarily the best possible rendering of these controls! You do have some freedom when you decide how to draw them, especially on the Web. See Chapter 9's introduction for further discussion.)

LISTS OF ITEMS

A wide variety of familiar controls allow users to select items or options from lists. Your choice of control depends on the number of items or options to be selected (one or many), and the number of potentially selectable items (two, a handful, or many).

Controls for selecting one of two options (a binary choice):

Checkbox

- Pros: simple; low space consumption.
- Cons: can only express one choice, so its inverse remains implied and unstated. This can lead to confusion about what it means when it's off.

Two radio buttons

- Pros: both choices are stated and visible.
- Cons: higher space consumption.

Two-choice dropdown list

- Pros: both choices are stated; low and predictable space consumption; easily expandable later to more than two choices.
- Cons: only one choice is visible at a time; requires some dexterity.

"Press-and-stick" toggle button

- Pros: same as for checkbox; when iconic, very low space consumption.
- Cons: same as for checkbox; also, not as standard as a checkbox for text choices.

Menu of two radio-button menu items

- Pros: very low space consumption on the main UI, since it's found on menu bars or pop-up menus.
- Cons: popup menus might be hard to discover; requires a lot of dexterity.

Controls for selecting one of N items, where N is small:

N radio buttons

- Pros: all choices are always visible.
- Cons: high space consumption.

N-item dropdown list

- Pros: low space consumption.
- Cons: only one choice is visible at a time, except when the menu is open; requires some dexterity.

N-item set of mutually exclusive iconic toggle buttons

- Pros: low space consumption; all choices are visible.
- Cons: icons might be cryptic, requiring tooltips for understanding; user might not know they're mutually exclusive.

Menu of N radio-button menu items

- Pros: very low space consumption on main UI, since it's found on menu bars or popup menus; all choices are visible.
- Cons: popup menus might be hard to discover; requires a lot of dexterity.

Single-selection list or table

- Pros: many choices are visible; frame can be kept as small as three items.
- Cons: higher space consumption than dropdown list or spinner.

Spinner

- Pros: low space consumption.
- Cons: only one choice is ever visible at a time; requires a lot of dexterity; and unfamiliar to naïve computer users. Dropdown list is usually a better choice.

Controls for selecting one of N items, where N is large:

N-item dropdown list, scrolled if necessary

- Pros: low space consumption.
- Cons: only one choice is visible at a time, except when menu is open; requires a lot of dexterity to scroll through items on the drop-down menu.

Single-selection list or table

- Pros: many choices are visible; can be kept small if needed.
- Cons: higher space consumption than dropdown list.

Single-selection tree or **Cascaded List**, with items arranged into categories

- Pros: many choices are visible; organization helps findability in some cases.
- Cons: may be unfamiliar to naïve computer users; high space consumption; requires high dexterity.

Custom browser, such as for files, colors, or fonts

- Pros: suited for browsing available choices.
- Cons: may be unfamiliar to some users; difficult to design; usually a separate window, so it's less immediate than controls placed directly on the page.

Controls for selecting many of N items, in any order:

Array of N checkboxes

- Pros: all choices are stated and visible.
- Cons: high space consumption.

Array of N toggle buttons

- Pros: low space consumption; all choices are visible.
- Cons: icons might be cryptic, requiring tooltips for understanding; might look mutually exclusive.

Menu of N check-box menu items

- Pros: very low space consumption on main UI, since it's found on menu bars or popup menus; all choices are visible.
- Cons: popup menus might be hard to discover; requires a lot of dexterity.

Multiple-selection list or table

- Pros: many choices are visible; can be kept small if needed.
- Cons: not all choices are visible without scrolling; high (but bounded) space consumption; user might not realize it's multiple-selection.

List with checkbox items

- Pros: many choices are visible; can be kept small if needed; affordance for selection is obvious.
- Cons: not all choices are visible without scrolling; high (but bounded) space consumption.

Multiple-selection tree or **Cascaded List**, with items arranged into categories

- Pros: many choices are visible; organization helps findability in some cases.
- Cons: may be unfamiliar to naïve computer users; requires high dexterity; looks same as single-selection tree.

Custom browser, such as for files, colors, or fonts

- Pros: suited for browsing available choices.
- Cons: may be unfamiliar to some users; difficult to design; usually a separate window, so it's less immediate than controls placed directly on the page.

List Builder pattern

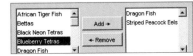

- Pros: selected set is easy to view; selection can be an ordered list if desired; easily handles a large source list.
- Cons: very high space consumption due to two lists; does not easily handle a large set of selected objects.

Controls for constructing an unordered list of user-entered items:

List or table with "Add" or "New" button

- Pros: "add" action is visible and obvious.
- Cons: higher space consumption; visual clutter.

List or table with **New Item Row** pattern (Chapter 6)

- Pros: lower space consumption; editing is done in place.
- Cons: "add" action is not quite as obvious as a button.

List or table that can receive drag-and-dropped items

- Pros: visually elegant and space-saving; drag-and-drop is efficient and intuitive.
- Cons: "add" action is not visible, so users may not know the list is a drop target.

Controls for constructing an ordered list of items:

Unordered list with "Up" and "Down" affordances
- Pros: rearrangement actions are visible.
- Cons: higher space consumption.

Unordered list that offers internal drag-and-drop for reordering items
- Pros: visually elegant and space-saving; drag-and-drop is efficient and intuitive.
- Cons: rearrangement actions are not visible, so user may not know they're available.

TEXT

Collecting text input from a user is one of the most basic form tasks. The controls typically are chosen according to the number of lines to be entered, whether or not the lines are predetermined choices, and whether or not the text will include formatting.

Control for entering one line of text:

Single-line text field

Controls for entering either one line of text, or a one-of-N choice:

Combo box
- Pros: quicker to use than a separate dialog box; familiar.
- Cons: limited number of items can reasonably fit in drop-down.

Text field with "More" button (you can also use it with a combo box instead of a text field)
- Pros: permits the launch of a specialized chooser dialog box—e.g., a file finder.
- Cons: not as familiar as a combo box to some users; not as immediate.

Control for entering multiple lines of unformatted text:

Multiline text area

GETTING INPUT FROM USERS

Controls for entering multiple lines of formatted text:

Text area with inline tags

- Pros: skilled users can avoid the toolbar by typing tags directly.

- Cons: not truly WYSIWYG (what you see is what you get).

Rich-text editor

- Pros: immediacy, since the edited text serves as a preview.

- Cons: use of toolbar is required, so it cannot always be keyboard-only.

NUMBERS

Because they often must follow more complex formatting rules, entering numbers on a form is slightly more complex than entering basic text. The choice of input options depends on the type of number you enter and its allowable range.

Controls for entering numbers of any type or format:

Text field using **Forgiving Format**

617 555-1212

- Pros: visually elegant; permits wide variety of formats or data types.

- Cons: expected format is not evident from the control's form, so it may cause temporary confusion; requires careful back-end validation

Text field using **Structured Format**

617 - 555 - 1212

- Pros: desired format evident from control's form.

- Cons: possibly higher space consumption; more visual complexity; does not permit any deviation from the specified format, even if user needs to do so.

Spin box (best for integers or discrete steps)

4

- Pros: user can arrive at a value via mouse clicks, without touching the keyboard; can also type directly if desired.

- Cons: not familiar to all users; you may need to hold down the button long enough to reach the desired value; requires dexterity to use tiny buttons.

Controls for entering numbers from a bounded range:

Slider

- Pros: obvious metaphor; position of value in range is shown visually; the user cannot enter a number outside the range.

- Cons: high space consumption; unobvious keyboard access; tick labels can make it very crowded.

Spinner

- Pros: values are constrained to be in range when buttons are used; low space consumption; supports both keyboard-only and mouse-only access.

- Cons: not familiar to all users; requires dexterity to use tiny buttons; needs validation; cannot visually see value within range.

Text field with after-the-fact error checking (can have **Input Hints**, **Input Prompt**, etc.)

- Pros: familiar to everyone; low space consumption; keyboard access.

- Cons: requires validation; no constraints on what can be entered, so you have to communicate the range the range by some other means.

Slider with text field (can take the form of a **Dropdown Chooser** with a slider on the dropdown)

- Pros: allows both visual and numeric forms of input

- Cons: complex; high space consumption when both elements are on the page; requires validation of text field when the user types the value.

Controls for entering a subrange from a larger range:

Double slider (can be used with text fields, as above)

- Pros: lower space consumption than two sliders.

- Cons: unfamiliar to most users; no keyboard access unless you also use text fields.

Two sliders (also can be used with text fields)

- Pros: less scary looking than a double slider.

- Cons: very high space consumption; no keyboard access unless text fields are used too.

Two spinners (can be linked via **Fill-in-the-Blank**)

- Pros: values are constrained to be in range when buttons are used; low space consumption; supports both keyboard-only and mouse-only access.

- Cons: not familiar to all users; requires dexterity to use tiny buttons; needs validation; cannot visually see value within range.

Two text fields with error checking (can use **Input Hints**, **Input Prompt**, **Fill-in-the-Blank**)

- Pros: familiar to everyone; much lower space consumption than sliders.

- Cons: requires validation; no constraints on what can be entered, so you need to communicate the range by some other means.

Because of the potential formats and internationalization issues, dates and times can be tricky to accept from users. Input options for dates or times include:

Forgiving Format text field

- Pros: visually simple; permits wide variety of formats or data types; keyboard access.
- Cons: expected format not evident from control's form, so it may cause brief confusion; requires careful back-end validation.

`Wed 7/21/2004`

Structured Format text field

- Pros: desired format evident from control's form.
- Cons: possibly higher space consumption; more visual clutter; does not permit deviation from specified format, even if user wants to do so.

`7 / 21 / 2004`

Calendar or clock control

- Pros: obvious metaphor; input is constrained to allowable values.
- Cons: high space consumption; may not provide keyboard-only access.

Dropdown Chooser with calendar or clock control

- Pros: combines the advantages of text field and calendar control; low space consumption.
- Cons: complex interaction; requires dexterity to pick values from a dropdown.

THE PATTERNS

As you might have guessed if you read through the control tables in the preceding section, most of these patterns describe controls—specifically, how you can combine controls with other controls and text in ways that make them easier to use. Some patterns define structural relationships between elements, like **Dropdown Chooser** and **Fill-in-the-Blanks**. Others, such as **Good Defaults** and **Autocompletion**, discuss the values of controls and how those values change.

A large number of these patterns deal primarily with text fields. That shouldn't be surprising. Text fields are as common as dirt, but they don't make it easy for users to figure out what should go in them. They're easiest to use when presented in a context that makes their usage clear. These six patterns give you many ways to create that context:

68	Forgiving Format	**71**	Input Hints
69	Structured Format	**72**	Input Prompt
70	Fill-in-the-Blanks	**73**	Autocompletion

The next three patterns deal with controls other than text fields. **Dropdown Chooser** describes a way to create a custom control; **Illustrated Choices** encourages visuals in lists and other controls; and **List Builder** describes a commonly reinvented combination of controls that lets users construct a list of items.

74 Dropdown Chooser

75 Illustrated Choices

76 List Builder

You should design the remaining patterns into the whole form. They apply equally well to text fields, drop-downs, radio buttons, lists, and other stateful controls, but you should use them consistently within a form (or within a dialog box, or even an entire application).

77 Good Defaults

78 Same-Page Error Messages

68 forgiving format

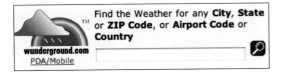

FIGURE 7-1 / From *http://wunderground.com*

what

Permit users to enter text in a variety of formats and syntaxes, and make the application interpret it intelligently.

use when

Your UI asks for data that users might type with an unpredictable mix of whitespace, hyphens, abbreviations, or capitalizations. More generally, the UI can accept input of various kinds from the user—different meanings, formats, or syntax. But you want to keep the interface visually simple.

why

The user just wants to get something done, not think about "correct" formats and complex UIs. Computers are good at figuring out how to handle input of different types (up to a point, anyway). It's a perfect match: let the user type whatever he needs, and if it's reasonable, make the software do the right thing with it.

This can help simplify the UI tremendously, in terms of how many brain cells a user has to use to figure it out. It may even remove the requirement for an **Input Hint** or **Input Prompt**, though they're often seen together, as in the example above.

You might consider **Structured Format** as an alternative, but that pattern works best when the input format is entirely predictable (and usually numeric, like telephone numbers).

how

The catch (you knew there would be one): it turns a UI design problem into a programming problem. You have to think about what kinds of text a user is likely to type in. Maybe you ask for a date or time, and only the format varies—that's an easy case. Or maybe you ask for search terms, and the variation is what the software *does* with the data. That's harder. Can the software disambiguate one case from another? How?

Each application uses this pattern differently. Just make sure that the software's response to various input formats matches what users expect it to do. Test, test, and test again with real users.

example

Figure 7-2 comes from Outlook's tool for setting up a meeting. Look at the "Start time:" and "End time:" fields at the bottom of the screenshot—you don't need to give it a fully defined date, like what appears in the text fields. If today is April 24, and you want to set up a meeting for April 29, you can type any of the following terms:

- next Thu
- thu
- 4/29/2004
- 4/29
- 5 days
- nxt thu
- 29/4/2004
- 29/4
- five days

And so on—there are probably other accepted formats, too. The specified date then is "echoed back" to the user in the appropriate format for the user's language and location, as shown in Figure 7-2.

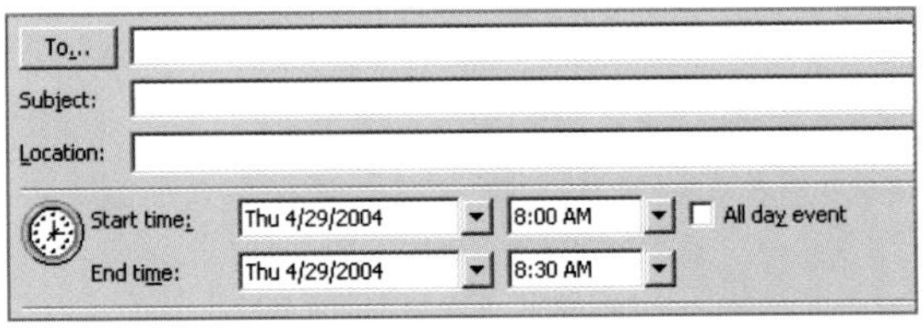

FIGURE 7-2 / Microsoft Outlook

69 structured format

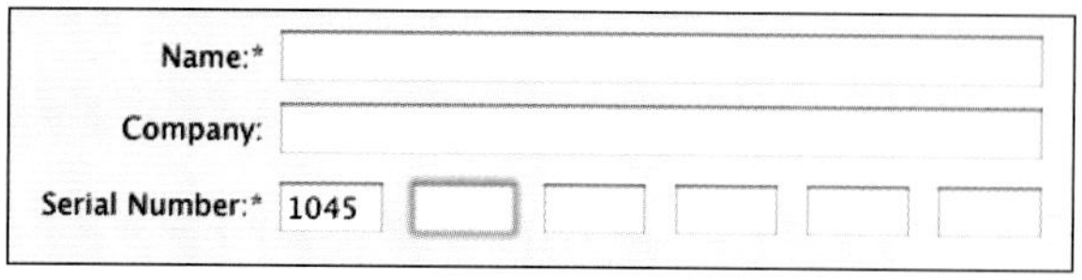

FIGURE 7-3 / Photoshop's installation screen

what

Instead of using one text field, use a set of text fields that reflect the structure of the requested data.

use when

Your interface requests a specific kind of text input from the user, formatted in a certain way. That format is familiar and well-defined, and you don't expect any users to need to deviate from the format you expect. Examples include credit card information, local telephone numbers, and license strings or numbers, as shown in Figure 7-3.

It's generally a bad idea to use this pattern for any data whose format may vary from user to user. Consider especially what might happen if your interface is used in other countries. Names, addresses, postal codes, telephone numbers—all have different standard formats in different places. Consider using **Forgiving Format** in those cases.

why

The structure of the text fields gives the user a clue about what kind of input is being requested. For example, she can mentally map the six text fields in Figure 7-3 to the six-chunk number written on her Photoshop CD case, and conclude that that's the license number she now needs to type in. Expectations are clear. She probably also realizes that she doesn't need to type in any spaces or hyphens to separate the six chunks.

Interestingly, this pattern usually gets implemented as a set of small text fields instead of one big one. That alone can reduce data entry errors. It's easier for someone to double-check several short strings (two to five characters or so) than one long one, especially when numbers are involved. Likewise, it's easier to transcribe or memorize a long number when it's broken up into chunks. That's how the human brain works.

Contrast this pattern to **Forgiving Format**, which takes the opposite tack: it allows you to type in data in any format, without providing structural evidence of what's being asked for. (You can use other clues instead, like **Input Hints**.) Structured Format is better for very predictable formats, **Forgiving Format** for open-ended input.

how

Design a set of text fields that reflect the format being asked for. Keep the text fields short, as clues to the length of the input.

Once the user has typed all the digits or characters in the first text field, confirm it for her by automatically moving the input focus to the next field. She can still go back and re-edit the first one, of course, but now she knows how many digits are required there.

You can also use Input Prompts to give the user yet more clues about what's expected. In fact, structured format fields for dates often do use **Input Prompts**, such as "dd/mm/yyyy".

At its simplest, Structured Format literally can take the shape of the data, complete with spaces, hyphens, and parentheses, as illustrated in the following table:

Telephone number	(504) 555-1212	 (504) 555 – 1212
Credit card number	1021 1234 5678 0000	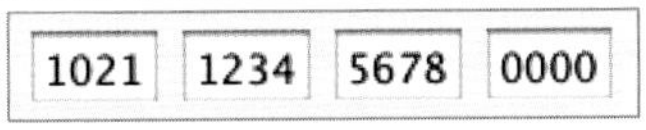 1021 1234 5678 0000
Date	12/25/2004	 12 / 25 / 2004
ISBN number	0-1950-1919-9	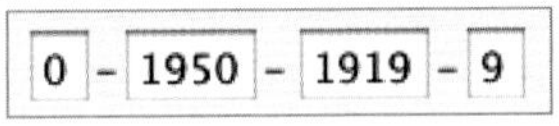 0 – 1950 – 1919 – 9

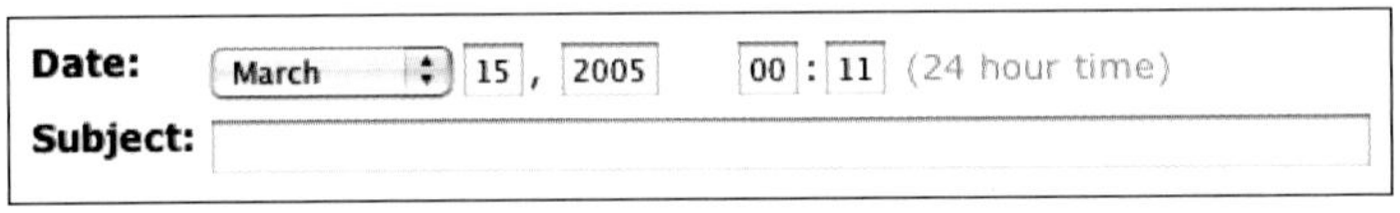

Date: March ⬍ 15 , 2005   00 : 11 (24 hour time)
Subject:

FIGURE 7-4 / For date input, LiveJournal uses Structured Format in combination with a dropdown to choose a month. It defaults to the current day and time. See *http://livejournal.com*.

70 fill-in-the-blanks

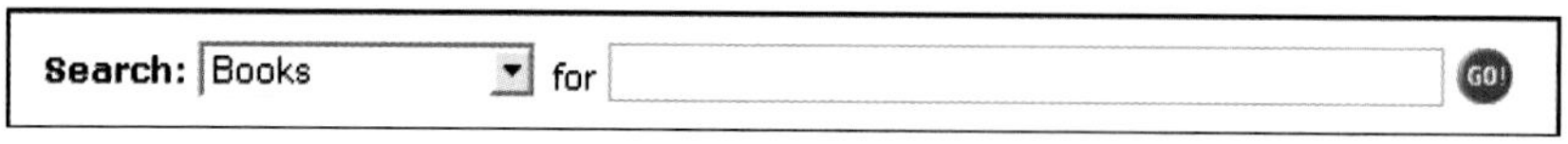

Search: [Books ▾] for [   ] (GO!)

FIGURE 7-5 / From *http://amazon.com*

what

Arrange one or more fields in the form of a prose sentence or phrase, with the fields as "blanks" to be filled in by the user.

use when

You need to ask the user for input, usually one-line text, a number, or a choice from a dropdown list. You tried to write it out as a set of label/control pairs, but the labels' typical declarative style (such as "Name:" and "Address:") isn't clear enough for users to understand what's going on. You can, however, verbally describe the action to be taken once everything's filled out, in an active-voice sentence or phrase.

why

Fill-in-the-Blanks helps make the interface self-explanatory. After all, we all know how to finish a sentence. (A verb phrase or noun phrase will do the trick, too.) Seeing the input, or "blanks," in the context of a verbal description helps the user understand what's going on and what's asked of him.

how

Write the sentence or phrase using all your word-crafting skills. Use controls in place of words.

If you're going to embed the controls in the middle of the phrase, instead of at the end, this pattern works best with text fields, dropdown lists, and combo boxes—in other words, controls with the same form factor (width and height) as words in the sentence. Also, make sure the baseline of the sentence text lines up with the text baselines in the controls, or it'll look sloppy. Size the controls so that they are just long enough to contain the user's choices, and maintain proper word spacing between them and the surrounding words.

This is particularly useful for defining conditions, as one might do when searching for items or filtering them out of a display. The Excel and Photoshop examples below illustrate the point. Robert Reimann and Alan Cooper describe this pattern as an ideal way to handle queries; their term for it is "natural language output."[1]

There's a big "gotcha" in this pattern, however: it becomes very hard to properly localize the interface (convert it to a different language), since comprehension now depends upon word order in a natural language. For some international products or web sites, that's a non-starter. You may have to rearrange the UI to make it work in a different language; at the very least, work with a competent translator to make sure the UI can be localized.

---

1 See their book *About Face 2.0: The Essentials of Interaction Design* (Wiley), page 205.

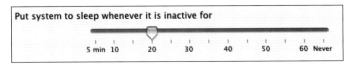

FIGURE 7-6 / The Mac OS X System Preferences has several places that use a simple Fill-in-the-Blanks approach. Here's one.

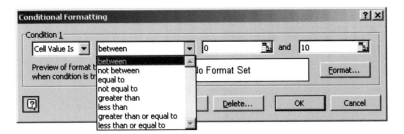

FIGURE 7-7 / This Excel cell-formatting dialog box lets you choose the phrases in this "sentence" from dropdown boxes. As the phrases change, the subsequent text fields—showing 0 and 10 in this example—might be replaced by other controls, such as a single text field for "greater than."

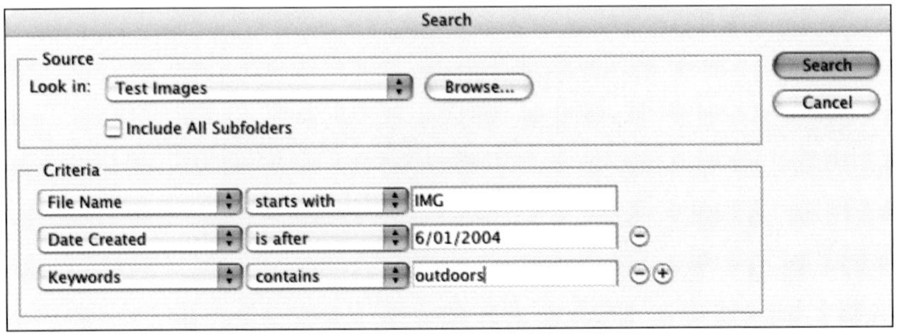

FIGURE 7-8 / Photoshop's image search dialog box uses a very similar approach to the Excel dialog, but this one uses multiple conditions.

71 input hints

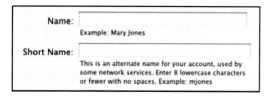

FIGURE 7-9 / Mac OS X System Preferences

what

Beside an empty text field, place a sentence or example that explains what is required.

use when

The interface presents a text field, but the kind of input it requires isn't obvious to all users. You don't want to put more than a few words into the text field's label.

why

A text field that explains what goes into it frees users from having to guess. If you visually separate the hint from the main label, users who know what to do can more or less ignore the hint, and stay focused on the label and control.

how

Write a short example or explanatory sentence, and put it below or beside the text field. Two examples conjoined by "or" works fine too. Keep the text small and inconspicuous, though readable; consider using a font two points smaller than the label font. (A one-point difference will look more like a mistake than an intended font-size change.)

Also, keep the hint short. Beyond a sentence of two, many users' eyes will glaze over, and they'll ignore the text altogether.

This pattern is often used in conjunction with **Forgiving Format**, as illustrated by the Word example below, or **Structured Format**. Alternative patterns are **Input Prompt** (in which a short hint goes into the control itself), and **Good Defaults** (which puts an actual valid value into the control). Input Hints permit longer, more permanent help texts than **Input Prompts**, but because no default value is present in the text field, the user is forced to consider the question and give an answer.

example

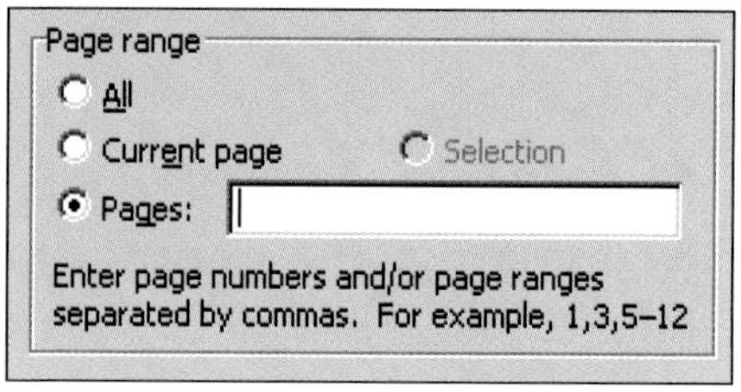

Page range
- All
- Current page   Selection
- Pages:

Enter page numbers and/or page ranges separated by commas. For example, 1,3,5–12

FIGURE 7-10 / The printing dialog boxes used by several Microsoft Office applications supply an Input Hint below a **Forgiving Format** text field—it takes page numbers, page ranges, or both. The hint is very useful to anyone who's never had to use the "Pages" option, but users who already understand it don't need to focus on the written text; they can just go straight for the input field.

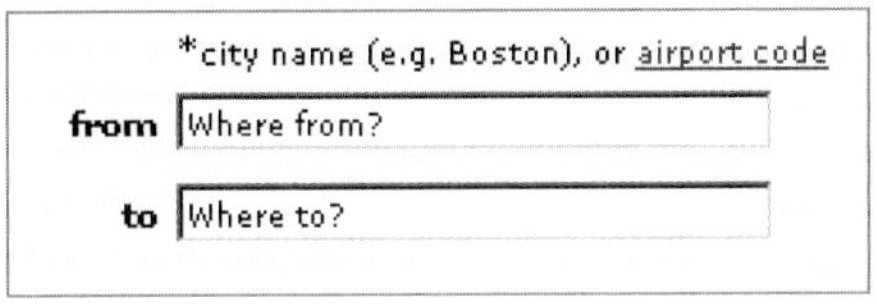

FIGURE 7-11 / From *http://orbitz.com*

what

Prefill a text field or dropdown with a prompt that tells the user what to do or type.

use when

The UI presents a text field, dropdown, or combo box for required input. Normally you would use a good default value, but you can't in this case—perhaps there is no reasonable default, as in the Orbitz form above. The user needs only a short reminder of what is required.

why

It helps make the UI self-explanatory. Like Input Hints, an Input Prompt is a sneaky way of supplying help information for controls whose purpose or format may not be immediately clear.

With an **Input Hint**, someone quickly scanning the UI can easily ignore the hint (or miss it entirely). Sometimes this is your desired outcome. But an Input Prompt sits right where the user will type, so it can't be ignored. The advantage here is that the user doesn't have to guess whether she has to deal with this control or not—the control itself tells her she does. (Remember that users don't fill out forms for fun—they'll do as little as needed to finish up and get out of there.) A question or an imperative "Fill me in!" is likely to be noticed.

An interesting side effect of this pattern is that users may not even bother to read the label that prefixes the text field. Look again at Figure 7-11. The labels "from" and "to" are completely superfluous, in terms of the form's meaning. Because the user's eye will be drawn first to the white text fields, those

prompts probably will be read before the labels anyway! That said, don't remove the labels—that prompt is gone forever once the user types over it, and on subsequent readings of this form, she may not remember what the control asks for.

how

Choose an appropriate prompt string, perhaps beginning with one of these words:

- For a dropdown list, use *Select, Choose,* or *Pick.*
- For a text field, use *Type* or *Enter.*

End it with a noun describing what the input is, such as "Choose a state," "Type your message here," or "Enter the patient's name." Put this phrase into the control where the value would normally be. (The prompt itself shouldn't be a selectable value in a dropdown; if the user selects it, it's not clear what the software should do with it.)

Since the point of the exercise was to tell the users what they were required to do before proceeding, don't let the operation proceed until they've done it! As long as the prompt is still sitting untouched in the control, disable the button (or other device) that lets the user finish this part of the operation. That way, you won't have to throw an error message at the user.

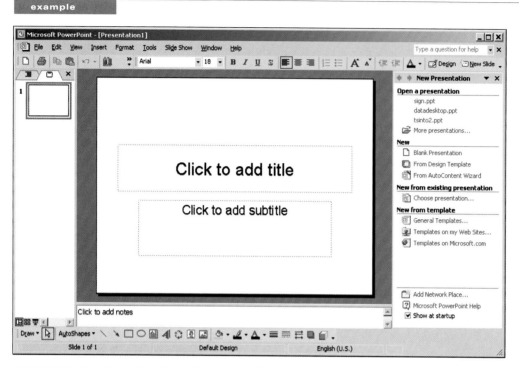

FIGURE 7-12 / Input Prompt has historically been unusual in desktop applications, but it's as good an idea in this context as it is on the Web. Note its use on a WYSIWYG editor's canvas here—it doesn't indicate a "required field" as such, but the application clearly communicates its intent to the user, who doesn't have to puzzle out what he should do next.

73 autocompletion

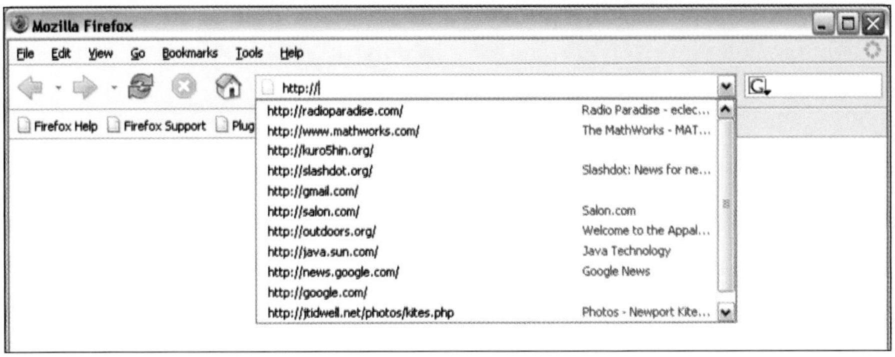

FIGURE 7-13 / Firefox's autocompletion for typed URLs

what

As the user types into a text field, anticipate the possible answers and automatically complete the entry when appropriate.

use when

The user types something predictable, such as a URL, the user's own name or address, today's date, or a filename. You can make a reasonable guess as to what they're attempting to type—perhaps there's a saved history of things this user has previously typed, for instance, or perhaps the user is picking from a set of preexisting values, like a list of filenames in a directory.

When the typed entries are long and hard to type (or remember), like URLs or email addresses, Autocompletion is particularly valuable.

Autocompletion is also common in text editors and command-line UIs. As users type commands or phrases, the application or shell might offer suggestions for completion. Code editors and OS shells are well-suited for this, because the language used is small and predictable (as opposed to a human language, like English); it's therefore easier to predict what the user tries to type.

why

Save the user the trouble of typing the whole string, and do it for him. You thus save countless seconds of work, and contribute to the good health of thousands of wrists. An additional benefit can be error prevention: the longer or stranger the string that must be typed, the greater the odds of the user making a typographical error. Autocompleted entries can avoid that problem.

how

With each additional character that the user types, the software quietly forms a list of the possible completions to that partially entered string. If the user enters one of a limited number of possible valid values, use that set of valid values. If the possible values are wide open, then one of these might supply completions:

- Previous entries typed by this user, stored in a preferences or history mechanism

- Common phrases that many users have used in the past, supplied as a built-in "dictionary" for the application

- Artifacts appropriate to the context, such as company-wide contact lists for internal email

From here, you can approach the interaction design of **Autocompletion** in two ways. One is to show the user a list of possible completions on demand, such as by hitting the Tab key, and let him choose one explicitly by picking from that list. Many code editors do this (see Figure 7-17). It's probably better used when the user would recognize what he wants when he sees it, but may not remember how to type it without help. "Knowledge in the world is better than knowledge in the head."

The other way is to wait until there's only one reasonable completion, and then put it in front of the user, unprompted. Word does this with a tooltip; many forms do it by filling in the remainder of the entry, but with selection turned on, so another keystroke would wipe out the autocompleted part. Either way, the user gets a choice about whether to retain the autocompletion or not—and the default is to not keep it.

You can use both approaches together, as in Figure 7-17.

Make sure that Autocompletion doesn't irritate users. If you guess wrong, the user won't like it—he then has to go erase the autocompletion, and retype what he meant in the first place, avoiding having autocomplete pick the wrong completion

yet again. These interaction details can help prevent irritation:

- Always give the user a choice to take the completion or not take it; default to "no."
- Don't interfere with ordinary typing. If the user intends to type a certain string and just keeps typing in spite of the attempts at autocompletion, make sure that the result is what the user intended to type.
- If the user keeps rejecting a certain autocompletion in one place, don't keep offering it. Let it go at some point.
- Guess correctly.

Here's one possible way to implement Autocompletion cheaply. You can turn a text field into a combo box (which is a combination of a typable text field and a dropdown). Each time the user enters a unique value into the text field, make a new drop-down item for it. Now, if your GUI toolkit allows type-ahead in combo boxes (as many do), the drop-down items are automatically used to complete whatever the user types. See Figure 7-13 above for a typical example; most web browsers now keep the most recently visited sites in a combo box where the user types URLs.

examples

To: dis|

To: discuss@interactiondesigners.com (Interaction Designers)

FIGURE 7-14 / Many email clients, of course, use autocompletion to help users fill in To: and CC: fields. They generally draw on an address book, contacts list, or a list of addresses you've exchanged email with. This example from Mac Mail shows a single completion suggested upon typing the letter 'c'; the completed text is automatically highlighted, so a single keystroke can get rid of it. You can thus type straight "through" the completion if it's wrong.

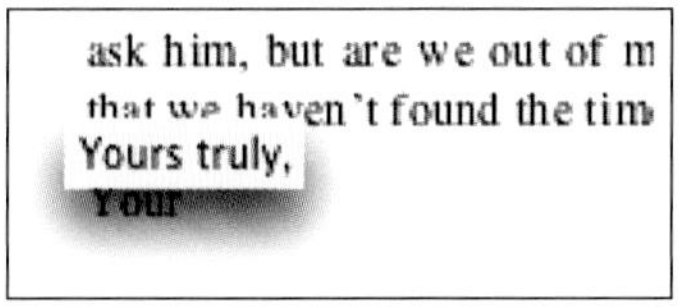

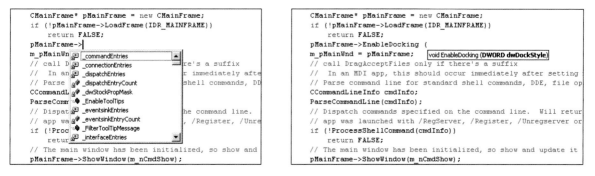

FIGURE 7-15 / Word has a built-in dictionary of words and phrases that it uses to suggest completions. In this picture, typing the word "Your" at the beginning of a line has caused Word to suggest "Yours truly," which is appropriate only for signatures of letters. Had Word been smarter, it might have noticed that the text in question was in the middle of a 10,000-word book chapter that bore no resemblance whatsoever to a letter. But again, you can type straight through the autocompletion, ignoring it.

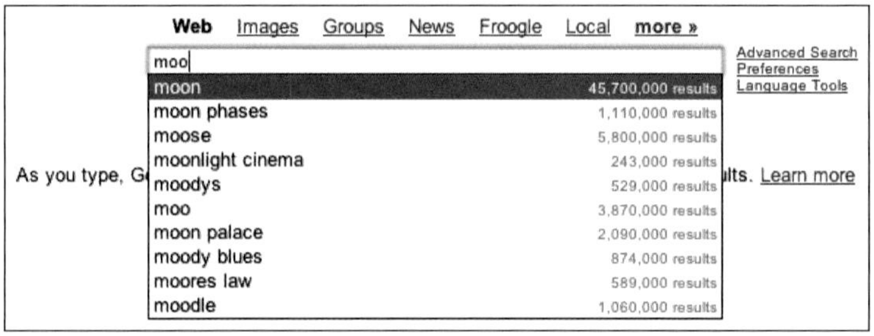

FIGURE 7-16 / In contrast to Mail and Word, Google Suggest makes autocompletion its defining feature. As you type, it shows you the most popular searches that match what you've typed thus far. Rather than being a mere typing aid, it actually turns into a way to navigate a small corner of the public mental landscape.

FIGURE 7-17 / Finally, code editors such as Visual Studio invest in very complex autocompletion mechanisms. Visual Studio's IntelliSense™ completes the built-in keywords of a programming language, of course, but it also draws on the functions, classes, and variable names defined by the user. It even can show the arguments to functions that you invoke (in the righthand screenshot). Furthermore, both "select from a list" and "take the one completion that matches" approaches are supported, and you can call up autocompletion on demand by typing Control-Space.

Autocompletion in Visual Studio thus serves as a typing aid, a memory aid, and a browser of context-appropriate functions and classes. It's very useful.

74 dropdown chooser

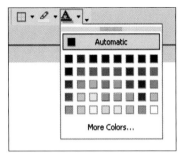

FIGURE 7-18 / Word's color chooser

what

Extend the concept of a menu by using a drop-down or pop-up panel to contain a more complex value-selection UI.

use when

The user needs to supply input that is a choice from a set (such as in the color example above), a date or time, a number, or anything other than free text typed at a keyboard. You want to provide a UI that supports that choice—a nice visual rendering of the choices, for instance, or interactive tools—but you don't want to use space on the main page for that; a tiny space showing the current value is all you want.

why

Most users are very familiar with the dropdown list control (called a "combo box" when used with a free-typing text field). Many applications successfully extend this concept to dropdowns that aren't simple lists, such as trees, 2D grids, and arbitrary layouts. Users seem to understand them with no problem, as long as the controls have down-arrow buttons to indicate that they open when clicked.

Dropdown choosers encapsulate complex UIs in a small space, so they are a fine solution for many situations. Toolbars, forms, dialog boxes, and web pages of all sorts use them now. The page the user sees remains simple and elegant, and the chooser

UI only shows itself when the user requests it—an appropriate way to hide complexity until it is needed.

(In general, I wouldn't recommend using it on UIs that are used primarily by computer novices. But Microsoft Office has trained its legions of users in Dropdown Choosers—color selectors and font selectors, for example, all take advantage of them—so just make sure your audience is comfortable with them.)

how

For the Dropdown Chooser control's "closed" state, show the current value of the control in either a button or a text field. To its right, put a down arrow. This may be in its own button, or not, as you see fit; experiment and see what looks good and makes sense to your users. A click on the arrow (or the whole control) brings up the chooser panel, and a second click closes it again.

Tailor the chooser panel for the choice the user needs to make. Make it relatively small and compact; its visual organization should be a familiar information-graphics format, such as a list, a table, an outline-type tree, or a specialized format like a calendar or calculator (see the following examples).

Scrolling the panel is OK if the user understands that it's a choice from a large set, such as a file from a filesystem, but keep in mind that scrolling one of these pop-up panels is not easy for people without perfect dexterity!

Links or buttons on the panel can in turn bring up secondary UIs—for example, color-chooser dialog boxes, file-finder dialog boxes, or help pages—that help the user choose a value. These usually are modal dialog boxes. In fact, if you intend to use one of these modal dialogs as the primary way the user picks a value (say, by launching it from a button), you could use a Dropdown Chooser instead of going straight to the modal dialog. The pop-up panel could contain the most common or recently chosen items. By making frequently chosen items so easy to pick, you reduce the total time (or number of clicks) it takes for an average user to pick values.

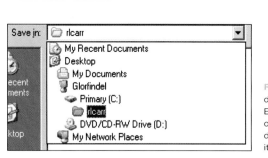

FIGURE 7-19 / One of the first non-list uses of a dropdown chooser was the directory selector in Windows Explorer. It is indented to look like a tree view. You cannot open or close its nodes, so it really behaves more like a dropdown list with indented items than an actual tree, but it was visually different from a dropdown list.

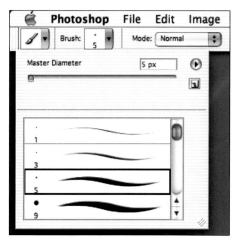

FIGURE 7-20 / Photoshop's compact, interaction-rich toolbars use dropdown choosers heavily. The Brush control is shown here; Opacity is shown in the next example. The Brush chooser is a selectable list with a twist—it has extra controls such as a slider, a text field, and a pullright button (the circular one) for yet more choices.

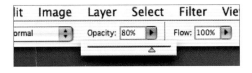

FIGURE 7-21 / The Opacity chooser is a simple
slider, and the text field above it echoes its value.
(Note the mysterious use of a right arrow instead of a
down arrow.)

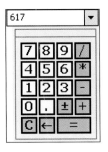

FIGURE 7-22 / A text field from Money.
Normally a user would just type a number
into this text field. But in the context of a
financial application, having a calculator
attached to a text field is very useful. A
user might type in a number and then
multiply it by 12, for instance.

FIGURE 7-23 / Even web sites
can get into the swing of things.
Orbitz's calendar dropdown is
slightly buggy (it appears far
away from the dropdown button
itself), but it's an effective
presentation for a date chooser.

75 illustrated choices

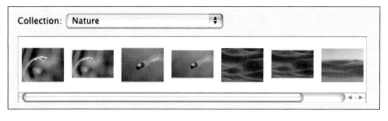

Collection: [Nature]

FIGURE 7-24 / Mac OS X System Properties

what

Use pictures instead of words (or in addition to them) to show available choices.

use when

The interface presents a set of choices that differ visually, such as images, colors, font families, or object alignment.

why

Why translate a visual concept into words, when showing it visually is so much more direct? You reduce the cognitive load on the user—they don't have to think about what "goldenrod" or "Garamond" might look like—while simultaneously making the interface more attractive.

how

First, each thumbnail (or color swatch) should be accurate. The user should get what he sees on the illustrated choice. Beyond that, show the differences that matter, and little else; there's no need for perfect miniature reproductions of the choices' effects. Show a simplified, streamlined, and exaggerated picture.

You can use illustrated choices in many controls: dropdown lists, radio boxes, scrolled lists, tables, trees, and specialized dialog boxes like color choosers. Ideally, you can show the user a set of illustrated choices all at once, in one single dropdown, list, or toolbar. A user then can compare them to one another immediately and easily. If you show them one at a time—which sometimes must be the case, as with the **Preview** pattern (see Chapter 5)—the user sees them sequentially over time, which isn't as good for comparing one to another.

Sometimes it's appropriate to show both the picture and the item's name. If the user would benefit from seeing both of them, do it—they'll learn to associate the name with the picture, and thus the concept. Interfaces can teach.

If you need custom icons or thumbnail pictures, consider getting a good graphic designer to do the artistic work. Make sure she is sensitive to the visual vocabulary of the whole application, and that she understands what the choices mean.

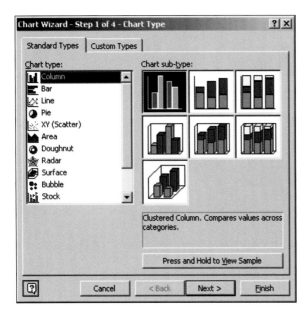

FIGURE 7-25 / When you create a chart in Excel, you see a Chart Wizard that first asks you to choose a chart type. This is a perfect use of Illustrated Choices: not everyone knows what a bubble chart or a radar chart should look like, but some people recognize the pictures of them. (Also note the use of a help text at the lower right, and the fact that the three-page elements together behave like a **Cascaded List**.)

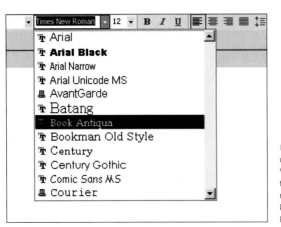

FIGURE 7-26 / A font chooser is a classic place to use Illustrated Choices. In this dropdown box from Word, the font names are written in their own fonts, thus sparing the user the need to look it up in a separate font dialog box or tool—few Word users would know the difference between Book Antiqua and Palatino without seeing examples of them.

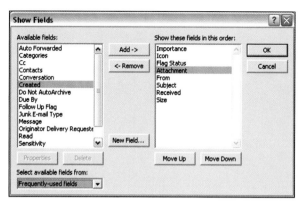

FIGURE 7-27 / A dialog box from MS Outlook

what

Show both the "source" and the "destination" lists on the same page; let the user move items between them.

use when

You ask the user to create a list of items by choosing them from another list. The source list may be long—too long to easily show as a set of checkboxes, for instance.

why

The key to this pattern is showing both lists on the same page. The user can see what's what—she doesn't have to jump to and from a modal dialog box, for instance (see the "Examples" section for an example of that).

A simpler alternative to List Builder might be a single list of checkbox items. Both solve the "select a subset" problem. But if you have a very large source list (such as an entire filesystem), a list of checkboxes doesn't scale—the user can't easily see what's been checked off, and thus may not get a clear picture of what she selected. She has to keep scrolling up and down to see it all.

how

Put the source list on the left and the destination list on the right. The items thus will move from left to right, which is a more natural flow than right to left. Between the two lists, put Add and Remove buttons; you could label them with words, arrows, or both.

This pattern provides room for other buttons, too. If the destination list is ordered, use Move Up and Move Down buttons, as shown in the example above. (They could have arrow icons, too, instead of or in addition to the words.)

Depending on what kind of items you deal with, you could either move the items literally from the source to the destination—so the source list "loses" the item—or maintain a source list that doesn't change. A listing of files in a filesystem shouldn't change; users would find it bizarre if it did, since they see such a list as a model of the underlying filesystem, and the files aren't actually deleted. But the list of "Available fields" in the Outlook example above does lose the items. That's a judgment call.

Implement drag-and-drop between the lists, if possible, and give the lists multiple-selection semantics instead of single-selection, so users can move large numbers of items from list to list.

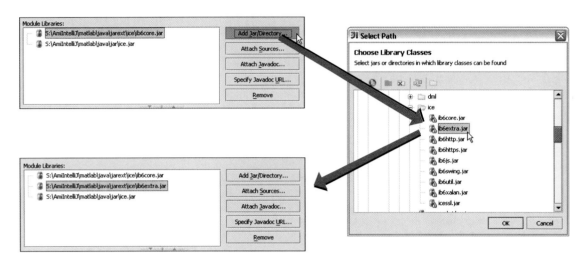

FIGURE 7-28 / IntelliJ IDEA is a complex Java development environment. It has an unfortunate dialog box, for which a List Builder might have been better suited. This example shows a fragment of that dialog box. The user's task is to select some number of .jar files from the filesystem; it may be a few, it may be many. Each time the user wants to add files to the "Module Libraries" list on the left, she has to launch a modal dialog box, shown on the right, where she can select the jar files in question. This can lead to many launches of that dialog box. (The dialog box permits multiple selection, fortunately, but if the user builds up that list slowly, it still will be launched too many times.)

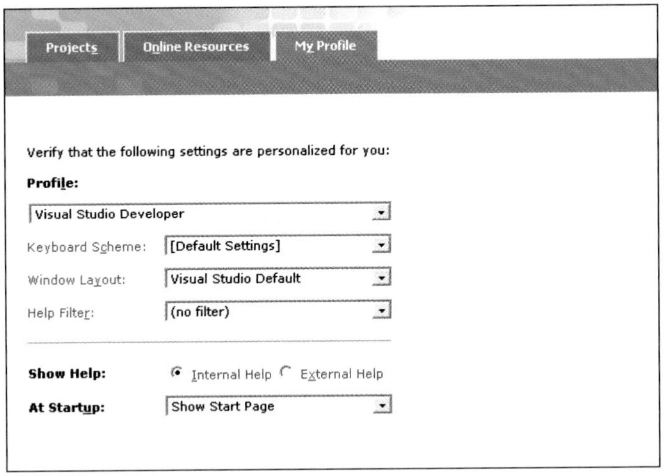

FIGURE 7-29 / Visual Studio profile screen

what

Wherever appropriate, prefill form fields with your best guesses at the values the user wants.

use when

Your UI asks the user any questions requiring form-like input (such as text fields or radio buttons), and you want to reduce the amount of work that users have to do. Perhaps most users will answer in a certain way, or the user has already provided enough contextual information for the UI to make an accurate guess. For technical or semi-relevant questions, maybe he can't be expected to know or care about the answer, and "whatever the system decides" is okay.

But supplying defaults is not always wise when answers might be sensitive or politically charged, such as passwords, gender, or citizenship. Making assumptions like that, or pre-filling fields with data you should be careful with, can make users uncomfortable or angry. (And for the love of all that is good in the world, don't leave "Please send me advertising email" checkboxes checked by default!)

why

By providing reasonable default answers to questions, you save the users work. It's really that simple. You spare the user the effort of thinking about, or typing, the answer. Filling in forms is never fun, but if this pattern halves the time it takes him to work through it, he'll be grateful.

Even if the default isn't what the user wants, at least you offered an example of what kind of answer is asked for. That alone can save him a few seconds of thought—or, worse, an error message.

Sometimes you may run into an unintended consequence of Good Defaults. If a user can skip over a field, that question may not "register" mentally with him. He may forget that it was asked; he may not understand the implications of the question, or of the default value. The act of typing an answer, selecting a value, or clicking a button forces the user to address the issue consciously, and that can be important if you want the user to learn the application effectively.

Prefill the text fields, combo boxes, and other controls with a reasonable default value. You could do this when you show the page to the user for the first time, or you could use the information the user supplies early in the application to dynamically set later default values. (For instance, if someone supplies a United States ZIP Code, you can infer the state, country, and sometimes the city or town from just that number.)

Don't choose a default value just because you think you shouldn't leave any blank controls. Do so only when you're reasonably sure that most users, most of the time, won't change it—otherwise, you will create extra work for everybody. Know your users!

Occasional-use interfaces like software installers deserve a special note. You should ask users for some technical information, like the location of the install, in case they want to customize it. But 90 percent of users probably won't. And they won't care where you install it, either—it's just not important to them. So it's perfectly reasonable to supply a default location.

Jeff Johnson discusses this issue at length in *Web Bloopers: 60 Common Web Design Mistakes and How To Avoid Them* (Morgan Kaufmann). He provides some hilarious examples of poor default values.

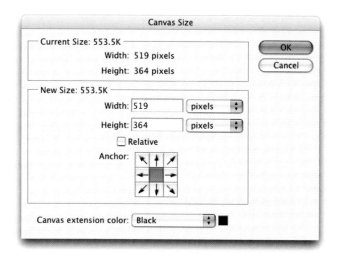

FIGURE 7-30 / When an image canvas is resized in Photoshop, this dialog box appears. The original image was 519 × 364, as shown. These dimensions become the default Width and Height, which is very convenient for several use cases. If I wanted to put a thin frame around the image, I can start with the existing dimensions and increase them by just two pixels each; if I want to make the image canvas wider but not taller, I only need to change the Width field; or I could just click OK now and nothing changes.

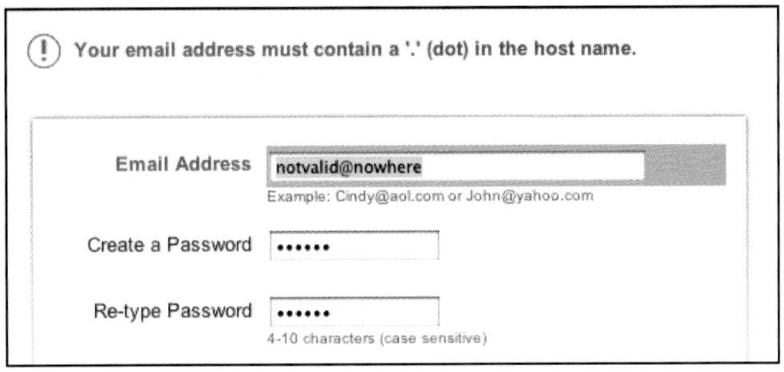

FIGURE 7-31 / Netflix's registration page

what

Place form error messages directly on the page with the form itself; mark the top of the page with an error message, and if possible, put indicators next to the originating controls.

use when

Users might enter form information that somehow isn't acceptable. They may skip required fields, enter unparseable numbers, or type invalid email addresses, for instance. You want to encourage them to try again. You want to point out typos before they become a problem, and help puzzled users understand what is asked for.

why

Traditionally, GUI applications report error messages to users via modal dialog boxes. Those messages can be very helpful, pointing out what the problem was and how you can fix it. The problem is that you have to click away the modal dialog box to fix the error. And with the dialog box gone, you can't read the error message anymore! (Maybe you're supposed to memorize the message.)

Then, when web forms came along, error messages often were reported on a separately loaded page, shown after you clicked "Submit." Again, you can read the message, but you have to click the "Back" button to fix the problem; once you do

that, the message is gone. Then you need to scan the form to find the field with the error, which takes effort and itself is error-prone.

Many web forms now place the error message on the form itself. By keeping both messages and controls together on the same page, the user can read the message and make the form corrections easily, with no jumping around or error-prone memorization.

Even better, some web forms put error messages physically next to the controls where the errors were made. Now the user can see at a glance where the problems were—no need to hunt down the offending field based just on its name—and the instructions for fixing it are right there, easily visible.

how

First, design the form to prevent certain kinds of errors. Use dropdowns instead of open text fields, if you can; offer **Input Hints**, **Input Prompts**, **Forgiving Format**, and other techniques to support text entry. Clearly mark all the required fields as required, and don't ask for too many required fields in the first place.

When errors do happen, you should show some kind of error message on top of the form, even if you put the detailed messages next to the controls. The top is the first thing people see. (It's also good for visually impaired users—the top of the form is read to them first, so they know immediately that the form has an error.) Put an attention-getting graphic there, and use text that's stronger than the body text: make it red and bold, for instance.

Now mark the form fields that caused the errors. Put specific messages next to them, if you can—this will require extra space beside, above, or below the fields—but at the least, use color and/or a small graphic to mark the field, as shown above.

Users commonly associate red with errors in this context. Use it freely, but since so many people are colorblind with respect to red, use other cues, too: language, bold text (not huge), and graphics.

If you're designing for the Web or some other client/server system, try to do as much validation as you can on the client side. It's much quicker. Put the error messages on the page that's already loaded, if possible, to avoid a page-load wait.

A tutorial on error-message writing is beyond the scope of this pattern, but here are some quick guidelines:

- Make them short, but detailed enough to explain both which field it is and what went wrong: "You haven't given us your address" versus "Not enough information."
- Use ordinary language, not computerese: "Is that a letter in your ZIP code?" versus "Numeric validation error."
- Be polite: "Sorry, but something went wrong! Please click 'Go' again" versus "Javascript Error 693" or "This form contains no data."

Register: Enter Information

1 Enter Information   2. Choose User ID & Password   3. Check Your Email

The following must be corrected before continuing:
- Last name - - Please enter this information.
- Address - Please enter this information.

Register now to bid or buy on **any** eBay site. It's easy and **free!**

First name
Zelda

⚠ Please enter this information.
Last name

⚠ Please enter this information.
Street address

City
Cambridge

State / Province   Zip / Postal code   Country
Massachusetts   02130   United States

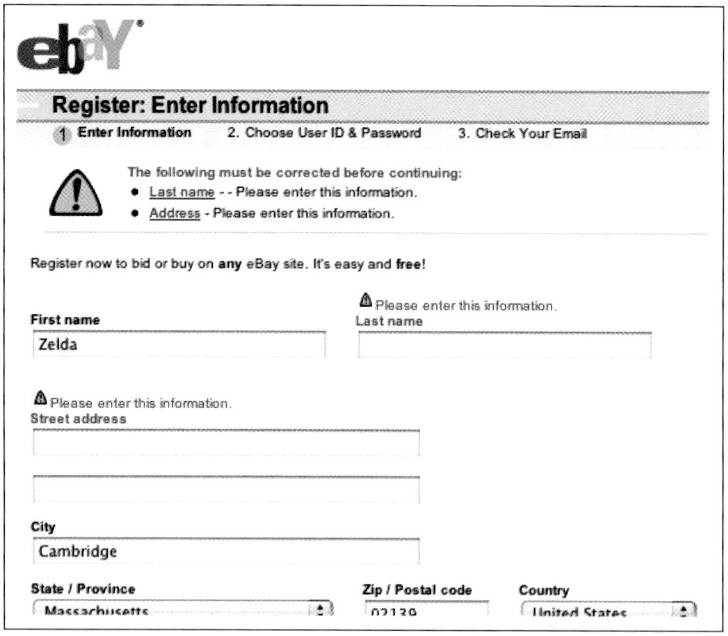

FIGURE 7-32 / The user registration page at eBay offers an excellent example of this pattern. The error summary at the top of the form catches the eye and lays out exactly what needs to be fixed before registration can proceed. (It even provides links to the fields in question.) Each of the problematic fields has its own error message, too. It's redundant, but that's okay in this case—some people will zero in on the two red-labeled fields before they finish reading the messages at the top.

08

BUILDERS AND EDITORS

This chapter covers ideas and patterns used in various "editor" idioms. Many users are familiar with them through common applications like Word and PowerPoint, but the ideas usually are much older or more widespread than these applications. The patterns in this chapter are drawn mostly from these idioms:

Page layout and formatted text editors
> For example, Word, Quark, and InDesign

Image editors
> Photoshop, the GIMP, Paint Shop Pro, Fireworks, and MacPaint

Vector-graphics editors
> Powerpoint, Illustrator, CorelDraw, Visio, and OmniGraffle

Web site builders
> Dreamweaver and GoLive

GUI builders and code editors
> Visual Studio, Eclipse, and Interface Builder

Generic text editors
> Notepad, Emacs, email composers, and millions of web pages

Despite the different media they edit, these idioms have a lot in common. They are, first and foremost, canvases—they offer the user an empty shell she can creatively fill, plus the tools to fill it with. Most of them are naturally structured around the **Canvas Plus Palette** pattern, from Chapter 2, which prescribes a blank canvas area next to an iconic toolbox.

Going back further, into Chapter 1, you might recall the **Incremental Construction** pattern and the concept of "flow." They are especially important for builder-style software. People who create things don't work linearly—they create a little bit, see how it looks (or works), change it, add more, delete some of it, and step back to take another look. When the tools are responsive and designed appropriately for the task, they fade from the user's awareness, and the user becomes fully absorbed in the creative activity.

To get there, a user has to be able to use the tools with skill and efficiency. Fortunately for users, most editors within a given idiom have evolved to become very similar, so skills and habits learned in one editor are "transferable" to others. There's no need to make your editor identical to another—there's still plenty of room for innovation in editor design. However, it's best not to reinvent too many wheels at once.

Then there's efficiency. Nothing disrupts flow like a needlessly long series of dialog boxes, wasteful and tiring mouse movements, or having to wait for software to think before it responds. In builders and editors, strive for *immediacy:* common actions are executed with minimal keystrokes or pointer motions, and gestures have instant results.

Many interaction-design decisions you make for any builder or editor will deal with WYSI-WYG editing, direct manipulation, modes, or selection. Getting these concepts right is critical for efficient, skilled use.

THE BASICS OF EDITOR DESIGN

Four elements are essential in most editors: the ability to do WYSIWYG editing; the ability to manipulate the interface and data elements directly; a variety of operational modes; and a wide range of options for selecting text or objects.

WYSIWYG EDITING

WYSIWYG is an acronym for "what you see is what you get" (but you probably knew that already). It makes some interfaces easier to use because the user doesn't have to do any complicated mental transformations at design time to figure out what the end result will look like.

WYSIWYG is best suited for images, vector graphics, video and animation, some GUI builders, and "hard" formatted text—the end products look the same to everyone, regardless of the context in which they are viewed.

But now think about HTML. When you design a web page, you may not have full control over the final product. Depending on how you've written it, your page may be subject to many end-user manipulations—style sheets, text sizes, window sizes, browser varieties, display devices, layout preferences, and even customized content. What does WYSIWYG mean when every viewer sees a different end result? That's an open question.

Also, if you design a text editor that produces formatted text, consider this: Almost everyone with a Windows computer has a copy of Microsoft Word, and that sets up some powerful expectations for how a text editor should work. On the other hand, every computer user has email, and most email editors produce plain text (and so they should, since email is fundamentally a plain-text medium). Then there are millions of web pages that edit message boards or blogs—mostly plain text, though some include simple tag-based formatting. Instant messaging also uses plain text.

On any given day, how many of the world's words are typed into Word, and how many into plain-text editors? Again, it's an open question. Don't underestimate the usability benefits of plain-text, non-WYSIWYG editors—they're simple to design and easy to use.

DIRECT MANIPULATION

"Direct manipulation" means that an interface lets the user grab, push, drag, drop, reshape, stack, paint, open, close, or otherwise handle the objects in the interface. A sense of physicality is key—even though the objects are virtual, and handling is done via mice or other devices, the user is under the illusion of direct physical engagement with those objects.

And a strong illusion it is! The next time you sit down at a windowed computer, put a paper sticky note on the screen. Try to ignore it for a while. At some point, your conscious mind probably will forget that it's not a window, and you'll try to grab it and move it with the mouse.

When designed well, direct manipulation is *immediate*—actions take place with no apparent wait time, which in practice means that the system responds in less than one-tenth of a second. And it is *precise*—users need to have fine control over the location of that pointer and the objects attached to it, as though it were a fingertip in real space.

Direct manipulation also should follow conventions. As mentioned earlier, people assume they can transfer common skills from one piece of software to another: for example, copy and paste, drag and drop, resizing via handles, and multiple selection via rubber-band selection.

MODES

An interface mode is a state in which input gestures do things other than what they normally do. For example, click-and-drag in a drawing program normally means "rubber-band select these objects." But in line-drawing mode, click-and-drag means "draw a line from here to here."

Some say that modes in an interface are bad, because they make it too easy for users to get into trouble. That's not always true. People who use graphic editors are used to them. In fact, I don't know how to design a complex graphics editor without them, if I have only a mouse and keyboard to work with—those input devices have to be functionally overloaded if you're going to implement a lot of different drawing features.

However, modes can go bad if:

- It's not made clear to a user that the interface is in a particular mode.
- The modes cause unnecessary work by being obnoxious to turn on and off.

You can easily solve the first problem with sufficient interface feedback. The mouse cursor should always represent the current mode, for instance. The user's attention will focus wherever the cursor is, so that cue is hard to miss. If you use buttons to turn modes on and off, render the "on" button differently from the others (e.g., show it as pressed in, not popped out).

Two mode-related patterns in this chapter try to solve the second problem: **One-Off Mode** and **Spring-Loaded Mode**. Both make it easy to turn a mode off; Spring-Loaded Mode makes it easy to turn a mode on, too. Contrast these patterns to a situation in which the user has to move the mouse pointer all the way to a palette in the screen corner, locate a tiny palette button, click it to turn a mode on, move the mouse back to the canvas, draw something, go back to the palette to turn another mode on, and go back to the canvas...ad infinitum. That's a lot of mouse motion. It's also a repetitive strain injury waiting to happen.

SELECTION

On its surface, selection seems simple to design. Long ago, conventions were established for many kinds of selection, such as text, list items, and graphic objects; people grew accustomed to them. The following table describes the most common conventions for object selection, within three groups of interface idioms:

- Text editors, including both plain and formatted text
- Vector-based graphics, most drawing programs, and GUI builders
- Lists, tables, and trees (which are covered in Chapter 6, but they're in this table so you can compare selection gestures)

The following table summarizes the most frequently encountered actions for common selection-related gestures. (Not all gestures affect the selection; the ones that don't are shown in gray.) These are the conventions your users most likely will assume your application will follow.

	Text editors	Vector graphics editors, GUI builders	Lists, tables, trees
Single click	Move text insertion cursor here	Select just this item	Select just this item
Double click	Select this word	Open or edit this item	Open or edit this item
Triple click	Select this line, or select this paragraph	N/A	N/A
Click, drag, release	Start selection here, end it there; select all text between them	Select everything inside the bounding box (known as "rubber-band", "marquee" or "marching ants" selection)	Drag this item from here to there
Shift-click	Start selection at the text insertion cursor, end it at the click point, and select all text between them	Add this item to the selection set	Add this item to the selection set, plus all intervening items ("contiguous selection")
Control-click	Varies from application to application	Varies from application to application	Add this item to the selection set ("discontiguous selection")

Now the fun begins. If you implement only these conventions, have you solved all the selection-related problems your users will encounter? Probably not. Think about the higher-level tasks that users might want to perform. For example, suppose:

- The user selects several items on a graphic editor, intending to align their left edges. But which shape's left edge? The first selected item? The last? How can the user tell? Some applications mark the first selected item as the "dominant" item. It looks different from the others, such as one that is drawn with green selection handles instead of blue (see Figure 8-1). When an alignment completes, the dominant item stays put, and the others are moved into alignment with it.

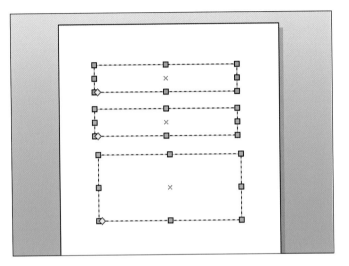

FIGURE 8-1 / Dominant selection in Visio

- Now let's say that a user wants to select a red region of an image. That region is many hundreds of pixels large, and it has a ragged edge, making it very difficult to select all the red pixels cleanly. The **Smart Selection** pattern helps with that scenario. If an application can anticipate the "chunks" of content that users want to select, it can help by selecting that chunk automatically. The chunk could also be a paragraph of text, or a grouped set of shapes.

In any case, get to know your users' common tasks. Anticipate the difficulties they may have with traditional selection, and augment your selection design to help with those difficulties.

THE PATTERNS

Most of this chapter's patterns fit into the functional groups described earlier. **Edit-in-Place** is very much a WYSIWYG approach to editing labels and text. **Smart Selection** and **Composite Selection** deal with selection mechanics, and **One-Off Mode** and **Spring-Loaded Mode** solve problems with mode switching.

 79   **Edit-in-Place**

 80   **Smart Selection**

 81   **Composite Selection**

 82   **One-Off Mode**

 83   **Spring-Loaded Mode**

Constrained Resize, **Magnetism**, and **Guides** address precision-related problems that users often face with direct manipulation. All three patterns help a user achieve a specific task—resizing an object correctly in the first case, and moving objects to precise locations in the other two.

 84   **Constrained Resize**

 85   **Magnetism**

 86   **Guides**

Paste Variations addresses a very specific design problem in an application's cut, copy, and paste feature. WYSIWYG editors tend to need it more than other kinds of applications.

87   **Paste Variations**

79 edit-in-place

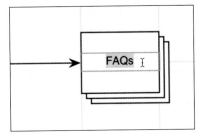

FIGURE 8-2 / OmniGraffle label edited in place

what

Use a small, dynamic text editor to let the user change text "in place": position the editor directly over the original text, rather than using a separate panel or dialog box.

use when

The builder UI contains text that the user may want to change sometimes. The names of objects, text elements in a graphic layout, labels, and even property values are good candidates.

why

Making the user go somewhere else—a place far away spatially, or disconnected from the original text, in another window—usually isn't a good idea. The user may not find the editor, for one thing. It also takes time to switch one's attention from one place to another, and the perceived complexity of the interface is increased.

That said, an alternative to this pattern is to edit the text in a separate panel, such as a **Property Sheet** (see Chapter 4) or in a dialog box. You should do this only if **Edit-in-Place** is too technically difficult, or if the text in question is so long and complex that it deserves specialized editing and formatting tools—fonts, text sizes, the kinds of things you'd find on text editors' toolbars.

how

When the user clicks or, more typically, double-clicks on the text to be edited, simply replace it with an editable text field containing the string. Anything the user types is then entered into the text field. End the edit session when the user clicks somewhere else.

Make sure the text field appears in precisely the same apparent location as the original non-editable string. If it seems to jump when editing starts, it may irritate users. (This situation doesn't seem like a big deal, but it can be.) Also, retain the same typeface as the original text, if you can. In short, make it as WYSIWYG as possible.

Usually a border appears around the text when the editor is invoked, indicating to the user that editing has begun. That may not even be necessary, though. Other cues may suffice: a text-entry cursor should appear (often blinking), and if a common user task is to replace the original string entirely, then the whole original string should be automatically selected when the editor appears.

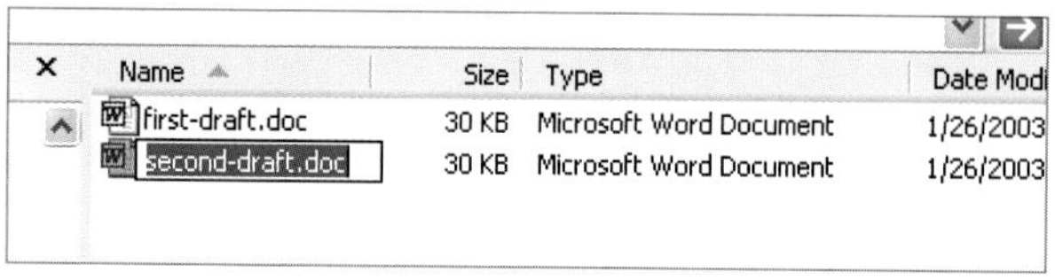

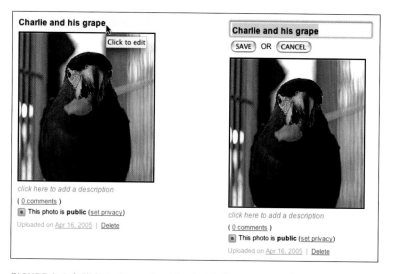

FIGURE 8-3 / Windows Explorer is where many people see Edit-in-Place for the first time. Explorer isn't an editor, but it establishes a precedent for how one interacts with Edit-in-Place. Explorer differs from most editors because you invoke Edit-in-Place via a "slow" double-click (not always easy to do, and not recommended), whereas most editors use an ordinary single or double click. But the rest is the same. The previous text is automatically selected, a box is drawn around the text, and a blinking text-entry cursor appears.

FIGURE 8-4 / Flickr isn't an editor either, but it allows users to edit picture titles and descriptions in place. What's interesting about it, from an interaction-design point of view, is how the edit session ends. Most applications end it when the user clicks somewhere else. The Flickr designers decided to make it more explicit: they offer Save and Cancel buttons that appear dynamically along with the text fields. First-time users will have no trouble figuring it out (once they learn they can click on the text in the first place).

FIGURE 8-5 / Photoshop's magic-wand selection tool selects a red area

what

Make the software smart enough to automatically select a coherent group of items, rather than making the user do it.

use when

The user works with selectable objects of any kind—text, pixels, geometric objects, or even tree items or table cells. The selectable items are organized into coherent visual groups, like words or sentences in a text editor, groups of vector graphics, or pixels of contiguous color in an image.

Normally, selection of all the items in one of these groups requires the user to click and drag the mouse pointer with some precision. This isn't always easy. For instance, lassoing all the red pixels might be difficult because they're not contained in a tidy rectangular area.

why

Not all users are good at fine, precise mouse movements. Also, sometimes circumstances make them hard or impossible for everyone! (Consider a laptop's trackpad, for example.) Once it becomes clear to the software that the user is trying to select a particular group of items—or when the user intentionally begins a smart selection—then the software ought to help out the user and select that group automatically. Let computers do what computers are good at, and let humans do what they're good at!

how

Figure out which UI gesture you ought to use to make a "smart selection." The gesture might be any of the following actions:

- A double click or double tap
- A single click while in a particular mode or tool, such as Photoshop's magic wand
- A single click while a key is held down
- The act of enlarging the selection out towards the boundaries of a group, as many text editors do

If larger groups contain the smaller groups, consider ways to enlarge the smart selection to the enclosing groups, too—like expanding the selection of a word to the selection of a sentence, and then a whole paragraph.

But be careful. When done thoughtlessly, smart selections can be irritating. Imagine the user's frustration when he tries to precisely select a group of pixels, but every time he comes close to a color boundary, the selection "snaps" out to where he didn't want it! The equivalent problem happens in some text editors; see the following example.

"There's no place like home."

"There's no place like home."

"There's no place like home."

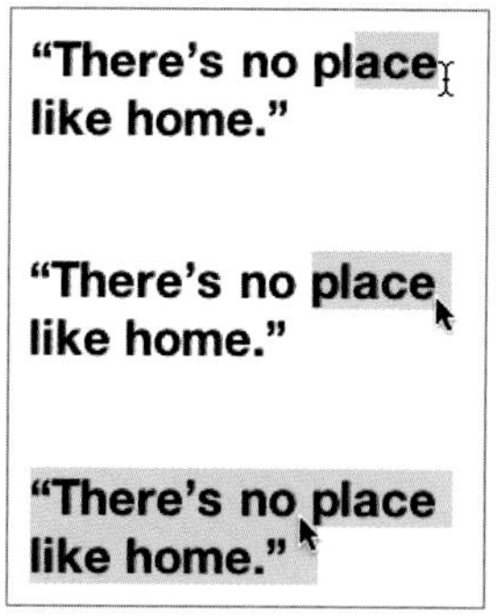

FIGURE 8-6 / Word does smart selection on words and lines. These screenshots show the results of a mouse click-and-drag (first), a double click on a word (second), and a triple click on the whole paragraph (third).

Note the inclusion of the trailing space when a whole word is selected. You wanted that space to be selected too, right? No? Well, that's too bad, because you can't *not* select it if you invoke smart selection via double-click. If you don't want it, you have to click-and-drag over the word yourself, and carefully stop before accidentally including that space.

This kind of behavior causes Word to tread the fine line between being appropriately helpful and being obnoxious. When you design software to make decisions for users, be sure you're correct most of the time, for most users, under most circumstances.

81 composite selection

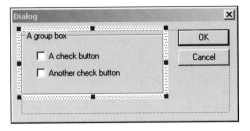

FIGURE 8-7 / Selecting a Visual Studio composite

what

Use different gestures—or mouse clicks in different screen areas, such as the composite's edges versus its insides—to determine whether you should select a composite itself or allow its contained objects to be selected.

use when

Your graphical editor may contain composite objects—things that you can move and otherwise manipulate, but happen to contain other objects. This is especially common in drawing programs and GUI builders.

why

When objects are on canvases, a single click normally selects the object. In this case, you want the user to be able to select child objects (or create new ones) inside the composite, but that means the user has to click on the composite's background. Should it select the composite, or not? The mouse click has two interpretations, reflecting the double role—parent and child—that the composite plays.

Obviously one of these interpretations has to win out; the user needs to be able to predict what will happen when he clicks the mouse on the composite's background. Two different kinds of selection—one for composites, and one for "leaf" objects that

are not composites—solves the problem (albeit in a brute-force fashion). The two selection modes are similar, but respond differently to mouse events like clicking and dragging.

how

Visual Studio (Figure 8-7) demonstrates the most common solution to this problem. A user cannot select its group boxes (which are technically not composites, but appear to be anyway) unless she clicks near the edge of the group box. Mouse clicks inside the object operate on the contents; if it's a click-and-drag, a lasso is started, and if it's just a click, the contained object is selected. She also can drag the group box by the edges; she can re-size only by the eight selection handles, at the corners and edge centers. This limits direct manipulation, but the mechanism is simple and easily understood once the user knows what's going on.

When a composite is selected, draw the draggable edges and resize handles in a recognizable way, like the dotted border in Figure 8-7. The visual cue sets expectations for the user.

FIGURE 8-8 / HTML tables are composites—they usually contain objects like text, images, or nested tables. So an HTML editor such as Dreamweaver needs to give the user access to both the table as an object, and its contents as objects. Here, the lefthand screenshot shows a click inside the table—such a click would select either an image or text. The example on the right shows table selection with a click on the table's edge.

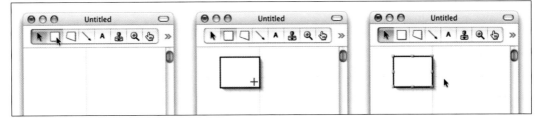

FIGURE 8-9 / One-off shape creation in OmniGraffle

what

When a mode is turned on, perform the operation once. Then switch back automatically into the default or previous mode.

use when

In the editor you build, users don't normally repeat or iterate over certain operations, such as object creation. Usually, a user performs the operation only once, and then he immediately wants to do something else, like manipulate the object he just created.

why

Users will find it annoying to switch into a mode, do one little thing, and then explicitly switch out of that mode again. Doing so often involves clicking on small "hit targets" in palette windows far away from the working canvas, which takes up time and energy. Too much "clickiness" in an interface is a known irritant.

Instead, the interface should do that which makes the user's job easier, even if it's not easy to program, or isn't consistent across all the palette items. Several builder programs use one-off modes, so your users likely will be familiar with the idea.

Also, modes are tricky. A user can forget which mode is currently active in a program, and take actions that have unintended consequences. When using one-off modes, that's less likely; the user can't get "stuck" in that mode.

how

The hardest part of implementing One-Off Mode is deciding which operations ought to use it. Object creation typically uses it. Zooming, lassoing, and paint strokes (despite being "objects" in the programming sense) typically don't. Find out which graphical editors your users are most familiar with, and see what those editors do.

This is a design decision best made when you really know users' work habits. If they do want to create several similar objects in a row, then having to go to the palette to start each individual object will irritate them.

Many applications that use a one-off mode have a "secret" version of the mode that allows multiple operations (thus behaving like a regular mode). You can often invoke it by holding down a key, like Shift, while clicking the mode's button, but it varies across applications.

An example walkthrough might clarify this concept. Consider a drawing tool in which mouse-clicking on the canvas normally selects objects underneath the mouse pointer.

1. The user clicks the "Create rectangle" button on a palette. The UI goes into a special creation mode, indicated by a rectangle cursor. Now clicking on the canvas will place the object and not select anything.

2. The user clicks down on the mouse button, to place the upper-left corner.

3. The user moves the mouse and releases the button to place the lower-right corner.

4. The UI, having noted the click-drag-release and created the rectangle, leaves the rectangle-creation mode and goes back to the default mode, in which clicking means selection.

5. The user now is free to select objects, move them, and resize them without having to go back to the palette to change modes.

FIGURE 8-10 / The shift key on a keyboard

what

Let the user enter a mode by holding down a key or a mouse button. When the user releases it, leave the mode and go back to the previous one.

use when

You build a graphical editor, or any interface that uses modes extensively. Sometimes a user wants to enter a mode temporarily—he might need to do something quickly, and then fall back immediately to the mode he was already in.

Your users are motivated to learn the interface well; maybe they use it every day. They don't mind learning and memorizing shortcuts to desired functionality.

why

One of the big problems with modes is that a user can forget what mode he's in. Without an obvious state indicator, like a special mouse cursor, he may take actions believing he's in Mode A when he's really in Mode B. Unintended consequences may result. You can partially solve that problem with **One-Off Modes**, of course, and also by constant reminders of what mode the user is in (like the mouse cursor). A user won't forget about that spring-loaded mode as long as he's physically holding down a key.

But a spring-loaded mode gives you another advantage: convenience. Again, like one-off modes, spring-loaded modes reduce the number of times the user has to go to the palette, click a little button, and go back to work. In this case, no such trip is necessary—the user just holds down a key, does whatever needs doing, and releases the key. Once learned, it takes very little effort. It's conducive to working fast and to a state of flow.

The problem with spring-loaded modes is that they're invisible. There's nothing on the interface—no labels or menu mnemonics—that announces their presence. The user has to learn them "the hard way," by reading manuals or learning from other people.

how

The mechanics here are pretty simple: invoke the mode while the user holds down a key. However, as with **One-Off Modes**, the hard part is choosing which modes deserve a spring-loaded alternative to normal operation. Know your users. What tasks do they do that require very temporary modes?

As in all interfaces, make sure that this "secret" keyboard gesture is not the only way to reach the mode in question. Make it an alternative to a palette button, for instance, or something done from the toolbar or menu bar.

examples

A Shift key is the classic example of a spring-loaded mode—while the key is held down, typed letters come out in uppercase. Release it, and you're back to lowercase. Contrast this key to Caps Lock, which is more like typical graphical-editor modes: press it to turn it on, and press it again to turn it off.

Photoshop, Paint Shop Pro, and Fireworks (and probably other drawing programs, too) all offer a spring-loaded mode for the eyedropper tool. Why? Imagine that you are trying to paint one region with the same color as another region:

1. While in the paintbrush mode, hold down the Alt key (or Option, depending on platform). The mode switches to the eyedropper.
2. Click on the color you want.
3. Release the Alt or Option key, and keep painting with the new color.

This is very quick and convenient. Your attention remains focused on the canvas, where you want it, and it's not diverted to the palette.

(Incidentally, Photoshop is packed full of spring-loaded modes like these. You can find them in books and quick-reference cards, but you may not find them just by hunting around.)

You can find another spring-loaded mode example in list-oriented interfaces, such as Windows Explorer, Mac Finder, and email clients. You can usually invoke multiple selection by holding down the shift or control key, and then selecting objects. Because the "click" gesture is interpreted differently—single selection versus multiple—these are two different modes, by definition.

If you're used to that, consider what would happen if you had to switch from single to multiple selection via a button on Explorer's toolbar (or Finder's), rather than holding down a key. You'd be going back and forth to that toolbar a lot! If you visited another application for a while, and then came back, could you recall whether you'd left it in single or multiple selection mode? Probably not, and thus you wouldn't immediately know what would happen when you clicked on filenames. You don't know whether the new selection would replace the current selection or be added to it.

84 constrained resize

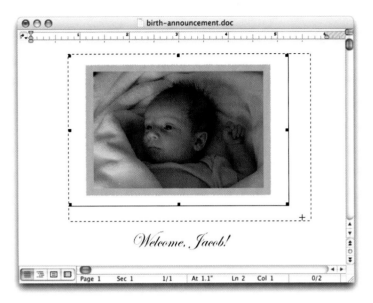

FIGURE 8-11 / Resizing a picture; Word preserves a picture's aspect ratio when corners are dragged

what

Supply resize modes with different behavior, such as preserving aspect ratio, for use under special circumstances.

use when

You build a graphical editor that lets the user resize objects interactively, such as by dragging a corner. But sometimes users want to preserve certain properties, like the object's aspect ratio, for instance—especially of pictures and formatted text—or the position of the object's geometrical center. Normal drag-the-corner interactive resizing makes this task difficult.

why

Quite simply, this technique can save the user a lot of work. If the UI constrains the resize to work in certain ways, such as by forcing the width and height to remain in the same proportion to each other, then the user can focus on what he really wants it to look like.

If the user doesn't have this degree of control over the interface, he might resort to doing the resize by typing numbers into a form. That works, but it's almost never as nice as direct manipulation. It breaks up the user's flow of work and forces him to think numerically instead of visually—something not everyone does well. Direct manipulation better supports **Incremental Construction** (see Chapter 1).

how

This technique is basically a modified resize mode, so it should behave much like your normal resize—usually by dragging a corner or edge of the object to be resized. How should you differentiate this mode from a normal resize mode? Consider using a modifier key; many applications go into a constrained-resize mode when you hold down the Shift or Function key while dragging a corner.

Or, if you think most users are always going to want the constraint, make it the default resize operation. Word does this with pictures and clip art; see Figure 8-11. Thus users don't accidentally end up with vertically or horizontally squished faces in their baby announcements.

As the user drags the mouse cursor, a resize box should be drawn to show the new dimensions and/or position. This box gives the user immediate feedback about what's going to happen; if the user is alert, he can even tell from the resize-box behavior whether or not the resize is constrained.

You can constrain a resize in several ways. Here are some possibilities:

- Retain the object's original aspect ratio (the ratio of width to height).

- Leave the object's geometric center in the same place, and resize symmetrically around it.

1 *About Face 2.0: The Essentials of Interaction Design* (Wiley), page 311.

- Resize by units larger than pixels. For instance, a GUI builder might require that a list box's height be some integral number of text lines. (Probably not a good idea in general, but if that's what you have to work with, the UI should reflect it.) The resize, by default, should "jump" from one size quantum to the next. Similarly, the graphical builder's canvas might use a Snap-to-Grid mechanism; again, the resize should jump between grid squares.

- Limit the size of the object. Once the user hits the size limit in one dimension or the other, don't let the resize box expand (or contract, as the case may be) any further in that dimension.

Alan Cooper and Robert Reimann describe this technique as "constrained drag."[1] The technique dates back at least to the mid-1990s.

examples

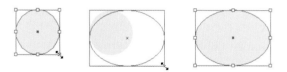

FIGURE 8-12 / Adobe Illustrator has at least two constrained-resize modes: one for preserving the object's aspect ratio, and one for preserving its geometric center. This figure shows a normal drag-the-corner resize, in its "before" (with grabbable handles), "during," and "after" states. The blue outlines, which change in real time as the user drags the corner, show what the object's new size and position would be, should the user release the drag.

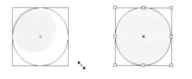

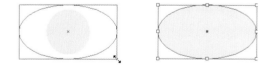

FIGURE 8-13 / These screenshots show the two constrained-resize modes. When the user holds down the Shift key, the aspect-ratio-preserving mode kicks in. When the user holds down the Alt key instead, the object can be resized freely in both dimensions, but the center stays fixed..

85 magnetism

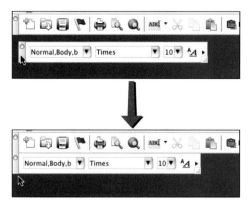

FIGURE 8-14 / A Word toolbar "snapped" into place

what

Make the objects "magnetic" to the things a user positions them against. When the user drags an object very near one of these things, it should stick.

use when

The user needs to position objects very precisely, such as next to other objects or against **Guides**. This often happens in graphic editors, of course, but it's also common in window managers and desktop frameworks, in which a user needs to move windows and palettes, for example.

why

Magnetism helps compensate for users' lack of perfect dexterity with a mouse. If the user really does want the moved object to end up right against another one—and you need to be sure about this—then the computer can help by doing it for her.

What magnetism does is make the mouse "target zone" effectively bigger than it really is. If the user tries to put one thing precisely next to another thing, the target zone is one pixel wide; beyond that, they either overlap or don't touch, and she has to keep trying to position it exactly right. But a one-pixel target is awfully tiny. If magnetism snaps the object into place when the user gets within, say, four pixels of the edge, then the target zone is two times four (i.e., eight) pixels wide. Much easier!

And much faster, too. This device also helps users who do have the dexterity necessary to place objects within one-pixel target zones. Magnetism saves them the time and effort they'd otherwise need to do that, and it makes the application feel more responsive and helpful in general.[2]

how

When the user drags an object close to another object's edge, make it snap to the other object. Likewise, when it's dragged away, keep it there for a few pixels, and then let it move away.

---

2 Martijn van Welie first described this pattern in his online patterns catalog: *http://www.welie.com/patterns/gui/magnetism.html*.

Objects that can be "magnetic" might include:

- Objects of the same type as the one moved, such as windows to windows or shapes to shapes.

- Canvas edges, margins, and screen edges.

- **Guides** and grid lines—devices that exist strictly for the purpose of aligning objects with one another.

- Easily detectable "hard edges" in picture layers, as seen in Photoshop.

examples

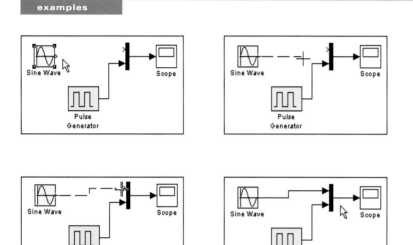

FIGURE 8-15 / Diagram builders and visual programming environments sometimes use magnetism to help the user link together a diagram. Here, you can use the Simulink application to put together a miniature signal-generator simulation. The user needs to connect the output port of the Sine Wave source to an input port of a multiplexer, shown as a dark vertical bar.

Without magnetism, this task would require the user to position the mouse on a very tiny target, click down on the mouse button, and then drag and release the connection to another very tiny target. However, the source output port actually is bigger than the few pixels shown. And as the user drags the connection—illustrated by a dotted line— toward the multiplexer's input port, the connection "snaps" into the input port as the mouse approaches within ten pixels or so. (Simulink even puts corners into the connection automatically.) In the last frame, the user has released the mouse button, finishing the connection.

86 guides

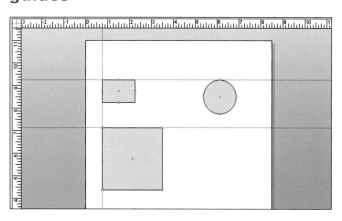

FIGURE 8-16 / Guides in Visio

Offer horizontal and vertical reference lines to help users align objects.

The user needs to position objects so they align with one another precisely, or against page margins. This is most common in vector-based drawing programs, GUI builders, page layout editors, and image editors.

Like **Magnetism**, guides can compensate for users' lack of perfect dexterity—they help users keep objects aligned. In addition, guides make it easier for a user to see that alignment is pixel-perfect. At low magnification, as in the Visio example above, a user can't see for sure that the two rectangles line up perfectly. But the guide assures that they do.

Some implementations of guides move the objects when the guide is moved. This is helpful because the user's original intent was almost certainly to keep those objects aligned to the same line, and by automatically moving the attached objects, the guide spares the user the work of dragging all those objects back to the guide's new location.

You shouldn't necessarily use guides as a substitute for traditional alignment tools (e.g., to align selected shapes on their bottom edges, or align selected shapes vertically by center), since those tools are faster for complex alignment tasks. Guides, however, are more true to the spirit of direct manipulation.

Finally, guides can communicate layout information between multiple authors of one document. If Amber starts a complex page layout, she might create guides along the margins and gridlines of that layout. Then when she hands it off to Bert to finish filling it in, he can see the guides defining those margins and gridlines.

Guides are reference lines that float "above" the canvas—they aren't part of the document being created, and they shouldn't look like they are. Most guides are brightly colored. Some are red, some are bright blue, and others are lime green; the idea is that they should be visible against whatever is underneath them. They are effectively zero-width, so always draw them a single pixel wide, and don't enlarge them under higher magnification.

Let users create guides that are either horizontal or vertical, and let them create as many as they'd like. Many applications provide rulers around canvases, as shown in the Visio example above, and guides often are created by dragging some affordance from the ruler (like those two crossed blue lines in the upper-left corner). Other applications afford guide creation from menu bars or toolbars. Then again, you may want to create them automatically, whenever an alignment task demands it—see the Word and Interface Builder examples in Figures 8-17 and 8-18.

Guides should be draggable whenever the user wishes to adjust the layout, so consider letting them be draggable in many different modes, not just one mode. Also consider the ability to lock them down so you can't move them by accident. Some applications, including Visio and Visual Studio, let users glue objects onto guides, so they're semi-permanently stuck; when the guide is moved, the objects move with it.

Guides work very well when combined with the **Magnetism** pattern found in this chapter. When a user moves an object close to the guide, the object snaps to the guide and aligns itself against it. This makes it far easier for a user to align things precisely to the guide.

Allow users to show and hide guides on demand, especially in WYSIWYG editors. After all, they're not part of the document itself. Also, they can contribute to visual clutter.

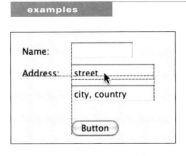

FIGURE 8-17 / Many GUI builders, including Visual Studio and the Mac Interface Builder, offer guides. In the Interface Builder, dotted blue guides automatically appear as the user drags interface elements around the canvas. The guides, which are "magnetic," actively encourage the user to place the controls so they are aligned with one another—when you see the guides appear, you know that you've aligned it correctly.

In this screenshot, the "street" text field is dragged nearly into alignment with the other text fields and with the "Address:" label. The guides helpfully push it the last few pixels into place.

FIGURE 8-18 / Photoshop's guides are drawn as thin cyan lines. These are created explicitly by the user (not automatically), and he can position them at precise pixel locations via a dialog box—quite useful in some scenarios. Users can also drag them. As shown in this figure, the guide doesn't have any physical width relative to the image, so it can stay a single pixel wide while the image is magnified.

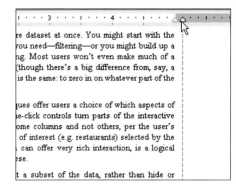

FIGURE 8-19 / Word's guides are created automatically. They control the locations of margins and indentations, and when they're moved, they change the way that text fills the page. A Word guide isn't visible until the user drags its affordance along the top ruler.

FIGURE 8-20 / Paint Shop Pro

what

Provide specialized paste functionality in addition to the standard paste operation.

use when

The user will paste things from the clipboard into the application. But he might intend to do one of several things with it, and each task requires a subtly different paste operation—he might paste it into a different format, for instance, or into a new destination document instead of an existing one.

This pattern is rarely used. Only a few applications need it, but it's a viable solution to a tough design problem.

why

Sometimes there's no getting around it: you have to support two or more paste-related task scenarios, and no amount of cleverness will help you reconcile them into one ultra-smart paste operation. You could pick one as the only way paste is done,

which would keep the design simple. But users who perform one of the other tasks will be out of luck. They'll have to do a lot of work by hand to get the pasted content to look right.

So you need to present two or more kinds of paste. One will have to be the default, because when the user hits Control-V (or whatever the paste accelerator is on your platform), something reasonable should happen—you can't just put up a menu or a dialog box on Control-V. Doing so will break users' expectations of immediate action. However, you can provide choices in some other way, in addition to the default behavior.

how

On the Edit menu, show the other paste variations in addition to the default paste operation. Label them with more detail; say exactly what they do. You could put them directly on the Edit menu—which is probably easiest to use—or you could put all the paste operations, including the default, into a cascaded or pull-right menu off of the Edit menu. (Cascaded menus require annoyingly precise mouse motions, however, so use them only if you need to reduce the number of top-level Edit menu items.)

examples

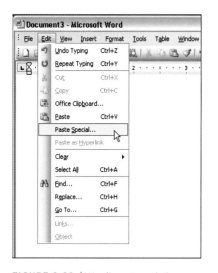

FIGURE 8-21 / Dreamweaver is a complicated website building program. You can edit a web page either in a WYSIWYG graphic editor, or in a text editor showing the HTML code itself, or both in one split window, as shown here; Dreamweaver keeps the two in sync. In this screenshot, I copied a piece of HTML code to the clipboard, tags and all.

Now what should happen if I just paste that code into the WYSIWYG half of the editor? It's just text, really. It has some pesky angle brackets in it (<h4>), but shouldn't it be copied literally, so you see "<h4>" in the web page? Or should it be interpreted as a level-4 header? Better yet, what if it were a custom tag that Dreamweaver doesn't know about, like <customheader>?

Maybe yes, maybe no. Dreamweaver can't read my mind. So it provides a paste variation: "Paste HTML". If I select that menu item, then Dreamweaver assumes it's code and doesn't show the tags in the web page. If I use the default Paste operation, Dreamweaver treats it as literal text and *does* show the tags in the web page.

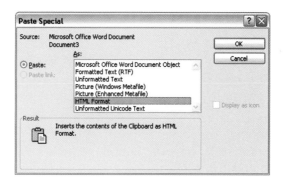

FIGURE 8-22 / Word's paste variations are so complex that they need to appear in a separate dialog box. Word's Edit menu displays two paste items: Paste, which is the default (and performed by Control-V), and Paste Special, which brings up the dialog box. For the items currently on the clipboard—text with some bold words in it—Word lists no fewer than seven destination formats! But as the user tentatively selects each format in that list, she can see a short description of the result. (In the case shown here, the description isn't actually all that helpful, but it *could* be.) Interestingly, the dialog box also shows the source of the clipboard items.

MAKING IT LOOK GOOD:
VISUAL STYLE AND AESTHETICS

In 2002, a research group discovered something interesting. The Stanford Web Credibility Project[1] set out to learn what causes people to trust or distrust web sites, and much of what they found made intuitive sense: company reputation, customer service, sponsorships, and ads all helped users decide whether or not a web site was credible.

But the most important factor—number one on their list—was the appearance of the web site. Users did not trust sites that looked amateurish. Sites that made the effort to craft a nice, professionally designed look made a lot more headway with users, even if those users had few other reasons to trust the site.

Here's another data point. Donald Norman, one of the best-known gurus of interaction design, concluded that "positive affect enhances creative, breadth-first thinking whereas negative affect focuses cognition, enhancing depth-first processing and minimizing distractions." He added that "Positive affect makes people more tolerant of minor difficulties and more flexible and creative in finding solutions."[2] Interfaces actually become more usable when people enjoy using them.

Looking good matters.

For many chapters now, we've talked about the structure, form, and behavior of an application; now we'll focus more on its "skin" or its "look-and-feel." Chapter 4, *Layout*, discussed some graphic design basics. That chapter covered visual hierarchy, visual flow, focal points, and the Gestalt principles of proximity, similarity, continuity, and closure. These topics form the foundation of page organization, and should not be shortchanged.

But there's more to a nice house than just its room layout, though. When you pay for a well-designed new house, you also expect beautiful carpets, paint colors, wall textures, and other surface treatments. Without them, a house can be perfectly functional but uninspiring. Completing the job means paying attention to detail, fit, and finish.

Beautiful details don't necessarily affect the efficiency with which people accomplish tasks in the house or interface (although research indicates that it sometimes does). But they certainly affect whether or not people enjoy it. That, in turn, affects other behavior—like how long they linger and explore, whether they choose to go there again, and whether they recommend it to other people.

You could even think about it as a moral issue. What kind of experience do you want your users to have? Do you want to give them an all-gray application that bores them, or a flashy ad-filled application that irritates them? Would you rather give them something they enjoy looking at, maybe for hours at a time?

1 See *http://credibility.stanford.edu*.

2 See Donald Norman, "Emotion and Design: Attractive Things Work Better," at *http://www.jnd.org/dn.mss/Emotion-and-design.html*. See also his book on the subject, *Emotional Design: Why We Love (or Hate) Everyday Things* (Basic Books).

Of course, far more than visual style influences a user's emotional response (affect). Chapter 1 began discussing other considerations, such as how well you anticipate their usage habits. Software can pleasantly surprise people with considerate design. Tightly packed layouts evoke a different affective response than sparse, open layouts. Language and verbal tone play a huge part in this response, as does the quality of the software itself—does it "just work," and is it fast and responsive?

A well-designed interface takes all of these factors into account. When content, meaning, and interactive behavior all work in concert with your visual style, you can evoke a chosen emotional response very effectively.

With products and web sites, stylistic elements are often designed to support *branding*. The design of any software product or site expresses something about the organization that produced it (even if it's a loosely-knit group of open-source developers). It might say something neutral, or it might send a focused message: "You can trust us," "We're cool," "We build exciting things." A brand identity encompasses more than just a logo and tagline. It runs throughout an organization's product designs, its web site, and its advertising materials—in fact, the brand's chosen color schemes, fonts, iconography, and vocabulary show up everywhere. When planned well, a complete brand identity is coherent and intentional.

A brand identity is important because it establishes familiarity and sets expectations for someone's experience with an organization's products. Ultimately, a good brand should make people feel better about using those products. Look at what Apple was able to do with brand loyalty: many people love Apple products and seek them out.

In any case, whether or not they are intended to support a brand, stylistic elements make statements about your product. They communicate attributes like reliability, excitement, playfulness, energy, calmness, strength, tension, and joy. What do you want to communicate?

This chapter discusses more visual design concepts, this time focusing less on formal structure and more on these emotionally based attributes. The chapter won't make an artist out of you—that takes serious practice and study. But the patterns capture some techniques commonly found on well-designed artifacts and explain why they work.

SAME CONTENT, DIFFERENT STYLES

To explore how styles evoke different visceral and emotional reactions, we can try applying different visual styles to identical content. The actual content isn't even that important— we're looking for immediate, pre-rational reactions here, not the impressions gained from reading and interacting with the content.

The "CSS Zen Garden" web site (*http://csszengarden.com*) offers us exactly that situation. Invented as a showcase for CSS-based web design, this site provides a single HTML page to all participants—everyone gets the same body text, the same HTML tags, and the same lists of links. Participants then create unique CSS files to define new visual designs for the page, and contribute them to the site. Visitors can browse through all the contributed CSS designs. It's a delightful way to spend an hour or three, especially if you're teaching yourself about visual design and trying to understand what you do and do not like.

The following eight figures present a sample of these designs. In each case, the basic content is the same; only the design has changed. Take some time to observe each one. When you look at each design, what is your immediate, visceral reaction? What words come to mind that describe the page? Does it draw you in, repel you, make you nervous, or delight you?

FIGURE 9-1 / Design 1: "Contempo Finery," by Ro London

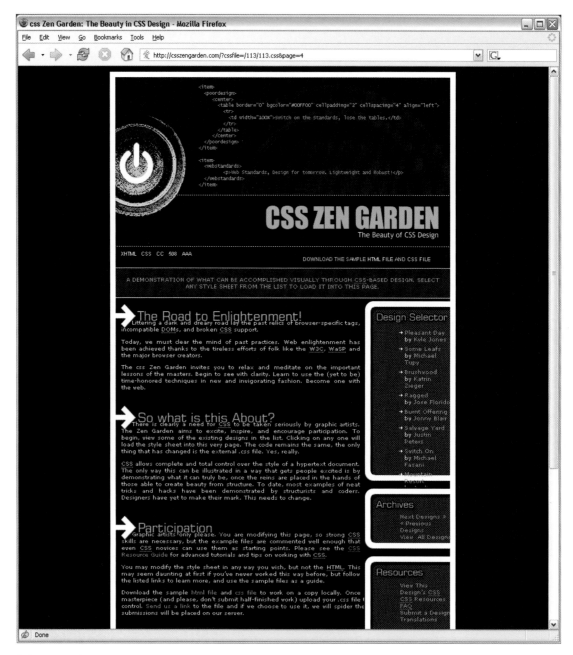

FIGURE 9-2 / Design 2: "Switch On," by Michael Fasani

FIGURE 9-3 / Design 3: "Pleasant Day," by Kyle Jones

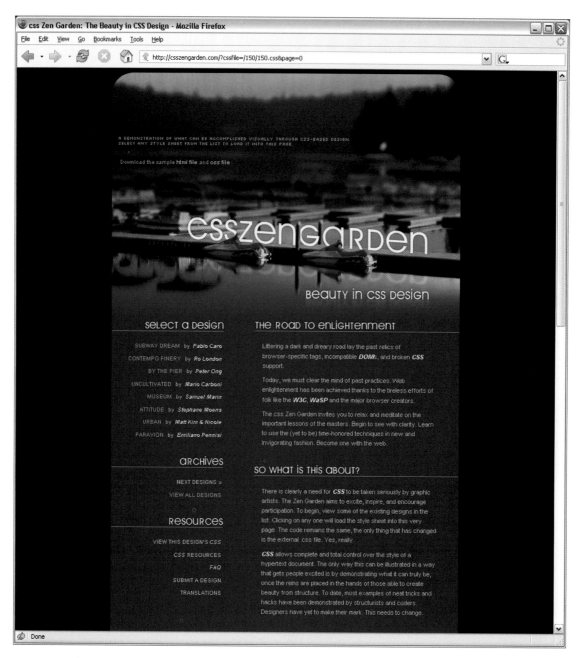

FIGURE 9-4 / Design 4: "By the Pier," by Peter Ong

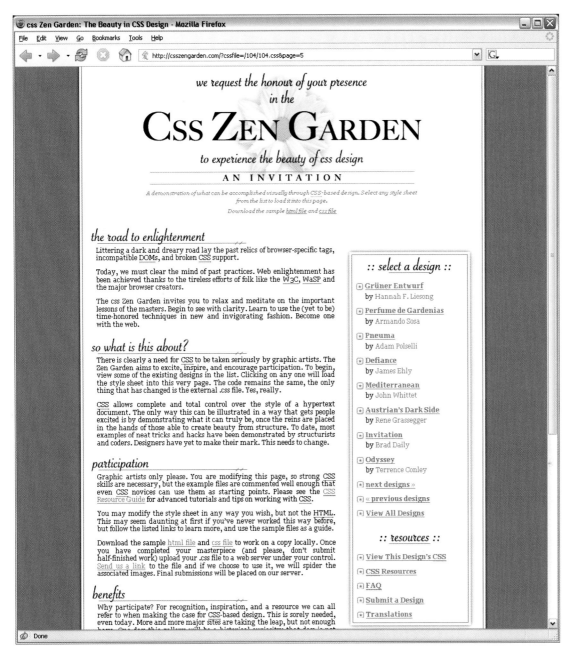

css Zen Garden: The Beauty in CSS Design - Mozilla Firefox

File Edit View Go Bookmarks Tools Help

http://csszengarden.com/?cssfile=/104/104.css&page=5

we request the honour of your presence
in the

CSS ZEN GARDEN

to experience the beauty of css design

AN INVITATION

*A demonstration of what can be accomplished visually through CSS-based design. Select any style sheet
from the list to load it into this page.*

Download the sample html file and css file

the road to enlightenment

Littering a dark and dreary road lay the past relics of browser-specific tags,
incompatible DOMs, and broken CSS support.

Today, we must clear the mind of past practices. Web enlightenment has
been achieved thanks to the tireless efforts of folk like the W3C, WaSP and
the major browser creators.

The css Zen Garden invites you to relax and meditate on the important
lessons of the masters. Begin to see with clarity. Learn to use the (yet to be)
time-honored techniques in new and invigorating fashion. Become one
with the web.

so what is this about?

There is clearly a need for CSS to be taken seriously by graphic artists. The
Zen Garden aims to excite, inspire, and encourage participation. To begin,
view some of the existing designs in the list. Clicking on any one will load
the style sheet into this very page. The code remains the same, the only
thing that has changed is the external .css file. Yes, really.

CSS allows complete and total control over the style of a hypertext
document. The only way this can be illustrated in a way that gets people
excited is by demonstrating what it can truly be, once the reins are placed
in the hands of those able to create beauty from structure. To date, most
examples of neat tricks and hacks have been demonstrated by structurists
and coders. Designers have yet to make their mark. This needs to change.

participation

Graphic artists only please. You are modifying this page, so strong CSS
skills are necessary, but the example files are commented well enough that
even CSS novices can use them as starting points. Please see the CSS
Resource Guide for advanced tutorials and tips on working with CSS.

You may modify the style sheet in any way you wish, but not the HTML.
This may seem daunting at first if you've never worked this way before,
but follow the listed links to learn more, and use the sample files as a guide.

Download the sample html file and css file to work on a copy locally. Once
you have completed your masterpiece (and please, don't submit
half-finished work) upload your .css file to a web server under your control.
Send us a link to the file and if we choose to use it, we will spider the
associated images. Final submissions will be placed on our server.

benefits

Why participate? For recognition, inspiration, and a resource we can all
refer to when making the case for CSS-based design. This is sorely needed,
even today. More and more major sites are taking the leap, but not enough

:: select a design ::

- **Grüner Entwurf**
  by Hannah F. Liesong
- **Perfume de Gardenias**
  by Armando Sosa
- **Pneuma**
  by Adam Polselli
- **Defiance**
  by James Ehly
- **Mediterranean**
  by John Whittet
- **Austrian's Dark Side**
  by Rene Grassegger
- **Invitation**
  by Brad Daily
- **Odyssey**
  by Terrence Conley
- **next designs »**
- **« previous designs**
- **View All Designs**

:: resources ::

- **View This Design's CSS**
- **CSS Resources**
- **FAQ**
- **Submit a Design**
- **Translations**

Done

FIGURE 9-5 / Design 5: "Invitation," by Brad Daily

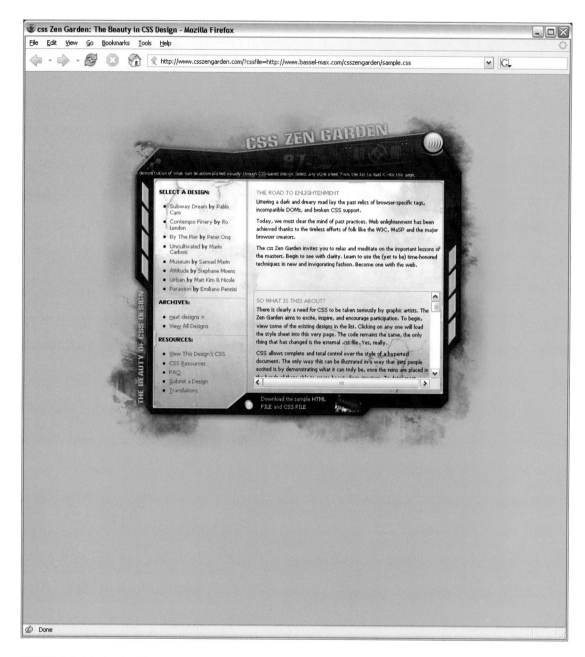

FIGURE 9-6 / Design 6: "Yellow Jet," by Bassel Max

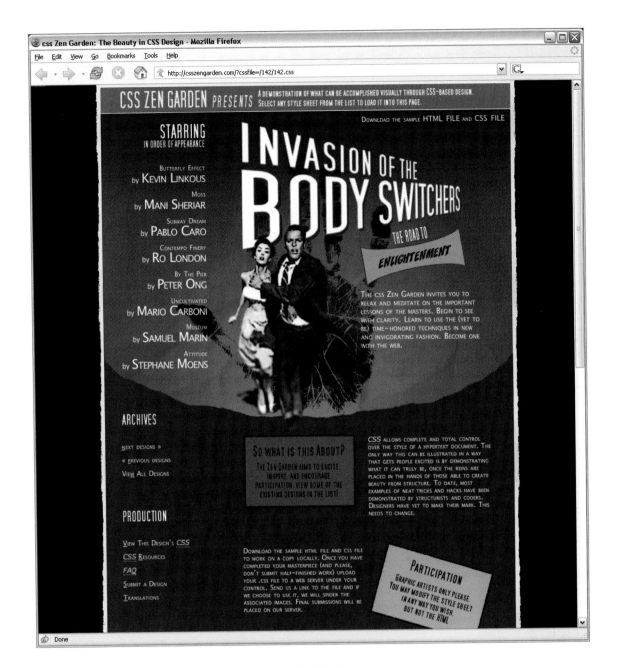

FIGURE 9-7 / Design 7: "Invasion of the Body Switchers," by Andy Clarke

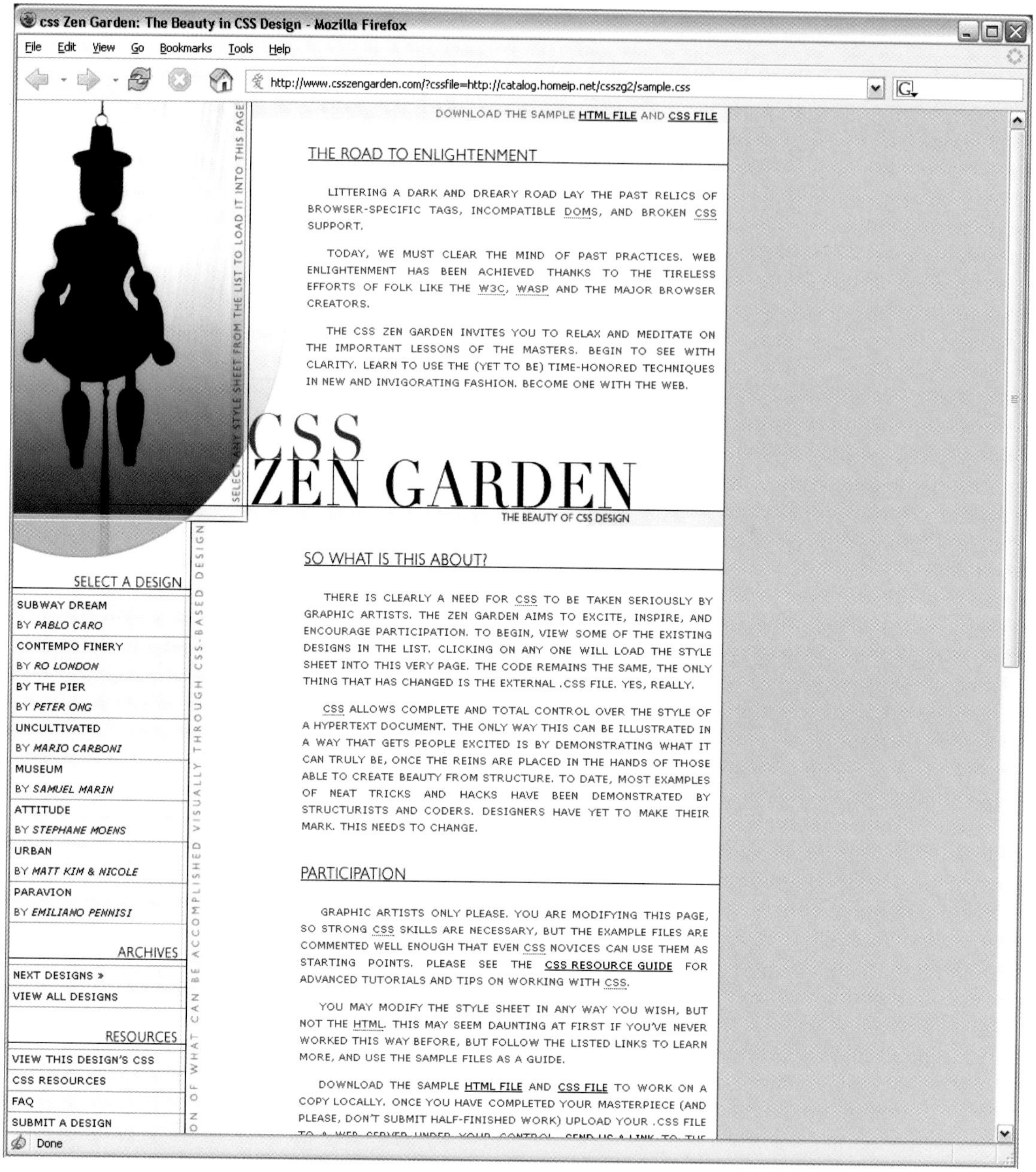
css Zen Garden: The Beauty in CSS Design - Mozilla Firefox
File Edit View Go Bookmarks Tools Help
http://www.csszengarden.com/?cssfile=http://catalog.homeip.net/csszg2/sample.css
DOWNLOAD THE SAMPLE HTML FILE AND CSS FILE
SELECT ANY STYLE SHEET FROM THE LIST TO LOAD IT INTO THIS PAGE
THE ROAD TO ENLIGHTENMENT
LITTERING A DARK AND DREARY ROAD LAY THE PAST RELICS OF BROWSER-SPECIFIC TAGS, INCOMPATIBLE DOMS, AND BROKEN CSS SUPPORT.
TODAY, WE MUST CLEAR THE MIND OF PAST PRACTICES. WEB ENLIGHTENMENT HAS BEEN ACHIEVED THANKS TO THE TIRELESS EFFORTS OF FOLK LIKE THE W3C, WASP AND THE MAJOR BROWSER CREATORS.
THE CSS ZEN GARDEN INVITES YOU TO RELAX AND MEDITATE ON THE IMPORTANT LESSONS OF THE MASTERS. BEGIN TO SEE WITH CLARITY. LEARN TO USE THE (YET TO BE) TIME-HONORED TECHNIQUES IN NEW AND INVIGORATING FASHION. BECOME ONE WITH THE WEB.
CSS
ZEN GARDEN
THE BEAUTY OF CSS DESIGN
A DEMONSTRATION OF WHAT CAN BE ACCOMPLISHED VISUALLY THROUGH CSS-BASED DESIGN
SELECT A DESIGN
SUBWAY DREAM
BY PABLO CARO
CONTEMPO FINERY
BY RO LONDON
BY THE PIER
BY PETER ONG
UNCULTIVATED
BY MARIO CARBONI
MUSEUM
BY SAMUEL MARIN
ATTITUDE
BY STEPHANE MOENS
URBAN
BY MATT KIM & NICOLE
PARAVION
BY EMILIANO PENNISI
ARCHIVES
NEXT DESIGNS »
VIEW ALL DESIGNS
RESOURCES
VIEW THIS DESIGN'S CSS
CSS RESOURCES
FAQ
SUBMIT A DESIGN
SO WHAT IS THIS ABOUT?
THERE IS CLEARLY A NEED FOR CSS TO BE TAKEN SERIOUSLY BY GRAPHIC ARTISTS. THE ZEN GARDEN AIMS TO EXCITE, INSPIRE, AND ENCOURAGE PARTICIPATION. TO BEGIN, VIEW SOME OF THE EXISTING DESIGNS IN THE LIST. CLICKING ON ANY ONE WILL LOAD THE STYLE SHEET INTO THIS VERY PAGE. THE CODE REMAINS THE SAME, THE ONLY THING THAT HAS CHANGED IS THE EXTERNAL .CSS FILE. YES, REALLY.
CSS ALLOWS COMPLETE AND TOTAL CONTROL OVER THE STYLE OF A HYPERTEXT DOCUMENT. THE ONLY WAY THIS CAN BE ILLUSTRATED IN A WAY THAT GETS PEOPLE EXCITED IS BY DEMONSTRATING WHAT IT CAN TRULY BE, ONCE THE REINS ARE PLACED IN THE HANDS OF THOSE ABLE TO CREATE BEAUTY FROM STRUCTURE. TO DATE, MOST EXAMPLES OF NEAT TRICKS AND HACKS HAVE BEEN DEMONSTRATED BY STRUCTURISTS AND CODERS. DESIGNERS HAVE YET TO MAKE THEIR MARK. THIS NEEDS TO CHANGE.
PARTICIPATION
GRAPHIC ARTISTS ONLY PLEASE. YOU ARE MODIFYING THIS PAGE, SO STRONG CSS SKILLS ARE NECESSARY, BUT THE EXAMPLE FILES ARE COMMENTED WELL ENOUGH THAT EVEN CSS NOVICES CAN USE THEM AS STARTING POINTS. PLEASE SEE THE CSS RESOURCE GUIDE FOR ADVANCED TUTORIALS AND TIPS ON WORKING WITH CSS.
YOU MAY MODIFY THE STYLE SHEET IN ANY WAY YOU WISH, BUT NOT THE HTML. THIS MAY SEEM DAUNTING AT FIRST IF YOU'VE NEVER WORKED THIS WAY BEFORE, BUT FOLLOW THE LISTED LINKS TO LEARN MORE, AND USE THE SAMPLE FILES AS A GUIDE.
DOWNLOAD THE SAMPLE HTML FILE AND CSS FILE TO WORK ON A COPY LOCALLY. ONCE YOU HAVE COMPLETED YOUR MASTERPIECE (AND PLEASE, DON'T SUBMIT HALF-FINISHED WORK) UPLOAD YOUR .CSS FILE
Done

FIGURE 9-8 / Design 8: "Rain," by Pierre-Leo Bourbonnais

THE BASICS OF VISUAL DESIGN

As you looked at the Zen Garden examples, you might have observed how they achieve such different impressions—a page's color scheme may cause you to either smile or cringe, for example. Using these examples as a touchstone, we can talk about some of the principles of good visual design.

You might recall that we've already covered some visual design principles in Chapter 4, *Layout*, and Chapter 6, *Information Graphics*. Those chapters explored how the human visual system responds *cognitively* to certain inputs. The time it takes for someone to click on an orange square out of a field of blue squares, for example, doesn't depend upon a user's aesthetic sense or cultural expectations.

But now we're talking about *emotional and visceral* reactions—does a single orange square add tension, brightness, balance, or nothing at all to a design? The answer depends on so many factors that it's genuinely hard to get it "right" without a lot of practice. The cognitive aspects of these design choices certainly play a part; for starters, you can make a page hard or easy to read (a cognitive effect). But each person is unique. Each person has a different history of experiences, associations, and preferences; and each person is part of a culture that imposes its own meanings on color, typography, and imagery.

Furthermore, the context of the design affects the user's response. Users see your design as a part of a genre (such as office applications, games, or e-commerce sites), and they will have certain expectations about what's appropriate, trite or original, dull or interesting. Branding also sets expectations. So here's the problem: as soon as you learn a "rule" for evoking an emotional reaction using a design principle, you can find a million exceptions.

That said, if you know your audience well, visceral and emotional responses are surprisingly predictable. For example, most readers of this book probably thought that the first CSS example was a calm, soothing design, but that the second one was noisier and more tense. Why is that?

The answer lies in a combination of many factors working in concert: color, typography, spaciousness, angles and shapes, repeated visual motifs, texture, images, and cultural references.

COLOR

Color is immediate. It's one of the first things you perceive about a design, along with basic forms and shapes. Yet the application of color to art and design is infinitely subtle—master painters have studied it for centuries. We can only scratch the surface here.

When devising a color scheme for an interface, first rule out anything that makes it impossible to read:

- Always put dark foregrounds against light backgrounds, or vice versa—to test, pull the design into an image tool like Photoshop and desaturate it (make it grayscale).
- Never use red versus green as a critical color distinction, since many colorblind people won't be able to see the difference. Statistically, 10 percent of men have some form of colorblindness, as do about 1 percent of women.
- Never put bright blue small text on a bright red or orange background, or vice versa, because human eyes can't read text written in complementary colors (on opposite sides of the color wheel).

With that out of the way, here are some very approximate guidelines for color usage.

Warm versus cool

Red, orange, yellow, brown, and beige are considered "warm" colors. Blue, green, purple, gray (in large quantities), and white are considered "cool." The yellow CSS Zen Garden in Design 6 feels vividly "hot," despite the cool gray metallic surface used behind the content itself. Sites and interfaces that need to connote respectability and conservativeness often use predominantly cool colors (especially blue). Still, warm and cool colors can combine very effectively to achieve a balanced look—and they frequently do, in classic paintings and poster designs.

Dark versus light background

The pages with light backgrounds—white, beige, and light gray—feel very different from the ones with very dark backgrounds. Light is more typical of computer interfaces (and printed pages); dark pages can feel edgier, more somber, or more energetic, depending on other design aspects. Actually, dark palettes are rarely used in form-style interfaces because desktop-native controls, such as text fields and buttons, don't look good on dark backgrounds.

High versus low contrast

Whether the background is dark or light, the elements on that background might have either high or low contrast against it. Strong contrast evokes tension, strength, and boldness; low contrast is more soothing and relaxing.

Saturated versus unsaturated

Highly saturated, or pure, colors—brilliant yellows, reds, and greens, for example—evoke energy, vividness, brightness, and warmth. They are daring; they have character. But when overused, they can tire the eyes, so most UI designers use them sparingly; they often choose only one or two. Muted colors, either dark or light (*tones* or *tints,* respectively), make up the bulk of most color palettes. The green-and-blue Zen Garden design, Design 3, gets away with two saturated colors by using white borders, white text, and dark halos to separate the green and blue. (Even so, you probably wouldn't want to stare at that green all day long in a desktop application.)

Combinations of hues

Once you start combining colors, interesting effects happen. Two saturated colors can evoke far more energy, motion, or richness than one alone. A page that combines one saturated color with a set of muted colors directs attention to the saturated color, and sets up "layers" of color—the brighter and stronger ones appear closer to the viewer, while the grayer and paler colors recede. Strong dimensionality can make a design dramatic. Flatter designs, with more muted or lighter colors, are calmer. See the **Few Hues, Many Values** pattern for more discussion.

TYPOGRAPHY

By choosing a font (properly called a *typeface*) for a piece of text, you decide what kind of voice that text is "spoken" in. The voice might be loud or soft, friendly or formal, colloquial or authoritative, hip or old-fashioned.

As with color, readability—the cognitive part—comes first when choosing type. Small text, or what's called "body text" in print and on web sites, demands careful choice. The following considerations for body text also apply to "label fonts" in GUIs, used to caption text fields and other controls.

- On computer displays, sans-serif fonts often work better at small point sizes, unlike print, in which the serifed fonts tend to be more readable as body text. Pixels aren't big enough to render tiny serifs well. (Some serifed fonts, like Georgia, do look okay, though.) Display technologies such as anti-aliasing affect legibility greatly, so test the candidate fonts on your application's destination platforms.

- Avoid italicized, cursive, or otherwise ornamental fonts; they are unreadable at small sizes.

- Highly geometric fonts, with circular letters (e, c, d, o, etc.), tend to be difficult to read at small point sizes. Those letters are hard to differentiate. Futura, Univers, and some other mid-twentieth-century fonts are like this.

- All-caps is too hard to read for body text, though it's okay for headlines and short texts, if the font is chosen carefully. Capital letters tend to look similar, and are hard for a reader to differentiate.

- Set large amounts of text in a medium-width column when possible—say around 10 to 12 English words, on average. Don't right-justify narrower columns of text; let it be "ragged right."

Now for the visceral and emotional aspects. Fonts have distinctive voices, or colors, if you prefer. They have different graphic characteristics and textures on the page. For instance, some fonts are dense and dark, while others are more open. Look at the thickness of strokes and the relative sizes of letter openings for clues. Some fonts have narrower letters than others, and some font families have "condensed" versions to make them even narrower. The separation between lines of text (the leading) might be distant or close, making the block of text look either more open or more solid.

Serifs and curves add another dimension to font color or texture. Serifs add a level of scale that's much smaller than the letterform itself, and that adds refinement to the font's texture—the thick sans-serif fonts look blunt, strong, or even coarse in comparison (especially Helvetica). The curves and angles used in each letterform, including those that form the serifs, combine to form an overall texture. Compare an old-fashioned typeface such as Goudy Old Style to another classic serifed font such as Didot; they look very different on the page (Figure 9-9).

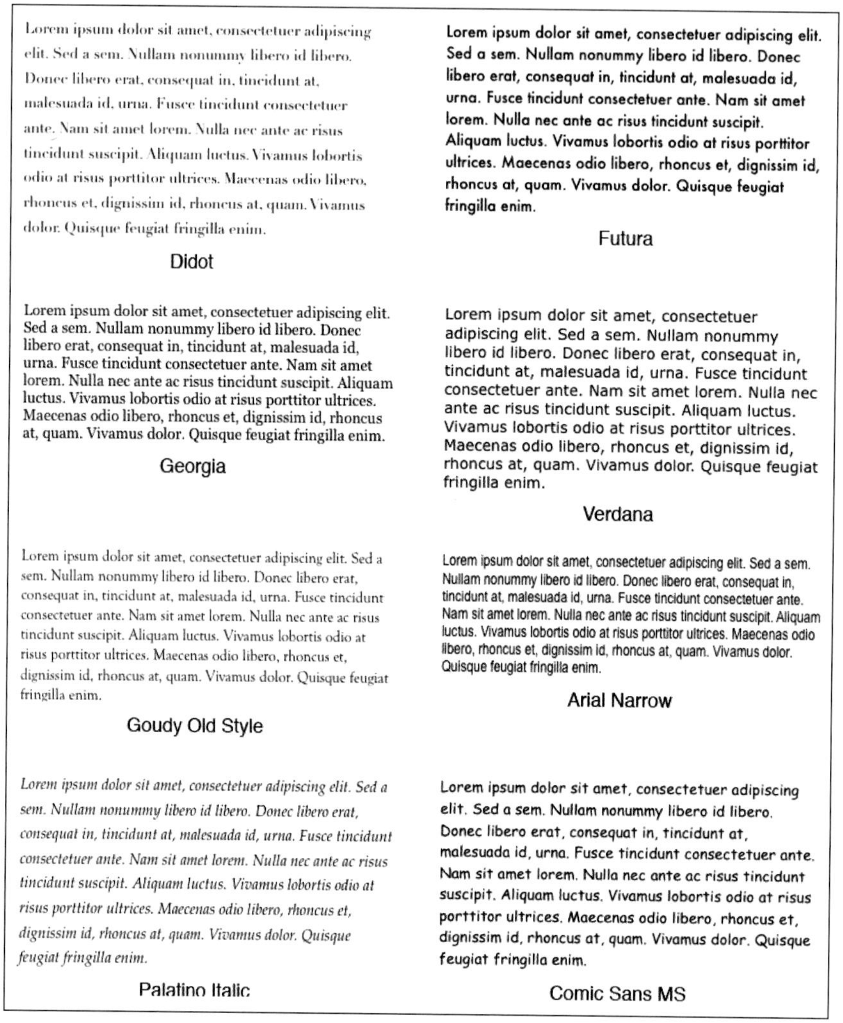

Lorem ipsum dolor sit amet, consectetuer adipiscing elit. Sed a sem. Nullam nonummy libero id libero. Donec libero erat, consequat in, tincidunt at, malesuada id, urna. Fusce tincidunt consectetuer ante. Nam sit amet lorem. Nulla nec ante ac risus tincidunt suscipit. Aliquam luctus. Vivamus lobortis odio at risus porttitor ultrices. Maecenas odio libero, rhoncus et, dignissim id, rhoncus at, quam. Vivamus dolor. Quisque feugiat fringilla enim.

Didot

Lorem ipsum dolor sit amet, consectetuer adipiscing elit. Sed a sem. Nullam nonummy libero id libero. Donec libero erat, consequat in, tincidunt at, malesuada id, urna. Fusce tincidunt consectetuer ante. Nam sit amet lorem. Nulla nec ante ac risus tincidunt suscipit. Aliquam luctus. Vivamus lobortis odio at risus porttitor ultrices. Maecenas odio libero, rhoncus et, dignissim id, rhoncus at, quam. Vivamus dolor. Quisque feugiat fringilla enim.

Georgia

Lorem ipsum dolor sit amet, consectetuer adipiscing elit. Sed a sem. Nullam nonummy libero id libero. Donec libero erat, consequat in, tincidunt at, malesuada id, urna. Fusce tincidunt consectetuer ante. Nam sit amet lorem. Nulla nec ante ac risus tincidunt suscipit. Aliquam luctus. Vivamus lobortis odio at risus porttitor ultrices. Maecenas odio libero, rhoncus et, dignissim id, rhoncus at, quam. Vivamus dolor. Quisque feugiat fringilla enim.

Goudy Old Style

Lorem ipsum dolor sit amet, consectetuer adipiscing elit. Sed a sem. Nullam nonummy libero id libero. Donec libero erat, consequat in, tincidunt at, malesuada id, urna. Fusce tincidunt consectetuer ante. Nam sit amet lorem. Nulla nec ante ac risus tincidunt suscipit. Aliquam luctus. Vivamus lobortis odio at risus porttitor ultrices. Maecenas odio libero, rhoncus et, dignissim id, rhoncus at, quam. Vivamus dolor. Quisque feugiat fringilla enim.

Palatino Italic

Lorem ipsum dolor sit amet, consectetuer adipiscing elit. Sed a sem. Nullam nonummy libero id libero. Donec libero erat, consequat in, tincidunt at, malesuada id, urna. Fusce tincidunt consectetuer ante. Nam sit amet lorem. Nulla nec ante ac risus tincidunt suscipit. Aliquam luctus. Vivamus lobortis odio at risus porttitor ultrices. Maecenas odio libero, rhoncus et, dignissim id, rhoncus at, quam. Vivamus dolor. Quisque feugiat fringilla enim.

Futura

Lorem ipsum dolor sit amet, consectetuer adipiscing elit. Sed a sem. Nullam nonummy libero id libero. Donec libero erat, consequat in, tincidunt at, malesuada id, urna. Fusce tincidunt consectetuer ante. Nam sit amet lorem. Nulla nec ante ac risus tincidunt suscipit. Aliquam luctus. Vivamus lobortis odio at risus porttitor ultrices. Maecenas odio libero, rhoncus et, dignissim id, rhoncus at, quam. Vivamus dolor. Quisque feugiat fringilla enim.

Verdana

Lorem ipsum dolor sit amet, consectetuer adipiscing elit. Sed a sem. Nullam nonummy libero id libero. Donec libero erat, consequat in, tincidunt at, malesuada id, urna. Fusce tincidunt consectetuer ante. Nam sit amet lorem. Nulla nec ante ac risus tincidunt suscipit. Aliquam luctus. Vivamus lobortis odio at risus porttitor ultrices. Maecenas odio libero, rhoncus et, dignissim id, rhoncus at, quam. Vivamus dolor. Quisque feugiat fringilla enim.

Arial Narrow

Lorem ipsum dolor sit amet, consectetuer adipiscing elit. Sed a sem. Nullam nonummy libero id libero. Donec libero erat, consequat in, tincidunt at, malesuada id, urna. Fusce tincidunt consectetuer ante. Nam sit amet lorem. Nulla nec ante ac risus tincidunt suscipit. Aliquam luctus. Vivamus lobortis odio at risus porttitor ultrices. Maecenas odio libero, rhoncus et, dignissim id, rhoncus at, quam. Vivamus dolor. Quisque feugiat fringilla enim.

Comic Sans MS

FIGURE 9-9 / Eight fonts, as rendered on Mac OS X. Notice the different sizes, densities, textures, and formalities.

Though it's not always easy to explain why, some fonts speak with a formal voice, while others speak with an informal voice. Comic Sans and other playful fonts are certainly informal, but so is Georgia, when compared to Didot. All-caps and capitalized words speak more formally than lowercase; italics speak informally. In the CSS Zen Garden designs shown earlier, Design 8 uses an all-caps, sans-serif font to speak in a cool and removed voice. Meanwhile, Design 5 (which uses Georgia) speaks in a warm and informal voice.

Cultural aspects come into play here too. Old-fashioned fonts, usually with serifs, tend to look—wait for it—old-fashioned, although anything set in Futura (a sans-serif font) still looks like it came from a 1963 science textbook. Verdana has been used so much on the Web that it's now standard for that medium. And Chicago always will be the original Mac font, no matter what context it's used in.

SPACIOUSNESS AND CROWDING

Some of the CSS Zen Garden designs use plenty of whitespace, while others crowd the page elements together. Spaciousness on a page gives an impression of airiness, openness, quiet, calmness, freedom, or stateliness and dignity, depending on other design factors.

Crowded designs can evoke urgency or tension under some circumstances. Why? Because text and other graphic elements need to "breathe"—when they're colliding against each other, or against the edges or borders of the page, they cause visual tension. Our eyes want to see margins around things. We get slightly disturbed by designs such as CSS Zen Garden Design 2 (the black one with white arrows), which shoves the headlines right against the text. Likewise, Design 6's compact layout somehow contributes to the busy, industrial feel of the page, though it doesn't have collisions like Design 2.

However, not all crowded designs evoke that kind of tension. Some connote friendliness and comfort. If you give the text and other elements just enough space, and reduce the interline spacing (leading) to the smallest amount that is comfortably readable, then you might achieve a friendlier and less rarified look. Design 5, the one with the daisy, illustrates this well.

ANGLES AND CURVES

A page composed of straight up-and-down lines and right angles generally looks calmer and more still than a page containing diagonal lines and non-rectangular shapes. Likewise, a page with many different angles has more apparent motion than a page with a single repeated angle on it—see Design 7 for an dramatic example. Design 6 uses angles to create uneasiness and visual interest.

Curves also can add motion and liveliness, but not always. A design made with a lot of circles and circular arcs can be calming and restful. But a curve swooping through a page sets the whole design in motion, and a few carefully chosen curves in an otherwise rectangular design add sophistication and interest. Design 8 uses a single large elliptical curve for a dramatic effect—it contrasts strongly against the otherwise rectilinear design, so its impact is high.

Wherever two curves intersect, notice what the geometrical tangents to those curves are doing. Are the tangents at right angles? That results in a calmer, more still composition; if they cross at a more acute angle, the design has more tension and apparent motion. (Again, these aren't hard-and-fast rules, but they're generally true.)

When using angles, curves, and non-rectangular shapes, think about where the focal points are: at sharp angles, where lines cross, and where multiple lines converge, for instance. Use these focal points to draw the viewer's eye where you want it to go.

TEXTURE AND RHYTHM

Texture adds richness to a visual design. As described in the "Typography" section, text forms its own texture,[3] and you can control the look of that texture by choosing good fonts. For many pages and interfaces, fonts are the most important texture element.

But other kinds of textures deserve attention too. Blank regions, like the strips of empty space down the sides of a web page, can look much better when filled with a texture. You also can use textures to surround strong visual elements and set them off, as done in Designs 6 and 7. Textures add visual interest, and depending on what they look like, they can add warmth, richness, excitement, or tension.

The most effective textures in interface design are subtle, not vivid checkerboards of eye-hurting colors. They use gentle color gradations and very tiny details. When spread over large areas, their impact is greater than you might think. Figure 9-10 shows some of the margin textures in the CSS designs. Single-pixel dots, parallel lines, and finely-drawn grids are nice geometric textures; they're easy to generate and render, and they add refinement to a design. See the **Hairlines** pattern.

Be careful when using textures behind words on a computer screen—it rarely works. All but the most subtle textures interfere with the readability of small text. You can put them behind large text, but watch the way the edges of the letterforms interact with the different colors in the texture, as that can visually distort the letters. Try fading a texture into a solid color as it approaches a block of text.

---

3 On an interesting etymological note, the English words "text," "texture," and "textile" all derive from the same Latin root, *texere,* meaning "to weave." Isn't that evocative?

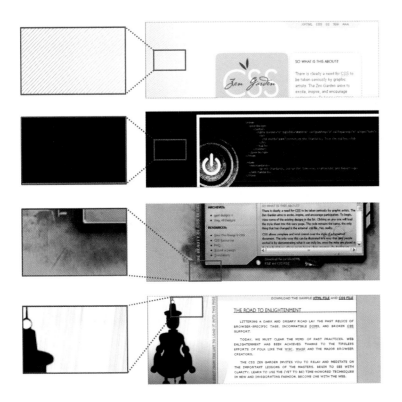

FIGURE 9-10 / Details of textures in four CSS designs

IMAGES

Each of the CSS Zen Garden designs reproduced here uses imagery. Some are photographs, and others are iconic semi-abstract pictures. In all cases, the images exist purely to set the mood of the design. These particular designs can go as far as they need to set that mood, since in the CSS Zen Garden, the design is more important than the content.

Your situation probably is different. In most applications and web applications, content and ease of use are more important than style. You should use purely decorative images sparingly and with great care on functional GUIs, since they tend to be distracting.

That said, you should look at the functional icons and images in your design—such as toolbar icons and **Illustrated Choices** (see Chapter 7)—and see if they make the emotional statement you want the whole design to make. Use the same criteria listed here: color, texture, angles, curves, spacing, and so on. Specifically, color schemes, angles, and curves should be consistent across an icon set. Don't make them look too much alike, though, or users won't see the differences easily. Larger icons usually "feel" better than small ones, partly because you can draw them more generously, and partly because of the crowding and space issues discussed earlier.

Back to decorative imagery. Photographs are extraordinary tools for evoking emotional responses. How many web pages have you seen showing happy, smiling faces? Kids flying kites? Competent-looking businesspeople in crisp suits? How about roads winding through beautiful mountain scenery? Sunsets or beaches? Rolling grassy hills under sunny blue skies? (You may find this one on something other than a web page.)

These kinds of pictures appeal to our deepest human instincts, and they all predispose the viewer to respond positively—as long as the context is right. If you try to put powerful images like these on an unassuming little utility application, users might laugh or criticize it as marketing overkill. This is a delicate area, and if you're not sure something works, test it with users.

CULTURAL REFERENCES

A design might remind you of something cultural—a brand, movie, art style, historical era, literary genre, or an inside joke. A familiar reference may evoke memories or emotions strong enough to trump all these other design factors, though the best designs make cultural references work in concert with everything else.

Design 7 might remind you of a 1950s movie poster. That's almost certainly deliberate. The feel of the page is informal, lively, and playful—note the angles, color, and typography. The emotional reaction from most American adults probably will be "silly," "nostalgic," "retro cool," or something like that. Everything in this design works together to produce a specific gut reaction. Some other CSS designs not shown here replicate the styles of Bauhaus, Art Nouveau, Dadaism, comic books, and even Soviet-era Communist propaganda posters.

Obviously, if you make overt cultural references, consider your audience. A 10-year-old will not get the 1950s movie-poster reference. Chances are good that a young adult in India won't either. But if your audience is sufficiently well-defined for you to know that a cultural reference will be familiar to them, then it can be a good "hook" to engage a viewer emotionally with your design.

Cultural references rarely are used in functional application designs, but you can see them in **Skins** for applications such as Winamp. Its library of user-contributed skins include a Klingon style, an iPod imitation, and one that looks like an Etch-a-Sketch. The user-contributed GNOME backgrounds and themes are a rich source of references, too.

You also can find cultural references in applications like Quickbooks, in which some pages are designed to look like checks and bills. They actually move beyond a stylistic treatment and become an interaction metaphor, but the metaphor still is entirely cultural—someone who's never seen a checkbook wouldn't respond in the same way as someone who has.

REPEATED VISUAL MOTIFS

A good design has unity: it hangs together as one entity, with each element supporting the others structurally and viscerally. That's a hard goal to achieve. I can't give you hard-and-fast rules on how to do it; it takes skill and practice.

But one thing that contributes greatly toward visual unity is the repetition of visual elements or motifs. We've already talked about angles and curves; you can use diagonal lines of the same angle, or lines with similar curvature, as repeated elements in a design. The **Corner Treatments** pattern talks about a common way to do this.

Also consider typography. Use only one main body-text font, though other fonts work very effectively in small areas like sidebars or navigation links. (Their contrast to the main font make them stand out.) If you have several headlines or titled sections, use the same headline font for them. You also can pull smaller graphic elements—line width and color, for instance—out of your fonts into the rest of the design. See the **Borders that Echo Fonts** pattern.

When similar groupings of text or controls repeat along a line, a visual rhythm results. You can see this especially in the "Select a Design" sections of Designs 3, 4, and 8. They show each of the design name/author pairs in a well-defined grouping, and then repeat that grouping along a column. You easily could accomplish the same effect with form fields, palette buttons, and other UI elements.

Rhythms like these can be powerful design tools. Use them with care, and apply them to groups of comparable things—users will assume that similarity in form means similarity in function. Incidentally, visual rhythm is what makes **Small Multiples** (Chapter 6) look so attractive when done well.

WHAT THIS MEANS FOR DESKTOP APPLICATIONS

Those of you who work on web sites might already be familiar with everything discussed so far. People expect web sites—and by extension, web applications—to have strong graphic styling, and you will rarely find them looking completely plain and neutral.

But what if you work on desktop applications? If you try to apply these principles just to the controls' look-and-feel—how the controls are drawn—you don't have many choices. Java applications get to choose from a few look-and-feel options, most of which are native looking or fairly neutral (like Swing's Metal look-and-feel). Linux applications have some nice choices, too, such as GNOME's application themes. But native Windows or Mac applications generally use the standard platform look-and-feel, unless you're willing to work hard to develop a custom one.

Given the situation, you can be forgiven for just using the platform look-and-feel standards, and concentrating your graphic design attentions elsewhere.

But some applications now look more "webbish" or "designery" than they used to, and they generally look better for it. Microsoft Money 2000 was one of the first mainstream applications to break the mold. Its designers chose to use background images in the top margins, gradient fills, anti-aliased headline fonts, and an unusual color scheme. Other applications have since done similar things. Winamp, as another example, has used creatively-designed skins for a long time; now most other media players have very distinctive looks, too.

Even if you do use a neutral look-and-feel for your actual widgetry, there still are ways to be creative.

Backgrounds

Inobtrusive images, gradient fills, and subtle textures or repeated patterns in large background areas can brighten up an interface to an amazing extent. Use them in dialog or page backgrounds; tree, table, or list backgrounds; or box backgrounds (in conjunction with a box border). See the **Deep Background** pattern for more.

Colors and fonts

You often can control overall color schemes and fonts in a native-looking UI, too. For instance, you might draw headlines in an unusual font, at several point sizes larger than standard dialog text, and maybe even on a strip of contrasting background color. Consider using these if you design a page layout with **Titled Sections** (Chapter 4).

Borders

Borders offer another possibility for creative styling. Again, if you use **Titled Sections** or any other kind of physical grouping, you might be able to change how box borders are drawn. Solid-color boxes of narrow widths work best; beveled borders look very 1990s now. See **Corner Treatments** and **Borders that Echo Fonts**.

Images

In some UI toolkits, certain controls let you replace their standard look-and-feel with custom images on a per-item basis. Buttons often allow this, for instance, so your buttons, including their borders, can look like anything you want. Tables, trees, and lists sometimes permit you to define how their items are drawn (in Java Swing, you have complete control over item rendering, and several other toolkits at least let you use custom icons). You also can place static images on UI layouts, giving you the ability to put images of any dimension just about anywhere.

The biggest danger here is accessibility. Operating systems like Windows let users change desktop color/font themes, and that's not just for fun—visually impaired users use desktop themes with high-contrast color schemes and giant fonts just so they can see what they're doing. Make sure your design works with those high-contrast themes. It's the right thing to do.[4]

Along the same lines, you might replace ordinary text labels with images containing unusual fonts, maybe with halos, or drop-shadow effects, or complex backgrounds. This is common in web pages. If you insist on using an image for text, you need to provide enough information with that image to let a screen-reader like JAWS read it aloud. (How exactly you do that depends entirely upon the UI technology you're using.)

Another danger is fatiguing your users. If you design an application meant to be used at full size or for a long time, then tone down the saturated colors, huge text, high contrast, and eye-catching textures—make the design quiet, not loud. More importantly, if your applica-

---

4 And, depending on who buys your software, it may also be the correct legal thing to do. The United States government, for example, requires that all software used by federal agencies be accessible to people with disabilities. See *http://www.section508.gov* for more information.

tion is meant to be used in high-stress situations, like a control panel for heavy machinery, strip out anything superfluous that might distract users from the task. Here, cognitive concerns are far more important than aesthetics.

That said, I hope this discussion gives you some ideas about how to make your desktop UI a little more interesting. Figure 9-11 gives you some examples of controls with custom look-and-feels that still are relatively usable.

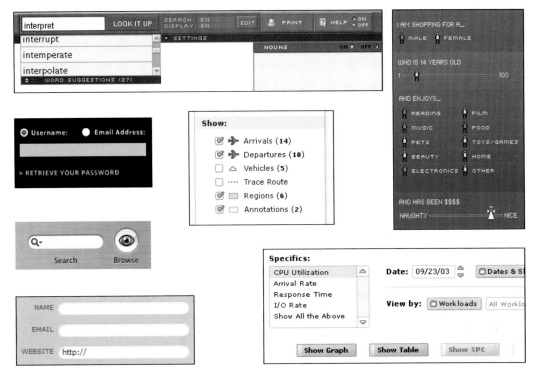

FIGURE 9-11 / Some nonstandard (but usable) controls

THE PATTERNS

All of these patterns except **Skins** draw on the concepts described in the introduction. They talk about specific ways to apply those concepts; **Corner Treatments**, for instance, captures one kind of repeated visual motif, and **Borders that Echo Fonts** captures another. **Deep Background** touches on texture choice, but so does **Hairlines**, and fonts are discussed in **Contrasting Font Weights**.

 88   Deep Background

 89   Few Hues, Many Values

 90   Corner Treatments

 91   Borders that Echo Fonts

 92   Hairlines

 93   Contrasting Font Weights

The **Skins** pattern is different. It deals more with meta-design—it says nothing about how you design the skin or look-and-feel of your application, but it does address how you design your application to let others replace your look-and-feel with their own designs.

 94   Skins

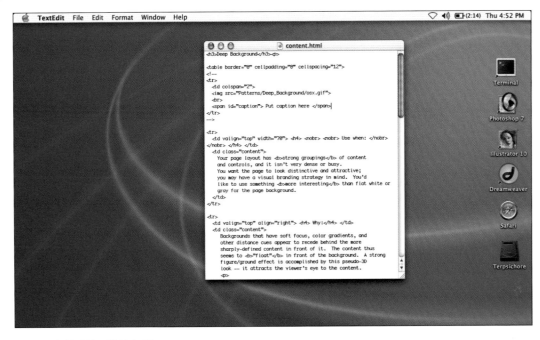

FIGURE 9-12 / Mac OS X desktop

what

Place an image or gradient into the page's background that visually recedes behind the foreground elements.

use when

Your page layout has strong visual elements (such as text blocks, groups of controls, or windows), and it isn't very dense or busy. You want the page to look distinctive and attractive; you may have a visual branding strategy in mind. You'd like to use something more interesting than flat white or gray for the page background.

why

Backgrounds that have soft focus, color gradients, and other distance cues appear to recede behind the more sharply defined content in front of it. The content thus seems to "float" in front of the background. This pseudo-3D look results in a strong figure/ground effect—it attracts the viewer's eye to the content.

Fancy explanations aside, it just looks good.

how

Use a background that has one or more of these characteristics:

Soft focus

Keep lines fuzzy and avoid too much small detail—sharp lines interfere with readability of the content atop it, especially if that content is text or small icons. (You can kind of get away with sharp lines if they are low-contrast, but even then, text doesn't work well over them.)

Color gradients

Bright, saturated colors are okay, but again, hard lines between them are not. Allow colors to blend into each other. In fact, if you don't have an image to use in the background, you can create a simple color gradient in your favorite drawing tool—it still looks better than a solid color. (You don't need to store or download pure gradients as images, either. On the Web, you can create them by repeating one-pixel-wide strips, either horizontally or vertically. In systems where you can use code to generate large areas of color, gradients generally are easy to program.)

Depth cues

Fuzzy detail and vertical color gradients are two features that tell our visual systems about distance. To understand why, imagine a photograph of a hilly landscape—the farther away something is, the softer and hazier the color is. Other depth cues include texture gradients (features that get smaller as they get farther away) and lines radiating from vanishing points.

No strong focal points

The background shouldn't compete with the main content for the user's attention. Diffuse (weak) focal points can work, but make sure they contribute to a balanced composition on the whole page, rather than distract the viewer from seeing the parts of the page they should look at instead. See Figure 9-13.

As you design an interface with a deep background, consider what happens when the user changes the size of the page. How will the background accommodate a larger (or smaller) size? Will it rescale to fit, or will the window just clip an unscaled image? Clipping is probably less unsettling to the user; it's how most web pages behave, and it feels more stable. Besides, you don't have to worry about changing aspect ratios, which is problematic with many images.

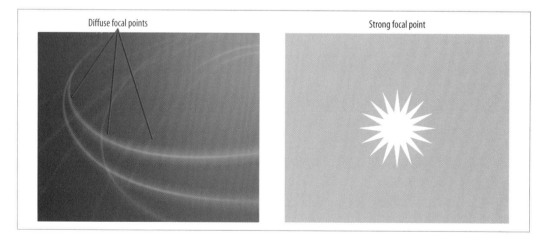

FIGURE 9-13 /Diffuse versus strong focal points

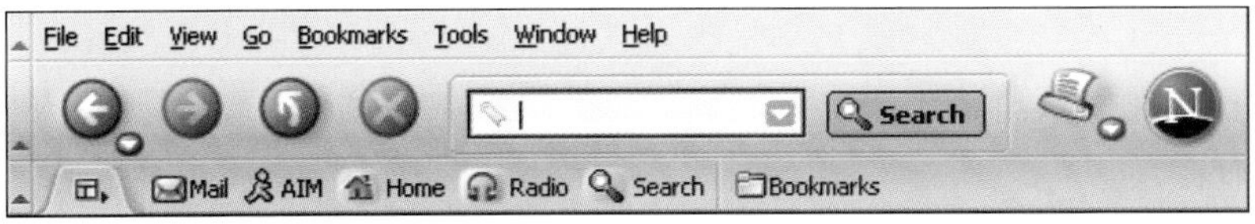

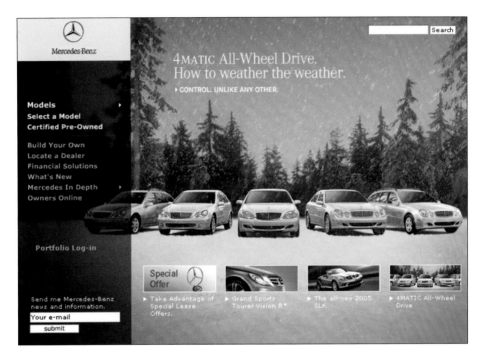

FIGURE 9-14 / The Netscape 7 look-and-feel shows the use of gradient-based sculpturing behind UI controls. The gradient works well with other visual features—barely-visible drop shadows, contouring around the "Home" and "Radio" buttons, and even the shading in the etched group box around the Search field and button—to create a finished "two-and-a-half-D" look.

FIGURE 9-15 / The Mercedes-Benz web site uses an image as a background. This image has some very strong focal points—the cars, of course—and they are the central feature of the page. But the outer parts of the image, which are much softer, are deep backgrounds for other content: the search box, the four small images at bottom, and the "4MATIC All-Wheel Drive" tagline.

The most interesting aspect of this figure is the darker band running down the lefthand side. The site needed a navigation bar with small text, but layering those links directly over the background image wouldn't have worked—the words may have been unreadable over small detail, and would have gotten lost in the composition. A translucent smoked-glass background highlights those white links by increasing contrast; it balances the page (which otherwise is right-weighted); it doesn't obscure the nice background image; and it adds a sense of layered depth. See *http://www.mbusa.com/brand/index.jsp*.

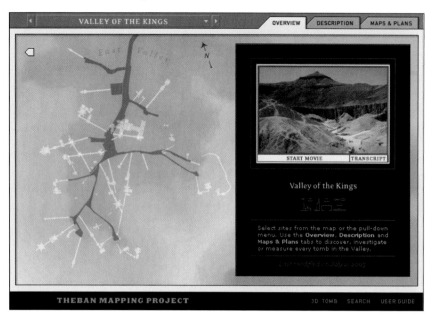

FIGURE 9-16 / From *http://thebanmappingproject.org*

what

Choose one, two, or at most three major color hues to use in the interface. Create a color palette by selecting assorted values (brightnesses) from within those few hues.

use when

You decide on a color scheme for an application or site. You want to avoid a flashy, rainbow-colored, "angry fruit salad" look, but you still want the interface to have some character.

why

Where colors are concerned, sometimes less is better. Too many color hues scattered throughout the interface, especially when they're bright and saturated, make a design noisy and cluttered. The colors compete for the user's attention.

But when you use many subtle variations on a single color, you can create a design that has depth and dimension. Consider the gray and brown colors used in the example above, reproduced in the color strip below (Figure 9-17). Notice how the darker and grayer shades appear to recede, and the lighter and brighter tints appear to move forward. This contributes to the pseudo-3D effects—such as beveling, drop shadows, and gradients—that form the contours of the UI.

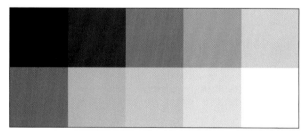

FIGURE 9-17 / The two hues used in the Theban Mapping Project UI

As mentioned earlier, pick one, two, or even three main hues. You get black and white for free, but gray counts. In fact, gray works very well in multiple values and brightnesses; it's a versatile color, especially if you add a little color to make it more blue (cool), or more beige (warm).

Within those hues, vary the color value to get a range of bright and dark shades. You also can vary the saturation at the same time; this can produce more subtle color combinations than you would get by varying just the value. Use as many of these colors as you want to compile a color palette for the application.

You can, of course, use other colors in the interface besides these hues. Just use them sparingly. Icons, ads, and other features that take up relatively small spaces don't have to fit this restricted color scheme. You might want to choose only one or two accent colors, too, like using red or cyan to mark points of interest. In fact, using a single hue for the "background" of the UI actually emphasizes these minor colors because they don't get lost in a sea of color hues.

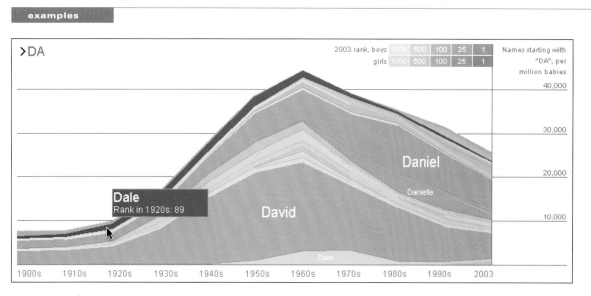

FIGURE 9-18 / This graph uses two hues, blue and pink, to show its data. Blue represents boys' names, and pink represents girls' names. Within those colors, the color value represents the popularity of those names in 2003. A third color, dark gray, shows the frame around the data—the grid lines, the numbers, and the title—and a dark blue highlights the selected name ("Dale").

This color combination is very effective, both cognitively and aesthetically. The hues and values mean something with respect to the data, and the coding is very easy to follow—you hardly even need the legend once you've looked at it once. Aesthetically, the whole thing has a layered richness that isn't garish, as rainbow hues would have been. And in American culture, people understand light blues and pinks as "baby" colors, so the emotional and cultural connection is there too. See *http://babynamewizard.com*.

FIGURE 9-19 / Even a single hue can produce designs with subtlety and interest. Here are two monochromatic examples from the CSS Zen Garden. (The green one technically has several green hues in it, some more yellowish than others, but the viewer's impression is of a single color.)

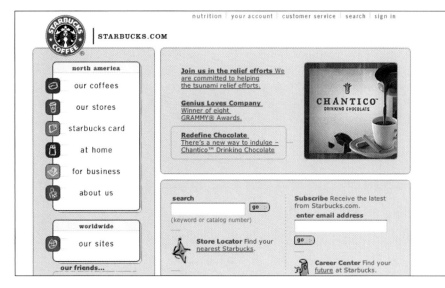

FIGURE 9-20 / Rounded corners on *http://starbucks.com*

what

Instead of using ordinary right angles, use diagonals, curves, or cutouts for some of the interface's box corners. Make these corner treatments consistent across the interface.

use when

The interface uses rectangular elements, such as boxes, buttons, and tabs.

why

The repetition of visual motifs helps unify a design. When you devise a single "corner" motif and use it consistently in many places, it gives a distinctive look to the whole design. It's certainly less boring than ordinary right-angled corners.

how

Many web sites use curved corners. Others use diagonal lines, and a few use cutouts. What you choose depends on the overall look of your site—do you have a logo, an image, or a font that has eye-catching visual elements to it? Use one of those visual elements. Are you going for something soothing (as curves often are), edgy, or energetic? Try out several different ideas.

Not all of the rectangular elements in the interface need to use corner treatments—don't use too much of a good thing. But group boxes or panels usually do, and tabs commonly are done this way too. If you use corner treatments on one group box, do them all, for consistency.

Furthermore, not every corner on a given box needs to use a corner treatment. Sometimes two opposing corners get it, such as the upper right and lower left. Sometimes it's just one corner, usually the upper left or upper right.

Everywhere the element is repeated, make sure it resembles the others. In other words, curved corners should use the same type of curve (though not necessarily the same radius). Angles should be the same angle—don't mix a 45-degree angle motif with a 20-degree angle, for instance.

examples

The Starbucks web site, shown at the top of this pattern, takes advantage of its circular logo by echoing that curve in rectangle corners all over the page—in panel borders, icons, and even the "go" buttons. The overall effect is restful and unified.

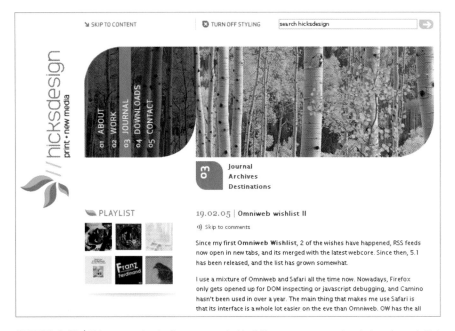

FIGURE 9-21 / This personal web site uses rounded leaf-like corners as a major design element. Not every corner is rounded, and not every curve has the same radius, but it's still a repeated motif. The design still works. See *http://hicksdesign.co.uk.*

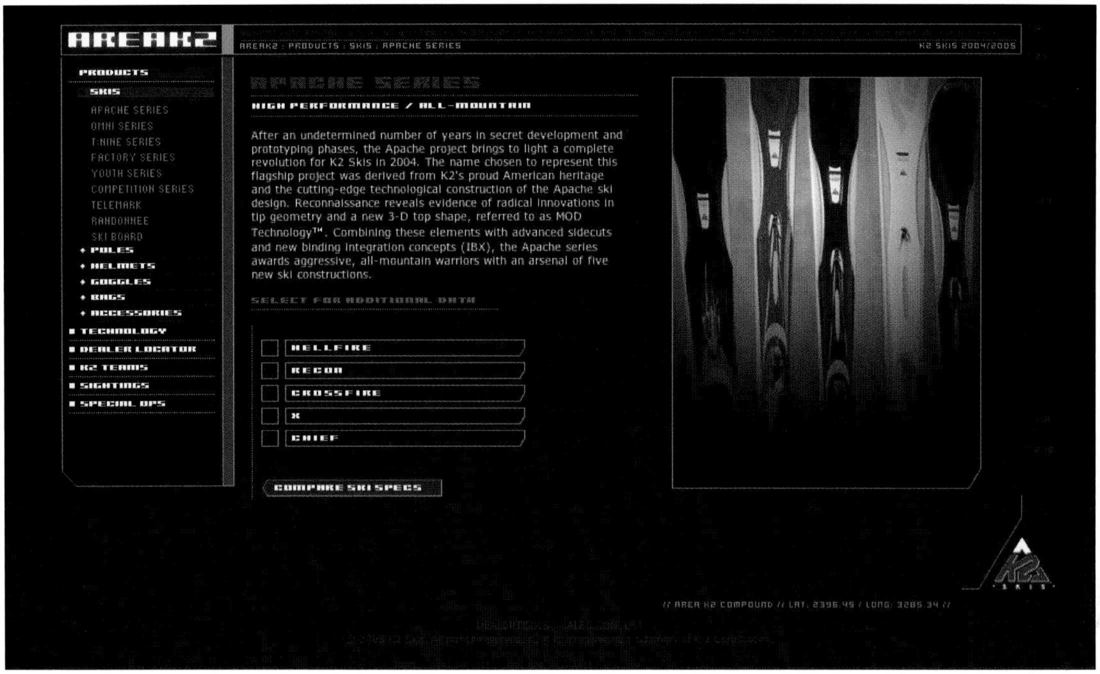

FIGURE 9-22 / This K2 site has an entirely different look. This one uses lime-green borders with angled bottom corners. Notice that most angles are on the lower-right corners, but to the far left, one is on the lower left corner. Also note that the angles are the same as those on K2's logo in the bottom right.

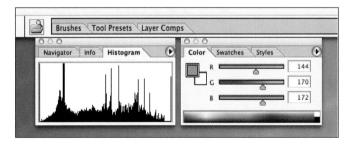

FIGURE 9-23 / Angles can be calm-looking, too. Here are two examples of angled corners used on tabs—one on a web page, and one on a desktop application. For tabs, angles make a lot of sense—they allow the tabs to overlap a bit visually without obscuring the entire right or left side of a tab.

FIGURE 9-24 / Angled tabs from Photoshop

91 borders that echo fonts

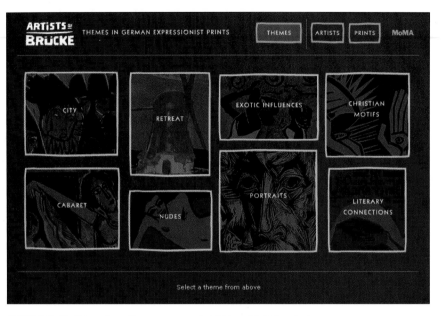

FIGURE 9-25 / From *http://www.moma.org/exhibitions/2002/brucke/*

what

When drawing borders and other lines, use the same color, thickness, and curves used by one of the design's major fonts.

use when

Your design contains a font carefully chosen for its visual effect, such as the font used in headlines, a title, or a logotype.

why

The repetition of visual motifs helps unify a design. Fonts and borders work at similar scales in a design—only a few pixels wide—and when they reinforce each other visually, their effect is magnified. When they clash (especially if you use many different kinds of borders), their contributions are weakened.

how

First, pick a font from your design. Title and headline fonts often work well, as do fonts used in logotypes, but sometimes body text works too. Observe its formal properties: color, primary line thickness, texture, curve radius, angles, and spacing.

Now try to draw borders and lines that use some of those same properties. The color should be the same as the font's, though you can cheat on thickness and make it a bit thinner than the font's strokes. If the font has pronounced circular curves, as many modern sans-serif fonts do, try using that same curve radius on the border corners.

If it's a particularly interesting font, ask yourself what makes it interesting. See if you can pull those visual elements from the font into the rest of the design.

You don't need to do this with all the borders in your interface, of course; just a few will do, especially if the lines are thick. Be careful not to make borders too thick or coarse. Thick borders make a strong statement, and after a point, they overwhelm whatever's inside them. Images usually can handle a thicker border than lightweight body text, for instance. You can use single-pixel lines effectively in combination with heavier borders.

examples

The example at the top of this pattern, Figure 9-25, uses borders that echo the logotype ("Artists of Brücke"). The logotype has a hand-drawn, rough-edged look to it. The rest of the UI's text is smooth and tiny; if the thick hand-drawn look hadn't been picked up elsewhere in the design, it wouldn't be such a strong design element. But since the borders work with it in concert, the whole page hangs together visually. It's a nice contrast to the thin smooth fonts and lines.

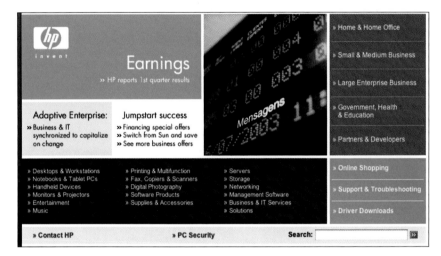

FIGURE 9-26 / You can see this pattern at work in many web sites where modern sans-serif fonts are echoed in thick, solid-color borders. The "Earnings" headline picks up elements of HP's logo font—white and four to five pixels thick—and the five-pixel white borders pick them up again. Here's something that's hard to see without a magnifier: the vertical lines in the "Earnings" font actually are only three pixels thick, but the font still looks similar to the five-pixel borders. Perception is more important than precision. See *http://hp.com*.

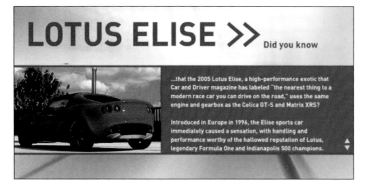

FIGURE 9-27 / This works similarly, though again, the font doesn't exactly match the thickness of the borders. But that's okay. See *http://www.planetkaizen.com.*

Thick diagonals around picture

Logo uses diagonals and right angles

Right angles in corners

Thick lines with diagonals

Yet more diagonals

FIGURE 9-28 / Dakine's web site mixes it up a bit. It uses many varied design elements, but the jagged white lines do in fact echo the logo font. Altogether, they lend a feeling of motion, tension, and edginess to the page, which was undoubtedly what its designers were after—Dakine sells sports equipment to a young demographic. See *http://dakine.com.*

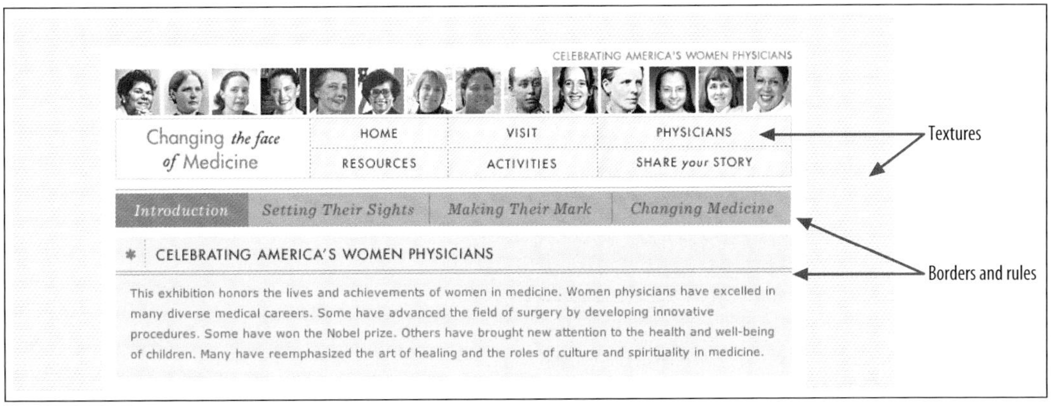

FIGURE 9-29 / From *http://nih.gov*

what

Use one-pixel-wide lines in borders, horizontal rules, and textures.

use when

You want a refined and sophisticated look to your interface.

why

When your design is made up of larger elements, such as blocks of body text, areas of different color, and images, hairlines add a level of scale to the design that may not be present otherwise. The design will look more refined.

how

Here are some of the many ways you can use hairlines in an interface:

- To demarcate **Titled Sections**, by underlining the titles
- To separate different content areas, either with horizontal or vertical rules, or with closed borders
- As guidelines to lead the eye through a composition
- Between areas of different background colors, to clarify the boundary between them

- In textures, such as a grid or a block of horizontal lines
- In icons, images, and drawn graphics
- As borders around controls, such as buttons

Hairlines look particularly good when placed near very thin sans-serif fonts. Remember that a gray line looks thinner than a black line, even if both are a single pixel wide. The same is true for other lighter colors, like the teal used in the NIH example at the top of the pattern. The less contrast between the line and its background, the thinner and lighter it appears.

Another way you can lighten a hairline—and add another texture while you're at it—is to make it a dotted line instead of a solid line. As of this writing, finely-drawn dotted lines are becoming common on the Web, even as underlines for links.

A trick to increase the tension and edginess in a design is to push a hairline flush up against the bottom of a line of text. Design 8 of the CSS Zen Garden designs does exactly that with its title and headlines (see Figure 9-8, back in the introduction to this chapter).

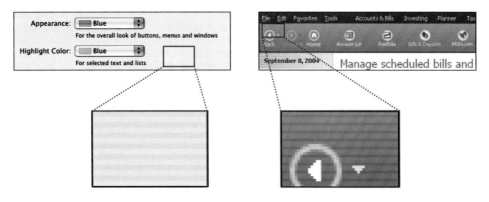

FIGURE 9-30 / Both Microsoft and Apple have used subtle hairline textures in their UI designs. Here are two examples—one from an OS X standard dialog, and the other from Microsoft Money. Both designs place small text against the textured background, which is a little risky. But the colors in these textures are so close that the difference is only barely detectable, so the texture doesn't interfere with readability.

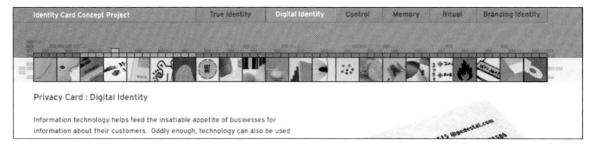

FIGURE 9-31 / IDEO's special identity-card web feature uses hairlines as a major design element, as does the NIH site at the top of the pattern. Notice that hairlines demarcate the title, the major navigation links ("Digital Identity"), the minor links (the square icons), and the decorative bricks. The design uses a horizontal hairline texture again behind the major links. These hairlines harmonize nicely with the small sans-serif font. See *http://www.ideo.com/identity/*.

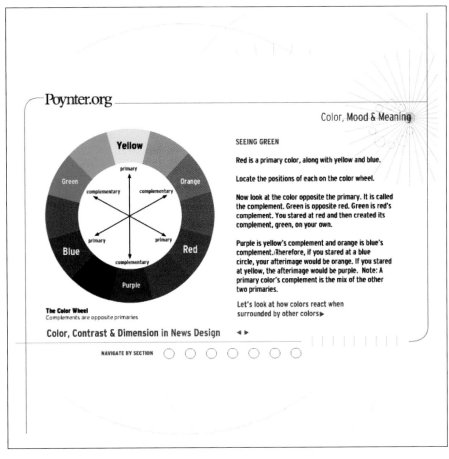

Poynter.org

Color, Mood & Meaning

SEEING GREEN

Red is a primary color, along with yellow and blue.

Locate the positions of each on the color wheel.

Now look at the color opposite the primary. It is called the complement. Green is opposite red. Green is red's complement. You stared at red and then created its complement, green, on your own.

Purple is yellow's complement and orange is blue's complement. Therefore, if you stared at a blue circle, your afterimage would be orange. If you stared at yellow, the afterimage would be purple. Note: A primary color's complement is the mix of the other two primaries.

Let's look at how colors react when surrounded by other colors▶

The Color Wheel
Complements are opposite primaries

Color, Contrast & Dimension in News Design ◀ ▶

NAVIGATE BY SECTION ○ ○ ○ ○ ○ ○ ○

FIGURE 9-32 / This design uses hairlines to frame the content and to create a strong focal point on the title ("Color, Mood & Meaning"). This time many of the lines are curved rather than straight, but the same principles apply. See *http://poynterextra.org/cp/index.html*.

93 contrasting font weights

FIGURE 9-33 / From *http://eg2006.com*

what

Use two contrasting fonts—one thin and light-weight, and the other heavier and darker—to separate different levels of information and add visual interest.

use when

Text makes up important elements on the page, and you want the page's organization to be very clear at first glance. You want the page to look dramatic.

why

When two fonts differ in weight, they form a strong and vibrant visual contrast. Aesthetically, contrast contributes to a dramatic and eye-catching look. High typographic contrast, which includes size, texture, and color—but especially weight—guarantees that your page will not look dull.

You can use this contrast to structure the text on the page. For instance, heavier-looking letters can form titles and headlines, thus helping build a visual hierarchy. The bold text in the above figure pulls the eye towards it. Thus, contrasting font weights contribute to the cognitive perception of the page as much as the aesthetics.

how

This pattern has many possible applications. This book already mentioned the use of bold text for headlines, but applications might include:

- Separating labels from data in a two-column listing
- Separating navigational links from information
- Indicating selection, such as selected links or list items
- Emphasizing words in a phrase
- Separating one word from another in a logotype

If you're using fonts that are larger than body text, such as the logotypes on the following page, make sure that the contrast is strong enough to be noticed. When the font family offers several weights, as does Helvetica Neue, pick fonts that are at least a couple of steps apart. If the contrast is weak, it looks accidental, not intentional. (The same goes for other font attributes. If you make two text elements different sizes, make them really different; if you want to mix font families, make sure they don't look too much alike!)

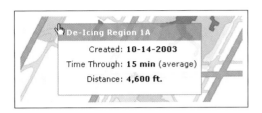

FIGURE 9-34 / Adaptive Path's home page has not one, not two, but three uses of contrasting font weights. The first is in the logotype—the heavier font weight and darker color emphasize the shorter word "path". The graphic figure underneath it adds additional emphasis. (Also note the use of **Deep Background** and **Hairlines** in this screenshot.)

The second usage is in the tagline, where the important words "value" and "experience" are heavily weighted. The design still uses spaces here to separate words, so the value of contrasting font weights is in the emphasis of some words over others.

The third usage is in the navigation bar, where the current page ("home," in this screenshot) gets a heavier font weight than the others. You should consider all the links to be one family of objects, but the current page ought to stand out, so the font is the same for all links except for the weight.

FIGURE 9-35 / When you work with data written in body text, you can use bold letters to separate labels from data. In this little window, users will be more interested in the data than the labels, so that's what gets the eye-catching bold text. See *http://lukew.com/ portfolio/*.

FIGURE 9-36 / Several more arbitrary examples of emphasis and separation: the Getty Images logo, a tagline from *http://microsoft.com*, and the CHI 2003 logo.

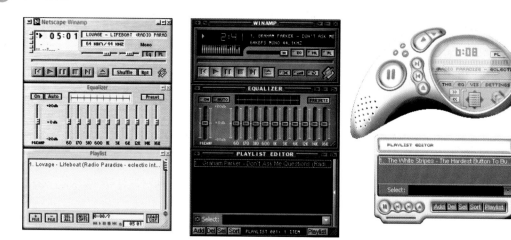

FIGURE 9-37 / Three Winamp skins

what

Open up the look-and-feel architecture of your application so users can design their own graphics and styles.

use when

Your user base includes a large population of people who know your interface well. For those people, the interface has relatively low cognitive requirements—it's not used in high-stress situations, for instance—so it's not necessary to make all widgets look standard.

Furthermore, these users like to tinker. They value style, and they are inclined to set software preferences to suit their tastes.

why

When people rearrange and customize their personal space, physical or virtual, they derive a sense of ownership of that space. This is a basic human need (though not all people act on it; many people are perfectly content with software's "factory settings"). Changing simple color and font preferences is one common way to customize someone's software environment, but skins go far beyond color schemes and fonts.

There's evidence all over the Internet that users really like skins. Actually, we're talking about two groups of users here: those who download and use skins, and those who not only use them but also design them. Those who design them see skinning as an opportunity to be creative, and to get their work out into the public eye. Many are graphic artists. These people may get to know your UI design very, very well.

In any case, there are numerous applications out there—most of them open-source, but Windows XP is one too—that are skinnable, and the sheer number of user-designed skins is enormous. The number of person-hours spent on these skins is testimony to the power of the creative impulse. For the skin designers, skinnable applications fulfill another basic human need: creativity.

how

Exactly how to design and implement a skinnable application depends entirely on the UI technologies you use, so it's very hard to generalize anything here.

First, remember that any native Windows XP application already is subject to skinning by a product called WindowBlinds (see *http://www.stardock.com/products/windowblinds*). It literally changes the way native controls are drawn.

Second, here's how application-specific skinning might work. Some skinnable applications let skinners define simple bitmap fragments, or "slices," that are fitted into the application frame at specific pixel locations. So a skinner might create images for corner tiles, horizontal slices (which are repeated along a horizontal line as many times as is necessary), vertical slices, and buttons in their various states: for example, checked, pressed, or rollover. ICQ skins work like this; see Figure 9-38. Your original page layout will remain stable in these cases.

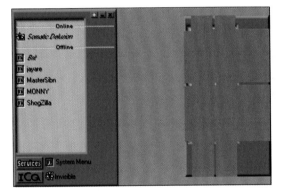

FIGURE 9-38 / Static bitmap skin implementation, courtesy of the tutorial at *http://www.geocities.com/bakerstr33t/*

However, some applications, including Winamp 3, allow skins to rearrange the location of controls, reshape the application frame, and even add new functionality. Some scripting is involved, and these skins are correspondingly harder to produce. And your UI gets rearranged! Your choices of functionality and navigation are preserved, but not much else is.

One objection often raised to skins is that they make interfaces harder to use. That's true about many badly designed skins. Ask yourself, though: How much does that matter? Does each application have to be cognitively perfect? (Default look-and-feels aren't perfect, though they're certainly more usability-tested than skins are.) For an application that someone already knows well and doesn't place high cognitive demands on, there's a point at which its basic usability is "good enough" and personal aesthetic preferences take over. When skins are available, people make that choice for themselves, whether or not they've educated themselves about usability.

To an extent, you can—and should, as part of a designer's responsibility—decide at which level to permit skinning. You may only allow icons to be changed. You may permit bitmap-level skinning that preserves layout, like ICQ. Or you may allow full customizability, like Winamp 3; it's up to you to decide if that kind of freedom is likely to make the interface criminally hard to use.

I'm going to speculate that excellent application design—for example, well-chosen functionality, easily understood organizational models, appropriate navigation, good page layout, and standard widgetry—can make an interface more resilient to bad skins. Design it as well as you can, and then put it out there for people to customize at a level you decide is appropriate. See what happens!

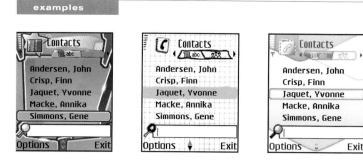

FIGURE 9-39 / Many high-end cell phones can have skins installed, along with ring tones and other customizations. This figure shows a few skins for the Nokia 6600. Note that all the text and buttons stay in the same places; only details like wallpaper, icons, and particular widget graphics are skinnable. See *http://mangothemes.com*.

FIGURE 9-40 / Start Menu details from four WinXP skins, found at *http://browse.deviantart.com/skins/windows/windowblindsxp/*.

WindowBlinds makes the entire Windows XP desktop skinnable, along with native applications, as mentioned earlier. These screenshots show some elaborate skins for Windows XP. Notice how they use many of the techniques and patterns discussed in this chapter: the use of only one or two main hues with many values, deep backgrounds and pseudo-3D detailing, dynamic curves and angles, and interesting corner treatments.

REFERENCES

If you want to learn more about some of the concepts discussed in this book, here are some references that can get you started. It's not a complete list by any means. It draws on a fairly small, well-known list of books and web sites, for simplicity, but many good references exist that aren't listed here (possibly because I don't know about them). You'll find the same books listed in several places—after all, many good design books cover multiple topics.

Introductory Design References

Krug, Steve. *Don't Make Me Think! A Common Sense Approach to Web Usability*, Second Edition. Berkeley, CA: New Riders, 2000.

Cooper, Alan, Robert Reimann. *About Face 2.0: The Essentials of Interaction Design*. Indianapolis: Wiley Publishing, Inc., 2003.

Norman, Donald A. *The Design of Everyday Things*. New York: Basic Books, 1998.

Shneiderman, Ben. *Designing the User Interface: Strategies for Effective Human-Computer Interaction*, Fourth Edition. Reading, MA: Addison-Wesley, 2004.

Williams, Robin. *The Non-Designer's Design Book: Design and Typographic Principles for the Visual Novice*. Berkeley: Peachpit Press, 2004.

Chapter 1: What Users Do

Krug, Steve. *Don't Make Me Think! A Common Sense Approach to Web Usability*, Second Edition. Berkeley, CA: New Riders, 2000.

Hackos, JoAnn T. and Janice C. Redish. *User and Task Analysis for Interface Design*. New York: John Wiley & Sons, Inc., 1998.

Holtzblatt, Karen, Jessamyn Burns Wendell, Shelley Wood. *Rapid Contextual Design: A How-To Guide to Key Techniques for User-Centered Design*. San Francisco: Morgan Kaufmann, 2005.

Carroll, John M. *Making Use: Scenario-Based Design of Human-Computer Interactions*. Cambridge, MA: MIT Press, 2000.

Cooper, Alan, Robert Reimann. *About Face 2.0: The Essentials of Interaction Design*. Indianapolis: Wiley Publishing, Inc., 2003. (The first section, "Know Thy User," is especially relevant.)

Csikszentmihalyi, Mihali. *Flow: The Psychology of Optimal Experience*. New York: Harper Perennial, 1991.

Schacter, Daniel L. *The Seven Sins of Memory: How the Mind Forgets and Remembers*. Boston: Houghton Mifflin Company, 2001. (The chapter on absent-mindedness talks about prospective memory.)

Chapter 2: Organizing the Content

McCloud, Scott. *Understanding Comics*. New York: HarperCollins, 1994. (Defines "idiom" for the comics and visual arts world.)

McCullough. *Digital Ground*. Cambridge, MA: MIT Press, 2004. (Defines "type" for architecture, and explains why the concept is important.)

Rosenfeld, Louis, Peter Morville. *Information Architecture for the World Wide Web: Designing Large-Scale Web Sites*, Second Edition. Sebastopol, CA: O'Reilly Media, 2002.

Wodtke, Christina. *Information Architecture: Blueprints for the Web*. Berkeley, CA: New Riders, 2002.

Jacobson, Robert, ed. *Information Design*. Cambridge, MA: MIT Press, 1999.

Lindholm, Christian, Turkka Keinonen, Harri Kiljander. *Mobile Usability: How Nokia Changed the Face of the Mobile Phone*. New York: McGraw-Hill, 2003. (Special considerations for the application design of mobile devices.)

Chapter 3: Getting Around

Jacobson, Robert, ed. *Information Design*. Cambridge, MA: MIT Press, 1999. (See especially "Sign-Posting Information Design," by Romedi Passini.)

Baxley, Bob. *Making the Web Work: Designing Effective Web Applications*. Indianapolis: Sams Publishing, 2002.

van Duyne, Douglas, James A. Landay, Jason I. Hong. *The Design of Sites: Patterns, Principles, and Processes for Crafting a Customer-Centered Web Experience*. Reading, MA: Addison-Wesley, 2002. (For this and all the remaining books listed here, find the chapters that deal with navigation and links.)

Johnson, Jeff. *Web Bloopers: 60 Common Web Design Mistakes, and How To Avoid Them*. San Francisco: Morgan Kaufmann, 2003.

Lindholm, Christian, Turkka Keinonen, Harri Kiljander. *Mobile Usability: How Nokia Changed the Face of the Mobile Phone*. New York: McGraw-Hill, 2003.

Cooper, Alan, Robert Reimann. *About Face 2.0: The Essentials of Interaction Design*. Indianapolis: Wiley Publishing, Inc., 2003.

Nielsen, Jakob. *Designing Web Usability*. Berkeley, CA: New Riders, 2000.

Krug, Steve. *Don't Make Me Think! A Common Sense Approach to Web Usability*, Second Edition. Berkeley, CA: New Riders, 2000. (This book has a good explanation of visual hierarchy.)

Chapter 4: Organizing the Page

Williams, Robin. *The Non-Designer's Design Book: Design and Typographic Principles for the Visual Novice*. Berkeley: Peachpit Press, 2004.

Faimon, Peg, and John Weigand. *The Nature of Design: How the Principles of Design Shape Our World: From Graphics and Architecture to Interiors and Products*. Cincinnati: HOW Design Books, 2004.

Hashimoto, Alan. *Visual Design Fundamentals: A Digital Approach*. Hingham, MA: Charles River Media, 2004.

Mullet, Kevin, Darrell Sano. *Designing Visual Interfaces: Communication Oriented Techniques*. Mountain View, CA: Sun Microsystems, Inc., 1995.

Solso, Robert. *Cognition and the Visual Arts*. Cambridge, MA: MIT Press, 1994. (The chapters on color, Gestalt principles, and eye-tracking are particularly relevant.)

Krug, Steve. *Don't Make Me Think! A Common Sense Approach to Web Usability*, Second Edition. Berkeley, CA: New Riders, 2000. (This book has a good explanation of visual hierarchy.)

Baxley, Bob. *Making the Web Work: Designing Effective Web Applications*. Indianapolis: Sams Publishing, 2002. (Chapter 10 discusses layout.)

Chapter 5: Doing Things

Norman, Donald A. *The Design of Everyday Things*. New York: Basic Books, 1998. (This book discusses affordances, among other things.)

Johnson, Jeff. *GUI Bloopers*. San Francisco: Morgan Kaufmann, 2000.

Gamma, Erich, Richard Helm, Ralph Johnson, John Vlissides. *Design Patterns: Elements of Reusable Object-Oriented Software*. Reading, MA: Addison-Wesley, 1995. (Defines the "Command" pattern, often used to implement three of Chapter 5's patterns.)

Cooper, Alan, Robert Reimann. *About Face 2.0: The Essentials of Interaction Design*. Indianapolis: Wiley Publishing, Inc., 2003.

Chapter 6: Showing Complex Data

Tufte, Edward. *The Visual Display of Quantitative Data*. Cheshire, CT: Graphics Press, 1983.

Tufte, Edward. *Envisioning Information*. Cheshire, CT: Graphics Press, 1991.

Tufte, Edward. *Visual Explanations: Images and Quantities, Evidence and Narrative*. Cheshire, CT: Graphics Press, 1997.

Fowler, Susan, and Victor Stanwick. *Web Application Design Handbook: Best Practices for Web-Based Software*. San Francisco: Morgan Kaufmann, 2004.

Cleveland, William S. *Visualizing Data*. Summit, NJ: Hobart Press, 1993.

Wildbur, Peter, and Michael Burke. *Information Graphics: Innovative Solutions in Contemporary Design*. London: Thames and Hudson Ltd., 1998.

Spence, Robert. *Information Visualization*. Reading, MA: Addison-Wesley, 2001.

Monmonier, Mark. *How to Lie With Maps*, Second Edition. Chicago: University of Chicago Press, 1996.

http://www.cs.umd.edu/hcil/ The University of Maryland's Human-Computer Interaction Lab has done wonderful work on information graphics, and will no doubt continue to do so.

http://www.math.yorku.ca/SCS/Gallery A sampler of the best and worst information graphics out there.

Chapter 7: Getting Input from Users

Johnson, Jeff. *GUI Bloopers*. San Francisco: Morgan Kaufmann, 2000.

Johnson, Jeff. *Web Bloopers: 60 Common Web Design Mistakes, and How To Avoid Them*. San Francisco: Morgan Kaufmann, 2003.

Fowler, Susan, and Victor Stanwick. *Web Application Design Handbook: Best Practices for Web-Based Software*. San Francisco: Morgan Kaufmann, 2004. (Chapter 3 talks about forms.)

37signals. *Defensive Design for the Web: How to Improve Error Messages, Help, Forms, and Other Crisis Points*. Berkeley, CA: New Riders, 2004. (Chapter 2, and Guidelines 9 and 10, discuss some of the same ideas used in this book's patterns.)

Baxley, Bob. *Making the Web Work: Designing Effective Web Applications*. Indianapolis: Sams Publishing, 2002. (Chapter 8 discusses forms.)

Chapter 8: Builders and Editors

Cooper, Alan, Robert Reimann. *About Face 2.0: The Essentials of Interaction Design*. Indianapolis: Wiley Publishing, Inc., 2003. (There really aren't many books that discuss this topic.)

Chapter 9: Making It Look Good

Norman, Donald A. *Emotional Design: Why We Love (or Hate) Everyday Things*. New York: Basic Books, 2004.

Shea, David, and Molly Holzschlag. *The Zen of CSS Design: Visual Enlightenment for the Web*. Berkeley, CA: New Riders, 2005.

Williams, Robin. *The Non-Designer's Design Book: Design and Typographic Principles for the Visual Novice*. Berkeley: Peachpit Press, 2004.

Bringhurst, Robert. *The Elements of Typographic Style, version 3.0*. Vancouver: Hartley & Marks, 2004.

Hashimoto, Alan. *Visual Design Fundamentals: A Digital Approach*. Hingham, MA: Charles River Media, 2004.

McCloud, Scott. *Understanding Comics*. New York: HarperCollins, 1994.

Other Patterns

Some well-known pattern languages and books are listed below. Only one, the well-known *Design Patterns,* deals directly with code, but there are scores of other code-related pattern books that you can look up easily.

Alexander, Christopher, Sara Ishikawa, Murray Silverstein, Max Jacobson, Ingrid Fiksdahl-King, Shlomo Angel. *A Pattern Language*. New York: Oxford University Press, 1977.

Alexander, Christopher. *The Timeless Way of Building*. New York: Oxford University Press, 1979.

Gamma, Erich, Richard Helm, Ralph Johnson, John Vlissides. *Design Patterns: Elements of Reusable Object-Oriented Software*. Reading, MA: Addison-Wesley, 1995.

van Duyne, Douglas, James A. Landay, Jason I. Hong. *The Design of Sites: Patterns, Principles, and Processes for Crafting a Customer-Centered Web Experience*. Reading, MA: Addison-Wesley, 2002.

http://www.welie.com/patterns/gui/index.html Martijn van Welie's pattern collection.

http://www.mit.edu/~jtidwell/common_ground.html The first precursor to this pattern book.

http://time-tripper.com/uipatterns/ The second precursor to this pattern book.

http://geography.uoregon.edu/datagraphics/patterns A small set of patterns for data visualization.

http://www.conservatoineconomy.org/ This large "pattern language for sustainability" has nothing to do with software, but everything to do with local and regional planning. It's a fine example of a working pattern language in another domain.

http://iasummit.org/2005/finalpapers/52.Presentation.pdf Entitled "Implementing a Pattern Library in the Real World: A Yahoo! Case Study," this paper describes not a single set of patterns, but a process for developing a useful set of corporate interaction design patterns.

http://usability.gov/guidlines/index.html The Research-Based Web Design & Usability Guidelines from the U.S. Department of Health and Human Services. It's not really a set of patterns, but it is a set of small, well-defined recommendations. Like the patterns in this book, some of the guidelines conflict with each other; you will have to use your judgment (and usability testing) to decide which are relevant to your situation and which aren't.

NUMBERS

80/20 rule, 57, 65

A

accessibility
high-contrast color schemes
and large fonts, 288
JAWS, 288
styles, 288-289
(see also keyboards)
**Action Panels, 132, 136, 140-
143**
actions/commands
Action Panels, 132, 136,
140-143
affordances, 135
Button Groups, 131, 136-141
buttons, 131, 136-141, 144-145
Cancelability, 136, 149, 151-152
Command History, 124, 136,
155-158
command line interfaces, 133
conventions, 135
creativity, 133-135
double-clicking, 132-133
drag-and-drop, 133
drop shadows, 135
dropdown menus, 132
idioms, 133
invisible actions, 132-133
interface architecture
lists of actions, 24-26
lists of subject categories,
26
lists of tools, 27
keyboards, 132-133
links, 132
Macros, 17, 136, 156, 158-159
menu bars, 131-132
mouse pointers, 135
Multi-Level Undo, 136, 153-155
Alternative Views, 40
Escape Hatch, 86

Macros, 157-158
Property Sheet, 122
users, 11
overview, 131
patterns overview, 136
pop-up menus, 132
Preview, 44, 136, 147-148, 233
Progress Indicator, 65, 136,
149-151
Prominent Done Button, 136,
144-145
scrollbars, 134, 139, 153
Smart Menu Items, 136, 146,
152, 154-155
toolbars, 132
tooltips, 135
typed commands, 133
visual impairment, 132
advice (user behavior), 18-19
affect, 270
**affordances (actions/
commands), 135**
alignment (layout), 94-96, 99
closure, 95-96
alternating row colors, 187
button groups, 137
styles, 269
continuity, 95-96
alternating row colors, 187
local zooming, 184-185
preattentive variables, 163
right-left alignment, 116
styles, 269
Gestalt theory, 94-96, 269
Prominent Done Button, 144
proximity, 94-95, 97
Action Panels, 141
alternating row colors, 187
button groups, 137
Datatips, 172
Multi-Y Graph, 198
responsive enabling, 126
right-left alignment, 116
styles, 269

similarity, 95, 97
button groups, 137
Multi-Y Graph, 198
preattentive variables, 163,
166
styles, 269, 287
visual hierarchy, 90-91
**Alternating Row Colors
(information graphics),
817-188**
**Alternative Views (information
architecture), 30, 39-41,
173**
analyzing user goals, 3-5
angles (styles), 279, 282-287
Borders that Echo Fonts, 302
Corner Treatments, 297-300
Skins, 311
shapes, 279
animation
Animated Transitions, 63,
84-85, 173, 185
progress indicator, 149
**Annotated Scrollbar
(navigation), 55, 63, 80-
81, 173**
**appearance, importance of,
269**
arranging. See sorting
audience. See users
**Autocompletion (controls),
127, 207-208, 227-229**
**axes (information graphics),
165, 171-172, 177, 198-201**

B

Back button, 10, 12, 14, 43
**backgrounds (styles), 280,
286-288, 290-293**
Deep Background, 288, 291-
293, 307, 311
Few Hues, Many Values, 295
Hairlines, 303-304
Baxley, Bob, 69